OXFORD

HORACE HART, PRINTER TO THE UNIVERSITY

JOHN WILLIAM BURGON

JOHN WILLIAM BURGON

LATE DEAN OF CHICHESTER

A BIOGRAPHY

WITH EXTRACTS FROM HIS LETTERS AND EARLY JOURNALS

Republished by
The Old Paths Publications, Inc
www.theoldpathspublications.com
2019

By EDWARD MEYRICK GOULBURN, D.D., D.C.L.

SOMETIME DEAN OF NORWICH

ISBN: 978-1-7336063-7-0

IN TWO VOLUMES: WITH PORTRAITS

VOL. II

Republished by
The Old Paths Publications, Inc
www.theoldpathspublications.com
2019

LONDON

JOHN MURRAY, ALBEMARLE STREET

LIBRARY ST. MARY'S COLLEGE

CONTENTS OF VOL. II.

CHAPTER II.

PAGE

THE OXFORD LIFE: FIFTH PERIOD .

(Vicarage of St. Mary the Virgin's [Oct. 15, 1863–Jan. 19, 1876].)

CHAPTER III.

THE CHICHESTER LIFE [1876–1888] .   123

CHAPTER IV.

THE CHARACTER — INTELLECTUAL, MORAL, AND SPIRITUAL   341

APPENDIX (A)   379
    (B)   382
    (C)   387
    (D)   392
    (E)   401
    (F)   407

INDEX   415

LIFE OF DEAN BURGON.

CHAPTER II.

ERRATUM.

Vol. II, p. 365, *footnote* 5, *line* 6, *for* Polytheist *read* Monotheist

Goulburn's Life of Burgon.

series of eminent men,—by one man so very eminent that he may be ranked with John Wesley, as one of the greatest leaders of religious thought, and originators of religious movement, whom the Church of England has produced since the Reformation. John Henry Newman's movement too, though taking quite a different direction from John Wesley's, had the same effect as the earlier one of stirring into a new activity, and quickening with a new life, even those ministers and members of the Church who were avowedly out of sympathy with it.

LIFE OF DEAN BURGON.

CHAPTER II.

THE OXFORD LIFE: FIFTH PERIOD.

Vicarage of St. Mary the Virgin's.

[*Oct.* 15, 1863—*Jan.* 19, 1876.]

"I was this day presented by the College" (the Provost and Fellows of Oriel College, the Patrons of the Vicarage of St. Mary the Virgin's) "to St. Mary's, and presume in due time that the other formalities will be got through." Thus wrote Burgon from his rooms in Oriel to his Brother-in-law, the Rev. Henry John Rose, under date October 15, 1863. The other formalities which he refers to were his Institution, which took place on October 29 of the same year, his Induction on the 4th of January in the year succeeding, and his Reading-in on the 17th of January. He had been preceded in the Vicarage by a series of eminent men,—by one man so very eminent that he may be ranked with John Wesley, as one of the greatest leaders of religious thought, and originators of religious movement, whom the Church of England has produced since the Reformation. John Henry Newman's movement too, though taking quite a different direction from John Wesley's, had the same effect as the earlier one of stirring into a new activity, and quickening with a new life, even those ministers and members of the Church who were avowedly out of sympathy with it.

On Mr. Newman's resignation of the Vicarage of St. Mary's in the autumn of 1843, the Reverend Charles Page Eden, "the Earnest Parish Priest," as Burgon styles him in his '*Lives of Twelve Good Men*,' succeeded ("a perilous undertaking, truly, it was, to succeed to that pulpit after such an one as John Henry Newman"), and held the post till the spring of 1850, when he was presented to Aberford in Yorkshire, also an Oriel College Living. Charles Marriott, "the Man of Saintly Life," another of the "Twelve Good Men" commemorated by Burgon, followed Eden in the Vicarage of St. Mary's, and held the position until, in the summer of 1855, a stroke of paralysis terminated, not indeed his life, but his ministerial career. From that time to Burgon's presentation to the Living in 1863, it was held by the Rev. Drummond Percy Chase, now Principal of St. Mary's Hall, who for some time had been desirous of devolving the post upon Burgon, but had with great considerateness held it on during his friend's tour in the East, and on his return thence, until he had sufficiently recovered his health to undertake the duties of the Parish. That Burgon was legitimately proud of being appointed to a post, which the tenure of it by so many distinguished men had rendered illustrious, goes without saying. Shortly after his appointment, the author remembers having met him at one of the dinners of "Nobody's Club" in London, when, as a newly elected member, he was required by one of the rules of the Club to give an account of himself and of his qualifications for membership. In his maiden speech he mentioned with pardonable pride his having been recently appointed to a post, illustrated by names all of them academically illustrious, and one of world-wide celebrity, and modestly said that, if his reputation could never be what theirs was, he would endeavour at all events to do his duty in his new vocation. But there was another and deeper consideration besides that of the lustre of his predecessors, which would make him thankful for his appointment to a parish of his own. Thirteen years ago, it will be remembered, he had written to Mrs. Hugh James Rose thus: "What I *do* desire is not to die till I have had the shepherding of a flock. In that task I am content to wear myself out" [see above, page 190]. "The shepherding" came to him at last in the shape of the Pastoral Charge of the chief Parish Church in Oxford—(chief it has a right to be called, on account of its being the University Church),—and thus his desire was fulfilled. But was it "a tree of life" to him, as the Wise Man says that the long-deferred "desire" is, when at length it "cometh" [Prov. xiii. 12]? Eventually, and in one sense, "Yes." He himself always pointed to his ministry at St. Mary's as the happiest and most useful,—the happiest, because the most useful,—period of his life. He "wore himself out" indeed in that cure, crowding into those twelve years the pastoral activities of an ordinary lifetime, but he found "contentment," deep and satisfying, in spending and being spent for others, and abundantly realised the truth of the promise that "he that watereth shall be watered also himself." At the outset of the new undertaking, however, he found all sorts of drawbacks and discouragements; there was none of the *couleur de rose* with which his imagination had invested a Parish of his own, when it was only in prospect. First, there was the reflexion, sure to be bitter to a heart so tender and loving as his, that the Oxford Vacations, which he had been wont to spend at his sister's house at Houghton Conquest (since his father's death he seems to have regarded Houghton as his home), would now be claimed, if not wholly, yet in great part by his Parish,—at all events that those long quiet weeks, sacred to study and the cultivation of family ties, must now come to an end for ever.

"I can think of nothing but you all," he writes to Mrs. Henry John Rose, under date Oct. 10, 1863,—"as usual when I come from dear Houghton; but this time more than any other; for there seems something very like the severance of the ties of more than twenty bright summers: no small portion of *any* life, and nearly half of *mine*! To dwell upon this aspect of the case is even keenly distressing to me. It cuts me like a knife to bend my thoughts steadily in that direction; and I will not recur to it again. But it cannot be right to shut one's eyes to the melancholy probability that Houghton —dear, dear Houghton—will never more be to me, as for so many years it has been, my *home*. I may come and go, and you may be kind enough to receive me from time to time; but the many consecutive weeks,—the calm, studious, quiet weeks, sweetened by your constant kindness and the society of the beloved children,—those many weeks of repose for mind and body,—alas! they seem to have come to an end."

And then the new position seemed to him at first to have much that was repellent in it. In the same breath in which he tells his Brother-in-law, "I was this day presented by the College to St. Mary's," he adds; "All at present is heavy, strange, lonely, and discouraging."

And in the letter to his sister, an excerpt from which has just been given to the reader, he goes on to say:—

"It is certainly the most anomalous, unattractive, queer place I ever heard of,—or, I suppose, you either. The parishioners are estimated variously by Chase, and the Provost, and the Churchwardens, at 300—400—500; while the Clergy List takes a bold leap, and calls it 1000. There are no poor in the Parish, and no schools as the necessary consequence..... I am warned that I shall find no soil to work upon, and cautioned against expecting a congregation. .... I listen and stare, and can hardly believe my own ears."

But he is not going to allow the grass to grow under his feet.

"I have resolved to attempt no changes on this side of Advent; but I will in the meantime visit the flock" (be it remembered that he was not even *presented* as yet, the date of the letter being October 10), "and convince myself whether it may not be practicable to feed the flock of CHRIST, even here!"

On Nov. 24, he writes to his sister of a change which he did make "on this side Advent[1]," notwithstanding the resolution he had announced to her in the previous month.

"I started an Afternoon Service last Sunday,—or rather revived the old Service. How hard it is to bring back the lost! I think there were scarcely fifty in that vast Church! And it used to be such a large congregation! However, the Evening Service is very popular. I am glad to see undergraduates there, in considerable numbers."

Those who knew him well might have augured with tolerable certainty that one of his first acts would be the revival of the Afternoon Service, that having been *the* Service at which Mr. Newman had been in the habit of delivering his celebrated Sermons, which attracted so large an audience from the various Colleges, and Burgon having always retained to the end of his life the most affectionate veneration for Mr. Newman's memory, though he never showed the smallest symptom of a disposition to follow him in his secession from the Anglican fold. Soon after the restoration of the Sunday Afternoon Service followed that of the Daily and Saints' Day Services; and Burgon, foreseeing that he should not be equal singlehanded to all the work which he contemplated

[1] Advent Sunday in the year 1863 fell on Nov. 29.

for the benefit of his parishioners, appointed the Rev. R. G. Livingstone, of Pembroke College, his first Curate. Mr. Livingstone was ordained to the Curacy of St. Mary's at the December ordination of 1863, and became the fast friend as well as the very efficient assistant of his Vicar. No amiable man, who had penetrated beyond the range of Burgon's polemical fulmination into the inner circle of his intimates, could resist the fascination of his affectionateness and geniality.

A.D. 1864. [Æt. 51.] In the year 1864, Burgon's '*Treatise on the Pastoral Office, addressed chiefly to Candidates for Holy Orders, or to those who have recently undertaken the cure of souls*,' made its appearance. It had been commenced, he tells us, in 1856 (three years after he had resigned his Curacy at Finmere), had been "laid aside for a long period," "resumed from time to time," and finally "brought to a close in 1864." He was not well in his saddle at St. Mary's, certainly had not had more than a month's experience of Pastoral work in a town, when this Treatise, which enters in considerable detail into each separate department of the duties of a Parish Priest, issued from the press. What strikes one at first sight as requiring explanation, is the very limited account of actual experience, on which the instructions and advices given in the Treatise are founded. He himself is evidently aware of this objection which might be advanced against the book; for he says in the Preface;—

"It will distress me if I shall be thought to have overstepped the limits of a becoming modesty: or if any should be offended because an individual invested with no authority has thus presumed to teach . . . . . I have confined my particular observations to that sphere of Pastoral labour with which alone I have been hitherto familiar,—namely, the cure of souls in agricultural parishes. But, in truth, whether in Town or

Country, human nature is found to be much the same; and, except in matters of detail, the same general principles are everywhere applicable."

And if it should be thought that even in agricultural parishes, his experience had been hitherto of the briefest, consisting only of temporary engagements at West Ilsley, Worton, and Finmere during the years 1849 to 1853 inclusive, at none of which places however did he ever permanently reside as licensed Curate, we have only to refer to the letters descriptive of his ministry in those places, which are given at the end of the Second Period of his Oxford Life, to see with how much justice those words of the Book of Wisdom may be applied to him in his Pastoral work; "He, being made perfect in a short time, fulfilled a long time." In those fragments of weeks (for this they were, and nothing more) which he devoted to West Ilsley, Worton, and Finmere, he crowded by his extraordinary energy the experience of years, and learnt about his parishioners, his work, his responsibilities, and the best means of meeting them, what it would have taken another man, of less fervent spirit and less intense self-devotion, ten years' continuous residence among the people to acquire. Add to which that he was not ordained till he was thirty-five years old, and accordingly came to the work with far more furniture in the way of general cultivation, and far more knowledge of human life and society, than falls to the lot of ordinary Clergymen, who receive the first grade of Holy Orders at the Canonical age of twenty-three. Burgon was a man of letters, a man of art, a man of high cultivation, and one who had moved in the literary society of the metropolis, before he put his hand to the work of the Ministry, and his intellectual and social maturity gave him a facility of acquisition, even in a comparatively new sphere of duty, which would have been wanting to a man of less advanced general experience. Any how the '*Treatise on the Pastoral Office*' is an extraordinary production, when considered as the result of a Pastoral experience so very brief in point of time, and so very fitful. A man who had studied a country Parish for twenty-five years of continuous residence in it could not write with more thorough mastery of his subject, nor (generally speaking) with sounder sense and better judgment. Needless to say that his idiosyncrasies, both as regards doctrine and manner,—the thing taught and the way of teaching it— run from one end of the Treatise to the other ; as in all his other writings, so in this, there is no mistaking who it is that writes. The First Chapter is devoted to the study of the Bible—the fundamental study, beyond all doubt, for those who would duly qualify themselves for the exercise of the Christian Ministry,—and the second to Inspiration, which gives the Bible its unique character of the Word of God. In these two Chapters, Burgon, deploring, with only too much reason, the shallow grounding in Holy Scripture of most of those who offer themselves for Holy Orders, does little else than reproduce in other, and perhaps rather simpler, words the same views of the Bible, its claims, and the right way of studying it, which he had already laid before the Church in his Sermons on "Inspiration and Interpretation." Next to the study of the Bible, he shows the necessity of the study of the Prayer Book, in its sources, in the changes through which it has reached its present state, and in its teaching,—the Prayer Book being " the authorized exponent of the Church's mind on all the chief points of doctrine." The foundation of sacred learning having thus been laid deep in the study of the Bible and Prayer Book, a course of reading is then recommended in Ecclesiastical History, in the works of the great English Divines, and, as far as possible, in the Fathers,—a too vast field, it might be thought, for the average young Clergyman[2]; but of course it is intended that each one should apply himself to that particular quarter of the field, to which he is drawn by his peculiar circumstances and prepossessions. The Eight Chapters which follow, and constitute the bulk of the book, give very pertinent and judicious advices on different branches of the Pastoral Work, Preaching and Sermon Writing, Pastoral Visitation of the Sick and the whole (to the universality and individuality of which

[2] The late Archdeacon Churton, then Rector of Crayke, who, as we have seen, had so highly eulogized Burgon's Biography of Tytler, while calling '*The Pastoral Office*' "a rich offering made to the Service of the Altar," thinks that the author has in some measure laid himself open to the objection which he makes [Preface, p. viii.] against Professor Blunt's '*Duties of the Parish-Priest*,'—that objection being that the Professor overloads the Parish Priest with too many subjects of study, and sets up a standard *impossible of attainment*. Burgon, Mr. Churton seems to think, lays himself open more or less to the same charge.

And in the same letter (dated Crayke, April 30, 1864), Mr. Churton hits one or two other blots in the work, in the way of chronological inaccuracy, which are here given in order that, should this very valuable Treatise ever be reprinted for the use of Candidates for Holy Orders, the trifling blunders, here indicated in Mr. Churton's own words, may be set right:—" In p. xi. I do not understand what you mean by speaking of Bp. Wilkins as a 'little later' than Rob. Nelson, or speaking of Pearson in terms that seem to imply that you consider him to have been earlier. The only Bp. Wilkins with whom I am acquainted is John Wilkins, the Natural Philosopher, famous for proposing a voyage to the moon, and Bp. Pearson's predecessor in the See of Chester, where he died in 1672. But his Treatise called '*Ecclesiastes*,' so far from being written (as you say, p. 172), 'a century and a half ago,' was first published in 1646. See Wood's '*Athenæ*,' iii. 969, ed. Bliss, where some later editions are also mentioned."

John Wilkins, Bp. of Chester, was born in 1614,—consecrated 1668,—died 1672.

John Pearson, who succeeded him in the see, was born in 1612,—consecrated 1673,—died 1686.

Robert Nelson, author of '*The Fasts and Festivals*,' was born in 1656,—died 1714.

last visitation he attaches great weight), Village Education and Catechizing, Preparation for Confirmation and First Communion, impressive reading of the Psalms and Lessons, and so forth. The chapter on Parochial Management, which recognises each Parish as presenting a separate problem of its own, and to be dealt with therefore not by any cast-iron rule, but in methods demanded by its own peculiar characteristics, treats very pertinently and sensibly of such humble subjects as the Village Feast, the School Feast, the Harvest Home, the Village Club and Reading Room, the Lending Library, the dealing of the Pastor with Dissenters, and the line he should take in visiting them. The Book is as exhaustive as it well can be on its own subject—the exercise of the Pastoral Office in a rural district—and, as being studiously moderate in its tone, and repudiating both the Ultra Protestant and Ritualistic extremes, may safely be recommended. On the one hand, Burgon is no Puritan. "Let preaching have all honour," he says; "but let it subordinate duly, and never be looked upon as the great business of the Sanctuary, the sole means of evangelizing a Parish. In Puritan times we learn that *la Prêche* was a name for Protestantism. In more recent days, we have perhaps heard of Church Services abridged, or indecently hurried over, in order that the performance in the pulpit might commence. All such self-glorification is a dishonour put upon GOD; and an omen of nothing but ill to the spiritual life of a people" [p. 204]. On the other hand Burgon is certainly no Ritualist. Witness the following:—

"*How attired* shall a man go forth to minister? A soiled curt surplice, stained with iron-mould, and unfurnished with hood or stole,—crumpled bands, tied askew,—and muddy boots,—form an unseemly accompaniment (to say the least) for one who is to conduct the services of GOD'S House,—however humble it may be. But is a man therefore driven into curious millinery, and the foppish extravagances of unpopular æstheticism? Need he appear in a surplice of peculiar cut,—a stole embroidered with red, green, or yellow crosses,—a hood so displayed that the crimson lining shall make him look positively smart,—or wearing some unauthorized, or at least questionable vestment? *Why* these mediæval tricks on the LORD'S Day' and in the LORD'S House? ..... Strange blindness, which sometimes overtakes a clergyman of self-denying zeal, and unmistakable piety, that he should fail to perceive that he is as thorough a fop, as affected and contemptible a puppy, in his own solemn way, as the most secular dandy in a London congregation³" [p. 307].

And as to more essential matters than costume, he maintains that a "strictly Choral Service," (meaning a Service "where, in addition to the Canticles, the Psalms are invariably chanted, and the prayers intoned,") "however indispensable in a Cathedral, is utterly out of place in an ordinary parish Church; and in the country, simply ridiculous" [p. 323]; that "to the whole system of

---

[3] The passage is given (not without hesitation) as a specimen of his somewhat intemperate language, when his controversial antipathies were aroused. It is obvious, however, to remark that "self-denying zeal and unmistakable piety" (which Burgon admits in this passage characterize many of the Ritualists) are hardly compatible with foppishness and puppyism. A zealous and devoted clergyman, leading the worship of his congregation, cannot really be a fop or a puppy, however much his costume might give such an impression to those who look only on the surface. There is something deeper than this in the vestments.

As regards the first appearance of Ritualism in Oxford, the Rev. Henry Deane, who has favoured the author with an able sketch of the religious movements in Oxford during Burgon's time, writes;—

"There was considerable change in the religious thought of Oxford during the years 1863-6. Ritualism had now begun to take hold of the undergraduate, and the High Churchman was nothing if not a Ritualist. The Seniors also had changed very much. Many were inclining to the new school of thought."

auricular confession, whether constant or periodical, the Church of England stands utterly opposed" [p. 220]; and that it is not "the office of the physician of souls to probe the hearts of those, who come to him 'to open their grief,'" but

"rather to lend a patient, yet most incurious ear, (the reverse of *inquisitive*, I mean) to the history of what does so weigh down a fellow-sinner ..... in silence and in love to *listen*:—next, if need be, with a faithful yet merciful hand to touch the sore which has thus been brought to light; yet not with judicial inquisitiveness (GOD forbid!), as having for our object the eliciting of one additional detail; but with brotherly sympathy rather, as supremely anxious to minister 'such ghostly counsel, advice, and comfort,' that the conscience of the other 'may be relieved,'" &c., &c. [pp. 221, 222].

The merits of the '*Treatise on the Pastoral Office*' did not go without recognition. The work elicited from Henry Phillpotts, Bishop of Exeter, the following Letter to the Author:—

"Durham, August 13, 1864.

"Dear Sir,—Forgive my taking the liberty of thus addressing you, as if I had the privilege of personal acquaintance. But I cannot regard as a stranger one to whom I am so much obliged, both individually, and as the bearer of an office to which I wish you were raised. For I know not who would be so likely to fulfil its duties as the author of the '*Treatise on the Pastoral Office*.' Yet you must pardon my brevity of acknowledgment of the value of that Book. I do not write without effort,— which I think you would not wish me to incur.

"I have not been able to read your Book entirely as yet. But I am grateful for it. If you do not become Bishop, may you be Professor of Pastoral Theology!

"God bless you! Believe me,

"Gratefully yours,

"H. EXETER.

"Rev. J. W. Burgon.

"If you ever come within reach of me (I return, D.V., to Bishopstowe, Torquay, at the end of this month), pray gratify me with giving me an opportunity of improving my acquaintance with a man, who has been enabled by God to confer so great a boon on our Church."

In the course of the next month "Henry of Exeter" shewed his appreciation of the '*Treatise on the Pastoral Office*,' in what may be thought a more substantial form.

"Exeter, Sept. 22, 1864.

"Dear Sir,—Let me intreat your permission to propose to you the Office of Principal of the Theological College at Exeter [4]. Your Predecessors have been the Bishops of Gloucester and of Ely; and I should rejoice more than I can express to be allowed to number you—I cannot say *after*, but with them—as Teachers of the duties and qualifications of the Clergy. . . . .

"I would wish to write more at length; but writing is inconvenient to me, almost to pain.

"Believe me, dear Sir,

"With warm esteem and respect,

"Yours most faithfully,

"H. Exeter.

"Rev. J. Burgon."

On the next day (Sept. 23), Burgon, after cordial expressions of gratitude "for this fresh mark of confidence from one whom I honour so profoundly, and sympathize

---

[4] It is observable that in the Preface to his '*Pastoral Office*,' Burgon, after some (not too severe) strictures on the want of furniture for the Pastoral Office, with which young men are allowed to take on themselves so arduous a charge, speaks gratefully of our Theological Colleges as having done something to supply a recognised need: "The complaint is of long standing: yet has no practical answer been hitherto given to it, except by the setting up of a few Diocesan Colleges,—institutions which claim our generous sympathy, and deserve to have a place in our prayers. They found an able advocate a century and a half ago in the person of Robert Nelson." Preface, p. x.

with so entirely," asks for "time to deliberate on so serious a step as quitting a cure in Oxford, and a sphere of undoubted usefulness. I will frankly confess that I find it very hard to see 'my way plain before me.'" On the 1st of October he definitively declined the offer, "having with regret arrived at the conclusion that my duty clearly is to remain where I am." He was right probably in the world's point of view, as well as in his own. In a University city the claims of a theologian to higher Church preferment are much more likely to make themselves generally known and recognised, than at the ecclesiastical centre of a remote provincial Diocese. At Oxford, he stood at the fountain-head of religious movement and controversy, ready, on the moment of the rise of a new theological error, to enter a firm and a learned protest for God's Truth, and also at the fountain-head of the best youthful life of England, ready to cast in at the very spring of that life the salt of Scriptural teaching and wholesome moral influence. Long years ago Professor Whewell struck this vein of thought, as regards the sister University of Cambridge, in commenting from the University pulpit on the text, "Behold, I stand by the well of water" (Gen. xxiv. 43).

A.D. 1865. [Æt. 52.]

Burgon's political allegiance to Mr. Gladstone, like that of many other members of the University, had been for some time past on the wane. But severe as was the strain which Mr. Gladstone had placed upon it, it did not even yet quite break down. Burgon supported Mr. Gladstone by his vote in the General Election of 1865[5]; but declined any longer to serve (as he had

---

[5] This General Election was not an appeal to the country on any particular question. The late Parliament had expired by efflux of time.

hitherto done) on his Committee. The University of Oxford at last shook herself loose of a member, who certainly had ceased to represent either her Toryism or her old-fashioned High Churchism. Sir William Heathcote was again returned, as a matter of course, but this time with Mr. Gathorne Hardy as his colleague, instead of Mr. Gladstone. The latter was in a minority of 180.

From a letter of Professor Seabury's[6] to Burgon in the June of this year, we gather that he was at this time giving a series of Lectures to his congregation on the Book of Genesis,—the foundation of these Lectures having been already laid in the Sunday Evening Bible Class, which (as we have seen in one of his letters to Mr. Hensley) he had eight years previously held for the citizens at the Town Hall [see above, p. 290].

"Let me entreat you," writes the Professor, "(I am sure you will pardon my freedom) to go on with your Homiletics on Genesis. It is what the Saint of the golden mouth would do, if he had now your position at Oxford. The formal Sermon (good in its place) should not be suffered to deprive God's people of familiar expositions of His Word. I did not hear your first Lecture; but

---

[6] The Rev. Samuel Seabury, D.D., was a theologian of great eminence and wide influence in the American Episcopal Church, and was the grandson of Bishop Seabury, its first Bishop. Dr. Seabury was the Professor of Biblical Learning and Interpretation of Holy Scripture in the General Theological Seminary of New York from 1862 to 1872, and held for thirty years the Rectory of the Church of the Annunciation in that city. He published several learned and valuable works, the best known of which are '*The Continuity of the Church of England in the Sixteenth Century,*' '*The Supremacy and Obligation of Conscience,*' '*The Theory and Use of the Church Calendar,*' and a tractate entitled '*Mary the Virgin.*' His son, the Reverend W. J. Seabury, the present Rector of the Church of the Annunciation, writes thus to the author:—"I well remember the occasion of my father's letter, having shared with him the hospitable kindness of Mr. Burgon, and having heard the Lecture referred to on the first Chapter of Genesis, which made an impression upon me not to be effaced."

the unmeasured gratification of Mrs. Seabury and my son, who did hear it, convinced me that God had given you access to the hearts and heads of your audience. And your second Lecture, which I heard, made me wish for a series of the same sort on the whole Book. And if the enemy comes in your way, don't spare him." (Perhaps there was less need for this exhortation in Burgon's case than there might have been in the case of some other expositors.) "The rasp of St. Jerome is sometimes of use; and as long as there are 'fools,' there ought to be a 'rod for their backs.'"

Burgon never seems to have done as Professor Seabury wished him, and completed his Expository Lectures on the Book of Genesis. Ten Lectures on this Book he has left behind him, the texts and subjects of which are given at the foot of the page[7]; and it is greatly to be desired that these, as well as the Lectures on the Acts of the Apostles, a series which he *did* complete, and which needs nothing but editing in order to its immediate publication, should be given to the world. The Book of Genesis, like the Acts of the Apostles, was a favourite Book with him. The simple but most stately and majestic Record of Creation, to the acceptance of which in its literal and obvious sense—the sense in which a child would accept it,—he clung (as we shall see) to the last moment of his life; and the inimitable

---

[7] SUBJECTS OF SERMONS ON GENESIS.

1. The Mosaic Record of Creation . . Gen. i. 1.
2. The Creation of Adam and Eve . ii. 7, 18–24.
3. The Temptation and Fall of Man . iii. 1–6.
4. The Promised Deliverer . . . . iii. 8–15.
5. Adam's Sentence . . . . . iii. 16–19.
6. Man an exile from Paradise . . iv. 1, 2.
7. The Offerings of Cain and Abel . iv. 3–7.
8. The Death of Abel . . iv. 8–10.
9. The Curse of Cain . iv. 11–16.
10. Enoch and Methuselah v. 21–27.

grace and beauty of the picture of patriarchal manners which is painted in the later part of the Book, and which, while it is no doubt pure history, is at the same time largely charged with type and figure, and has spiritual mysteries underlying every page of it,—these passages of Holy Writ had at all times an irresistible attraction for a mind so imaginative, and so susceptible of impressions from the sublime and beautiful, as was his.

Burgon's position as a Parish Priest was rendered more difficult than it otherwise would have been, by the circumstance that St. Mary's was the Church not only of his Parish, but of the University also, where on every Sunday in Term time two Sermons were preached before members of the University of all grades (preceded by nothing but the Bidding of Prayer prescribed in the fifty-fifth Canon, and the Lord's Prayer), for which convenient hours must somehow be found. The University had undoubted rights in the Church no less than the Vicar and Churchwardens,—rights which had been recognised in a practical shape by large sums contributed out of the University Chest towards the restoration of the fabric. By long prescription the hours appointed for the University Sermons had been half-past ten in the morning and two in the afternoon. College discipline required of all undergraduates on Sundays attendance at Morning Prayers in their respective College Chapels at 8 a.m.; but attendance at the University Sermons was not enforced except at two or three Colleges, where the students were obliged in the course of the week to produce Sermon Notes, as an evidence that they had been present at one of the University Sermons at least, and had given some attention to it.

Accordingly, attendance at the Sermons being at most

Colleges voluntary, but few Undergraduates presented themselves, except when some preacher of eminence and notoriety had been announced in the previous week. Many of the better Tutors, who were in earnest about the spiritual and moral welfare of their pupils, and who also desired such arrangements as might secure to the College Servants the opportunity of attending Divine Service on Sundays, thought that the system might be improved by a change in the hours of the University Sermons, and of Sunday Morning Prayers in the College Chapels. The Rev. Charles Waldegrave Sandford, then Senior Censor of Christ Church [8] (the College not only largest in numbers, but also first in rank from the circumstance of its connexion with the Cathedral Church), addressed a letter to the Vice-Chancellor, sketching the outline of such a change as he thought might be conducive to the spiritual interests of the Undergraduates and the College Servants, without however committing himself to details. We gather from his letter the interesting fact that "the Undergraduates had lately addressed memorials to the authorities in their several Colleges, praying for a weekly Communion." Mr. Sandford provided in his scheme for a compliance with this gratifying request. The proposal which he threw out for consideration and discussion in the Hebdomadal Council was, that there should be in College Chapels a weekly celebration of Holy Communion at 8 a.m., to be attended, not as a matter of College discipline, but by such Undergraduates as might desire it; that the Morning Prayer in the College Chapels should be at 10 (instead of, as hitherto, at 8 a.m.); and that the Morning University Sermon should be moved from 10.30 a.m. to 12 (noon). He also recommended that sermons of a

[8] Now Bishop of Gibraltar.

more familiar and less ambitious character than those usually preached before the University should be occasionally given in the College Chapels, in which case he thought that the Afternoon University Sermon (almost always feebly attended) might be dispensed with. In this way he hoped that the Sunday breakfast parties and luncheons, which occupied so large a portion of the Sunday morning of many Undergraduates, might have impediments thrown in their way (inasmuch as every Undergraduate must be in Chapel from 10 to 11), while the request of the right-thinking ones for a weekly Communion would be acceded to. This was just one of those alterations which, while seeming at first sight exceedingly desirable, are found to be impracticable without putting other things seriously out of joint; but there can be no question that the proposal was one, both from the obvious aim of it, and the high character of those who supported it, which amply deserved the consideration that Mr. Sandford solicited for it. The Vicar of St. Mary's had been consulted, it appears,—most pointedly consulted,—nay, and listened to upon the subject;—had not this been done, the proceeding would have been not only uncourteous in a high degree, but inconsiderate and inequitable. But, though means had been taken to soothe and conciliate him, it cannot be denied that in the three letters which he wrote on the subject, and specially in that in which he fulminated against Mr. Kitchin[9] for the support given by him to Mr. Sandford, Burgon expressed himself with an asperity quite uncalled for. It is possible that his feelings of repugnance to Mr. Sandford's suggestions may have been prompted in some measure (all unconsciously to himself) not only by the supposed encroachment upon his rights

[9] Now Dean of Winchester.

as Vicar of St. Mary's, but also by his regarding the spiritual welfare of the undergraduates as his peculiar sphere, in which, during the whole of his maturer Oxford life, he had striven to make his mark at the cost of great personal self-sacrifice. He loved the undergraduates dearly, it is true, and laboured hard for them; but others loved and laboured for them too; and it would be most unjust not to recognise how deeply the young life of Oxford in those days was indebted to such men as Professor Heurtley, Mr. Linton, Mr. Christopher (both of the latter Parish Priests like Mr. Burgon), and the late universally lamented Canon Liddon. The faithful chronicler of Burgon's Life could not pass over this incident unnoticed; but the reader who is curious to know more of the particulars must consult the six Pamphlets, the titles of which are given at the foot of the page [1].—We pass from

---

[1] 1. '*The University Sermon and College Services.*' A Letter addressed to the Vice-Chancellor, by Charles Waldegrave Sandford, M.A., Senior Censor of Christ Church, Oxford; Chaplain to the Lord Bishop of London; and late Whitehall Preacher. Oxford: John Henry and James Parker, 1865.

2. '*Mr. Sandford and the University Sermon.*' A Letter addressed to the Rev. the Vice-Chancellor, by the Rev. John W. Burgon, M.A., Fellow of Oriel, and Vicar of St. Mary the Virgin's. Oxford: John Henry and James Parker, 1865.

3. '*Mr. Burgon and the University Sermon.*' By G. W. Kitchin, M.A., late Censor of Christ Church; Examining Chaplain to the Lord Bishop of Chester; and late Select Preacher. Oxford: John Henry and James Parker, 1865.

4. '*Mr. Kitchin, Mr. Sandford, and the University Sermon.*' A Second Letter addressed to the Rev. the Vice-Chancellor, by the Rev. John W. Burgon, M.A. Oxford: John Henry and James Parker, 1865.

5. '*The University Sermon and College Services.*' A Letter addressed to the Vicar of St. Mary the Virgin's, by Charles Waldegrave Sandford, M.A., Senior Censor of Christ Church, Oxford; Chaplain to the Lord Bishop of London; and late Whitehall Preacher. Oxford: Messrs. Parker and Co., 1866.

6. '*The Oxford Sunday.*' A Letter to Mr. Sandford in Reply. By the Rev. John W. Burgon, M.A., Fellow of Oriel, and Vicar of St. Mary the Virgin's. Oxford: James Parker and Co., 1866.

It may be observed that in No. 3,

the subject with the reflexion that this was not the first time in the history of the Church, nor will it be the last, when good men, really seeking the same high and holy ends, have come to a sharp parry and thrust of words. Burgon's aptness to be betrayed, when writing, into intemperate expressions towards opponents, was one of the foibles of his truly great, and noble, and attractive character, and gave a wholly erroneous impression of him to those who were only superficially acquainted with him. "Oh that thou wouldst dip thy foot in oil!" said one of his most ardent and enthusiastic admirers respecting Burgon, wishing for him the blessing of Asher (Deut. xxxiii. 24). It certainly is to be desired that he had dipped his pen in it more frequently.

The early part of the year 1867 carried away the old and venerated friend who had baptized Burgon, and had in later life been his correspondent and trusted counsellor,—the Rev. G. C. Renouard, Rector of Swanscombe. Thus he writes of this event in his Journal:—

1867.
[Æt. 54.]

> "Very many were the tender memories of other years which seemed gathered with that dear old friend into the grave. O what a long catalogue of remembrances there were and are! He is almost the first person I can remember; and he survived my parents, and almost all my other oldest friends,—as Rogers, Hamilton, Smyth, Millingen, and so many, many more. He departed

Mr. Kitchin, while censuring Burgon's attack upon Mr. Sandford as "sharp and somewhat flippant," admits, "One cannot help liking Mr. Burgon, even when his parochial sympathies set him to lay a sleeper in the track of the University train."

It is also only fair to say that in No. 5, whatever view may be taken of the merits of the question at issue, Mr. Sandford has set a model of the way in which Christian Controversy should be conducted, the tone of his Pamphlet being, while he firmly maintains his own ground, most courteous, reasonable, dignified, and perfectly inoffensive towards his antagonist.

Feb. 15, 1867, *æt.* 86, and was buried in the corner of the new part of Swanscombe Churchyard on the 21st."

A natural association of ideas would connect the remembrance of Mr. Renouard with that of his young sister Kitty; for it was, as it will be remembered, from Renouard's house and Churchyard that he had been summoned away thirty-one years ago to Kitty's deathbed. [See *sup.* pp. 54, 55.]

"On my return from dear Mr. Renouard's funeral," he writes in a special and very long memorandum, giving the account of the removal of his sister's body to the Holywell Cemetery in Oxford, "a sudden inclination, which I could not explain, came over me to go and pass half an hour in Bucklersbury with our Uncle and Cousins. We spoke of the most recent changes in the metropolis. 'Yes; St. Stephen's, Walbrook, will infallibly come down one of these days,' said Uncle John. The words seemed to go through me. All the way back to Oxford I revolved the matter, devised a plan" (for the removal of Kitty's body from a site which might within a few years be desecrated by the demolition of the Church standing over her remains, and the conversion of the site into a London thoroughfare), "and acted upon my resolve the very next day." Having obtained the required "faculty" and the necessary sanctions from the clergymen of St. John the Baptist, Oxford, (to which parish the portion of the cemetery in which his father and mother had been buried belonged) and of St. Stephen's, Walbrook, he plans with the assistance of a stonemason "a sepulchral chamber" of stone, procures "four huge Yorkshire flags, eight feet long, four feet high, and six or seven inches thick," to be held together by "a strong iron cramp, secured with lead, at each of the four corners," and causes to be "engraved upon a slab of Mansfield stone," destined to "fit into and fill up the western side of the tomb," a Latin inscription of twenty-two lines, of which he gives the following translation :—

" ✠ The resting-place of a most sweet and excellent little girl, Catharine Margaret Burgon, youngest daughter of Thomas Burgon, Esq., and Catharine Margaret his wife,—who fell asleep in CHRIST on the 28th day of April, 1836. She lived only seven years, six months, twenty-one hours. Her sacred remains I removed at the end of thirty-one years from the Church of St. Stephen's, Walbrook, in London, to this place, in order that close beside her parents, whom she loved so dearly, she, their deeply lamented daughter, might rest. For our dearest mother sleeps in peace in the adjoining grave, and at her left hand sleeps our father also. 'They were lovely in their lives; and in death they were not divided.'

" O ye who succeed us, I implore and adjure you by the Coming of our LORD JESUS CHRIST, disturb not these so dear remains! O reader, O by-stander, one and all, O disturb them not. J. W. B."

By Tuesday evening, 9th of April, 1867, the sepulchral chamber was nearly ready for its proposed occupant; and "on Wednesday morning I was at St. Stephen's, Walbrook, before 9 o'clock. You may suppose with how much agitation of mind I approached *this* part of my task . . . . . What if any unsuspected difficulty should arise?" It did arise; but was surmounted. Several years ago, when interment in Churches had become illegal, the steps leading down into the vault had been bricked up and the aisle above "floored with solid concrete." "The singular liberality and kindness of Mr. Windle, the Rector, had," however, "ordered an opening for me to be effected with crowbars, so that I descended through the vaulted brickwork, which makes the roofing of the vault." A sexton and mason, who are on the spot to assist him, report that though they had found several coffins with the name of Burgon on the plate, none bore the Christian name of Catharine Margaret. With the help of "a guttering candle, and a little sketch which I had made in 1836," he finds the coffins of the other members of his family, in the position of which he had made a note thirty-one years ago; but in the spot where he remembered having deposited Kitty,—" A coffin was there; *but it was not hers*! I felt bewildered and giddy; and the men kept repeating how long they had looked in vain, until I felt sick too." But he is not to be daunted by the apprehension of failure. "I informed the men that, if I stayed for a fortnight, I *would find* what I wanted. So I bade them go and bring four or five strong men, and a pound of candles, and make haste back." Deeply dispirited, notwithstanding his gallant resolution, he rouses himself to "scrutinize every smallish coffin within three or four yards of the place, and presently saw one with a baby's body resting on it. I cannot express the joyous emotion with which, on pushing that little body aside, I first read the beginning of one of *her* names—then the next—then our surname and the date. I blessed GOD; sprang out of the hole in the floor; sent a boy after the men; and, to be brief, in half an hour more the treasure I was in search of had been deposited on the floor of the aisle, quite safe!"

Transported to Oxford in a hearse, the body was laid in the chapel of the Holywell Cemetery, till the sepulchral chamber was quite completed. "On the sides of the chamber, I employed a man to paint in vermilion the words, ✠ JESUS · CALLED · A ⊕ LITTLE · CHILD · UNTO · HIM. ✠"

When everything was ready for the interment, on the evening of Saturday, April 13, the Eve of Palm Sunday, he himself in the presence of his nephew, William Francis

THE OXFORD LIFE: FIFTH PERIOD. 25

Rose, and two friends who had kindly assisted in the preparation of the sepulchral chamber, read the Funeral Service (mindful perhaps of the slovenly way in which it had been read on occasion of the previous interment), "while dearest Billy threw the dust on the body." "The strength of the little sepulchral chamber elicited remarks from all. It looked like something destined to last for ever!"

To those who might be disposed to ask why so large a space should be devoted to an incident of purely domestic interest, the author would reply that the object of a Biography is to exhibit the mind of the subject; and how very large a portion of Burgon's mind this "Translation" of the little sister occupied, may be judged by the long and detailed memorandum he has drawn up of the transaction, only a very rapid outline of which has been presented to the reader.

The first Lambeth Conference, summoned by Archbishop Longley in the autumn of this year, which was attended by seventy-six Bishops of the Anglican Communion, elicited from Burgon one of his characteristic Sermons[2], which he inscribes to the Most Reverend Robert Gray, Metropolitan of South Africa, a Prelate for whom he always entertained what he professes in the Inscription,—a "profound respect and admiration." The Sermon justifies the tone of the Encyclical Letter put forth by the Conference, which had created some disappointment, as being (so it was said with something

---

[2] '*The Lambeth Conference, and the Encyclical.* A Sermon preached at St. Mary the Virgin's, Oxford, on the Eighteenth Sunday after Trinity, (Oct. 20th), 1867, after publicly reading, by command of the Lord Bishop of the Diocese, the Pastoral Address of the Archbishops, Bishops, Metropolitans, and Presiding Bishops assembled at the Lambeth Conference. By the Rev. John W. Burgon, M.A., Fellow of Oriel College, and Vicar of St. Mary the Virgin's, Oxford. Oxford and London: James Parker and Co., 1867.

of a sneer), "judiciously confined to innocuous commonplaces." This, says Burgon, is only because "it enunciates the old Truths, rehearsing them not only in their integrity, but also in their simplicity," and because it "warns" both "against subtracting from the Deposit," and also "from overlaying Evangelical Truth with mere human inventions and new Articles of Faith." Very emphatic is the Vicar of St. Mary's Anti-Erastianism. While he would "sooner cut off his right hand than promote any severance between the Church and the State [3], the Church," he teaches his people, "is not the creature of the State, any more than the State is the vassal of the Church. The Church's Doctrine may not be decided by Lay Tribunals, neither are her formularies to be interpreted by secular Judges; who really, (to speak the plain truth in plain English), do not understand them; do not so much as understand the very language in which they are written. [I am content to rest this assertion on the judgment which they delivered in the famous Gorham case]."

Two events in Burgon's history occurring at the end of the year 1867 gave him, according to his own testimony in his Journal, great satisfaction,—the first the Ordination of the nephew mentioned above [4], whom he had watched over with fatherly care and affection; the second his own election to the Gresham Professorship, an office which he held till his death. Here is his notice of these two incidents in his Journal.

"Oriel, Sunday Night, Dec. 22, 1867.—I cannot lie

---

[3] In the following year (1868) he preached at St. Mary's and published a Sermon on '*Disestablishment: the Nation's formal rejection of God*,' which may be consulted by those who desire to know more of his views on the connexion of Church and State.

[4] William Francis Rose, ordained to the Curacy of Holy Trinity, Windsor;—now Vicar of Worle, Weston-super-Mare.

down to-night without recording the infinite goodness of GOD to me in suffering me to see my dearest W. F. R. ordained Deacon this day at Christ Church. He assisted me at St. Mary's this evening. *Laus Deo!*

"How can I fail also to record my election (on Wednesday, 11 Dec.) to the Gresham Professorship of Divinity—an office I have so much longed for, and now so rejoice to have obtained?

"Praise the LORD, O my soul, for both these great mercies. J. W. B."

But what *is* the Gresham Professorship of Divinity? the curious reader may be inclined to enquire. Burgon's own '*Life of Sir Thomas Gresham*,' which he published, as we have seen, in 1839 (twenty-eight years previously to his appointment to the Professorship), gives full particulars on this head. Suffice it to say here that Sir Thomas Gresham, the founder of the Royal Exchange, who died Nov. 21, 1579, ordained by will that the property of his great mansion house in Bishopsgate Street, as well as the rents arising from the Royal Exchange, after Lady Gresham's life interest in them, "were to be vested in the hands of the Corporation of London and the Mercers' Company. These public bodies were conjointly to nominate seven professors, who should lecture successively, one on every day of the week, on the seven sciences of divinity, astronomy, music, geometry, law, medicine, and rhetoric. The salaries of the lecturers were amply defrayed by the profits arising from the Royal Exchange, and were fixed at £50 per annum;—a more liberal remuneration than Henry VIII had appointed for the Regius Professors of Divinity at Oxford and Cambridge, and equivalent to at least £400 or £500 at the present day" ['*Life of Gresham*,' vol. ii. pp. 437, 438]. From a complaint made as early as 1647, in "a little quarto tract of eight pages, entitled '*Sir Thomas*

Gresham, his Ghost,' to the effect that 'the lecturers were so superbiously pettish, that they will resolve no Quære that may advantage the Dubitour,'" it would seem to have been a recognised practice for pupils who had difficulties to address questions to the Lecturer, and have them answered on the spot for the benefit of the class. This conversational method of conducting the Lectures continued down to Burgon's time, and, as is testified by persons who attended his class, he was usually [5] most

[5] Not absolutely always. His polemical antipathies were strong, and, when roused, put him out of the condition of mind in which calm argument is possible for a man. The author has been told an amusing story of Burgon's dealing with one of his "Dubitours" at a Gresham lecture. A member of the class, with some general knowledge of the questions of modern controversy, started an objection to what the lecturer had propounded. Burgon, at all times somewhat intolerant of opposition, gave a further exposition of what he conceived to be the truth, and tried to settle the matter by his own *Ipse dixit.* "Well, at all events," exclaimed the *Dubitour*, "A. B. holds it to be so" (naming a very eminent and well-known Rationalistic Divine, highly placed in the Church of England); "for I consulted his book about it before I came away." "A. B.," cried Gresham's Lecturer in Divinity, making his long arms perform a whirligig, and forming his lips to express the escape of vapour,— "A. B.!! Pouf-f-f-f-f-f-f!"

He cannot be said to have been patient "towards those that oppose themselves," however exceedingly so towards those who submitted meekly to receive instruction from him. Take the following incident, sent to the author by a widely known and highly esteemed beneficed clergyman :—

"It was about the year '71 or '72 that a lady of my acquaintance, who had gone to live at Oxford with her husband, asked me to write to Burgon, requesting him to allow her to call upon him in any doubt or difficulty. Both she and her husband had been brought up as strong Dissenters, and had come to me some years before for advice and counsel. I did not know Burgon ; but that want of knowledge never has hindered me from helping one who desires or needs help ; and so I wrote to him, and explained how matters stood. He wrote a kind reply, saying that, if she attended his Church (which was the case) and would come to the Vestry some day after Matins, he would see her. She soon knocked at the Vestry door, and was seen by him : he asked what her doubts or difficulties were, and spoke at some length in reply to them ; and when he stopped, she said, 'But, Mr. Burgon—.' His answer was quick and sharp, 'No *buts*!—*go*—do.'"

kind, patient, and painstaking in the replies made by him to enquirers. The Professors were originally, by the terms of the bequest, housed in the College, each of them having separate lodgings in that large mansion, which Gresham probably had built with a view to the corporate life, of which he purposed it ultimately to be the home; but the provisions of his will, full of wise forethought and desire to extend the blessings of Learning to his fellow-countrymen, were no better regarded than those of great Founders generally are, and a ruthless Act of Parliament gave powers, first for the demolition of the College, said to have grown old and ruinous (why was it ever allowed to become so?) and then [8 Geo. III. cap. 32] for the leasing of the ground to the Crown for a perpetual rent of £500 per annum. See all the details of these disreputable proceedings, and Burgon's wail of lamentation over them, in the last Appendix of his Second Volume, No. xxx. p. 500.

He gave his Inaugural Gresham Lecture, Jan. 17, 1868. [A.D. 1868. Æt. 55.] In the same year appeared his '*Plea for a fifth Final School*,' in a letter addressed by him to the Vice-Chancellor of the University. The establishment of this

"fifth Final School" was a subject which lay very near his heart, bearing as it did upon the better qualification of Candidates for Holy Orders, who would naturally avail themselves of the opportunity of obtaining Academical distinctions in Theology, which this new School would hold out. A few words of explanation are here necessary for such readers as are not familiar with the educational system of Oxford. In the year 1807, when first, second, and third Classes were first awarded as Honours to those who had distinguished themselves in the Examination for the first (or Bachelor's) degree, there were two Schools only (that is, two departments of subjects), in the first of which every undergraduate must pass an examination, and in either or both of which he might gain a Class,—*Literæ Humaniores*, vulgarly called Classics, and *Disciplinæ Mathematicæ et Physicæ*, vulgarly called Mathematics. So things continued for more than forty years, till in the year 1850,—after considerable resistance from many thoughtful members of the University, and among them from Burgon himself (see his letter to Mr. Renouard above, pp. 211, 212), the system of Examination for the B.A. degree was extended, so as to include two new Schools (or departments of subjects), one, Law and Modern History, the other Physical Science. This was a fundamental change, a subversion of the old theory and principle of Academical Education, though at first sight it might not appear to be so. For that theory and principle were, that Degrees in "Arts" merely stamped a man as qualified by discipline of the mind and general culture (which it was supposed that Classics and Mathematics were the best instruments of conveying) for the prosecution of such studies as might be called professional, the four recognised studies (besides "Arts") in which degrees were given being Theology, Law, Medicine, and Music. "Arts" were the preliminary of these;—the necessary foundation, upon which alone any of these several superstructures could with safety be reared. This theory, be it sound or unsound, was entirely disturbed, when to the subjects of study intended merely for mental discipline, were added two new ones, of the highest value and importance indeed, but departments of knowledge rather than instruments of training,—Natural Science one, the other Law and History. However, the old educational principle having been abandoned, and other subjects besides Classics and Mathematics being recognised as qualifying for the B.A. degree, and Classes being given for proficiency in them, it was felt by Mr. Burgon and others that Theology, the highest of all studies, would labour under a disadvantage, if in it alone proficiency was not signalised by any honour conferred in connexion with the B.A. degree. If men might graduate with distinction in Law and History, and in Natural Science, why not also in Divinity? A young man destined for Holy Orders would then feel that, in devoting himself to Theological study for a year previously to his first degree, he would be laying in a good foundation of sacred learning, for that which was to be the pursuit and business of his life. The great Bishop Pearson had complained of the University authorities two centuries ago;—"Year after year ye thrust forth youthful aspirants to Holy Orders, to whom ye refuse neither University degrees nor testimonials, but whom ye are not careful to furnish with even a smattering of Divinity before they leave your walls." Burgon attempts to shew that neither the large staffs of Theological Professors at Oxford and Cambridge, nor our Theological Colleges, nor training in a large town Parish under an experienced Parish Priest, will of themselves suffice to meet this long-standing evil, and proposes "that henceforth, just as men's attainments in Mathematics, History, Law, Chemistry, are ascertained by public examination; and as special proficiency is rewarded by a Class; so exactly shall it fare with them in respect of their Theological attainments."

By strenuous exertion on Burgon's own part, and that of others who thought with him, the Statute instituting a Final School of Theology, and prescribing that the Vice-Chancellor and Proctors, jointly with three of the Theological Professors, should nominate the Examiners, and prescribe the Books to be examined in

was passed in the year 1870. Five years later (in 1875) he reviewed the operation of this School in his '*Plea for the Study of Divinity in Oxford*⁶'; and found it by no means entirely satisfactory. On a recent occasion, "out of forty candidates in the Divinity School only twenty-six satisfied the Examiners," fourteen failing to obtain the certificate of having passed the Examination, or, in the slang Academical language, " being plucked ";—and of the twenty-six who *did* obtain the certificate, "the Examiners could not find *one* deserving of the distinction of a First Class" [p. 13]. He traces up "the general lack of Enthusiasm for Sacred Learning and Sacred Enterprise" mainly to the recent Academical Revolution, the effect of which had been to inundate the Colleges with lay Fellows, thus depriving them of persons interested in Divinity and competent to teach its early rudiments; indicates what he conceives to be "neglected fields of Inquiry in English Theology" (one of them Liturgical lore, another the furnishing of the Fathers with a complete Index of Texts [pp. 33, 31]); and advocates the endowment of four new Theological Professorships, Textual Criticism, *Modern* Ecclesiastical History, Liturgical Divinity, and Syriac [pp. 40-44]. But the Bible, regarded and dealt with as God's Inspired Word, is the essential basis of all Divinity ;—this is the one foundation. "I take upon myself to assert that until the dignity of Holy Scripture is more faithfully recognised (by teachers and learners alike), no real progress in Divinity will be made either here or elsewhere" [p. 52].

But great wrong would be done to Burgon, if it were to be for a moment supposed that the keen zest with which

---

⁶ By John William Burgon, B.D., Vicar of St. Mary the Virgin's, Fellow of Oriel College, and Gresham Lecturer in Divinity. Pro Ecclesia Dei. Oxford and London: James Parker and Co., 1875.

The Oxford Life: Fifth Period.

he threw himself into all Academical movements (and his lot was cast upon times astir with Academical movements such as, for the number and importance of them, had probably never been before), distracted him from the demands which his Parish made upon him. He was first and before all things else a diligent Parish-Priest,—diligent in every one of the Pastoral functions. At the close of the year 1868 he writes to his sister on Innocents' Day, proposing to come to her at Houghton for a short respite:—

"I shall be quite worn out. There was Christmas Day with all its previous worry; and that brought two Sermons and five Services: four Services (early Communion and Sermon) on Saturday and Monday: the same on Friday next" (New Year's Day): "on ew Year's Eve, a Service and Sermon; and yesterday of course" (Sunday, Dec. 27) "full work. I feel quite worn out. Eight Sermons and Eight Celebrations in eight days is heavy work for a tired man in an empty College."

In the spring of the next year [1869] we find him lithographing and sending round to every undergraduate [A.D. 1869. Æ. 46.]

who had lodgings in his Parish a most characteristic letter, earnestly entreating "that you will abstain as far as possible from giving *Sunday entertainments* of any sort in your rooms," on the ground that "only by your compliance can the Family with whom you lodge enjoy the opportunity of going to Church, and making Sunday —what God meant it to be to all His creatures—a day of rest." A few days later, we find from a letter addressed to him by Dean Mansel (April 23, 1869), offering to receive him at St. Paul's Deanery, when next he comes up to London for the Gresham Lectures, that he is raising subscriptions for the restoration of St. Mary's organ, two schemes for which, a partial and a more comprehensive one, he submits to those whom he asks to subscribe. To which alternative, when laid before him, the witty Dean characteristically replies thus:—

"THE GREAT ORGAN QUESTION
Decided on the principles of Bacon (Gammon).
Of whole and part, if 'tis confest
  The greater costs the larger sum,
Let *Instauratio Magna* rest,
  And give us *Novum Organum*."

And as to his diligence in Pastoral Visitation, he undoubtedly endeavoured to do, and probably succeeded in doing, what the small number of the Parishioners of St. Mary's made practicable for the Vicar,—that is, in acquainting himself not only with every family, but with every individual in the Parish. The author remembers his saying how hard he had found it to get access to the domestic servants in his Parish, and how he had in some measure achieved this by going his rounds in the morning as the maidservants were washing the doorsteps. He would stop, and after bidding "Good morning" to a girl thus engaged, and saying a few ordinary words about the weather, &c., not long enough to detain her seriously from her occupation, would put a tract in her hand, and bid her read it, and say, "When I come this way another morning, we will have a little bit of talk about it." This at least shews that he did not inculcate on others high aims in the exercise of the Ministry without strenuously endeavouring himself to act up to them[7].

The public events of the year 1869 were such as might well stir up almost frantic indignation in the breast of

---

[7] The Rev. Henry Deane writes to the Author (April 29, 1890) as follows:—"To my knowledge Burgon has sat up the greater part of the night, watching an infant which he had privately baptized. The infant is now a very promising man, and likely to take a First Class. He told me this story."

the old fashioned Tory and old fashioned High Churchman; and Burgon was both of these. The chief of these events was the Disestablishment and Disendowment of the Irish Church, of which measure the late Earl of Derby had spoken so pathetically, as to the horror with which it inspired him, in the last speech which he ever delivered in the House of Lords:—

"My Lords," he said, "I am an old man, past the allotted space of threescore years and ten; and if it be for the last time that I have the honour of addressing your Lordships, I declare that it will be to my dying day a satisfaction that I have been able to lift up my voice against a measure, the political impolicy of which is equalled only by its moral iniquity,"—

words which the noble Earl afterwards followed up by a protest sent in at the time of the Third Reading. Against this measure, while yet it was only in process of concoction, but engrossed to itself a large share of public attention, and was the talk of every tongue, Burgon had entered his usual trenchant protest in a Sermon preached at St. Mary's in the October of the previous year. The Sermon might be taken as an undesigned setting forth of the "moral iniquity," which Lord Derby was afterwards to find in the measure. Its title was '*Disestablishment: the Nation's formal rejection of God* [8].'—But a measure which galled him still more was in store for the end of the year 1869, and a measure emanating from the same Minister, who having shewn his respect for the status and property of a branch of the National Church, by depriving her of the one, and confiscating the other, was now (for had he not always posed as an advanced High Churchman?) to offer what seemed like a studied

[8] The author regrets that having endeavoured in vain to procure a copy of this Sermon, he is unable to give more than a conjectural account of its contents.

insult to the solemn judgment of the Church's synods and hierarchy. '*Essays and Reviews*' had been synodically condemned in Convocation, every Bishop on the Bench joining in the censure of the work, with the exception of two, and these explaining that they did so only from considerations of expediency, while one of the two [9] characterized the work as "subversive of the faith of the Gospel, as well as in contradiction to the doctrine of the Church of England." But all this shall not debar Essayists and Reviewers from receiving the highest honours which the Church has to give, and from sitting in her most dignified chairs of office. The see of Exeter having fallen vacant by the death of Dr. Phillpotts, one of the Essayists and Reviewers, the foremost among them, if any thing is to be augured (which however is doubtful) from the position of the Essays in the joint volume, was called upon by the Prime Minister to receive consecration as Bishop of Exeter. This opened Burgon's mouth wide, as those who knew him would know that it was perfectly sure to do, in obstreperous clamour against all persons concerned. No sooner had the majority of the Chapter of Exeter "sanctioned" Mr. Gladstone's "flagitious and tyrannical abuse of official prerogative" by accepting the Crown's nominee, than he put forth (Nov. 12) his '*Protest against Dr. Temple's Consecration to the Office of a Bishop in the Church of Christ*,' making the protest in the Name of the Blessed Trinity, in the hope and with the prayer that "so flagrant a scandal, so deplorable a calamity, may not befall this Church of England." In a second Protest, dated Dec. 4, he replies to a Manifesto, which Archbishop Tait had published in the newspapers, "in order, as it seems, to allay public anxiety" about the appointment; censures the Archbishop for his "im-

[9] Bishop Jackson of Lincoln, afterwards translated to London.

petuous partisanship" in "writing to persuade the Dean and Chapter of Exeter to elect" the Prime Minister's nominee; and implores the Bishops by every thing that is holy not to grant Consecration, and thus "cast this fatal stumbling block in the way of us all." In a third Paper, dated February 24 in the succeeding year, after the Consecration had taken place, he examines the '*Explanation*' which the new Bishop had given to the public, and in which, while he announced the withdrawal of his Essay from circulation, he pointedly disavowed recantation of the views maintained in it, and regret for having published it. The futility of this '*Explanation*' Burgon seeks to shew, his Essay being entitled '*Dr. Temple's "Explanation" examined*,' and bearing the motto, "Is not the hand of JOAB" [*sc*. Archbishop Tait] "with thee in all this?"—Finally, he administered a most severe reprimand[1] (of questionable propriety surely, as addressed by a Presbyter to a Bishop) to the then Bishop of London (Dr. Jackson), who, despite his 'own strong language as to the mischievousness of '*Essays and Reviews*' [See above, p. 380, footnote 4], had consented, in common with the Bishop of St. David's, the Bishop of Worcester, and the Bishop of Ely, to act on the Commission for the Consecration of Dr. Temple issued by Archbishop Tait in his own serious illness. Eight other Bishops of the

---

[1] '*Protests of the Bishops against the Consecration of Dr. Temple to the See of Exeter: Preceded by a Letter to the Right Hon. and Right Rev. John Jackson, D.D., Bishop of London*,' by the Rev. John W. Burgon, M.A., Vicar of St. Mary the Virgin's, Fellow of Oriel College, Oxford, and Gresham Lecturer in Divinity. "This shall be written for the generation to come." τὰ ἀρχαῖα ἔθη κρατείτω. Oxford and London; James Parker and Co., 1870.

The Letter is dated ORIEL, *Christmas*, 1869, and the Prefatory Notice, HOUGHTON CONQUEST, AMPTHILL, Jan. 12, 1870.

Province of Canterbury,—to their everlasting credit be it recorded,—four of them officially under their hand and seal [2], four in communications of a more informal character [3],—had announced themselves as dissentient from the Consecration, while Bishop Wilberforce of Winchester, in a letter to Burgon, confirmed the prevailing report that he too was dissentient, and had declined to act on the Archbishop's Commission. Four Bishops had avowedly taken up the position of neutrality. The number of the Comprovincial sees which were filled at that time was only seventeen; so that, *even counting the neutral Bishops as consentient*, there was a majority of one against the Consecration,—nine dissentients against eight consentient. And it should be added that four of the dissentients, in announcing their dissent, had appealed to the fourth Canon of the Council of Nice [4], as a Law of the Universal Church, which prescribes that no Consecration shall take place in any Province without the consent of all the comprovincial Bishops, given in writing, if it should be impracticable for them to attend personally and join in the Consecration. Under these circumstances it cannot excite surprise if so grave a scandal roused Burgon's wrath, and drew out all the natural combativeness of his disposition; but it would certainly have been well if, instead of taking matters so summarily into his own hands, he, being nothing more at that time than a Fellow of an Oxford College and a beneficed Clergyman, had fallen into line behind other men more highly placed, who felt the scandal

---

[2] Bp. Ellicott of Gloucester and Bristol, Bp. Selwyn of Lichfield, Bp. Atlay of Hereford, and Bp. Christopher Wordsworth of Lincoln.

[3] Bp. Ollivant of Llandaff, Bp. Campbell of Bangor, Bp. Magee of Peterborough, and Bp. Claughton of Rochester.

[4] The Canon, with a literal translation of it, is given at page 11, *note* 1, of Burgon's Pamphlet.

as keenly as himself, and were exerting themselves to the utmost in the way of protest and, if it might be, prevention. Whether he concurred in the constitutional opposition made to the appointment at Bow Church, under the auspices of Bishop Trower, does not appear. But we find a letter of Dean Mansel's to him about this time, in which the Dean, while sympathizing with the opponents of the Consecration, refuses to concur in Burgon's proposal to memorialize the Archbishop against it, and mildly reproves him for being unjust to those, who had laboured in the same cause before he put his hand to the plough. It was 'a true bill.' The Dean hit a blot, no doubt, in the attitude which his friend assumed upon this critical occasion in the history of the Church. The love of being prominent in any movement,—we may perhaps say, a claim, *quite unconsciously put forth*, to the leadership of it, undoubtedly transpires in the Papers referred to above. Burgon speaks as if he stood alone, or nearly alone, in his protest, ignoring the fact, which yet was notorious, that the proposed appointment had given a shock far and wide to the feelings of Church people, both laity and clergy, and that it was a certainty that some one of high position in the Church would head some movement against it, as indeed we find Dean Mansel himself had done. Similarly, in the movement against '*Essays and Reviews*' Burgon took but the slightest notice of any agency except his own, forgetting that, almost from the first appearance of the publication, two volumes of antagonistic Essays had been preparing by clergy and others, more or less competent, and more or less highly placed. On that occasion, however, there was a reason for his separating himself from others who in the main agreed with him,—namely, that the peculiar views of Inspiration, which formed the staple of his book, were shared by only a small minority of those who yet held '*Essays and Reviews*' to be a most mischievous publication. No such reason existed in the case before us; and we can only allege, in explanation of the tone of his protests, that very strong characters like his are not made for co-operation, but for taking the lead, and that this coming forward into the front rank, to bear the brunt of the battle, has its uses, as against that shrinking and reticence, which waits to see, before it moves in a great cause, what other people will do, and thinks it will be time enough to speak when persons in eminent position have spoken. There is an interesting anecdote of a clergyman of resolute and uncompromising character, who in the last century succeeded in stopping an improper Episcopal appointment by the mere threat of opposition at Bow Church—a threat to be followed up, if the appointment were persisted in, by publication far and wide of the circumstances which made the appointment improper[5]. Meanwhile, if there were faults in this

[5] The clergyman was the Reverend Richard Venn, then Rector of St. Antholin's in the City, father of the more celebrated Henry Venn; and the appointment he objected to was that of Dr. Rundle to the See of Gloucester. Dr. Rundle 'lay under the suspicion of Arianism,' says Lord Hervey. But Mr. Venn's objection to him was, that in general conversation some fourteen years previously he had spoken profanely of the Scriptural incident of Abraham's offering up Isaac, 'asserting that, had he been a Justice of the Peace living at that time, he should have thought it his duty to have laid Abraham by the heels, as a knave or madman, for such an act.' Mindful of this speech, Mr. Venn expressed his determination to appear publicly at Bow Church, and oppose the Confirmation of Dr. Rundle, if his election (by the Dean and Chapter of Gloucester) should give him the opportunity. Venn's decision of character was so well known that it was thought wise, if possible, to induce him to withdraw his opposition either by bribes or threats. On one occasion, when his wife and little boy (the afterwards famous Henry Venn) were in the room, a gentleman, either commissioned by the Lord Chancellor, whose interest at Court had procured Dr. Rundle's

(as in other) "Protests" of Burgon, we may yet admire the ardent love of the Truth, the fearless outspoken manliness, the absolute unworldliness (for preferment seldom waits upon vehement condemnation of the course taken by persons in high places) which transpires in every paragraph of them, as also the entire absence from them of any feeling of unkindness towards the persons declaimed against.

nomination, or by some of the Chancellor's friends, called at St. Antholin's Rectory, and hinted that the Deanery of Wells was soon likely to be vacant, and that it would not be impossible to obtain it, through the Chancellor's influence, for Mr. Venn, provided he would desist from his opposition to Dr. Rundle's advancement. 'Let the Chancellor know that I scorn his bribe,' was Mr. Venn's reply. The gentleman then changed his tone, and brought to bear upon Mr. Venn the terrors of incurring the indignation of so influential a personage as the Lord Chancellor;—'You will be ruined, Mr. Venn, you will be ruined, and all your family!' Richard Venn with great calmness turned to his wife, who was working by his side, and said, ' My dear, could not you support yourself and me by your needle?' 'Yes, if it were necessary.' Then turning to the boy, Henry Venn,—'Harry,' said he, 'would not you like to be a waterman?' 'Yes, Papa, very much.' 'There, Sir, report what you have heard to the Chancellor, and tell him I defy him.' The appointment of Dr. Rundle to the see of Gloucester was not persisted in. Sir Robert Walpole, the Prime Minister, begged the Lord Chancellor to relinquish his suit in favour of Rundle;—he might be got out of the way by being made a Dean, or an *Irish* Bishop;—and accordingly in the next year Rundle was made Bishop of Derry.

The foregoing particulars are taken from a most reliable source, the (unpublished) '*Parentalia*' of the Rev. John Venn of Clapham (son of Henry, and grandson of Richard), with excerpts from which the author has been favoured by the great kindness and courtesy of Dr. Venn of Bournemouth (the great-great-grandson of Richard Venn). The opposition to Dr. Rundle is mentioned in Lord Hervey's '*Memoirs of the Reign of George the Second*' [vol. i. pp. 447-455. *Ed.* Croker, London, 1848]. He mentions Venn, but makes Gibson, the then Bishop of London, the chief agent in the opposition, whereas it was Mr. Venn who originally brought Dr. Rundle's case before the Bishop; and he attributes inferior motives to both Mr. Venn and the Bishop,—to the former the motive of desiring to curry favour with the Bishop in order to get better preferment. The whole tone of Lord Hervey's treatment of the subject is thoroughly cynical and sneering.

"I was very frequently with him," writes Dr. Yule[6], formerly one of Burgon's Curates, "during the period of the controversy about Dr. Temple's appointment to the see of Exeter; and I can testify to the personally affectionate manner in which Burgon always spoke of him, while strenuously, and—as some perhaps thought—unduly, protesting against his Consecration. But with him affection,—the deepest even—was not allowed to prevail where the maintenance of the Faith was concerned. Indeed to my thinking, his ready defence of the Truth, together with his loving disposition, afford the key to the understanding of his character. His writings furnish abundant proof of the first; but only those, who (like myself) have been so fortunate as to be intimately connected with him privately as well as officially, can form any idea of the wealth of affection, which lay concealed under his impetuous zeal for God's Truth, so well aided by his fearless, if often scornful, pen."

The reader's attention has been already called (see above, pp. 149, 150) to a passage in one of Burgon's letters, in which he expresses his appreciation of the beauty and nobleness of the Bishop's character, an appreciation which all those who have the privilege of knowing him will cordially endorse. What follows in Dr. Yule's communication to the author, falling in as it does both with the point of time at which we have now arrived, and with the subject of the Essays and Reviews, may be here presented to the Reader.

"Nor should his ready wit be overlooked. In, I think, the year 1870 several of the Essayists and Reviewers dined together in London, the Master of Balliol (Mr. Jowett) being of the number. Somehow a Friday was chosen for the banquet; and by a strange coincidence a Friday in Lent, which, by a stranger chance still, proved

[6] Rector of Shipton-on-Cherwell, Oxford.

THE OXFORD LIFE: FIFTH PERIOD. 43

to be St. Matthias' Day[7]. Soon after, Burgon put forth the following Epigram :—

> ' When *false Apostles* wish to dine,
>   How plain they show their secret bias,
> With *Lent* and *Friday* to combine
>   The Festival of St. Matthias!' "

Another characteristic incident in Burgon's life belonging to the year 1870 is thus recorded by Dr. Yule.

A.D. 1870.

[*Æt.* 57.]

"In the debate as to the conditions, under which Keble College should be admitted to the privileges of the University, Mr. Burgon took a leading part. One of the chief opponents of the measure was the late Professor Thorold Rogers, whose reply to Burgon's speech was full of personal allusions, not in the best taste. This, as might be expected, excited Burgon very much; and neither Livingstone nor I, who, as it happened[8], sat one on each side of him, could restrain him from jumping up to answer Rogers. It was in vain that many called out that he had already spoken, and exhorted him to take no notice of what had been said. Speak he would, and speak he did, the Vice-Chancellor allowing him to do so. Drawing up his figure to his full height, he said with studied deliberation; 'Mr. Vice-Chancellor, I only wish to say that if the words which have fallen from the last speaker, had been uttered by any other member of this House, I should have been—*hurt*!'—and then he sat down amid roars of laughter, in which I must add Professor Rogers joined heartily."

One more incident of this year deserves to be recorded, if it were only on account of an anecdote connected

---

[7] Dr. Yule is under a mistake as to the year. Not in 1870, but in 1871, did the Festival of St. Matthias (Feb. 24) fall on a Friday. The previous Wednesday (Feb. 22) was Ash Wednesday, the first day of Lent.

[8] Mr. Livingstone *had been* Burgon's Curate (having been ordained to the Curacy in December, 1863). Dr. Yule had succeeded Mr. Livingstone as Curate of St. Mary's in June, 1868,—*was* his Curate therefore in 1870.

with it. Burgon was a Candidate in this year for the Professorship of Exegesis (Exposition of Holy Scripture), the very post for which the bent of his mind and the direction of his studies qualified him. We may be sure that the position would have been in every way congenial to him. But he was not destined to hold it. An aspirant of great brilliancy and of the highest order of qualifications (the late Canon Liddon) was elected to the vacant Chair. Burgon must have felt a keen disappointment, which with his usual transparency of character he was at no pains to conceal.

"When I was an undergraduate," writes the Reverend C. Jerram Hunt, "Dean Burgon was my very good friend, and in all ways most kind to me." (How many, many undergraduates have borne the same testimony!) "One day he asked me to call on him, as he had a book for me. I did so: but he told me he would not give me the book then, but in three days' time. As the book (Scrivener's '*Introduction to the Criticism of the New Testament*') was lying on his table, I was a little surprised. But when I called again, Mr. Burgon explained that in the interim the Professor of Exegesis had been elected (Dr. Liddon); that he had been a Candidate; and that he had hoped to have written in the title-page of his present, 'From the Professor of Exegesis.' . . . . . The incident seems to me to be an illustration of that exceeding simplicity and *naïveté* which were so characteristic of Dean Burgon."

Reviewing the year 1870 in his Journal, Burgon writes thus:—

"The past year has been the most memorable I can recall. The public events of that year have been altogether without parallel. The Fall of the Emperor Napoleon, the sudden collapse of his dynasty, the subjugation of France . . . . . this, on the one hand; and then, side by side, and immediately depending upon it, the overthrow of the Pope's temporal power, which followed upon the promulgation of the profane dogma of Papal Infallibility. So there has been the German Empire rising on the ruins of the French Empire, and the sovereignty of Victor Emmanuel supplanting the sovereignty of the Bishop of Rome."

This thought on the public events of the last year, which seems to have been much upon his mind, he expanded in a Sermon preached in his Parish Church on
A.D. 1781.
New Year's Day, 1871, and entitled '*The Review of a Year.*' [*Æt.* 58.] In this Sermon he calls attention to the

"remarkable coincidence that *the very next day* after the promulgation of the dogma of Papal Infallibility, took place the declaration of war between France and Prussia; —the immediate effect of which was to withdraw from Rome the arm of flesh on which she had hitherto leaned, and to open her gates to the forces of Victor Emmanuel."

To these four topics of European interest,—the fall of the French and the rise of the German Empire, the promulgation of the new dogma and the overthrow of the Pope's temporal power,—he adds his animadversions on three domestic movements, the movement for the Revision of the Authorised Version, "in which an avowed Socinian was invited to take part [9],"—a sure omen, in his

[9] In the July of this year (1871) he appears to have put forth a Protest against the Westminster Abbey scandal, to which he solicited signatures. Judging from the letters of several eminent men among the orthodox, in which, though entirely agreeing with him as to the scandal, and the wrong done to the Church thereby, they decline to affix their names to the Protest, it does not seem to have been a judicious manifesto. It assumed that "the avowed Socinian" had been personally invited to the Celebration of the Holy Communion, with which the proceedings of the N. T. company were inaugurated,—an assumption which some of his correspondents think was hardly borne out by the fact that the circular giving notice of the Celebration had been sent to Dr. Vance Smith as to the other Revisers. Others are of opinion that he should have taken his stand further back, and should have protested, not against a Reviser's being invited to partake of the Holy Communion, but against

view, of eventual failure,—the proposed New Lectionary, to which he always entertained the strongest antipathy, and the provisions of the Elementary Education Act, which "formally *divorces* Religion from Education," and which he regards as the first public avowal of England that she is "a nation without a Religion,"—a proclamation "that henceforth the little ones who come to *her* for Education shall grow up without belief in GOD the FATHER, their Creator; GOD the SON, their Redeemer; GOD the HOLY GHOST, their Sanctifier." Strong speaking, no doubt, and brave speaking; entirely after the manner of John William Burgon. He was absolutely innocent of the art of hedging and trimming, and cared not one jot whether his words were acceptable or distasteful to those "who seemed to be pillars" in Church and State.

It should be added that '*The Review of a Year*,' shows the deep interest which, in the capacity of a Christian Pastor, he took in current events, and the responsibility which he conceived to rest upon him of leading the thoughts of his flock upon such events in a right direction.

"The establishment of a School Board in Oxford," writes the Rev. Henry Deane, "gave Burgon some work this year. Miss Smith, the sister of the late Professor Henry Smith, had been elected a member of the Board. This gave rise to Burgon's Sermon on '*Woman's Place*,' dated Feb. 13, 1871; and the last paragraph[1], p. 12,

an avowed Socinian's having been invited to become a Reviser at all. Bishop Trower, however, a divine of sound judgment and of temperate views, affixed his signature. "I sign it," he writes, "however unworthy, as a Bishop of the Church."

[1] "No! The thing to which I directed your attention at the outset in the way of warning, and which now in conclusion I would faithfully warn you against again,—is the unfeminine, the unlovely method of these last days (I will not stigmatize it in any stronger way)—which, forsaking the place and the province

('Woman herself, I mean,') was a distinct reference to Miss Smith, who was a friend of Burgon's, one of the kindest and most charitable among the ladies of Oxford, and an admirable member of the School Board."

"Miss Smith's Sermon," as it came jocosely to be called, is really a valuable one, and needed at the present day even more than it was at the time it was delivered. The text (Titus ii. 5) in five brief words defines woman's sphere, and, as involved in that sphere, the distinctive duties to which God has called her—"To be keepers at home"; and there is one thought in it, which throws light both upon certain passages of the New Testament, and upon the movements of men's minds in the Apostolic age. It may have been, the preacher thinks, the exceeding honour which is placed upon woman in the Gospels by the Mystery of the Holy Incarnation, and by lifting her to exactly the same level with man, as regards the terms of salvation and the hopes of glory, which made it necessary for St. Paul "once and again, to rebuke with something like sharpness the over-eager self-assertion of the other sex, waking up to a proud sense of its newly-recovered privilege, and almost giddy (so to speak) at finding itself placed on such a pinnacle of honour."

No one knew better than Burgon how bitter is the

GOD Himself assigned to Woman,—(the way of privacy, the unobtrusive charities of Home, the acts which shun notoriety, the distaste for popular applause,)—is acting as if some new Gospel had been discovered, which inculcated a diametrically opposite course. Let me hope that I am not alone in confessing that I fairly *loathe* this new development, while I deplore it also: wishing above all that she in whose power alone it is to check this growing evil,—(Woman herself, I mean)—would interfere to put it down and tread it out; if not through a high Christian instinct of what is lovely and what is right, at least in obedience to the ordinary instinct of self-preservation, self-regard, self-respect."

experience of Death's removing one dear form after another, until at length the family tree is almost stripped bare, what remains being but "as the shaking of an olive-tree, two *or* three berries in the top of the uppermost bough, four *or* five in the outmost fruitful branches thereof." In his Journal of Jan. 27, 1871, he thanks GOD that his brother and his sister Emily were then at Houghton with him, "and so (except dearest Helen"—Mrs. Higgins—) " we are all together." "Little Kitty" was the only sister he had yet lost, and we have seen how the loss of her wrung his heart for many a long year afterwards. Now, in that visit to Houghton in the January of 1871, he looked his last upon Emily Mary[2]. After the family gathering she returned to Canterbury, where she resided, and on the 6th of May, Burgon (as also his brother and Mr. Higgins) received a telegram from her physician, announcing imminent danger, and requesting his presence forthwith. He could not reach Canterbury till between three and four p.m., and before he arrived all was over.

"While the whole thing was sudden and shocking to an inexpressible extent," (thus he writes in his Journal), he finds solace in the evidence given "of her pious and affectionate state of heart and mind," by the ejaculatory prayers which she put up in the hearing of her attendant amid the sufferings of pleurisy. And he recognises GOD'S "providential love to her in sparing her all the bitterness of parting" (with the members of her family), "all the effort to exert herself when exertion would have been agony, all distraction of mind, all sorrow at the sight of our sorrow," &c.

On Thursday, May 11, he brought the body to Oxford,

[2] See the family tree, giving the names of his sisters and brother, Vol. i. p. 8, note 4.

THE OXFORD LIFE: FIFTH PERIOD. 49

and deposited it in the Chapel of the Holywell Cemetery, where Kitty had lain before, and on Friday, May 12,

"we buried the dear sister at her father's feet. H. J. R., C. L. H." (Mr. Rose and Mr. Higgins), "and the two boys" (Mr. Rose's two sons, Hugh James and William Francis) "were the mourners present; but many kind hearts a long way off mourned with us, I am sure."

Thinking it desirable, as his almost exclusive study for some time past had been Theology, that he should graduate in Divinity, Burgon now proposed himself for the degree of Bachelor in that faculty (to the degree of Doctor he never proceeded, feeling probably that the fees demanded for the Doctorate might, with his limited income, be better spent in another form). It was at that time required from candidates for the Bachelor's degree, that they should read two exercises publicly in the Divinity School, as evidences of their competency in the Faculty of Divinity. The then Regius Professor of Divinity, Dr. Payne Smith[3], suggested to him that, as St. Mark's Gospel had always been his favourite book of the New Testament, and as he had been for some time past collecting materials for a work which should vindicate the genuineness of the last twelve verses of that Gospel, he should take those verses as the subject of the two exercises now required of him. Burgon accepted, nothing loth, the task of vindicating the genuineness of these twelve most important verses,—all the more so, because it was known that the most eminent textual critics of the New Testament Revision Company looked askance upon them, and would probably, as indeed they have done, insinuate a question as to their genuineness

---

[3] Now Dean of Canterbury.

into the minds of unsophisticated English readers[4]. He had been already for some years studying the manuscript evidence for and against the verses which so many of the learned felt disposed to obelize,—that is, to question their having appeared in the original autograph of St. Mark, even if they were willing to allow that they had been added at a very early date by some one who thought the narrative to be incomplete without them. Accordingly his exercises for the Divinity School were all but ready to his hand when they were wanted; he had but to open his desk, bring out the manuscript notes which he had accumulated there, and throw them, or a portion of them, into the form of two dissertations. These dissertations he read publicly in the Divinity School, on July 3 and 4 of this year [1871], and as the Epistle Dedicatory (addressed to Sir Roundell Palmer, Q.C., M.P.) and the Preface are both dated July, 1871, the work itself must have passed through the Press shortly after, showing that it had been concocting long before. "I have conscientiously laboured at it," he says in the Preface, "for many days and many nights, beginning it in joy, and ending it in sorrow." The sorrow which attended the end was his sister's death, as is clearly marked by the poem, "L'Envoy," which he appends to

---

[4] What else would a person of ordinary education, but altogether ignorant of Manuscripts, infer from the fact of a break being made in the printing of the Revised Version after St. Mark xvi. v. 8, and of this note's appearing in the margin of v. 9, "The two oldest Greek manuscripts, and some other authorities, omit from v. 9 to the end,"—but that the last twelve verses *are untrustworthy*? In order to place anything like a fair view of the evidence before the reader, it would have been necessary to add something of this kind to the note: "It should be said, however, that the two oldest Greek manuscripts are full of blemishes, both in the way of omission and interpolation." See how Burgon shows this in Chapter VI. of his '*Last Twelve Verses.*'

the work, and in which he asks her to "tell the Evangelist of her brother's toil[5]." What the "joy" was, which marked the commencement of the work, is more questionable. In the poem it is intimated that three springs had decked the trees with blossom,

> "Since I, like one that striveth unto death,
> Find myself early and late, and oft all day
> Engaged in eager conflict for GOD'S Truth;
> GOD'S Truth to be maintained against man's lie.
> And lo, my brook which widened out long since

---

[5] "O Sister, who ere yet my task is done,
Art lying (my loved Sister!) in thy shroud,
With a calm, placid smile upon thy lips,

Open those lips, kind sister, for my sake,
In the mysterious place of thy sojourn,

And tell the Evangelist of thy brother's toil;
Adding (be sure!) He found it his reward.
Yet supplicates thy blessing and thy prayers,
The blessing, saintly Stranger, of thy prayers,
Sure at the least unceasingly of mine!"

This idea of a request made to one of the Saints in another world to remember in favour of a person what that person had done in illustrating the Saint's work or writings, is not peculiar to Burgon. Dr. Pusey, Burgon himself tells us, not many weeks after his son's death, said to Canon Liddon in the course of conversation, "I cannot help hoping that if dear Philip" [a son of the Doctor's] "is allowed, now or hereafter, to be anywhere near St. Cyril in another world, St. Cyril may be able to show him some kindness, considering all that Philip has done in these later years to make St. Cyril's writings better known to our countrymen." [See '*Lives of Twelve Good Men*' (CHARLES LONGUET HIGGINS), vol. ii. p. 418, footnote 8, where this saying of Dr. Pusey's is cited from the Preface to vol. ii of Liddon's '*English Translation of Cyril.*'] It is cited à propos to Mr. Higgins, when lying on his deathbed, having said to Burgon, when he entered his room,—' "I suppose, Johnny, you will inquire for S. Mark immediately,—won't you?" "What? In Paradise, do you mean?" "Yes, to be sure," he rejoined, raising his head slightly from the pillow to smile and nod.' (*ibid.* p. 418). Such things have a grotesque sound; but query whether the grotesqueness may not come from the fact of our not realising the things of another world, which saintly men do realise?

Into a river, threatens now at length
To burst its channel and become a sea."

The probabilities are that the joy to which he referred was his election to the Gresham Professorship at the close of 1867, and upon the duties of which he entered in 1868. It is likely enough that he took the resolution of vindicating the genuineness of the concluding section of the Gospel according to St. Mark, as an occupation in every way befitting of the position which he now held; and worked at it (amid divers other engagements, parochial and polemical) with that energy and tenacity of purpose which so remarkably characterized him, until at the time of his sister's death it was well nigh completed. In a letter addressed to Miss Monier Williams (now Mrs. Samuel Bickersteth), a most attached member of his congregation at St. Mary's, and of one of his Bible classes, this is the account he gives of his labours on St. Mark, of their duration, and of the date of the publication. The letter is dated from Houghton, whither (as "I began to feel *very like a mummy*,") he had come in the Oxford Long Vacation "to get a little change of scene and occupation,"—and a little society also,—for "there is no telling," he says, "how lonely it is living alone in College." . .

"But I was going to tell you about myself and St. Mark (for we never parted company for an hour), and the plain truth is he almost wore me out. I rose every morning at five, and got two hours work before breakfast; studied all day; visited my parishioners in the evening; and so *Da Capo, Da Capo*, till Aug. 4. . . . You will understand that the book (which I have been three years about!) is at last done. It will not be published till October; but it is printed; and I shall neither see nor hear any more about it till October, when I return to Oxford." The letter is dated Aug. 15.

'The Last Twelve Verses of St. Mark' is indeed a grand monument of Burgon's genius, of his acumen as a textual critic, and of the extent and indefatigable industry of his researches, and while we may hesitate to admit the claim which he makes for himself in the Epistle Dedicatory—(the " claim to have shown, from considerations which have been hitherto overlooked, that the genuineness of these verses must needs be reckoned *among the things that are absolutely certain*,") we think that an unprejudiced reader will rise from the perusal of the work with a firm conviction that the main objections alleged against the genuineness of the passage have been successfully met, and that the evidence in favour of its having been part of the Evangelist's original autograph is immensely greater than anything which has been adduced on the other side. In conformity with his own principles of textual criticism, he appeals not to manuscripts only, but to the citations made by the early Fathers[6], as well as to the early versions, and finds

---

[6] This is the proper place in which to insert a Postscript to Dr. Scrivener's '*Adversaria Critica Sacra*,' with a sight of which he has been good enough to favour the author, before the work itself has been actually completed. It runs as follows:—

"*September* 29, 1890.

"My lamented friend and fellow student, the late Very Reverend J. W. Burgon, Dean of Chichester, very earnestly requested me, that if I lived to complete the present work, I would publickly testify that my latest labours had in no wise modified my previous critical convictions, namely, that the true text of the New Testament can best and most safely be gathered from a comprehensive acquaintance with every source of information yet open to us, whether they be Manuscripts of the original, Versions, or Fathers; rather than from a partial representation of three or four authorities which, though in date the more ancient and akin in character, cannot be made even tolerably to agree together.

"I saw on my own part no need of such avowal, yet (*neget quis carmina Gallo?*) I could not deny Dean Burgon's request. The Dean's capital argument arising from the fact that the text used by Patristic writers is often purer than primary manuscripts written one or two centuries

both Fathers and versions bearing favourable witness to the verses in question. He shows the utter untrustworthiness of the Vatican and Sinaitic manuscripts (in which the verses are wanting), from their numerous omissions, interpolations, corruptions, and perversions of the truth; then, passing to the internal evidence of the genuineness of the verses, shows that in them we meet with every principal characteristic of St. Mark's manner, and calls attention to the striking resemblances of style and thought between the first chapter of St. Mark's Gospel and its closing section; then appeals to the early Lectionaries, that of the East, *which is older than any extant manuscript*, giving the last twelve verses of St. Mark as the lesson for Matins on Ascension Day, and also as one of the eleven Gospels for Easter Day; and finally suggests, as the most probable explanation of their omission from the Vatican manuscript, that a marginal Lectionary-mark (το τελος, the end), indicating the end of the *Liturgical* Gospel for the second Sunday after Easter, was supposed by the scribe who made that copy to mean that the Gospel itself ended there, and that what he found after that was a later and unauthorized addition. He would therefore transcribe no further; but left a column blank[7], to show that there was

younger than they (see p. 2, note 1) needs, of course, much care in its application, and can only be insisted on when the context renders it quite clear what the reading before the elder writer actually was. Such a case (and it is by no means of rare occurrence) as the following seems to me absolutely conclusive. In John iii. 13 the clause ὁ ὢν ἐν τῷ οὐρανῷ, omitted by some four manuscripts (Codd. אBC. and 33), three at least of them being the production of an age deeply steeped in Arianism, is vindicated by Hippolytus, who flourished a full century before the date of the most ancient of them; while the theological inference drawn by him, ἀποσταλεὶς ἵνα δείξῃ τὸν ἐπὶ γῆς ὄντα εἶναι καὶ ἐν οὐρανῷ leaves no possible doubt as to the reading of the copy which Hippolytus had before him."

[7] The "plan" of the scribe, who

The Oxford Life: Fifth Period. 55

something after the word END, which he did not venture to reproduce, as his doing so might seem to give it authority.

It is needless to say that this great argument of Burgon's, in support of the genuineness of an important section of the New Testament, received the warm commendation of those best qualified to form a judgment in such matters.

"I have to thank you," writes Bishop Christopher Wordsworth from Riseholme (Oct. 7), "for a Volume, which (if I mistake not) will constitute a new era in the history of the science of the criticism of the Sacred Text. It has rendered a double service to Holy Scripture and the Church. It has restored twelve verses to their proper place in the Canon of the New Testament and in the Creed of the Church. And it has also recalled us to a sounder estimate of the value of our critical authorities, and will constrain many, I trust, to revise their principles of Biblical Criticism, and will stimulate many to labour in the same field of patient research into the testimony of the Old Lectionaries and Ancient Fathers, —a mine which (as you justly observe) has hardly

---

wrote the Vatican Manuscript, "is found to have been to begin every fresh book of the Bible at the top of *the next ensuing column* to that which contained the concluding words of the preceding book. At the close of St. Mark's Gospel he has deviated from his else invariable practice. He has left in this place one column entirely vacant. It is *the only vacant column* in the whole manuscript;—a blank space *abundantly sufficient to contain the twelve verses, which he nevertheless withheld.* *Why* did he leave that column vacant ? *What* can have induced the scribe on this solitary occasion to depart from his established rule ? The phenomenon,—(I believe I was the first to call distinct attention to it,)—is in the highest degree significant, and admits of only one interpretation. *The older MS.* from which Cod. B was copied must have infallibly *contained* the twelve verses in dispute. The copyist was instructed to leave them out,—and he obeyed; but he prudently left a blank space *in memoriam rei.* Never was blank more intelligible ! Never was silence more eloquent ! "—Burgon's 'Last Twelve Verses of St. Mark,' p. 87.

been worked at all as yet with anything like adequate care.

"It cannot, I think, be doubted, that some of our present countless Cursives were transcribed from very early MSS., and in many places may represent a Text older than what we possess in any extant Uncials. With affectionate gratitude to you, and with praise and thankfulness to the Divine Teacher whose scholar you are, I am, my dear Friend, Yours always,

"C. LINCOLN."

Here is the testimony of the late Canon Cook, assuredly no mean authority on such questions, to the '*Last Twelve Verses of St. Mark.*' The letter containing it was recently found in one of the Volumes of the '*Speaker's Commentary*' in the Chapter Library of Chichester:—

"Exeter, Oct. 4, 1875.

"My dear Sir,— . . . . .

"I am very glad to have occasion to write to you, that I may tell you with what intense interest, and I trust profit, I have just read your work on the '*Last Twelve Verses of St. Mark's Gospel.*' You have lifted a heavy weight from my shoulders; for, much as I distrusted the judgment and fairness of some of the critics who condemn that portion of the Gospel, I was unable to stand up against their combined forces. Your arguments are unanswerable; some of them entirely new to me; all of them ingenious, and for the most part convincing. I shall have to study your work carefully, since owing to unforeseen circumstances I am compelled to write the Commentary on St. Mark myself. You will not expect that I shall agree with you on all points: e. g. I feel quite satisfied that the narrative portion is independent of St. Matthew, derived partly from a common source, partly from St. Peter's personal teaching. But I feel that you penetrate so deeply into the character of the Evangelists that every hour spent with you will be full of profit. Glad indeed shall I be to become personally better acquainted with you, though I fear you will often think me cold-blooded, wanting in energetic faith and burning zeal.

"Yours truly,
"F. C. Cook."

Sir Roundell Palmer's acknowledgement of the book, which is inscribed to him with a flattering Epistle Dedicatory, because the author "desires to submit his argument to a practised judicial intellect of the loftiest stamp," is so remarkable, as showing the reasonableness of demanding the strongest proof, whenever the genuineness of a traditional passage of Holy Scripture is called in question, and the great improbabilities involved in a conclusion adverse to the genuineness of this particular passage, that it will be well to exhibit it by itself at the end of the Period.

The late Earl Beauchamp, writing from Madresfield Court, Oct. 22, shows his high appreciation of the value of the work in a form at once discerning and practical.

"In the present crisis of Christianity," he writes, "it is of the last importance to maintain the genuineness of v. 16." ['He that believeth and is baptized shall be saved,' &c.] "It is not as in the days of Pope,

'For *modes* of faith let graceless zealots fight';

but faith itself in God, as He is revealed, is denied to be more pleasing to Him than doubt. It would be impertinent in me to express an opinion on your book; but I think it very desirable it should be translated into Latin; and it would give me much pleasure to subscribe (say) £50 towards that object."

It is much to be regretted that this suggestion, however Burgon may have entertained it, was never acted upon; for such a work makes an appeal to the scholars of Europe, not to English scholars only, in favour of the genuineness of a most important section of the New Testament, and Latin is the language common to all scholars of whatever nationality.

In a later paragraph of the letter to Miss Williams already quoted [see p. 52], he writes—

"Did I tell you that I mean, if I live, to visit Florence this summer? I expect to start with my nephew in September, and to be away for a month. It is such a pleasure giving *him* pleasure! All the family seem to approve of the plan. So in about a month I hope we shall start."

Accordingly, in less than a month he and his nephew did start. On September 20 he writes to Miss Washbourne (a lady who did him good service as an amanuensis, and whom he addresses as "My dear Secretary") from Padua[8], where he is "collecting materials for a Second Edition of" his '*Last Twelve Verses*' (though the First Edition had not yet actually appeared), "and searching for and collating manuscripts." On October 17 he

---

[8] This was not Burgon's first journey to the continent in quest of Manuscripts. In the preceding year (1870) he had visited Paris in company with his nephew (Rev. W. F. Rose), and worked in the Bibliothèque Impériale, his special interest at that time being the manuscript containing Victor of Antioch's '*Commentary on St. Mark*,' which he wished to consult in connexion with his forthcoming work on '*The Last Twelve Verses*.' The journey of 1871 was in the nature of a *tour*, the uncle and nephew having visited in the course of it, not only Florence and Padua, but also Turin, Milan (where they made the acquaintance of Dr. Ceriani), Modena, Ferrara, Parma, Bologna, Siena, and Basle, and working at manuscripts in the Libraries of all these cities. In the September of 1872 they visited Munich, and went thence through the Dolomite country to Venice, making an expedition by the way, incidental to their main purpose of examining Manuscripts, to Ravenna.

While doubtless the change of scene and association which these tours necessitated was a great refreshment to Burgon, his work in the Libraries was probably as close and assiduous, and put as great a strain upon him, as any of his studies at home.

writes again to the same lady from Paris, "hoping to be at home shortly." In the year following (as may be now mentioned by anticipation) he made a similar tour in September. On the 9th of that month he writes to Miss Washbourne from the Rhine, telling her that he is going "to inspect MSS. at Munich and Venice." Arrived at Venice, he again writes that he is examining MSS. in a room of the Library, "all to myself with my nephew." In these tours Burgon got through a very large amount of research for, and collation of, Manuscripts, utilising for that purpose every day and almost every hour of his time. At page 224 of Dr. Scrivener's *Plain Introduction to the Criticism of the New Testament for the use of Biblical Students* [3rd Ed. 1883], we find that twenty Italian manuscripts were added by Burgon to the list of cursive copies of the Gospels given in Dr. Scrivener's earlier editions—these additions being announced in letters addressed to Dr. Scrivener in the '*Guardian*' of Jan. 29 and Feb. 5, 1873. Doubtless these twenty Italian manuscripts were brought to light by the enquiries which Burgon made in his autumnal tours of 1871, 1872. In point of research for and acquaintance with Cursives, he probably excelled every other English student of his time.

On the last Sunday of the year 1871 (which was also the last day of the year), Burgon preached his Sermon on the New Lectionary, which might legally supersede the old one on the next day, although it was left optional with the clergy for the next seven years to use the old one still, should they see fit to do so. It was on this occasion that on closing the Book after the reading of the Second Lesson, he said with that plaintive cadence of the voice, which he knew so well how to assume,—a cadence full of pathos, but not without a dash of querulousness,—

"Here endeth—the Old Lectionary,"—the further words "and more's the pity," which are usually attributed to him, never having been actually uttered, however much his accents may have seemed to imply them. Certainly the Sermon indicated very unequivocally his own conviction that "the more *was* the pity" that "the Lectionary of our fathers passes from us to-day." "I am profoundly convinced," he says, "that the new Lectionary is open to so many and such grave objections that we should be better without it than with it." "I hold that *the serious curtailment of the amount of Scripture which will henceforth be listened to in Church*, is in itself a blot which entirely eclipses every other proposed advantage of the New Lectionary." "I entreat you to seek, by increased private study, to remedy the loss you will henceforth daily sustain at the hands of the men who have given you 'the new Lectionary.'"—Yet, strong as his objections were to the Revised Lectionary,—only less strong than those which he entertained against the Revised New Testament—and, while he held, too, that the Revisers had gone altogether beyond the terms of their commission "in inventing an entirely new Lectionary for the Church of England," and that its adoption, having been carried by only a casting vote in the Southern Convocation, could scarcely be regarded as the Church's act at all, it is interesting and instructive in the way of example to observe how loyal he is to whatever is imposed by even the semblance of authority.

"Do any enquire why then I *adopt* this new Lectionary, —seeing that I disapprove of it so heartily, and for seven years am not compelled to employ it ? I answer, Because I hold that a worse thing by far than unskilfully constructed Tables of Lessons, is a divided Church. The Bishops have requested their Clergy to employ these

Tables, and in such matters they are to be obeyed. No vital principle is directly imperilled by compliance,—as would be the case if they were so ill-advised as to require the suppression of one of the Church's three Creeds." (He is thinking about the Athanasian Creed, to the abandonment of the public recitation of which some of the Bishops were known to be favourable, and the maintenance of which he felt himself bound "earnestly to contend for" in the coming year.) "Rather than do *that*, not a few of us would probably think it our duty to resign our cures."

Other men, while entertaining similar objections to the New Lectionary, considered themselves quite warranted in not adopting it till, in 1879, it became compulsory. This was the course taken by the author in Norwich Cathedral, and against which Burgon thus remonstrated with him in a private letter :—

"I really must affectionately entreat you," he writes, "to reconsider your practice of not using it. Believe me it is best,—*it must be best*—to set an example of submission to, i. e. of *acceptance of* Law." (Certainly; but the Old Lectionary was as much *Law* as the New until Jan. 1, 1879.) "It *will bring a blessing* to have submitted. After all, it is but the measuring out of the same blessed Scriptures which offends me,—as it does you. Would you not eat your mutton, because my servant carved it badly?

"Do you know how *I* avenge myself on the short Lessons. *I read them wondrous slow.* At all events, I will not be deprived of my choicest privilege—the public reading of Holy Scripture—because Mr. " [one of the Revisers] " has contrived a bad subdivision of the Chapters."

It may be here mentioned by anticipation, so that there shall be no need to recur again to the subject of the Revised Lectionary, that two years previously to its becoming compulsory,—that is, in 1877—three intimate friends, all of whom concurred in strongly objecting to the New Tables of Lessons, joined in putting forth three Essays, detailing each from his own standing-point what they conceived to be its sins of omission and commission. The late Bishop of Lincoln (Christopher Wordsworth) led the way, and Burgon (then Dean of Chichester), with the present writer, nothing loth, followed suit. Burgon in his Sermon had "carefully abstained from entering into a detailed examination of the New Lectionary"; but in his Essay he does so, saying comparatively little of what he conceived to be the objectionable principles underlying its structure, which he had sufficiently handled already in his Sermon of six years ago. Of course the joint literary enterprise led to much correspondence between the parties, in which Burgon was as clever, as grotesque, as cordially affectionate as ever. "I like the notion of our writing," he says, "without concert or comparison; for I think it will ensure variety, and give force to what we say: but we *must* compare our lucubrations in the end,—or—you remember what happened to the Kilkenny cats! In quite plain English, we may contradict one another!" The saintly and learned Bishop, who was the captain and pilot of this very tiny cock-boat, also writes about the enterprise quite in his own character:—

"There is something said in a certain place about 'a threefold cord.' Not that I feel any confidence in our carrying our point; but it is, in my judgment, always well to leave on record *a proof that things did not go unchallenged*. I recall with delight the opening sentence of Hooker's '*Preface*[9].' . . . . What is *quite*

---

[9] "Though for no other cause, yet for this; that posterity may know we have not loosely through silence permitted things to pass away as in a dream, there shall be for men's information extant thus much con-

certain is, the subject deserves prayerful thought. I confess I turn to *such* matters with a sense of downright relief, after the perplexing spectacle presented by the doings of such gentlemen as Mr. ——" (one of that band of advanced Ritualists, whose cases from time to time exercise tribunals, and most unhappily! open gaols).

The '*Threefold Cord*' has long since been forgotten, but the only survivor of those who twisted it recalls many pleasant and some amusing incidents to which that ephemeral production gave rise,—specially the genial and delicious frankness with which a dear friend of his, one of his then Colleagues in the Chapter of the Church of Norwich, exclaimed, on receiving a copy;—" All that is wanted is, that you should write after your names on the title-page, THE THREE MOST IMPRACTICABLE MEN IN THE CHURCH OF ENGLAND." Impracticable or not, the writer must avow that he is proud to have had his name associated, however temporarily, and however unworthily, with those of two such devout Christians and orthodox Theologians as Christopher Wordsworth, late Bishop of Lincoln, and John William Burgon, late Dean of Chichester.

The year 1872 furnished Burgon with trials in two points, in both of which he was especially susceptible, the domestic affections and orthodoxy. In the latter part of the month of January, he had met his only brother Thomas Charles[1], three years younger than himself, at the house of their younger sister in Bedfordshire, Turvey Abbey. "Tom" had been to school with him at Blackheath; and one or more of his early schoolboy

A.D. 1872.
Æt. 59.

cerning the present state of the Church of God established amongst us, and their careful endeavour which would have upheld the same." ['*A Preface to them that seek* (as they term it) *the Reformation of the* *Laws and Orders Ecclesiastical in the Church of England.*' By Mr. Richard Hooker.]

[1] See the Family Tree, Vol. i. p. 8, note 4.

letters bear pathetic testimony to his affection for, and quasi-parental interest in, his brother. At Turvey, though cheerful and able to live with the family, Thomas Burgon, who had "profound functional derangement, often let fall remarks which terrified me. I have since ascertained that he distinctly foresaw his own coming dissolution, and desired to prepare us for it. I embraced him for the last time on Saturday, 27 January, after a very early dinner." On Ash Wednesday (February 14), when the services of the Church on that holy day were demanding Burgon's attention; "I received a letter saying he was very poorly, and a telegram soon after implying that he was gone! I repaired to Turvey instantly, and found that soon after 2 a.m. he had departed." On Monday, February 19, he brings the body to Oxford, where on the following day it is interred in the Holywell cemetery, side by side with the remains of the other members of his family.

"And now all is done; and the beloved parents and their three children are lying together. O that I may be laid close beside them! . . . . Let me only add that he died with a good hope, resigned, trustful, faithful, and in charity with all. He was *a very humble Christian*, and I am persuaded he entered into his Saints' rest. All that belongs to his last days has been comfortable unspeakably. O that I had been a better brother to him, —more large-handed and more large-hearted! But I loved him well, and he knew it. I shall wear the sorrow of this present hour until I depart this world myself."

Scarcely were the days of mourning for his brother ended, than the troubles of the Church called him again to arms. His Letter, entitled '*An Unitarian Reviser of our Authorized Version, intolerable,*' which appeared originally in the '*Guardian*' newspaper, was published by him in a separate form under date *Friday before Holy-week* [March 22, 1872]. It is an appeal to Dr. Ellicott, Bishop of Gloucester and Bristol, the Head of the Company for the Revision of the New Testament[2], to "clear himself of complicity in the grievous scandal" of admitting on the Company "one who openly assails the fundamental doctrine of the Christian Religion" (the Divinity of Christ), either by "insisting on the removal of this Unitarian Teacher," or by "withdrawing himself from the Revising body." The scandal (a very serious one, no doubt, and calculated deeply to shock and offend all who believe the Church's dogmatic Faith to be her security, as also to throw the gravest suspicion on the result of the Revisers' labours) was now nearly two years old; and, as has just been said, Burgon had already dealt with the same grievance in the columns of the '*Guardian.*' What may have been the circumstances which moved him to renew a protest previously made, does not clearly appear. Judging from the few words of Introduction to the Letter, it would seem as if he thought a n' objection might be taken up to the scandal, on the ground that the co-optation into the Revising Company of "members of the various Sects" had been irregular, was never formally sanctioned by Convocation, and was thus *ipso facto* invalid. Anyhow, some circumstance or other seems to have excited him (though always very susceptible of such excitements) abnormally, and to have prompted

---

[2] The other Bishops who served on the New Testament Revision Company are all addressed through their representative, the Chairman:— "You, the successors of the Apostles, while engaged in the work of interpreting the everlasting Gospel, have knowingly and by choice associated yourselves with one who not only openly denies the eternal Godhead of our LORD, but in a recent publication is the open assailant of that fundamental doctrine of the Faith, as well as of the Inspiration of Holy Scripture itself." [P. ?.]

him to some injudicious course of action: for we find one of the Bishops on the Company (in entire sympathy with him as to the outrage done to the Church by the unhappy co-optation of a Socinian), writing thus to him (April 10);—

"I earnestly entreat you to cease your intended action for the sake of the great cause for which you live. I have done all that I could . . . . . I never attend the Company because of the Socinian's presence. *But* I still deeply lament your course. Your threatened agitation can only cause and widen scandal, and envenom ill-feeling."

Probably this was a just remonstrance. These occasions unduly excited Burgon, and led him oftentimes in his excessive zeal for the Truth, to speak not only injudiciously, but without calm consideration and self-control. Nevertheless, it may be thought that such vehement protests as he was in the habit of uttering are not without their uses in that wonderful system of Divine Providence, which subordinates to its own ends "the unruly wills and affections of sinful men," and that a few such champions, so bravely outspoken, so utterly careless of obloquy, so utterly without human respect, are needed to counteract the general indifference of professing Christians to the truths which ought to be dearer to them than life, and the miserable spirit of compromise, which is ever ready to acquiesce in the admission of a little error and a little wrong, and in the demolition first of one, and then of another of the barriers which secure our faith and our liberties. "What a splendid watch-dog he is!" said one in the author's hearing, after perusing and throwing on the table one of the Burgonian Philippics;—"How loud and furiously he barks, when the smallest danger threatens the Church, or the Faith

THE OXFORD LIFE: FIFTH PERIOD. 67

which is entrusted to the Church's keeping!" Yes! it is the business of a watch-dog to bark furiously, and even to fly at the throat of pilferers and thieves; and of al-pilferers and thieves there are none who more rouse the indignation of honest God-fearing men, than those who would rob the Church of her faith, and the Christian of his hope, by the gradual depredations of Rationalism. Anyhow, the accompanying admirable letter of the late Canon Liddon shows that Burgon, in his feelings of horror at the constitution of the New Testament Revision Company, had among his sympathizers and abettors, some of the very best men whom the Church of England could boast. It would appear from a private note enclosed with the letter [3] that Burgon had asked Canon Liddon to give an opinion which might be published, upon his '*Earnest Remonstrance and Petition addressed to Bishop Ellicott.*' Canon Liddon in reply sends him the following letter, which the author considers himself fortunate in having obtained permission to publish, before the lamented death of the writer[4]. While the Canon takes at least as strong a view of the scandal as Burgon does, his tone throughout is perfectly calm, considerate, and just to the Nonconformists, and to Dr. Vance Smith most courteous and conciliatory.

[3] "3 Amen Court, E.C., 11 April, 1872. My dear Burgon, I hope that this letter will do. I do not think that I can say less without failing in sincerity. Ever yours, H. P. LIDDON. Rev. J. W. Burgon. If you print it, will you send me a proof?"

[4] "Oct. 22, 1889. 3 Amen Court, St. Paul's, E.C. . . . . . If you think my letter to Burgon worth publishing, pray publish it. So far as I know, it has never been published. What it says, might of course have been said much better;—but I adhere to its drift entirely."

"3 Amen Court, St. Paul's, E.C.,

"April 11, 1872.

"My dear Burgon.—You ask me to tell you whether I concur in the remonstrance which you have addressed to the Bishop of Gloucester and Bristol on the admission of an Unitarian Minister to take part in the Revision of our Authorised Version. Silence would be welcome to me for very many reasons, but silence, I cannot help feeling, would imply a great want of the moral courage, in which I am already too painfully deficient. We all of us express ourselves in our own way; and in your letter there are some phrases and sentences which it would not have been natural in me to have employed. But with the substance and drift of your remonstrance I cannot but heartily agree; and I desire to be allowed to assure you of the respect which I entertain for the unworldly and fearless devotion to Truth, which on this, as on other occasions, leads you to encounter much unmerited obloquy in the way you do.

"That it is the duty of the Church of Christ, in every land, to offer to the people as accurate a rendering into the vulgar tongue of God's Holy Word as she can, is a point on which we are all agreed. That our Authorised English Version admits of some real and very considerable improvements is, I think, also undeniable, although of course much difference of opinion would necessarily arise as to the nature and number of the improvements that are really required But if, after consideration, it was the deliberate opinion of the Church's rulers that the required improvements are of so vital a character as to warrant the unsettlement of those old associations and habits of devotion, which have gathered around our present Version, there ought to have been no question as to the way in which effect should have been given to this conviction. It would have been natural to ask a Committee of Churchmen to revise the Church's Version of the Bible. If such a Revision had been made, and accepted by Nonconformists, we Churchmen must have rejoiced very sincerely that a link of sympathy so venerable, so precious, traversing our diff   and in itself a pledge, as we trust, of healthful union in the future, had not been forfeited by the necessary improvements. If, as is certainly the case, there are Nonconformist or Jewish scholars who could render us solid assistance on particular points, these gentlemen would, I cannot doubt, have allowed a committee of Churchmen to ask them for an opinion, without feeling that they were slighted by not being invited to join the Committee.

"Unhappily, this unambitious and straightforward course was not adopted. The enterprise was discussed as if it were a literary rather than a religious one; the new translation was to be made for 'English-speaking races,' rather than for the children of the Church of England. It followed that persons, who are not members of the Church, were associated, on perfectly equal terms, with her Bishops and Clergy in the work of Revision, in order to give it this literary and imperial character. There were several motives which led men, from some of whom we might have looked for better things, to favour this proceeding; but among these, two, as I believe, were especially powerful. Of these, one was the desire to make use of the opportunity thus presented, with a view to strengthening the political position of the 'Establishment.' It was hoped that the denominations, whose representative men had sat side by side with scholars and dignitaries of the Church in the Deanery at Westminster, would never be so ungrateful as to support Mr. Edward Miall in the House of Commons. It would be difficult, as yet, to offer any opinion upon the actual or probable success of the experiment. But I should have thought that well-informed Dissenters know what these principles are from which they conscientiously dissent, and that they are hardly likely to respect the Church more than they do, when they find that she is ready to throw her distinctive principles somewhat ostentatiously to the winds, under the stress of a real or apprehended political danger.

"Besides this, there was the desire to make capital out

of so promising an occasion for the cause of 'undogmatic Christianity.' If invitations to join the Revising Companies had been addressed only to Trinitarian Nonconformists, this object would have been very imperfectly attained. Whatever our differences with Independents and Baptists may be, as to the nature of the Church of Christ, and of the Christian Sacraments, we are, I rejoice to know, entirely at one with them, in our belief in the Most Holy Trinity, in the True and Eternal Godhead of Jesus Christ our Lord, and in the atoning efficacy of His Precious Death. In the interests of the Anti-dogmatic School, it was necessary that these central truths should be tacitly assumed to be of very inferior importance to literary considerations, and this was secured by the invitation addressed to Dr. Vance Smith to join the New Testament Revision Company.

"Of that gentleman many hard, and, as I cannot but think, wholly undeserved things have been said among ourselves. He is an accomplished and courteous scholar, who differs from us Christians, in that he does not believe that Jesus Christ is very and eternal God. I have often thought that, had I been in his position, I should have acted just as he did. He may well have reflected that, when a body of persons with very different religious convictions consent to act together for a religious object, it is only the smallest creed which escapes discredit. Dr. V. Smith's creed has suffered more[5] by his presence in the Revising Company. If Bishops and Deans were willing to postpone religious to literary considerations, that was not Dr. Vance Smith's affair. If Dr. V. Smith was invited to receive the Holy Communion, he did not, as it seems to me, compromise himself by accepting a compliment to his literary accomplishments. He naturally and very properly objected to say the Nicene Creed, which he did not believe; but what

---

[5] In publishing this letter, the author does not like to alter Canon Liddon's autograph in any particular; but it would seem as if in this sentence the "more" must have been a slip of the pen for "nothing."

objection. from his point of view, could there be to his eating a little bread and wine publicly in a beautiful Gothic building replete with national associations? We have no right to expect a man to admit the force of motives, which are really based on our own faith,—a faith which he would scout as a stupid superstition. But, alas! what apology can be suggested for the Churchmen, who invited a man who has spent his life in denying the Godhead of our Blessed Saviour, to join with them in the holiest act of Christian fellowship? What for those who have since, in whatever way, abetted the invitation? When, since the Reformation, has the faith of our Church been more cruelly wounded? When has a slight to our ascended Lord and King, more patent to all men, more eloquent, been offered Him by any section of the English Clergy? And, as you observe, it is not a thing done and over;—it is perpetuated. Every time that this Company of Revisers meet, our shame as a Church is published to the world; and it is not difficult to foresee the graver difficulties which must arise, when their labours are at length completed. How can this Socinian-Episcopal translation ever command the confidence of faithful Churchmen? How can we ever approach it, if we do approach it at all, but as jealous critics, who see in it not a precious gift leading us to clearer knowledge of the Highest Truth, but an object of legitimate, inevitable suspicion? How many passages will at once occur to both of us, in which we shall expect to trace the hand of heresy almost as a matter of course!

" It may be too late now to do anything. I do not think that Dr. Vance Smith ought to suffer anything that could be construed to his discredit. He has acted with perfect honour, from first to last. Whether Prelates who still prefer, before the world, to receive and to teach the Faith of Nicæa, but whose actions are (apparently to us) inconsistent with loyalty to that Faith, will listen to your solemn and earnest remonstrance, is more than I can say. Whether they do or not, you will find in your own heart, and in the thankful acknowledgments of thousands of devout Christians, a justification for your faithfulness,—at great personal cost, I well know,—to our Saviour's honour.

"I am,
"My dear Burgon,
"Ever yours most truly.
"H. P. Liddon.
"The Rev. J. W. Burgon."

The debates in Convocation on that much-vexed question, the retention of the Athanasian Creed as a devotional formulary to be recited periodically in the course of Morning Prayer[6], made the year 1872 one of unusual interest and importance in the annals of the Church. The question was arrived at by Convocation, in the course of its discussion of the Report of the Ritual Commissioners, who, as regards the Athanasian Creed, had proposed (though some thought that they exceeded the terms of their commission in proposing) that a note should be appended to it explanatory of the so-called Damnatory Clauses. This course had very weighty suffrages in its favour. Bishop Christopher Wordsworth, while cordially advocating the retention and public recital of the Creed, and bringing all his vast stores of erudition to bear on its defence, yet in that beautiful charity to the scruples of others which, no less than his learning, was a part of his character, proposed a note of

---

[6] There seems to have been no proposal in any quarter to eliminate the Creed from the Book of Common Prayer. The Bishop of St. David's (Thirlwall), the great opponent of its public recital, says in his speech in Convocation, upon which Burgon so severely animadverted: "I am not aware that anyone has suggested its removal, or that anyone wishes to see it removed from the monuments of the Church, or that it should not be held in as much veneration and respect as ever. All that is desired is that it should not form part of the public services of the Church." *Chronicle of Convocation: Sessions* Feb. 7-13, 1872, p. 73.

The Oxford Life: Fifth Period.

his own very much to the same effect as that of the Commissioners. The six Divinity Professors at Oxford[7] submitted another form of explanatory note of a similar scope, while one of them, Dr. Pusey, in a private letter to Burgon dated "Thursday in Easter Week" [April 4], "1872," thus defends the appending of an explanatory note:—

"What are our Commentaries but explanations of our LORD's words, in which, among others, we explain those words of His in St. Mark and St. John, on which the warning clauses are founded? It implies no defect in the Athanasian Creed to explain its meaning, since it does not, to explain our LORD's."

The Bishop of Winchester also (Wilberforce, who had been translated from Oxford in the end of 1869) had suggested at the discussions of the Ritual Commission, though he did not formally propose, a very suitable explanatory note, the first clause of which[8] was intended to meet the objections of those who maintain that in using the words, "The Holy Ghost is of the Father and of the Son," we condemn the entire Eastern Church, which denies the double procession of the Holy Ghost.

---

[7] Dr. Ogilvie (Pastoral); Dr. Heurtley (Lady Margaret's); Canon Mozley (Regius); Dr. Pusey (Hebrew); Canon Bright (Ecclesiastical History); Canon Liddon (Exegesis). Their note was: "That nothing in this Creed is to be understood as condemning those who, by involuntary ignorance, or invincible prejudice, are prevented from accepting the faith therein declared." *Chronicle of Convocation: Sessions* Feb. 7-13, 1872, p. 47.

[8] "For the avoiding of all scruples in the use of [this Confession of our Christian Faith], be it enacted that the words—*the Holy Ghost is of the Father and of the Son: neither made, nor created, nor begotten, but proceeding*— do not declare the Holy Ghost to proceed from the Son, so as in any way to contradict the Catholic doctrine that the Father alone is the fountain-head of the Triune Godhead." See *Chronicle of Convocation: Sessions* Feb. 7-13, 1872, p. 81.

Bishop Christopher Wordsworth, probably the most learned theologian then on the Bench, took the lead in defending the continued use of the Creed, while Bishop Thirlwall, gifted perhaps with the keenest and most vigorous intellect of all his Episcopal brethren, was the chief maintainer in the Upper House of its unsuitability for recitation in the Public Service of the Church.

It often happens that men of great intellectual power will, in maintaining a thesis, overlook something which lies immediately under their hand, and which must of necessity be perfectly familiar to them. And so it seems to have come to pass with that strong intellectual gladiator, the late Bishop of St. David's, in part of his argument in Convocation against the public recitation of the Creed. After making the most of the very high authority of Jeremy Taylor, which was unequivocally on his side, he proceeded to judge the Creed on its own merits, and invited his brother Bishops to take notice that no loss of dogmatical teaching would be incurred by striking out "the longest series of propositions contained in it," these propositions being only "rhetorical amplifications."

"The plan, your lordships see, is to enumerate a variety of divine attributes, and then to make the assertion that the Father is such, the Son is such, the Holy Ghost is such, and yet they are not Three, but One. I know of no reason whatever in the nature of things why this should not have been prolonged to the extent of the whole Creed; because *it seems to have been by pure accident that the author, whoever he was, confined himself to these particular illustrations*[9]."

---

[9] *Chronicle of Convocation*, Sessions Feb. 7, 8, 9, 10, 12, 13, 1872, p. 76. The italics are those of the present writer.

But the Bishop must have known, at least as well as any of his auditors, though he did not call it to mind at the moment,—it was not ready at hand to him,—that the successive dogmatic statements of the Creed took their rise, as an historical fact, from the oppositions of heresy,—whether Sabellian, Arian, Macedonian, or Apollinarian—which successively elicited them. So far from the "rhetorical amplifications" being due to "*pure accident*," they were due to the exigencies of the Church, who found them necessary from time to time, in order to meet encroachments which were made upon her faith. This slip of a very learned and able prelate (for it cannot be supposed to have been anything more) laid him open to the severe animadversion of Burgon. In a vigorous pamphlet, published on St. Mark's Day, and entitled, '*The Athanasian Creed to be retained in its integrity: And why*[1],'—after maintaining the Creed and the public use of it against Dean Stanley's somewhat rabid attack upon it, he turns to the Bishop of St. David's, and mercilessly exposes his slip in Convocation by citing a long and valuable passage from a Sermon of Dr. (afterwards Archbishop) Laurence, which exhibits the historical genesis of the successive dogmatic statements of the Athanasian Creed, in the rise of the heresies above referred to. This Sermon, preached in 1816, and entitled, '*The consequences resulting from a simplification of Public Creeds considered*,' was entirely *ad rem* to Burgon's argument with Bishop Thirlwall, and he evidently chuckles over the having unearthed it so opportunely.

---

[1] "Being the substance of Two Sermons preached at St. Mary the Virgin's, Oxford, April 14th and 21st, 1872, and now inscribed (without permission) to his Grace the Archbishop of Canterbury. By John W. Burgon, B.D., Vicar of St. Mary the Virgin's, Fellow of Oriel College, and Gresham Lecturer in Divinity.... Oxford and London: James Parker & Co., 1872."

"Finding the point under discussion ready done to my hand, and so very ably done, in the pages of (I suppose) a forgotten Sermon by a very eminent Divine, I thought it better for every reason to suffer the dead man to deliver his testimony here for the second time, and in his own recorded words[2]."

Bishop Thirlwall was not unnaturally made angry by Burgon's attack upon him, and not the less angry because the Bishop of Winchester, in the Upper House of the Convocation of Canterbury, took up much the same ground as Burgon, in regard of the alleged "rhetorical amplifications" in the Creed. In the Summer Sessions of Convocation (July 2), he spoke sorely and somewhat bitterly, in explanation of his own meaning, and in exposure of Burgon's method of conducting controversy. And much as Burgon's pamphlet on the Athanasian Creed may be admired and valued for its ability, and for soundness of the line which it takes, it is thought that even the reader who sympathizes with his argument will deeply regret the way, in which he allowed himself to speak of a prelate, venerable not by his office only, but by his age, his ability, his learning. And, while he, or any other Presbyter, had a perfect right to assure the Archbishop, as he does in his Prefatory Letter, that for himself he *did* take the warning clauses of the Athanasian Creed "in their plain and literal sense," the language of sorrowful censure in the last paragraph of that letter, as if he had been the Archbishop's spiritual father, instead of one of his spiritual sons, is surely wrong both in taste and principle. On the other hand, his independence of judgment in taking a line of his own on this as on other questions, even where some of his best and most valued friends materially differed from

[2] P. 34, *footnote* ^e.

The Oxford Life: Fifth Period.

him, cannot fail to be admired. He argues most acutely and convincingly against an Explanatory Note, though both the Bishop of Lincoln and Dr. Pusey (one of them a dearly loved, and both of them deeply venerated friends) had determined in favour of this solution of the difficulty, and as to the note proposed by the six Oxford Professors of Theology, with all of whom he was on intimate terms, he writes thus pertinently:—

"On behalf of what is called 'involuntary ignorance,' a great deal no doubt is to be said. But then it ought to be quite superfluous to say it; for if the ignorance be *really* involuntary, what need to introduce any mention of it at all? 'Invincible *prejudice*' on the other hand strikes me as quite a different matter. For, Which is meant? the prejudice which a man *will* not overcome,— or the prejudice which he absolutely *cannot* overcome? If the latter, it is surely needless to mention it: if the former, it is clearly (as in Pharaoh's case), a highly aggravated form of wickedness." [Pp. 20, 21.]

It may be added that Burgon does not omit to quote at some length the very important testimony to the great value of the Athanasian Creed, borne by the late lamented Bishop Cotton, of Calcutta, in his charge of 1863, in which he shows how "the errors rebuked in this Creed resulted from tendencies common to the human mind everywhere, and especially prevalent in this country." The passage is too long for citation; but it may be safely said to be of such importance in the controversy respecting the Athanasian Creed, that no man is qualified to pass judgment on the merits of this great Confession of Faith, who has not both read and deliberately weighed it. Burgon received cordial thanks for his pamphlet from several eminent divines,—among others Archdeacon Freeman, and Archdeacon Churton, the latter of whom, in a letter dated May 3, 1872, speaks of the publication as "a right valuable contribution to the theological literature evoked by this controversy. Your notice of Bishop Thirlwall's cavils, as answered by anticipation by Archbishop Laurence, is both effective and instructive."

In the end of this year, Burgon headed the opposition in the Oxford Convocation to the appointment of the Dean of Westminster (Stanley), as a Select Preacher before the University. The ground of the opposition was the sympathy with the rationalising and latitudinarian school, which the Dean had shown on several occasions. Socially loveable and attractive in an unusual degree, the most picturesque and fascinating historical writer of the day, and gifted with intellectual endowments of the highest order, the truth must yet be told that Dean Stanley was no theologian, had not the habits of mind which are the essential qualifications of a Divine. Apart from particular acts which gave great offence to those who were jealous for God's Truth and for the integrity of the Church's faith, he was not unreasonably complained of by Burgon as "the avowed champion of a negative and cloudy Christianity, which is really preparing the way for the rejection of all revealed Truth." The nomination of Select Preachers at Oxford (preachers, that is, chosen to supply the lack of service of such Masters of Arts in Priest's Orders as do not wish to take their turns of preaching) is in the hands of a Board consisting of the Regius and Margaret Professors of Divinity, and the two Proctors, and presided over by the Vice-Chancellor, who has a *veto* upon each nomination. But no nomination is valid, unless Convocation (the legislative body of the University approves

THE OXFORD LIFE: FIFTH PERIOD. 79

of it, and sanctions it by a majority, in case of its being objected to. Burgon and four other members of Convocation with him, one of them of Professorial rank, and another the Senior Tutor of one of the foremost Colleges, announced to the Vice-Chancellor their determination to oppose Dean Stanley's nomination [3], and requested him to appoint a day for the polling, which might suit the convenience of non-resident members. The Vice-Chancellor insisted on regarding this as a proposal to pass a "censure upon those whose duty it was to nominate Select Preachers," and especially upon himself, who was "required to approve of each name before it was submitted to Convocation." In the correspondence which passed on the subject, and was afterwards published [4], Burgon assured but did not succeed in convincing him that, while he and his friends intended to exercise their constitutional right of objecting to a particular name, no sort of censure was intended, and that non-resident members would be summoned from the country "for the sole purpose of confirming or cancelling what some considered to be a highly improper nomination." The "highly improper nomination" was eventually confirmed by a majority of sixty-two, to the sorrow and dismay of the orthodox. But Burgon, though his party was in a minority, was right in the point at which he was at issue with the Vice-Chancellor. The exercise of a

---

[3] The names besides Burgon's appended to the letter in which this announcement is made are those of C. P. Golightly, Edward C. Woollcombe, Montagu Burrows, and H. R. Bramley.

[4] '*Correspondence between the Very Reverend Henry George Liddell, D.D., Vice-Chancellor of the University of Oxford, and Mr. Burgon, concerning a Privilege of Convocation in respect of the nomination of Select Preachers.*' Oxford and London: James Parker and Co., 1872. The Prefatory Words of this Paper are dated Oriel, Dec. 5, 1872, and have the signature J. W. B. appended to them.

constitutional privilege by some members of a legislative body cannot fairly be regarded as a censure upon those who propose to them a measure which they refuse to concur in. Members of the House of Commons, who vote against a measure initiated in, and brought down from, the Lords, do not thereby censure the Peers who passed, and especially the Peer who introduced the measure, however much they may repudiate it as opposed (in their view) to the public weal.

The close of the year 1872, saw the appointment by authority of what has since become an annual observance in our Church. Friday, December 20, was set apart as *"A Day of public Prayer to Almighty God for the increase of the supply of Missionaries, and for His blessing on their Work."* It cannot be said that the Vicar of St. Mary the Virgin's allowed his controversial writings to engross him to the neglect of his parish; for we find him providing for his Parishioners four Services on that day. three of them accompanied with short Sermons, in addition to an early and a mid-day Celebration of the Holy Communion. He exhorted his people to avail themselves of the opportunities thus offered t a printed Address, which probably did not differ much from the hundreds of similar Pastorals issued all over the country, except it be in the pointed reminder that Fasting, as well Almsgiving, should go along with Prayer on such occasions, and that "self-denial in respect of meat and drink should be practised on a day of public Intercession."

The year 1873 was ushered in by an event which deprived Burgon of a much-loved relative and most congenial friend. On January 31, the Venerable Henry John Rose, B.D., Archdeacon of Bedford, and Rector of

Houghton Conquest, who had married Burgon's eldest sister, passed away in his 73rd year. The Archdeacon had made his mark in literature; and his attainments in Hebrew and Syriac were so considerable that he was invited to join the company nominated for the Revision of the Authorised Version of the Old Testament, "who first put their hands to the work on the 30th of June, 1870 [5]." Of his eminence as a scholar and a Divine, his labours as an editor and writer, his warmth of heart, equability of temper, fairness of mind, and of the graceful hospitality dispensed by him at his country Parsonage, Burgon himself has preserved a brief memorial in his Postscript to the Memoir of Hugh James Rose, the Archdeacon's elder brother ['*Lives of Twelve Good Men*,' vol. i. pp. 284-295].

Burgon was one of those men who are able to work with good effect at several wholly different pursuits simultaneously. We do not find that his diligence as a Parish Priest put any bar in the way of the prosecution of those abstruse studies, and that laborious recourse to the fountains of Theology, to which he had consecrated his life. How true it is (of Englishmen certainly, if not of Germans) that good literary work is often done, not by men of leisure, whose lives seem to allow room for it, but by those who are cumbered with some active pursuit, and can only give to literature their *horæ subsecivæ* and their vacations! Here is a glimpse of Burgon's life during his autumnal holiday at Turvey, given by himself to Miss Washbourne, whose assistance to Burgon, in the capacity of a secretary and amanu-

---

[5] Preface to the Revised Version of the Old Testament. Ten members of the original company (Archdeacon Rose among them) were removed by death before the Revision was completed on the 20th of June, 1884.

ensis, has been already noticed under the year 1871. (The reader will observe that, Archdeacon Rose having passed away, Houghton was no longer open to him as a holiday resort; but in one respect this loss was compensated by the circumstance of his elder sister's, Mrs. Henry John Rose, coming with her daughters to reside near him in Oxford).

"Turvey Abbey, Sept. 20, 1873.
"My faithful Secretary,— ......

"I will tell you how I pass my days. I rise at 6 a.m., come down by 7, and set to work in the Library. The housekeeper brings me a cup of tea [6], and at half-past 8 dear Charles and Helen appear,—and *scold* me. Breakfast over, *at it again* till 1.15, when we lunch. Then, *at it again*, till they pull me out for a drive. Then dinner—and *drawing-room*;—so I cannot go on writing. But I pick out the texts of the Gospels in a volume of Cyril and in Eusebius till 10. Then Prayers; and at 10.30 I *try* to go to bed. Next morning D. G. *allegretto*;—and so daily.

"After this you will wonder that I have not got a deal that wants transcribing. The truth is I have been preparing five letters for '*The Guardian*,' besides the one [No. xi.] just now in type; and I find that the printer can decipher my horrid scrawl. But as soon as I can get at *my Book* (*our* Book) [7] again, I shall be obliged to

---

[6] In another letter to his "Secretary" in the ensuing year, he says of this old and faithful servant;—"N.B. Old Jane, who brings me in a cup of tea, and eke some bread and butter, at 7, becomes to me one of the most interesting females in Creation."

[7] "*Our Book*" is that which he regarded as the great work of his life,—a work on the '*True Principles of the Textual Criticism of the New Testament*,' which he appears to have conceived and undertaken shortly after the publication of his '*Last Twelve Verses of St. Mark*.' He once observed to the lady, to whom this letter is addressed, that he had first been set upon the undertaking by Bishop Charles Wordsworth's (of St. Andrews) asking him to explain his views on Textual Criticism.

In preparation for this *magnum opus*, he made, with the efficient assistance of his "faithful Secre-

worry you *out of your life.* There will also *soon* be the residue of Cyril, Eusebius, and Gregory of Nyssa; and then I shall be able (thank GOD) to make some progress. I feel *goaded on*, and never tire."

The five letters for the '*Guardian*,' alleged by him to his "faithful Secretary," as calling him off from work in which she could assist him, belonged to a series of Twenty-one Letters to Dr. Scrivener, which appeared in that Journal,—the first fifteen of them in the year 1873, —the last six in the succeeding year [8]. They were the fruit of his laborious researches in foreign Libraries during his autumnal tours, already noticed, of 1871,

tary," his nieces, and occasionally one or more Undergraduates of his College, Indices to all the references to, or quotations from, the New Testament, made in the writings of the Fathers,—it being one of Burgon's leading principles of Textual Criticism that the true Text cannot be otherwise ascertained than by consulting not only manuscripts and ancient versions, but also the citations made from the Fathers. This involved his looking through all the Greek and Latin folios of the Fathers, and marking the texts in the margin. Then the folios passed into the hands of his assistants, who arranged the references in the order of the Books of the New Testament, and copied them out; so that it might be only the work of a minute to ascertain how Cyril, or Eusebius, or Gregory of Nyssa, quoted such and such a text, and *what was the generally accepted wording of that text at the time that particular Father wrote.* The result was the compilation of nearly twenty folios of enormous bulk, bound in stout dark red leather, and with handles at the back, to lift them by, of the same material. There is reason for regret that these valuable tomes, before being presented to the nation, were not placed at the disposal of the Reverend Edward Miller, Rector of Bucknell, who has undertaken the herculean labour of editing the great work which Burgon has left incomplete,—and the appearance of which will in all probability mark a new era in Textual Criticism, and perhaps even extort a tardy recognition from some of our own scholars, who, without independent research, have borrowed their methods of Biblical Criticism from Germany.

[8] The dates of the numbers of the '*Guardian*,' in which these Letters appear, are:

In 1873, Jan. 15, 22, 29; Feb. 5; Aug. 13, 20, 27; Sept. 3, 10, 17, 24; Oct. 1, 22, 29; Nov. 19.

In 1874, Jan. 7, 14; Feb. 18, 25; March 25; April 1.

1872. The series is headed, "Manuscript Evangelia in Foreign Libraries"; and his object, he tells the reader, was "partly to call attention to the most serious mistakes I have noticed in the labours of my predecessors (the result evidently, for the most part, of haste and inadvertence), partly to supply important details which previous critics have overlooked." He was shown over the Library of Milan by "the learned Dr. Ceriani," and at Florence "Dr. Anziani most obligingly promoted the object of a nameless and most troublesome stranger." He entirely fulfilled his purpose, collating more or less thoroughly almost every Codex he handled, correcting numerous mistakes of Scholz, Tischendorf, and others, and bringing to light many copies of the Gospels and other parts of the New Testament, and several Lectionary Books, the existence of which was previously unknown.

The close of this year gave Burgon occasion to declare himself as much opposed to the Romanising and Ritualising tendencies in the Church, as he had hitherto showed himself to be to the Rationalism which was slowly on all sides undermining the Faith, and derogating from the honour and perfection of God's holy Word. On Wednesday and Thursday, the 1st and 2nd of October, in the year 1873, was held the Oxford Diocesan Conference, the proceedings of which elicited from Burgon two Sermons [9], preached on the 12th and 19th of the month, and published by him with a word of Preface dated on the 28th. The gist of the Conference, he points out in the first of these Sermons, lay in two Resolutions,

---

[9] "The Oxford Diocesan Conference; and Romanizing within the Church of England: two Sermons preached at St. Mary the Virgin's, Oxford, Oct. 12th and 19th, 1873, by John W. Burgon, B.D., Vicar of St. Mary the Virgin's, Fellow of Oriel College, and Gresham Lecturer in Divinity." Oxford and London: James Parker and Co., 1873.

one in favour of " some organization of parochial Councils to confer with the Clergyman on the conduct of their Ecclesiastical affairs," the other "accepting as sound the principle of the Public Worship Facilities Bill" (thrown out in the Lords), the object of which was to enable any twenty-five parishioners, who might happen to be dissatisfied with the Pastoral Administration of their Incumbent, to set up independently of him, and in defiance of his wishes, a separate Church and Clergyman of their own, if they could only succeed in obtaining the sanction of the Bishop [see p. 9]. Burgon explains that to both these resolutions he personally entertained the strongest repugnance: but he discerns underlying both of them (and there is no doubt he was right in his discernment) the " growing impatience of the faithful Laity at the Romanising movement within the Church of England, which is even now making its way in many quarters unrestrained, and even unrebuked" [p. 12]. In the second Sermon, "taking up a position directly hostile to many of my personal friends" [Preface, p. 5], he launches out with his usual plain speaking and intrepidity against the Romanising practices and tenets which were being introduced and inculcated; against the representing Tradition as an unwritten Word, of co-ordinate authority with the written [p. 18]; against Saintworship and Mariolatry [p. 19]; against enforced habitual Auricular Confession [pp. 19, 20]; against Transubstantiation, and all the observances and ceremonial in connexion with the Holy Communion which are grouped round Transubstantiation, such as the Vestments, the Eastward position, Fasting Communion, and Non-Communicating Attendance, as well as the phraseologies unknown to our own Book of Common Prayer, such as High Mass and Low Mass [pp. 22, 23]. As to the doctrine of the Presence in the Holy

Communion, he will go no further than to say that Christ is really present in it to the faithful recipient, that to such an one His presence " is awfully real,—an objective reality of the most transcendent kind " [p. 29]. But he will not allow of a localized Presence; Christ is "present in the heart, *not in the hands*," according to the words of "the Author's *last* edition of '*The Christian Year*,'" —words which were tampered with after his death [pp. 30, 33]. By those words the great poet-theologian is to be judged, and not by his treatise on '*Eucharistic Adoration*,' "a singularly weak and unfortunate production, every way unworthy of the honoured name it bears" [p. 32]. While Burgon speaks thus vehemently, according to his wont, he takes especial care not to allow it to be thought that he has any sympathy whatever with the Low Church School. "With Clergymen who deny the doctrine of Baptismal Regeneration," he writes, "and apparently think *anything* good enough for the House of GOD, I have far less sympathy than I have with the Mediævalists themselves. Such persons are simply out of court" [Preface, p. 5]. Holding "that Romish Teaching may be popularly described as the systematic exaggeration, or rather caricature of the Truth" [p. 18], he never shows a tendency to deny the truth, of which a particular tenet or practice is an ugly distortion. Thus, while speaking in the strongest way against the miserable casuistry of fasting Communion, according to which even a "cough lozenge has been forbidden, on the plea that to take it into the mouth were to dishonour the reception which is to follow," he appeals to his flock to bear him witness that "I specially invite you to communicate at 6, or at 7, or at 8 o'clock; remarking generally that it is more reverent, for those who are able, to communicate fasting than full; and for every reason that it is better, for

THE OXFORD LIFE: FIFTH PERIOD.

such of you at least as conveniently can, to come early than to come late. (As for after-dinner Communions, I consider that they are not to be tolerated, as they certainly *never* are necessary)" [pp. 27, 28].—It should be remembered that in that year (1873) the gradual growth in our Church of Romish tenets and practices had aroused the serious alarms of many faithful and wise Pastors besides Burgon. It was the year of Bishop Wilberforce's sudden death by a fall from his horse on the 19th of July,

("The whole land wore the garb of grief
    For that great wealth departed—
Her peerless Prelate, Statesman, Chief,
    Large-souled and tender-hearted;
The man so eloquent of word,
    Who swayed all spirits near him;
Who did but touch the silver chord,
    And men perforce must hear him[1].");—

and the awful and distressing incident served to call attention to the last words of wise and loving counsel, which the Bishop had addressed to the Rural Deans of his Diocese at Winchester House, only four days before his death[2]. Those words were directed against that part of the Romish system "which required confession to a priest from every one, especially before communicating, as a condition for the obtaining forgiveness of sins," and showed the social and moral mischief which such confession was calculated to do, and the specific difference between it and that resort of a conscience unable to quiet itself, and requiring comfort and counsel, to "some discreet and learned minister," which the Church of

---

[1] Lines by the Bishop of Derry and Mrs. Alexander. "In Memoriam Samuel Wilberforce, Bishop of Winchester." [See '*Life of Bishop Wilberforce*,' by his son, vol. iii. p. 437.]

[2] '*Life of Bishop Wilberforce*,' vol. iii. pp. 419, 420.

England *does* recommend. In a Sermon preached before the University in 1855 on "the Principles of the English Reformation" (a long extract from which Burgon appends to his pamphlet), and earlier—in his correspondence with Dr. Pusey in 1850,—the Bishop had taken precisely the same ground. But the movement in favour of Private Confession had still gone on working its way, spite of these strong protests against it from strong men. "It came this year," Bishop Wilberforce's biographer tells us, "within the official cognizance of the Episcopate; a discussion upon it took place in Convocation, and on July 4 the Episcopate agreed upon a Declaration which was made public on July 23[3]." Thus Bishop Wilberforce did not live to see its publication, though he had helped to draw it up.

The domesticity of Burgon's character was so great, and his interest in the servant class, and his clinging attachment to old servants so strong,—as testified to by his beautiful little book of Sermons on '*The Servants of Holy Scripture*' (S.P.C.K.),—that it does not seem out of place just to notice in this Biography the death of the old, trusty, and trusted servant of the Church, "Rebecca," who had, under six consecutive vicars (Hawkins, Newman, Eden, Marriott, Chase, Burgon), acted as "sextoness" and pew-opener at St. Mary the Virgin's[4]. Thus he

---

[3] '*Life of Bishop Wilberforce*,' vol. iii. p. 418.

[4] He tells us in his own characteristically comical way, in the Life of Provost Hawkins ('*Lives of Twelve Good Men*,' vol. i. p. 397, *footnote* 8), how trying to this dear old lady were "the ways" of the different Vicars under whom she had served.

"She was a very crabbed-looking individual" (writes one of the attendants at the Bible Classes which Burgon used to hold in the chancel of his Church), "but wonderfully patient and good in waiting on the coldest nights till the Bible Class was over. And then it was; 'Good-night, my dear; good-night, dear Rebecca,' and (turning to me), 'You know she's my wife; we live at St. Mary's.'" This was the kind of frolicsome joke with which Bur-

THE OXFORD LIFE: FIFTH PERIOD.

writes about her death to Miss Monier-Williams (now Mrs. Samuel Bickersteth), an attached and much-loved member of his Bible Class for young ladies. The letter is dated "St. James's Day," [July 25] "1874.

"I ought to add a word about dear Rebecca. She died peacefully and happily, and was quite conscious to the last. I am going to put a cross of stone to her memory [5], and all the parishioners (Mamma and Papa are one) are to give a shilling apiece towards it.... You will like to know also that I have had water laid on to the Cemetery, which was getting quite burned up from the long drought."

The next month we find him at Turvey once again, writing to his "faithful Secretary" (Miss Washbourne) in terms which seem to show that his work, through her effective assistance, had made considerable progress since his letter of September 20 in the last year.

"Turvey Abbey, Aug. 28, 1874.

"My dear Secretary,—I am very grateful to you for the kind letter I received from you this morning. I will not disguise from you the pleasure it gives me to think of Cyril as a *fait accompli*. What a fat fellow, and what a useful one, he will be! I promise myself a great deal

gon was always bubbling over... On one occasion, when the Militia had attended Service at St. Mary's, they struck up, in marching back from the Church, "The girl I left behind me." It was irresistible. "That's Rebecca," exclaimed Burgon, as the notes of the well-known tune burst on his ear.

[5] This was done. Rebecca's headstone tapers into a circle, within which is a cross. The epitaph is:—
Rebecca Hawkins,
For Thirty-Six Years Sextoness of St. Mary's,
Fell asleep July 18, A.D. 1874,
Aged 63 years.
'Not now a servant, but above a servant, a sister beloved.'
On the back of the stone is the single name REBECCA in large capitals.

What a delicate and gentle touch, quite worthy of Burgon's head and heart, is given to the simple epitaph by the accommodation to this old and trusty Church-servant of St. Paul's words about Onesimus!

of benefit from the use of those laborious pages of yours; and I only feel genuine concern to think that the task must have taxed your strength unduly......

"I am working away very hard. I wake at 5; rise instantly; and at 6 am in the library. I open the windows for five minutes, to look out on the lawn and let in the fresh air. And O how fresh it is! and how lovely the matin prime! The gossamer on the grass, drenched with dews of night—the cattle feeding on the upland—all the birds exuberant in song—lengthy shadows over the lawn—and everything at peace! ... I cannot say how refreshing it is to me to work on in quiet for several long sunny hours in this pleasant home.—Farewell, and GOD bless you!

"Yours gratefully,
"J. W. B."

A.D. 1875.
Æt. 62.

Burgon's '*Plea for the Study of Divinity in Oxford*' has been already noticed by anticipation, when speaking of his '*Plea for a Fifth Final School*' in 1868 [see above, p. 376]. It was very mainly through his agency that this Fifth Final School (for examinations in Divinity, and for conferring honours for proficiency in that Queen of Sciences) had been established. He had watched over the experiment with an almost parental solicitude that it should turn out a success, and in the November of 1874 wrote three papers on the subject in the '*Oxford Undergraduates' Journal.*' These papers seem to have been thought by the Editor of so much value, that he caused them to be printed at his own expense in a separate form as a pamphlet. [See the *Avant-propos* to the '*Plea for the Study of Divinity.*'] The contents of this pamphlet having been noticed previously, more need not now be said of it than that it is one long wail over the excessively slender furniture of the younger Clergy for the discharge of the most onerous and responsible of all trusts, and over the declension of the Oxford Colleges, in virtue of the recent revolutionary changes, from the ideal of the Founders, which was in most instances to make them Seminaries of the Church, and sheltered retreats for students in Theology.

And now his career at Oxford,—a career in which he had toiled so incessantly for the spiritual good, both of his parishioners, and of the members of his University, and had won so many hearts both of Townsmen and Gownsmen, not more by the services rendered to them than by the deep and tender affectionateness with which he had rendered them,—was to be cut short by the offer of a Deanery, which opened to him much more leisure for the studies so dear to him than he had ever yet enjoyed, and relieved him of direct Pastoral responsibilities, if to remove a man from a sphere of work truly congenial to him can ever be rightly called relief. In a brief note, dated Nov. 1, the then Premier (Mr. Disraeli) announced that he "proposed with" Burgon's "permission to submit" his "name to the Queen to fill the Deanery of Chichester," which had been recently vacated by the death of the deeply venerated and greatly lamented Dean Hook. Burgon had never coveted this or any other preferment (rarely indeed has professional advancement been so little of a consideration to a distinguished clergyman as it was to him); nor, if the truth must be told, did he altogether like the position in itself; but he was moved to accept it, partly by the reflexion that his work, which had lately multiplied upon him, was somewhat overtaxing his strength already, and partly by the desire to make a home for his sister and her daughters, who, since leaving Houghton Conquest, had been residing near him at Oxford. On the eleventh of November came another equally brief missive from the Premier to announce that the Queen had been pleased to confer upon him the Deanery, and that he (Mr. Disraeli) would "take the necessary steps to carry into effect her Majesty's commands."

But Burgon shall himself assign the reasons which moved him to leave his beloved Parish, College, and University, as he gave them to Miss Monier-Williams, to whom he wrote probably more *à cœur ouvert* than to any one else outside his own family. He writes from his College, March 9, 1876, nearly two months after his installation at Chichester, which is explained by the circumstance that he had arranged to spend the Lent of 1876 amid his old surroundings, and to take a prolonged farewell of his beloved flock and his many Oxford friends. After speaking of "the shower of letters" [congratulations] "such as he never saw on his table before," he proceeds thus:—

"The effort of replying to them made me quite ill; for I could not help telling them all that at the end of thirty-three years of happy life,—happy and most *contented* life,—it is impossible to sever so many bonds, and begin a fresh career elsewhere, without a tremendous pang. Some will ask; Then why do you go, if you feel it so much? I have asked myself that question again and again, and still return myself the same answer. I am sure my dearest Parents would have wished me to go; and I think I owe it to *them* not to refuse such an offer[6]. Yet more: I desire

---

[6] If any other Clergyman besides Burgon, having attained the age of 63, had stated that one of his reasons for accepting a Deanery was, that "he owed it to his Parents" (one of whom had died eighteen, and the other twenty-two years before) "not to refuse such an offer," one would have been disposed to think the remark not quite genuine, and that he was deceiving himself as to the intensity of his filial affec-

beyond all things to provide an honourable shelter for my sister and my loved nieces ; and what better thing than a Deanery can be imagined for them? but the weightiest reason is behind. I am *convinced* that it is the Divine guidance I should go to Chichester. The position is so *wholly* unsought, or rather comes to a man who had so carefully disqualified himself for being a recipient of honours of this kind[7], that it is clearly *thrust* upon me. The very fact that I am disinclined to go makes me feel I *ought* to go. And the awkward circumstance that the income (£1000) is *insufficient* for the dignity, completes my reasons for going. I am not bribed, nor yielding to any seductive influences, nor obeying inclination, nor beckoned on by ambition. No ; I see an invisible Hand beckoning me on; and something says to me that I am *here* overtaxing my strength, especially on Sundays, as well as that I have here done as much probably as I should do by living on here for a few years more. Those few years *may be* employed more for GOD's honour and glory, and the welfare of his Church, at Chichester, than here in Oxford would be possible.

"I will be so confiding to you as to tell you that *my own* highest dream was a Canonry at Christ Church. But see how plainly this is not GOD's plan for me! Ogilvie " [the late Professor of Pastoral Theology] "died when Gladstone was in power ; and *he* named King. Well ; surely Ogilvie would have lived for two years more, had it been the Divine Will for me to go to *that* side of 'Tom Quad!' . . . . A few weeks after I had accepted Chichester, Mozley" [the Regius Professor of Divinity,—a post which Burgon would greatly have

tion and veneration. But those who knew John William Burgon intimately know that such a sentiment is *in the most perfect keeping with his character, and just what was to be expected from him under the circumstances.*

[7] Here again it is absolutely true that he had carefully disqualified himself for being a recipient of this world's honours and dignities. A man who aims at preferment must never let fly as passionately as he did against what he considered to be erroneous or wrong. Cautiousness in expressing his feelings must be the policy of a man on his promotion, and of such cautiousness there was not one single atom in Burgon's mental composition.

delighted in] "becomes paralysed. Surely Hook might have died three months later; and I might have had a prospect of the Regius Professorship!—No; I see the hand of a Divine Power in all this; and rejoice in being able to see it, and to walk by faith in this matter."

Burgon's strong claims to the preferment he so tardily received, together with the well-understood grounds of the delay, were duly recognised in a *communiquée*, known to come from the pen of a very competent writer, thoroughly acquainted with the facts, to 'The Churchman,' an American newspaper published in Hartford, Connecticut. The *communiquée* is dated Nov. 13, 1875, two days after the Deanery had been conferred upon him.

"The appointment to the Deanery of Chichester of the gentleman whose name I see attached to articles in 'The Churchman,' appears to call for a few special words. The Rev. John William Burgon, who has just received this preferment, is indeed one of our representative men, and might well have been made a Dean, or at least a Canon, any time during the last twenty years; but the significance of the preferment at this moment is great. It shows that the Government has determined to break through the trammels of a spurious public opinion propagated by a so-called liberal press, and to think for itself in Church matters. Mr. Burgon has committed what those who write for our papers would fain make to be considered the unpardonable sin of taking up consistently and powerfully the independent Anglican line, as against the Stanley school, and that of the Ritualists. His noble protests against the appointment of Dr. Temple to a Bishopric, and Dean Stanley to the Select Preachership at Oxford, may occur to the minds of your readers. It was thought impossible that the Queen, who avowedly protects and fosters this pernicious school, would ever consent to the promotion of its chief opponent; and it must be admitted that she has evinced great generosity in so doing; though indeed, in these days, a Prime Minister, with right upon his side, can hardly be resisted even by Royalty."

The Article goes on to refer to Burgon's various works, specially the '*Plain Commentary*,' the '*Short Sermons for Family Reading*' (both of them as well known, and as widely circulated, in America as in this country), and above all '*The Last Twelve Verses of St. Mark's Gospel*,' which "stamped him at once as one of the most learned critics of the Sacred Text in Europe," and which "has remained unanswered."

"It displayed the most intense intimacy with the whole literature of the Bible, and vast personal labour pursued on the spot in Rome and elsewhere. It formed a fitting crown to the numerous other books of the author on the Inspiration of the Holy Scriptures, and against the attacks of the writers of '*Essays and Reviews*.' Yet the press seemed to have no conception of this position. No article in the '*Quarterly*,' or '*Guardian*,' or any other influential paper or periodical, appeared to vindicate the work that had been done. When the Revisers of the Authorised Version were gathered to their work. Mr. Burgon's name was not amongst them. He had given too much offence to the new school of High Churchmen, and he did not pronounce the shibboleth of the Low. He had defied the school of Stanley and Colenso. So he seemed destined to remain in comparative obscurity, an Oxford leader, a revered preacher, a teacher of Undergraduates, an active Fellow of a College, but even at Oxford not a Professor, not a Canon of Christ Church, not a Head of a College. At last, when he has already lived a good long life, cheerily working on, recognised or not, he is suddenly singled out, and placed on high in the seat of dignity and honour which Hook so gloriously filled. Mr. Disraeli has done an honour to the whole English-speaking family."

Excerpts from letters to Miss Williams, one belonging to the year 1874, the other to 1875, are subjoined to this Chapter. The latter is presented to the reader with a little hesitation, arising from the fear that some persons might be led to ascribe to Burgon what in truth was very far from him—an unseemly levity on sacred subjects. As in Latimer, as in Rowland Hill, and many others of the best and most earnest men, nothing could prevent the humour, the fun and frolicsomeness which was in the man, from coming out and presenting itself on what sometimes seemed to be inopportune occasions; but it was accepted by those who loved and venerated him as part of his character, and did not prejudice in any measure the serious impressions which their hearts and consciences received from his teaching.

To Miss Williams.

"Oriel, St. Thomas' Day, 1874.

"Dearest little Girl,— . . . . . .

"As for idleness, I am of opinion that a *little* mental inactivity now and then is a good thing. It does more than unbend the bow. It fairly gives it strength and spring when it is next bended. I am always struck with our Saviour's invitation to His Disciples to come apart with Himself, and to '*rest awhile.*' We have also to learn that intellectual work is not the only—no, nor is it the highest—work we can do. There are other things to be done besides that. Social kindness is one of those things—and to swell the merriment of a family party is an admirable way of passing a few days at Christmas. The snare is when levity and laughter become the *habit*, amusement the *business*, of life.

"All here is in a very peculiar state. There is skating on the ice, snowballing in the quiet walks, slides on every pavement, and *falls* here and there. A robe of white is spread over the whole of the country, and that much-wished-for thing, *an old-fashioned Christmas*, has at last made its appearance. I shrewdly suspect that nine-tenths of the public prefer these old-fashioned things in theory to the actual experience of them.

"And now farewell! Remember me lovingly to all: but most lovingly of all, remember me yourself.

"Ever your faithful and affectionate friend,

"J. W. B."

To Miss Williams.

"Turvey Abbey, Aug. 23, 1875.

"My dearest little Girl,— . . . . .

"The essential condition of teaching well is to have first *thoroughly taught oneself*. To teach *interestingly* requires some genius: but *that* you and I have in perfection. So I may as well proceed.

"Seriously. Read over first the bit you are going to explain, so *very* carefully to yourself, that you could stand a very severe examination in it. Notice all the curious points—and there are always plenty in Scripture; and then *insist on the children seeing all those points*, by asking them short unexpected questions, and abusing them if they cannot answer them.

"But of course you must never ask them anything above their powers.

"Have a quantity of tickets. (A card cut up will do; but paint it, or at least take care that they cannot easily *forge* tickets.) Give a ticket for every right answer, or at least every *clever* answer, and let twelve tickets (suppose) represent a penny. Sixpence or a shilling on a Sunday I think well spent in making a class attentive. And you will find that this plan will galvanize the little beggars, and make them as eager as mustard.

"I think I had better explain by a pack of random questions on next Sunday morning's First Lesson. Let me see. Oh, it is 2 Kings ix.

"ELLA *loquitur*:—Ver. 1 . . . What do you mean by 'loins'? Show me your 'loins.' Very well. Now 'gird' them. Stand up, you little jackass, and gird up your loins this instant. Who has got a handkerchief? Now tie three together, and let him do it. The boy who girds up his loins best shall have a mark.

"Now why did he bind up his loins? [Then explain about the long drapery, and tell them in confidence that if you were pursued by a bull and wanted to run, you would of course 'gird up.' Be furnished with some picture of Orientals in petticoats.]

"Now shut your books. 'Children of the prophets.' Who were they? [Men brought up in a school of the prophets.] Refer them to 2 Kings ii. 3, 5, 7, 15; vi. 1, &c.

"Now how did he come to be talking with one of these children of the prophets? [If any boy were to remember that Elisha had *called* him, I would give him two tickets, perhaps three.] What was in the box that Elisha gave him? Where was he to carry the box? Where was he to go? Find the place on the map.

"Ver. 2. Who was Jehu's grandfather? Did Elisha expect that Jehu would be sitting or standing? Don't look in your book. If you do, I'll kill you. [Such threats keep the children awake on a hot afternoon.]

"Ver. 3. I suppose we don't know *where* the oil was to be poured,—do we? Do you think you understand how the whole thing was to take place? [The little beggars will say they do.] I don't believe you do, though, you little ass. At all events I'll try you. Now then *I* will be Elisha. But *who* will be Jehu? and *who* will be the son of the prophets? Good! You two, now stand up. The rest of you shall be Jehu's brethren. [Then you must act Elisha—give the boy your smelling-bottle. And if he does not do the right thing—*and a very striking and graphic thing indeed he has to do*—I would say that instead of tickets they deserve to be *thrashed* all round.] Next Sunday I shall try you all again; and I will cut off the head of every one who cannot act *the anointing of Jehu*.

"Seriously.—I think the dear old girl will understand what I mean. There will be no asking for 'the story.' They will be so astonished at your method, that, unless my memory deceives me, they will become like new creatures. O the fun of seeing their dear stupid faces devouring each succeeding verse, in anticipation of the strange searching ordeal of the Teacher!

. . .

"Give my best love to dear Mamma, and eke to dear Papa, and think of me ever, darling old Girl, as your very affectionate and faithful friend,
"J. W. B."

The narrative part of this Chapter being now completed, it only remains to exhibit Burgon in the several capacities which he filled in Oxford, and in the good and kind deeds which he was the means of doing there. What was he as a Vicar towards his Curates? As a religious instructor of young men and young women? The answers to these questions will be given in communications made to the author by Clergymen formerly associated with him, by attendants at his Bible Classes, and by others who crossed his path more incidentally.

I.

Let the Reverend Dr. Yule, portions of whose paper have been already submitted to the reader, speak of Burgon as a Vicar. Thus he writes:—

"I was with Mr. Burgon as Curate of St. Mary the Virgin's, Oxford, from June, 1868, to October, 1871, and during the whole of that time he was most kind and affectionate to me Those who are only acquainted with him by his writings, especially his controversial ones, will never be able to believe in the deep personal affection he was capable of. As one instance out of many, I should like to mention that for nearly the whole of the first year of my being in Holy Orders, he, sitting with me in the Chancel after the 8 a.m. service on every Friday morning, corrected the Sermon I had prepared for the ensuing Sunday afternoon. I am fortunate in possessing many books given to me by him, in each of which he has written some affectionate words on the title-page, together with my name.

"In the copy of '*Blunt's Undesigned Scriptural Coincidences*' formerly belonging to him, and now in my possession, he has written on the fly-leaf opposite to the title-page, as a commentary upon the title *Undesigned Coincidences*,— '*Unsuspected*, but designed from all Eternity.' This brief sentence in pencil seems to me a complete epitome of Burgon's theological method."

II.

The Reverend R. G. Livingstone, Burgon's first Curate, thus writes of his Bible Classes for Undergraduates, of his Public Catechizing, and the fulfilment of his College duties at Oriel as Censor Theologicus. Mr. Livingstone's remarks on the first and third of these points are supplemented in the footnotes from an interesting communication made to the author by the Reverend T. P. Brandram, Vicar of Rumboldswyke, who, as formerly an Undergraduate at Oriel, used to attend the Sunday evening gatherings in Burgon's rooms.

"The first time that I ever saw Dean Burgon, so far as I can remember, was in January, 1857, when I entered Oriel College. He was then Junior Treasurer, and I had to go to him to pay him some fees. He asked my name on that occasion, and then *more suo* referred to the verse where St. Peter in his First Epistle speaks of 'a living stone.' The brief interview terminated with a few kindly words of advice, and an invitation to come to his rooms on the following Sunday, and to spend an hour or so in quietly reading and studying a chapter of the Bible.

"Let me try to describe to you what took place on one of those Sunday evenings in Burgon's rooms. We went there about a quarter past eight. Usually there were, I think, about fifteen or sixteen young men present—possibly on some occasions as many as nineteen or twenty. His College rooms would hardly hold more. There were one or two outsiders, who came very regularly, but the great majority of those who attended were Oriel Undergraduates. Afterwards the numbers greatly increased, and Burgon's lectures (if I may so call them) were given no longer in his own rooms, but in the large Common Room—ultimately, in the years immediately preceding his departure to Chichester, in the College Hall. I can only describe what took place in his own rooms—those well-remembered rooms in the front quadrangle of Oriel, on the first floor of the first staircase to the right, as you enter the College, the two windows looking out on the open space before Canterbury Gate.

"Proceedings began with tea, and half-an-hour or three-quarters passed very pleasantly in conversation on all sorts of topics—our host, of course, leading the conversation, and taking the principal part in it, enlivening his remarks with delightful stories of old Oxford times, sometimes discussing measures of present interest to the University, very often criticizing one or other of the two University Sermons, which he, and a great part of his audience—for those were the days of Oriel 'Sermon Notes'—had heard that morning or afternoon at St. Mary's. I wish I could give you some idea of the charm of his manner on those occasions—his kindly wish to bring all present into the conversation, and to interest them in it. I seem to see him still—ever mindful of his hospitable duties—when he thought it was time to replenish our cups, going round the room, where several of us sat at detached tables—generally with a teapot in each hand, and saying 'You'll have another cup?' and then, as if he detected some distrust on our part of the quality of the beverage which the brace of teapots contained, 'You know, I'm as strong as Hercules still.'

"At or about 9 o'clock the decks were cleared, the tea-things removed, the remnant of the currant cake—a dainty which invariably appeared on these occasions—deposited in a cupboard near the door, whence it emerged on the following morning, when a deputation of little Blue-coat girls regularly tripped down to College, and carried off what remained to regale themselves and their school companions therewith.

"The reading began with the repetition of a Collect, that for the Second Sunday in Advent if I remember aright, and of the text, 'Open Thou mine eyes that I may see the wondrous things of Thy Law.' And then our friend plunged at once *in medias res*. He was commenting on Genesis at the time that I went to these Sunday evening gatherings, and so careful and minute was his method of procedure that at the end of four years we had not quite arrived at the end of the book. Of course it will be remembered that these Sunday readings took place only eight times in the Term, twenty-four times in the year. Still, in the course of ninety-six evenings he had not finished commenting on the first book in the Bible. Not a sentence, not a word was slurred over, not a verse, not a chapter omitted, not even the chapter containing the catalogue of the Dukes of Edom. His plan was to make the Bible its own interpreter, constantly referring his hearers to parallel passages in other parts of Holy Scripture. And the result was that, though our attention was mainly fixed on one book, yet we came to know a good deal about other books of the Bible, which in any way helped to illustrate the particular portion of Holy Scripture which we were studying. I do not think he often referred to Patristic interpreters: but there was one commentary on which he set great store, Ainsworth's '*Annotations*[8].'

---

[8] "Annotations upon the Five Bookes of Moses, the Booke of the Psalmes, and the Song of Songs, or, Canticles. Wherein the Hebrew words and sentences are compared with, and explained by the ancient Greeke and Chaldee Versions, and other Records and Monuments of the Hebrewes : But chiefly by conference with the Holy Scriptures, Moses his words, lawes, and ordinances, the Sacrifices and other Legall ceremonies heretofore commanded by God to the Church of ISRAEL, are explained. With an Advertisement touching some objections made against the sinceritie of the Hebrew Text, and allegations of the Rabbines in these ANNOTATIONS. As also Tables directing

He always had this folio open before him, his Bible resting upon it, and he frequently quoted in terms of high approval observations and suggestions made by the old writer. He was fond of repeating how greatly Bishop Pearson esteemed Ainsworth's work [9], and in his own '*Treatise on the Pastoral Office*' he speaks very highly of the book [1].

"He leaned very much, as might be expected, to the mystical method of interpretation, never ignoring the plain primary meaning of a passage, but still always delighting to see in it some typical foreshadowing of an event recorded or of a doctrine fully unfolded in the Gospel. Beyond any student of Holy Scripture that I ever met with, he aimed at finding, and rejoiced to find, illustrations of the famous saying ; 'In Vetere Testamento Evangelium latet.'

unto such principall things as are observed in the Annotations upon each severall Booke. By HENRY AINSWORTH. Luke 24, 44. *All things must be fulfilled which are written in the law of* MOSES, *and in the Prophets, and in the Psalmes.* LONDON, Printed for *John Bellamie*, and are to be sold at his shop in *Cornehill*, at the Signe of the three Golden Lions neere the ROYALL EXCHANGE. 1627."

Henry Ainsworth, one of the most learned Hebrew and Rabbinical scholars whom this country has ever produced, was a founder of the body called Independents. He afterwards fled to Holland, where he sided with the exiled Brownists, and taught in the Church at Amsterdam. He died quite suddenly in 1622, and was suspected to have been killed by the machinations of the Jews, who could not endure the evidence which he adduced for our Lord's Messiahship, not only from the Old Testament, but from their own writers. Burgon by no means overestimated his '*Annotations.*' The author has been assured that the demand for this old book in Oxford, consequent on Burgon's recommendation of it among his friends and at his Bible Classes, had the effect of sending up the price considerably.

[9] Bishop Pearson, however, speaks not of the merit of the '*Annotations*' of Ainsworth, but of the excessive literality of his translations of the Hebrew. And he evidently thinks his translations sometimes to be *too* literal. "Mr. Ainsworth, who translated the Pentateuch *nearer the letter than the sense,*" &c. See what he says in vol. i. ART. v. p. 392 [Oxford : University Press, MDCCCXXXIII].

[1] " On the Pentateuch, for reverence, learning, and fulness, I know of nothing better than the '*Annotations*' of Henry Ainsworth—a folio which may be easily met with," &c., '*Pastoral Office,*' chap. i. p. 32.

"I remember, when we came to the chapters giving the brief account of the Antediluvian Patriarchs, his exhibiting an elaborate table prepared by himself, which displayed the age of each man drawn out to scale, and showed at a glance how few were the human links in the chain of oral tradition between Adam and Abraham.

"I distinctly remember how beautifully he discoursed on the chapters describing the mission of Eliezer, Abraham's steward, to Padan Aram. By a comparison of texts (Gen. xvii. 17 ; xxi. 5 ; xxiii. 1 ; xxiv. 67 ; and xxv. 20); he brought out a touching trait in the character of the Patriarch Isaac—his tender devotion to his mother's memory. He showed that he was thirty-seven at the time of his mother's death, forty at the time of his marriage: and the tone of his voice as he read and commented on the final clause of the twenty-fourth chapter, ' Isaac was comforted after his mother's death,' revealing almost in spite of himself one of the deepest feelings of his own nature, still lives in my memory.

"At this distance of time, I cannot do more than recall the general impression which these readings in Burgon's rooms made on me, and, I am sure, on all who attended them. We could not but notice the profound reverence with which he regarded the Bible as being from first to last, through every part of it, the Word of God—the unspeakable importance which he attached to everything which it contained. A name, a word, a date was of importance and interest to him because he found it *there*. But besides this, it was nothing short of a revelation to me to discover that the study of the Bible could be made so full of interest and brightness—so attractive, as he made it. I had been accustomed all through my boyhood and youth to see the Bible carefully and devoutly studied, and had been taught both by precept and example that it was a duty so to study it. But as I look back to the Bible readings to which I was accustomed, I am impressed chiefly by the extraordinary dulness and dryness which characterized them. With Burgon this state of things was entirely reversed. For dulness and dryness he substituted a vivacious style of comment, he caused the characters of the Old Testament to live, as I had never seen them made to live before; and he thus helped to make a duty and occupation, which had previously seemed dull and heavy, full of interest and attractiveness. Whether others, whose experience in their early days was different from mine, will endorse what I have said I do not know. I only describe what I myself felt. And to the man who taught me so much, and showed me how attractive the study of the Bible might be made, I owe a debt of gratitude which no words can express.

"At 10 o'clock Burgon used to bring his remarks to a close, and immediately afterwards the little gathering dispersed [2].

[2] The Rev. T. P. Brandram, of Rumboldswyke, who has also kindly favoured the author with his reminiscences of these Bible Classes of Burgon's, writes: "We were invited, not encouraged, to ask questions; nothing like discussion took place; and we were made to feel that we were there to hear Mr. Burgon have his say, and very interesting his say was. During the time that I attended he travelled slowly from Gen. xxvii. to the end of the Book. There was no attempt made to deal with any of the moral difficulties, which parts of the history included in the above chapters present. This was not Mr. Burgon's line at all. One of the valuable parts of his Lecture lay in his frequent references to the Septuagint, about which I suspect most of us were at that time very ignorant."

Another attendant on these Classes says of their effect: "I don't think any of us went down at the close of the Term, who was not permanently impressed with the inexplicable accuracy (inexplicable except on the hypothesis of its full inspiration), the all-pervading wisdom, and the organic unity of the Bible. . . . Precious were those hours in Oriel. The teacher, though subtle and penetrating, struck no sparks of brilliancy to illuminate himself, but simply drew us on and drew us out. His one anxiety was that the Bible might be made to produce its own complete impression upon us. The same men usually came, and he knew us each personally. At the end of the Lecture we each shook hands with him;—but at the end of Term he always closed with the two beautiful Collects for St. Michael's Day and for All Saints."

The following notes of the teaching given in Burgon's Bible Classes, kindly furnished by Mr. Brandram, will give a better idea of them than any description:—

"Gen. xxviii. 14. Notice 'the West' placed first. May not this point to the spread of the Gospel in the Gentile world Westward?

xxix. 10. We see here a

"He allowed no engagement to interfere with his Sunday Readings. Once, and only once, do I remember his being absent. He was imperatively called away from Oxford for the Sunday, but on that occasion he got a friend (Dr. Chase, I think) to take his place. On another Sunday he was once very poorly—so poorly that, marvellous to relate, he was not present at any of the services at St. Mary's. But in spite of my earnest remonstrances, he would go—wrapped it is true in rugs, and taking all sorts of precautions—across the quadrangle to the College Hall, in order that he might have his usual Sunday reading.

"It was wonderful how the necessary strength was supplied to him to discharge Sunday after Sunday, at the end of a very laborious day, this self-imposed duty. The Sunday began at St. Mary's with a Celebration of the Holy Communion at 7 a.m., at which he was always the Celebrant. At 10.30 came the Morning University Sermon, at which, as well as at the Afternoon University Sermon at 2 p.m., he was bound, as Censor Theologicus, to be present. There were, besides, three full parochial services, at 11.30, at 4, and at 7. At each of these he never failed to be present. At the first and third service he invariably preached: at the second he *catechized*

mark of Jacob's strength of body. He himself rolls away the stone from the well's mouth, which we are told in v. 8 could not be rolled away till all the flocks had arrived. Jacob again shows his strength of body in wrestling with the angel.

Gen. xxix. 17. 'Tender-eyed.' ὀφθαλμοὶ ἀσθενεῖς (lxx.); weak-eyed;—no allusion to a soft expression of eye.

xxx. 3. Note in reference to this verse ('She shall *bear* upon my *knees*') the words γόνυ, γίνομαι, gigno, genui, gener.

Gen. xxxi. 53. 'The God of Nahor.' Laban swears by a *false* god, as we learn from Joshua xxiv. 2.

xxxvi. 24. 'That found the *mules* in the wilderness.' Hot watersprings, bearing this name.

xxxix. This chapter of Joseph's purity is set in beautiful contrast to the last of Judah's incontinence.

1. Attention called to the heading of the chapter, and the obsolete expression, 'Joseph is *chested*.'"

THE OXFORD LIFE: FIFTH PERIOD. 107

the children[3]. At all three he read both lessons—a duty which he never delegated to anyone; and at the morning and afternoon services he took a considerable part of the Prayers. And yet at 8.30, when his duties as Vicar of St. Mary's were ended, one saw him hurry away from the vestry to his rooms or to the Hall of Oriel, in order to meet his young friends and spend at least an hour and a half with them, first in pleasant general discussion, and then in the minute study of a portion of Holy Scripture.

"During the time that I was an Undergraduate, and for several years afterwards, Burgon held a College office which brought him into close contact with the Undergraduates. He was Censor Theologicus. There was an institution at Oriel, peculiar or almost peculiar to the College, called 'Sermon Notes.' The Undergraduate

---

[3] Burgon had the rare gift of so catechizing children as to make them attentive, and to adapt to their capacities (occasionally in a somewhat grotesque form) the instruction he instilled. The author remembers having once been present at St. Mary's when he was catechizing his Choristers. Something in the catechizing having led up to the subject of Holy Scripture, and the sentiments with which the Bible should be regarded, he said, "Some people use a fine long word, 'Bibliolatry,' which they say is a sin,—only another kind of idolatry. Bibliolatry means worshipping the Bible. Now I am not at all afraid of your worshipping the Bible *in any wrong sense*,—I quite allow you to worship it as much as you like. I'm only afraid that you won't worship it enough. It is God's own Word, inspired by Him; and we owe to His Word the same reverence which we owe to Himself."

Of course, like all other Catechists, he got answers occasionally which, however ingenious in themselves, showed that the Catechumen had not in the least seized the point of his instruction. One of these instances he loved to recount, to the great amusement of himself and his hearers. After carefully explaining to his boys the mystical meaning of David's taking five stones in his scrip (the five stones representing the Pentateuch, out of one book of which,—that of Deuteronomy—our Lord in His temptation drew the passages whereby He defeated the Tempter)—after laboriously inculcating this upon the children, he suddenly turned upon them and said; "Well, come now! *you* tell *me—why* did David take *five* smooth stones out of the brook, when he went to meet the giant?" Boy (thoughtfully): "Mayhap 'e thowt there mut be *some more on* 'em about."

members of the College were expected to go to one or other of the University Sermons, and on the Monday following to send up to the Censor Theologicus an analysis of the discourse which they had heard. In the course of the week the Sermon Notes were returned to the writer, a brief criticism, written in red ink, being appended, under which were the well-known initials J. W. B.... One day Burgon thought that he had detected a case of copying. He sent for the young man, whom he believed to be the culprit, and said to him 'I think, Mr. So and So, you have copied your Sermon Notes from Mr. ——,' naming another Undergraduate. The young man denied the charge, and said he had not copied. Burgon at once expressed his sincere regret for having wrongfully accused him, assuring him that he fully believed his statement, and that he was certain that the similarity between his Sermon Notes and those of the other man admitted of a perfectly innocent explanation. The young man withdrew. Burgon heard him slowly descend the staircase. A moment or two afterwards he heard the footstep of some one slowly coming upstairs. The door opened and the same Undergraduate re-appeared. 'What I told you just now,' he said, 'was not true. I did copy.' fidence, with which he had been treated, made it impossible for him to persist in the untruth[4].

"It would be a serious omission, in describing those old Oriel days, to leave unrecorded Burgon's great hospitality. Breakfast was the meal to which he was in the habit of inviting his friends—and what pleasant breakfasts his were! How plentiful and generous the style in which he regaled his guests! Nothing could be simpler or more frugal than his own fare when he was by himself—his breakfast consisting only of his 'Commons'

---

[4] Speaking of Burgon as *Censor Theologicus*, whose business it is to look over the Sermon Notes, the Rev. T. P. Brandram says; "He must have read through our notes, —no slight task—with considerable care. For instance, when I made the preacher (the Rev. C. P. Chretien) say that our Lord, 'when He took our body, condescended to the veil of our ignorance,' Mr. Burgon's annotation was,—' Only as the *Son of Man*—Remember.'"

of bread and butter—the only thing to be noticed being the cup of real oriental china made in true oriental fashion without a handle, which stood beside his solitary plate. Very different was the fare which he set before his guests: for them there was no lack of good cheer. But how can I describe the master of the feast? I despair of conveying anything like an adequate impression of what he was—of his attention to all the duties of a host—of his geniality—his powers as a conversationalist—the happy way in which he illustrated any topic which was started, by some appropriate anecdote—the dramatic way in which he told his stories, enhancing the effect by various tones of his voice, the play of his features, the sympathetic movement of his hands. Any story of his which I try to re-produce seems so flat and tame, compared with the impression which it made on me when I first heard it from his lips. How he made us laugh with his comical descriptions of persons and scenes that he set with wonderful vividness before us! But it would be a great mistake to suppose that he was only or even chiefly a teller of good stories. The stories were distinctly subordinate to the general aim and purpose of the conversation—they were called into requisition to illustrate the particular topic under discussion— they were means to an end—the end often a very high one indeed. I remember once, at one of these Undergraduate breakfasts, Burgon was talking of the good which was always present, if one could only discover it, in natures even the most unpromising—and how that good should be sought out, and, if possible, developed and made the starting-point for further improvement. And he urged repeatedly with great earnestness that there was no one, however degraded, without some spark of good not wholly quenched

within him—to quote his own phrase which he once or twice repeated, 'There is a green spot in every man's nature, if only you could find it.' Some one at the table told the story of a party of Australian miners—the rudest, coarsest, roughest human beings one could imagine—who were yet melted into tenderness, when a newly arrived emigrant showed them a primrose plant which he had brought with him from England, and thereby awakened old half-forgotten memories of home within their breasts. Burgon added another illustration, derived from a most unlikely source, the history of the Emperor Nero! The story was that after Nero's fall, when his statues and monuments were torn down by order of the Senate, and every kind of dishonour done to his memory, it was found that some one had gone by night and strewed violets over his grave. Inquiry was made, but it was never discovered who had done this. And then Burgon enlarged upon the incident, speculating who it was that had done this deed, and what feeling had actuated him: and finally he came to the conclusion that even Nero had some good point about him—that he had at some time or other befriended some one who had needed his help—and that this person had never forgotten the kindness, but when he was overthrown and abandoned by every one, still cherished his memory, and came secretly and scattered violets over his dishonoured grave. 'Yes' he added, 'there is a green spot in every man's nature, if only you could find it.'"

We cannot terminate our notice of Burgon's Bible Classes for the Undergraduates without adding that this part of his work was a source of high enjoyment to himself. On March 9 of the year 1876 he writes to Miss Monier-Williams, in a letter from which some excerpts have been given already;—

"O how I shall miss that gathering on Sunday evenings! True it is that at 9 I feel very tired; but every bit as true is it that every atom of fatigue vanishes the instant I enter the Hall, and see the dear young chaps in their places. Yes, and the fatigue does not return until the last of them is gone!"

III.

The following particulars of Burgon's life as a Parish Priest have been kindly furnished to the author by the

Rev. George Henry Gwilliam, who was associated with him as Curate of St. Mary's in 1874, and in charge of whom he left the Parish in 1876, until his successor should be appointed.

"During the latter part of the summer of 1875, I was in sole charge while the Vicar was at his sister's, at Turvey Abbey. . . . The weather being intensely hot, and many of our people absent from Oxford, I found the Sunday Afternoon Service so poorly attended that I ventured to question the necessity of continuing it during the summer. In reply I received a characteristic letter, from which I quote as follows:—'Your natural feeling about the afternoons and the empty Church I have two words to say about. The experience and thoughts of many years may not be quite unworthy of attention in your eyes.

"'(1) Pains taken over a Sermon are NEVER thrown away. GOD may—and will—for your reward, send you the *one* person whom your words may reach. He at least, and His holy Angels are present, and we preach at least *for Him*, as we minister *to Him*—WITH them. Next;

"'(2) Whenever you put by a sermon which was preached to very few, be advised always to *note that circumstance on the blank cover* (*I* always do). The practical sequel is that *that* sermon is very nearly *as if it had never been preached*, and certainly may be made one of your sermons at the *Morning Service* at St. Mary's (D.V.) next year.'

"It is singular how unwilling he was to enter the pulpit without a manuscript. I have seen him writing some addition to his sermon while I was saying the Prayers, rather than extemporise it in the pulpit. Yet he occasionally took off his glasses, and added some extemporised explanation; and *once*—yet only once (it was on Ascension Day) I heard him deliver a brief unwritten address. Then he showed how well he could speak without manuscript, if so disposed.

"He would draw a favourable comparison between

the best Anglican preachers and those of ancient days; and I have heard him say that he felt sure that Chrysostom and Augustine must have received into Paradise with open arms such men as Andrewes, and Hall, and Beveridge, because they would recognize in them fellow-workers who used the same methods of teaching as they had employed centuries before. . . . .

"Burgon was immensely popular in the circle of those who knew him intimately. He was quick-tempered, and his plainness of speech offended many; but most of his parishioners loved him dearly. At Parochial gatherings all bitterness of controversy was laid aside, and he was at his best. Coming back once from the Churchwardens' Dinner at Kennington Island, he kept the boat's company in such roars of laughter at his stories and jokes, that one of them had to declare he could handle his oar no longer, if Mr. Burgon made him laugh so."

The following reminiscences of Burgon's preaching and reading by a clergyman, an excerpt from whose paper has been already presented to the reader, give all the little traits which make a portraiture vivid:—

An Undergraduate's Testimony.

"I am one of a host of men who owe their acquaintance with the late Dean to his enthusiastic interest in Undergraduates. His first desire was to do them good. His next, I believe, was to send forth from Oxford a body of young clergymen sound in the faith through a deep conviction of the Inspiration of the Bible. And the means which he employed were the pulpit and private intercourse.

"I used regularly to attend his Sunday Evening Sermons at St. Mary's. In the pulpit he was deeply serious; by which should be understood something quite distinct from what is commonly known as an 'earnest style.' It was not the preacher, but your Parish *Priest* and friend who stood above you, and in homely but beautiful English was bent on enlisting your attention for things of the gravest importance.

The Oxford Life: Fifth Period. 113

"His voice was poor, and he was not always easy to be heard; yet he insisted on retaining unflagging attention, which (truth to tell) he always did, for his Sermons were full of interest; and, if he observed it to droop for a moment, the authority of the Parish Priest would come out. 'Attend now!' 'Now, listen to what I am going to say!' 'Pay attention, now; I'm not going to bawl!' uttered in his quick and authoritative little manner, which was always irresistibly comic, but had an instant effect on the congregation. Before the University it would be something more respectful—e.g. 'You are invited to observe, if you please,' uttered, nevertheless, with the force of the imperative. His voice was the one obstacle to brilliant success as a preacher. And the fact that his Sermons before the University were generally very well attended by the senior members, as well as the younger men, must be accepted as testimony to the purity of his language, the clear cogency of his reasoning, the entire originality of his theme and of his methods, his reputation for Biblical and Patristic learning, and his unique and powerful individuality.

"But on Sunday evenings, before his own congregation, his Sermons were of a plain parochial character, although scholarly, and full of fresh material quarried by himself from original sources. When I heard him, towards the close of his cure at St. Mary's, he preached very much from the Gospels. The interesting pictures of Gospel incident would receive a few fresh touches from his research; graphic details would often be filled in, and vivid side lights, borrowed from c
the text, thrown upon the scene, all enabling his people to grasp the reality of the marvellous records. Practical lessons were duly and pointedly enforced—often in a pungent sentence or two—as he went on. (I am writing from memory, not from any perusal of his published Sermons.) Then came the close, with a few deep fervent sentences uttered deliberately, sometimes with emotion, while he closed his manuscript; and in a marked way, peculiar to himself, removed his glasses very slowly, which seemed to say to us, 'One more Sermon to your account.'

"During the final hymn he stood back half propped up against the corner of the pulpit—he had been going since early morning, and had not yet done ; and I can still see that tall, grave, scholarly form, standing in that historic pulpit in the M.A. gown, bent a little forward, apparently in solemn reflection. while the choir beneath him were singing ' A few more years shall roll,'—a hymn which oftener than any other followed the Sermon.

" But if Dean Burgon was arresting in the pulpit, he was also striking at the lectern. He was a beautiful reader. and it was here that his profound reverence for the sacred Scriptures—every word of them—exhibited itself. The first time that I ever heard him open his lips was to read the first lesson, Daniel xii. ; and the impression made upon me was that no Sermon could follow that. It seemed as if the service should appropriately end there. His rendering of verse 2 was sublime. He always read as if some Heaven-sent revelation had been lowered before his eyes, not a word of which he had ever seen before, yet each word pregnant with meaning "

IV.

We have yet to hear from those who attended them some account of his Bible Readings for young ladies,—a class assuredly in which he was no less interested than in young men. The principal figure in these classes was the lady who has kindly placed at the author's disposal some of the most characteristic and beautiful of all Burgon's letters, thus contributing to this work one of its principal features of interest. She is good enough to permit the publication of part of a letter from herself to the author, in which she explains the origin of her intimacy with the late Dean Burgon, and in so doing gives a picture of his public and private instructions which is full of beauty and interest.

Mrs. Samuel Bickersteth (*née* Monier-Williams)
to the Author.

"The Vicarage, Belvedere, Kent, April 2, 1890.
"Dear Sir,— . . . . . .

"To me Dean Burgon was goodness itself. I think, when I was seven years old, he fancied he saw some resemblance in me to a little sister he had lost and tenderly loved. From that time I spent an hour in his College rooms every Sunday afternoon, until he was made Dean of Chichester (and I was 17 years old).

"I went to the four o'clock service at St. Mary's, where his delightful and racy catechizing of the choir boys was always full of interest. He gave each choir boy three-pence, if he attended that service, and these threepenny pieces I distributed in the Vestry after service. We then walked together to Oriel, Mr. Burgon, my governess and I, to find six Charity girls awaiting him at the Porter's Lodge. From his smaller sitting-room, an untidy little place, full of papers, books, dust and confusion (which he always in joke called his 'drawing-room'), he produced cake which was given to the girls.

"Then came the pleasure of my afternoon,—when sitting on his knee, or on a stool at his feet, he taught me Divinity (and who could teach as he could?), or Church History, Church principles, the Harmony of the Gospels, and other Bible study. The talk was varied by instruction on every conceivable subject.—He would show me old MSS., explain Codex A, or Codex B, point out the beauties of some picture of a Madonna, or some sculpture, with which the walls of his rooms were adorned, and would send me home with a mind awakened to every kind of interest.

"During the week to meet him in the streets (*always* in his cap and gown) was a great delight,—something was sure to follow—a game of hide-and-seek round the trees opposite Keble; a turn in some Fellows' garden, not generally open to the public, and where he would know every tree and plant, and everything, and everybody of interest connected with the College; a visit to some Chapel or Hall; or perhaps even to a pastry-cook's shop. If to this last, we were followed by a small crowd of ragged children to whom he gave handfuls of cake and buns.

"Then every Friday he had a Ladies' Bible Class in our house, to which I, even when a child, was admitted. I sat on a stool at his feet, and had to look up all his references. And very quick and particular he was, expecting me to know the order of the Books in the Bible as well as my alphabet. Sometimes he only commented on one verse, during the whole hour's Bible lesson, so carefully and critically did he go into the subject. I shall never forget my preparation for Confirmation, when he held a class in St. Mary's Chancel. He told us such funny stories, asked such quick sharp questions, never allowing us to take our eyes from his face, and yet withal was so solemn in all he said, going to the root of the whole matter. Then those quiet Holy Communion services in the Chancel of St. Mary's, where according to old custom we did not leave our seats, but the fair linen cloths were placed all round the Chancel, over the broad book desks. He would come down, and as he administered the Sacred Elements, he would tenderly lay his hand on the head of each lad who might be present, or on the hand of each girl who knelt there.

"He used to call me his 'little sweetheart,' and I think he guided every step of my life until he left us,— but staunch Churchman as he was, anything savouring of Roman Confession was abhorrent to him."

Here is a communication from Miss Miller, Principal of the Oxford Diocesan Training College, which illustrates the vivacity of the teaching given in his Bible Classes, and also exhibits the feature of humour which occasionally lighted up his Sermons, as it has done that of many distinguished preachers.

"The first time I saw Mr. Burgon was when—in 1867 (?)—he preached at Fenny Stratford on the 'Intermediate

State.' Those who may have heard him discourse on this congenial topic will understand the pleasant enlightenment so coming as to the preacher himself—before known only by repute as a good and able divine quaintly devoted to contention. Fuller illustration was happily gained when, a few years later, I found myself in the near neighbourhood of St. Mary's, at Oxford, and for several years rejoiced in the ministrations of the good Vicar. These included Bible Classes, at which the method followed was perhaps open to criticism in some respects, exuberant life and nature in the teacher being somewhat too defiant of educational art, and pupils being very imperfectly responsive, afraid—some to show their ignorance, others, their knowledge; but the very protest against prevalent conventionalism had its own special value, and we came away, if but dimly conscious of progress made, and more or less dissatisfied with ourselves, yet with quickened faculties, and hearts roused and warmed,—as how could it be otherwise, on coming in contact with one so taught of GOD—his own soul aflame with love of Truth as set forth in the Holy Book [5] ?

"Years before, I had heard the remark that the *vis comica* was more or less characteristic of the best men,—said in reference to Hugh James Rose, but no less true of his friend, John William Burgon. Whatever one's traditional sense of propriety might be, in attendance on Sermons, how completely was it overborne and put to flight by some pointed allusion, as irresistibly funny as it was innocent and unexpected! If for the moment shocked at one's own want of self-control, it was at least satisfactory to note that the properest folks were in the same predicament—a broad grin being apparent in every direction. One might have thought oneself safe in Lent,—the subject being 'Conviction of Sin,' and the preacher in dead earnest. But how could he help it?—'Convic-

---

[5] Those of us who joined the classes held at Prof. Monier-Williams's, will not forget our common debt to Mrs. Samuel Bickersteth, then a child, who, sitting at the feet of the revered teacher, did her best to atone for the shortcomings of us older ones;—"'ow, Ella, what do *you* say?" being the usual last resort in the general silence.

tion,' said he, 'might arise in many ways,—through some striking event in one's life, enforced reflection in illness, reading, conversation with friends,' (then lightly, as if barely worth mention) 'a sermon even.' Such attempt at illustration, apart from the inimitable look and tone of the speaker, reminds one of the dried specimens shown in a *hortus siccus*, as compared with the living plants, but unfortunately it is all that can now be offered. It was this same lively preacher that pressed upon one's attention earnestly, in private, the paramount importance of easing the work of thought for young ones by the provision of favourable conditions,—a vital matter which still claims the serious consideration of all who profess to educate them in any true or worthy sense.—It was by Mr. Burgon's advice that I sought State aid for my small training school, weighted however with an injunction to 'hold my own,' which has proved a less easy matter, on the whole, than the good man could possibly have foreseen. I trust however that —as time goes on—the results of the work thus feebly attempted will be such as fully to justify the advice given,—one's aim being always for the recognition and training of 'life,' in the fullest sense of the word, and as so strikingly exemplified in every word, look, and movement of the adviser himself.

"Susanna A. Miller.
(Principal of the
Diocesan Training College at Oxford.)
"Sept. 1889."

Another lady who attended his Bible Class in the Chancel of St. Mary's (for at the same period that one class was held at Mrs. Monier-Williams's, another was held in the Chancel) writes thus;—

"You may have noticed a vine and a fig-tree at the porch of St. Mary's. At the Bible Class one day the Dean told us he had had them planted there for us; and would we always, as we passed in and out, look at them and think of the lessons they taught us, as well as of his teaching when he was far away? Needless to say, I always do look at them, and often, when passing the Church, I go on that side of the road to see them better. When he had the stone placed in the chancel floor in memory of Amy Robsart[6], he gave us a short account of her and showed us the stone."

V.

This long Chapter on Mr. Burgon's Oxford life shall conclude with a few anecdotes which did not fall naturally into any place in the narrative, but which the author thinks to be quite worth preserving.

1. HIS FONDNESS FOR ANIMALS.
(From Rev. H. D. Pearson.)

"Burgon was not only, as you say, fond of children, but also of dumb animals. The Rev. Arthur Brook, formerly Rector of Hackney, told me that the only time he ever met Burgon was in the High Street at Oxford. Brook was on his way to St. Mary's; so was Burgon; and there was a miserable dog on the pavement. Burgon stopped to look at it, and hailed Brook. 'Do take care of this poor animal,' said Burgon, 'I am obliged to go to St. Mary's at once; I cannot see to it: will you be a good Samaritan?' Brook, who was a young Undergraduate, did what he was asked to do, sought out some veterinary surgeon, placed the dog with him;

---

[6] J. W. B. was from his early days specially romantic on the subject of Amy Robsart. "One afternoon," writes the Rev. H. D. Pearson, Vicar of St. James's, Clapton, to the author, "he made an expedition" (when an Undergraduate at Oxford) "with Sir William Honyman, the Hon. Henry Skeffington, my brother, and myself, to 'The Ragged Staff,' an inn of very humble pretensions at Cumnor. Burgon was fired with the thought of Amy Robsart. As to Tony Foster, I believe that Skeffington was a descendant of that hero, who, according to the brass tablet in the Church of Cumnor, is described as *vir piissimus*, I think,—at all events as very different from *pessimus*. We ransacked the farmhouses near for eggs; and with the ham of the inn these made a very good repast for us. Burgon was quite in his element, overflowing with poetry and romance."

then went to St. Mary's, and heard a good part of Burgon's sermon."

(From Rev. T. P. Brandram).—"He used to like to see the members of his Bible Class at breakfast, now and again. On one occasion, I remember some one had the face to ask him whether he could recollect ever having been cruel to animals. He became very grave, and said, 'Yes: twice. The first time it was dreadful,—yes, too dreadful for anything. The second time was when I was living in a tall London house. I went one day into my room, and saw the cat sitting at an open window. Her back was towards me, and the impulse irresistible. I crept up, and gave her a push!'"

2. Courtesy to Undergraduate Guests.

(Henry Wagner, Esq.)

"Dean Burgon was the first and almost the only 'Don' to seek me out and show me kindness, when I went up to Oxford. One of my earliest recollections is my meeting him in Oriel Lane, and his bidding me to dine with him that day in the Common Room to meet (a gratuitous assertion on his part) 'a great friend of yours,' Canon Wordsworth (afterwards Bishop of Lincoln); and how Dr. Wordsworth, fresh from Rome, and full of the Vatican Codex, and his work in the Library there, persistently talked *Codex*, with an absolutely unconscious rudeness quite ignoring me; and how the position would have been very trying to a shy youngster, had not Burgon, after some vain attempts to bring the conversation back and down to my undergraduate level, with his quick sympathy thrown me across the table a most humorous look of mock despair, with a comic shrug of the shoulders, and, I had almost thought, a *wink*.

"And my last recollection is my having sent him a date he wanted in connexion with C. Marriott, and a post-card from him in acknowledgment, on which he said, 'Never you attempt to write the lives of Twelve Good Men; or they will surely be your own death,'—followed so very soon after by the coincidence of his own."

3. Sensibility to Pathetic Scriptural Incidents.

(Rev. T. P. Garnier.)

"It was in the Long Vacation of (I think) 1869 or 1870, when our own Chapel at All Souls was closed, that I used to attend the 8 o'clock a.m. service at St. Mary's. On one occasion the late Dean was reading the Lesson of the day, which contained the account of the 'woman which was a sinner' washing our Lord's feet with her tears. When he came to the passage, 'Simon, seest thou this woman? I entered into thine house; thou gavest me no water for My feet: but she,' voice began to falter, and he ended by breaking down, covering his face with his hands, and for a time could not proceed. The few who were there that day had been admitted behind the veils of conventional life to the 'inner man.'

4. The Claims sometimes made upon him.

(As told by Burgon himself to Mr. Ryman Hall, a member of his congregation, and by him written down from memory.)

"When leaving St. Mary's Church after Morning Service one Sunday, a gentleman walked up to me, and with a decided American accent said, 'Stranger, have you got any leisure?' 'Well; let me see; it is now a quarter past one o'clock. I have to get my luncheon, and be back at the University Sermon at 2 o'clock. At 3 o'clock I ought to be . . . . . . At 4 o'clock I have an Afternoon Service. At 6, if I have time, I shall have some dinner. Anyhow, I must be at Church again at 7 for Evening Service, which will last until half-past 8. Then, on returning to my rooms, I shall find 20 or 30 Undergraduates waiting for me, and I shall be engaged with them until about 11. Oh! at 11 I shall have some leisure!' 'Ah! I'll come to you at 11.'

"The usual routine of the day's work went on, and—tired as a dog, you know—I had just turned the men out of my rooms at 11 o'clock, having quite forgotten the enquirer of the morning, when I heard steps on the stairs and a knock at my door. 'Come in';—and in came the man, and again asked, 'Have you got any leisure now?' Tired as I was, I said, 'Oh, yes! come in. Now, my dear Sir, will you kindly tell me what you want of me?' 'Well; can you convince me of the truth of Christianity?' 'What, Sir! do you really come to me at this time of night to ask such a question as that?' 'Yes, stranger, that's what I came for.' 'What do you mean, Sir? What are your doubts? What *do* you mean, Sir?' 'Well;—the Gospels, they contradict one another.' 'The Gospels contradict one another!! Now I pin you to that, Sir! *Where* do they contradict one another?' 'Oh! so and so.' 'My *dear* Sir! that is too easy! Do think of something else!' 'No: that's enough: explain that first!' I explained it at once, of course; it was too ridiculous. He then mentioned something else, to be as easily made clear to him; and so we went on, ding-dong, hammer and tongs, until the College clock struck 2, when he rose to go, saying, 'Well, I guess if anyone has convinced me of the truth of Christianity, it's you;—you are so *beastly positive*. Good night!' Before leaving, he told me he was a Clergyman of the American Church; but from doubts that arose in his mind he had thrown up his living, and had travelled a great deal. He never lost an opportunity of hearing a preacher of whom he had heard favourable mention; and if he found him an earnest man, he always made a point of asking him if he could convince him of the truth of Christianity."

SIR ROUNDELL PALMER'S ACKNOWLEDGMENT OF THE '*Last Twelve Verses of St. Mark*' IS HERE SUBJOINED, AS PROMISED ABOVE, p. 57.

"Blackmoor, Petersfield, Oct. 19, 1871.

"Dear Burgon,—On arriving here on Saturday, I found your kind and acceptable present: for which, (and for your letter, and the too favourable mention made of me in the 'Inscription'), I beg you to accept my sincere thanks. I will bear in mind your wish, as to keeping the book to myself, till it is regularly published.

"I have already seen enough of it, to be satisfied, that it is a work of value and importance. But I cannot pretend to say, that I am a wholly unprejudiced judge of the argument, if it is a prejudice for one, who is no professed critic, nor learned in manuscripts, to have already a pretty strong opinion of his own upon the subject. I think it reasonable, whenever the authority of any text of Scripture, which has been generally received in the Church from a remote antiquity, is assailed, upon (alleged) critical grounds, to require from the assailant strong proofs: and, in the present instance, the preliminary difficulties in the way of the critic appear to me to be so great, as to be absolutely insuperable by that kind of evidence, which alone is, or can be, alleged. The improbability of either of the three hypotheses, (1) that this Evangelist deliberately ended his Gospel with the words ἐφοβοῦντο γάρ,—(2) that a work of this nature and importance was left incomplete, when so very near the end, contrary to the intention of the writer,—(3) that the verses in question are a successful substitution by some impostor, of a new conclusion, different in substance as well as style, for the original text, irrevocably lost almost as soon as written, of which neither record, tradition, nor trace remains,—appears to me to amount to a moral impossibility: and I can only explain to myself the facile reception, by professed Biblical critics, of theories involving such great difficulties, (as to their original authors), by that credulity of the incredulous, when the objects of belief are themselves and their own imaginations, of which we daily witness such extraordinary instances; and (as to their followers) by the eagerness of men, who have not really sounded the depths of a question. to take up at second-hand those novelties, which pass in the world for the latest discoveries of the wise, and by that natural law, which produces *currents* of (so-called) scientific or critical opinion, through the abu e of the same principle of *authority*, which all *pretenders* to science so much delight in setting aside.

    "Believe me ever
     "My dear Burgon
      "Yours faithfully
       "ROUNDELL PALMER."

CHAPTER III.

THE CHICHESTER LIFE.

1876.

JOHN WILLIAM BURGON was installed Dean of Chichester, Jan. 19, 1876. He did not, however, set out for Chichester till after Easter (which in this year fell upon April 16), partly as having many arrangements to make in reference to the removal of his sister and her daughters from Oxford to the Deanery, and partly as desiring to spend one more Lent and Eastertide with his flock at St. Mary's, many members of which loved him with a devotion which he so ardently reciprocated. In the earliest days of January, and while he was yet only Dean-Designate, he paid a visit of two nights to the Deanery at Norwich, "to learn Dean-craft," as Dean Hook expressed it, when the writer of these pages, on his appointment to the Deanery of Norwich, paid *him* a visit at Chichester for the same purpose. During this visit Burgon's spirits seemed to be at flood-tide. Doubtless, unfeignedly grieved as he was at being torn away from his beloved Oxford, he felt the relief from the strain of overwork which a Deanery would give, and also delighted in the prospect of leisure for his theological studies, which the position would bring with it. But with all this exuberant buoyancy and light-heartedness, there was a skeleton in the cupboard, which stalked out occasionally and haunted him. The misunderstandings with the Canons, soon to end in painful dissensions, had already begun. He complained bitterly, and (as was his wont) somewhat passionately, that his request to see the Statutes of the Cathedral Church of Chichester, of which he was to be the guardian and administrator, had been refused, and that his Colleagues had not been slow to inform him, both by letter and word of mouth, that the position of Dean of Chichester was only that of first among equals, and that he must look upon himself as no more than one of five, having not even the privilege of a casting-vote in Chapter. If this latter piece of information was not relieved of its defiant character (as possibly it was) by courteous expressions of personal goodwill, and brotherly welcome, one can quite understand its making him sore, while his being refused a sight of the Statutes (if this were indeed the case) certainly needs explanation. These and other complaints were ultimately formulated in two pamphlets printed by him for private circulation three years afterwards, the first of which is headed, '*Chichester Cathedral. Suggestions submitted to the Cathedral Commissioners*, 1879.' The author is truly glad to be dispensed by their intended privacy from referring any further to these pamphlets, which, as dealing with jealousies and quarrels for "pre-eminence" among brethren in the Christian Ministry, are not agreeable or edifying reading. He feels nevertheless that his fidelity as a biographer obliges him to give some general account of these painful differences, and of the misapprehensions in which they took their rise, and he is fortunate in having obtained such an account from Canon Awdry, a warm friend and loyal supporter of Burgon's, who joined the Chapter at a later date (Nov. 1879), and who had fullest access to accurate information upon the subject, such as no one outside the

Capitular Body could possibly have. Thus Canon Awdry writes:—

"The history of Dean Burgon's relations with his Chapter from first to last was this. He declared war upon his Residentiary Canons by sending them one of those scoldings with which we were all familiar before he came into residence, and when, to use his own phrase, he 'was not yet Dean,' but only Dean Nominate. It was evident that he was entering upon his office with the idea that he was Rector and the Canons were his Curates. The immediate result was the firm union for self-defence of men, whom it would have required a stroke of genius to have united in any other way. Troubled times followed. The Dean knew very little of the Statutes and customs of the Cathedral, which were very hard to know, for little or no part of them had then been printed, and the most important documents relating to them were in the University College Library and at the British Museum, while others had to be hunted up in the Bishop's Muniment Room and the ponderous tomes of the Chapter Act Books. With the Constitution of the Cathedral, and the Chapter precedents, the Senior Canon was very familiar. He had analysed and tabulated them, and was editing part of them. The Chapter had certainly got out of hand, and though much good work had been done in late years, notably, the rebuilding of the central tower and steeple[7], yet things were done from time to time too much on individual responsibility, with some of which the exquisite taste of the new Dean was reasonably offended. In the collisions which occurred the Dean's impulse was almost always in

---

[7] Under Dean Hook, and mainly through his exertions. The spire fell on February 21, 1861. "One thing I have determined," wrote the Dean to Vice-Chancellor Wood; "I will rebuild the spire, if I beg my bread, if God will but preserve my life for the seven years which remain till I am three-score-and-ten." A great meeting was held at Brighton, March 22, 1861, at which £14,300 was raised in the room, the estimate being for £50,000. In November, 1867, the Cathedral was re-opened after the rebuilding of the spire. [*See* Prebendary Stephens' '*Life and Letters of Hook*,' vol. ii. pp. 407, 410, 441. Ed. 2.]

the right direction, but he was no match for the calm knowledge of the then Senior Canon, and after struggling impetuously for some time like a fly in a spider's web, he almost always ended technically in the wrong.

"Not long after I became a Canon Residentiary, Dean Burgon had a long illness [8], induced chiefly, as it seemed to us, by fret and worry at the sea of useless controversy in which he was struggling at Chichester, and at the meetings of the Cathedral Establishment Commission, whilst he felt his life ebbing away, and the great work on which he was bent [9] still undone. He recovered, however, and the change which took place in the Chapter very soon after gave him a sense of confidence and freedom from restraint and irritation, which enabled him to plunge once more with a good heart into his proper literary work."

[Canon Awdry then mentions the appointment of Dr. Crosse to a Canonry (in March, 1882)—a change in the *personnel* of the Capitular Body peculiarly acceptable to the Dean; and after highly eulogizing Dr. Crosse, and his happy art of carrying other men with him, while he seemed to follow them, continues thus]:—

"Such was the man that came among us, and into whose arms Dean Burgon almost immediately threw himself. The Dean felt himself safe. The lead was gladly accorded to him in everything, and when he was in danger of a blunder, he was saved from any great mistake and still left with the lead, and all was done with tact and delicacy. Had Dean Burgon asserted authority over his Chapter, as inherent in his office, at the end of his tenure as he did at the beginning, I doubt whether any very material improvement in his position and his peace of mind could have been brought about; but we all

---

[8] Canon Awdry is probably under a slight mistake as to the date. The illness, of which a notice will be found under 1879, took place in that year. It was recent, and no doubt much talked of, at the time of the Canon's Installation, Nov. 28, 1879.

[9] His work on '*The Principles of the Textual Criticism of the New Testament*,' which, alas! he has left unfinished.

desired better order in the affairs of the Cathedral, and one of the things most needed with a view to this was that nothing of any consequence should be done without the Dean, and that he should have as large a measure of initiative. and be as visibly our head as possible. By no longer raising questions of principle and of the Cathedral Constitution, on which we were not in agreement, he obtained his proper place as our natural leader, and left the Dean's position stronger than he found it, and more nearly what it ought to be.

"The position of a Dean, particularly in a Cathedral of the old Foundation, is and must be very difficult, and was more complicated at Chichester by inconvenient precedents than in the other Cathedrals with which I am much acquainted. It was no small honour to a man of Dean Burgon's impulsive and uncompromising temperament that he ended his term of office on terms of friendship and affection with his Bishop and with his greater and lesser Chapters."

And now let us return to the Norwich visit, in which, his bright and sanguine mind soon throwing off the vexation arising from the prospect of Capitular troubles and conflicts, he displayed the spirits of a boy, and made himself the life and soul of the little parties of friends who were asked to meet him. He was an accomplished retailer of anecdotes, and one of those which he told at a breakfast party will never be forgotten by the hearers. He related how a friend of his had resorted to some conjurer's entertainment. Pressing into the exhibition-room in a pushing, struggling throng of people, he felt somebody at his coat pocket; and putting his hand there he found, instead of the subtraction of his pocket-handkerchief which he had expected, that two small wooden dolls had been introduced. "Oh, no doubt," thought he, "the conjurer is going to make game of me by pretending that he has conjured these dolls into my pocket; but I will be more than a match for him." Panting and puffing into the exhibition-room immediately in front of him was a stout gentleman, whose coat-pocket presented every now and then, as he struggled with the crowd, an inviting aperture. In this aperture the two dolls were very gently ensconced, so that the wearer of the coat was entirely unconscious of the process;— under "Mr. Fagin's" own supervision and drilling the transfer could not have been more adroitly made. The narrow straits of the door having been passed, the man who had disposed of the dolls so cleverly took care to seat himself as far as possible from the stout gentleman, to the contents of whose pocket he had made a contribution. Very soon after the beginning of the entertainment, the conjurer pulled out two dolls, and said he would order them to go into the pocket of one of the spectators. "Abra-Cadabra, Fi, fee, fo, fum, pass into the pocket of that gentleman yonder!" Whereupon he seemed to throw the dolls into the midst of his audience, but really passed them up his sleeve by legerdemain. "And now," added he, "I think if that gentleman" (pointing out the visitor, into whose pocket he had himself put two dolls) "will do me the favour to look in his pocket, he will find that he has got the dolls." Burgon here acted the visitor, exhibiting his coat-pockets in proof of their being empty. Standing up on his chair at the breakfast-table, and turning his back, he pulled out the linings of the pockets, and showed them to us in their empty and flaccid state. And then, turning round and fronting us, he said; "No, I don't carry about dolls in *my* pocket; but I shouldn't wonder if that stout gentleman yonder should find a doll or two in his." Then he acted the stout gentleman, who, he explained, was also a little irritable; "What, me, Sir? what do you mean, Sir? *I* carry dolls!" And then he put his hands into his pocket, and made believe to bring out the dolls, with a look of amazement, and horror,—a quasi-guilty look, which, as he did it, was indescribably ludicrous. The audience, he continued, were convulsed. But oh! the poor conjurer! How heavily the wheels of his entertainment seemed to drag all the night afterwards! Outdone in a trick by one of his spectators, who might, for all he knew, be a great adept in legerdemain, a Prospero or a Merlin! He was performing in the presence of one who knew his secrets. and might perhaps expose them all publicly, and prevent his having spectators any more! Nerveless and spiritless, he contrived to drag on to the end of his programme; and then as the visitor, who had so put him out of countenance, was passing out with the rest of the people, a boy, who assisted in the conjuring, touched his sleeve. and said his master would be greatly obliged by an interview in his private room. "By all means," said the visitor, and was ushered into a room at the back of the platform. Pale and looking care-worn the conjurer grasped his hand. "My dear good Sir, I'll give you FIVE POUNDS down on the spot, if you'll show me how you did that trick!" "My dear good Sir," was the reply, "if you would give me FIFTY POUNDS down on the spot, I *wouldn't* show you how I did that trick."

It will be remembered also by those who met Burgon at another small party at Norwich, when the talk turned upon sleeplessness, a state of which he had had no small experience, how he imitated in the most lifelike manner the sound of a gnat hovering within the bed-curtains, now more distant, now coming nearer,—and at length settling down upon his victim and poisoning and inflaming his blood. One has heard of some great preacher (was it Mr. Spurgeon himself?) who, in describing to his congregation the conflict of David with Goliath, imitated the gesture of slinging in so life-like a manner that the congregation in the gallery could not help ducking their heads, under the impression that the smooth stone out of the brook was coming in among them. The writer distinctly remembers that when Burgon's gnat was winding in mazy dance about the room, and seemed by the altered sound of his drone to be getting close up to the company and preparing for an assault, one felt a strong inclination to dive under the tablecloth as if under bed-clothes.

"The year 1876," writes the Rev. Henry Deane, to whose Review of the state of thought and religion in Oxford, from 1846 to 1876, the author is already so much indebted, "was remarkable in the religious history of Oxford, as being the occasion of the first Mission on the new system which had been held in Oxford;—a mission planned conjointly by Ritualist and Evangelical clergy. The matter was warmly discussed in the Ruridecanal Chapter, at which Burgon said; 'You say in your circular that you cannot declare the whole counsel of God to your people in 52 weeks; and now you get down two missioners to do it for you in one week.' Two sermons" (one preached at St. Mary's to his own congregation, Feb. 20, the other before the University on Quinquagesima Sunday, Feb. 27, both printed in a single pamphlet) "were the outcome of the Mission. In the first of them ('*Home Missions and Sensational Religion*') he says of Missioners" (of Missioners in general, not of those employed at Oxford); "'With a few honourable exceptions, they prove to be gentlemen conspicuous neither for their learning nor for their attainments.' This charge he justifies in a footnote; 'There lies before me the favourite (penny) '*Hymnal Parochial Missions and Retreats*,' &c., &c. The colophon of this precious document is as follows:—AD MAJORAM (*sic*) DEI GLORIAM.' He said to me afterwards, 'Perhaps all they meant to do was to make an attempt at a rhyme.' I suggested that it was a printer's error. 'No,' he said, 'I don't believe they knew any better.'"

His main objection to the new system of Missions (for to the old system, as set on foot by and worked under Bishop Wilberforce, he is careful to explain that he had no objection; but, "retaining the old name, we have drifted into something essentially different,") was the (certainly very questionable) practice of an Incumbent's "handing over his flock for so long as the Mission lasts to the spiritual oversight of a stranger." Accordingly, while the Mission was carried on at St. Mary's as at other Churches, it was by himself and his Curates, the services of the Missioner being not called into request; and in this course he was kept in countenance, he tells us, by his three brother Incumbents of St. Peter's-in-the-East, All Saints', and St. Giles's. His strictures upon the two methods adopted by the modern Missioner,—one being "the Confessional," which he holds in thorough Protestant abhorrence, and the other the inculcation of "the unscriptural tenet that the instantaneous and effectual Conversion of the soul to GOD is quite an ordinary phenomenon in the spiritual life of individuals,"—are worth reading, if it were only as exhibiting his own thoroughly well-balanced views of religious truth, and the fearless uncompromising way in which he put them forth. The second Sermon, entitled '*Humility—ad Clerum*,' is the annual "Humility Sermon" preached before the University, for which there is a separate endowment, and in the course of which the preacher is obliged to introduce certain texts, as one of the terms of the endowment[1]. The want of humility in

---

[1] The endowment is for two Sermons, one on Humility, to be preached on Quinquagesima Sunday, the other on Pride, to be preached on the Sunday next before Advent. It yields £5, which is divided between the two preachers, who thus receive (including the £5 5s. given out of the University Chest to preachers before the University) £7 15s. apiece. Burgon was called upon in 1880 to take "the Pride Sermon." [See under that year.]

the Clergy, and specially in the more able and gifted Clergy, which leads them to preach and write on the loftiest of all topics from their own theorizings, without the slightest study of the science of Divinity, and to settle beforehand what Holy Scripture *ought to say*, instead of entirely prostrating the heart and the understanding before what it *does* say, is the topic of this Sermon; while in the latter part of it the lawlessness of a certain section of the Clergy (again traceable to their want of humility), and the entire departure of the Ritualists from the first principle of the Tractarian movement—reverence for authority—and from the early teaching of Mr. Newman, are very explicitly and not too severely censured. Verily our new Dean was not slow to show his colours.

It was not in Burgon's nature to forget old friends, more particularly such old friends as had shown him kindness in trouble. Mr. Finn, the English Consul at Jerusalem, with the members of his family, had been, as we have seen, instrumental in saving his life when he was attacked by the Jerusalem fever in 1862. The year 1876 found Mrs. and Miss Finn in England, and at Oxford. What need to say that Burgon renewed his acquaintance with these ladies, and showed them all that graceful hospitality, which was quite one of his characteristic accomplishments?

Here are Miss Finn's reminiscences of her visit to Oxford, with which she has been good enough to furnish the author.

"On March 12, 1876, my mother and I were at the morning service at St. Mary's, Oxford, and heard Dean Burgon read the first lesson, Gen. xxvii. to v. 41 [2]. When

---

[2] March 12 was in 1876 the Second Sunday in Lent. Gen. xxvii. to v. 41 is the First Morning Lesson for that Sunday *according to the New Lectionary*. It is clear therefore that during the first seven

he had read the words, 'When Isaac was old and his eyes were dim,' he paused, sighed, removed his glasses from his eyes, and after carefully rubbing them, put them on again. The effect was irresistibly funny. The whole chapter, and the Sermon on the history of Rebecca which followed, were read with much pathos ; and in his own peculiar fashion he conjured up the whole scene before us, bringing out the tenderness in Rebecca's character, and her sorrows.

"On the following Tuesday morning we breakfasted with him in his rooms at Oriel, the floor piled with books,—but the table loaded with every imaginable good thing,—and in the centre the Founder's cup filled with flowers.

" The record in my diary of the conversation is, ' Long discussion on slang, and then on the proportions of the Temple Area.' The latter was a subject that interested us both deeply, and he told those present of the wonderful beauty of the stained glass windows in the ' Dome of the Rock,' which stands on the site of the Temple at Jerusalem. He explained how the jewelled effect of the glass was produced by refraction from the tiles in which each pane was set,—which my mother was the first to observe, and had pointed it out to Mr. Burgon on the spot."

We have seen how lively an interest Burgon took in the spiritual welfare of the Undergraduates, and how much of his time he devoted not only to instructing them in the Holy Scriptures, but also to cultivating their acquaintance, and seeking to gain an influence over them. It would have been strange indeed if many of them had not responded to such self-sacrificing and

---

years of the New Lectionary, when it was optional with the clergy to use either the Old or the New, Burgon used the New, greatly as he disliked it, in preference to the Old, *in deference to authority.* See his letter to the (then) Dean of Norwich, which is given above, vol. ii. p. 61. The New Lectionary came into use Jan. 1, 1872, and became imperative Jan. 1, 1879, having hitherto been optional.

disinterested efforts in their behalf. But they did so most warmly and cordially, and were on the point of getting up a testimonial to him in acknowledgment of his services. He declined this in a letter to a representative of theirs, who had written to him on the subject, and who, having graduated, was about to present himself for Ordination. The letter is not only characteristic throughout, but seems to be a commentary on the text, " I seek not yours, but you." Here are some excerpts from it:—

To a young B.A.

" Oriel, March 7, 1876.

" Dear Mr. Knollys,—. . . .

" No ; I dislike very cordially 'testimonials,' as they are called. . . . . You will remember me when I am gone, I hope. I shall never forget all of *you*. My happiest moments have been spent in teaching some of you. None but images of brightness and pleasure are connected in my memory (and will be till I die), with the Undergraduate members of the University. If you wish to show me your goodwill, do it in *this* way; help one another to live pure lives. Discourage every form of vice and sin. When freshmen come up, get hold of them, and influence them for good. Be zealous for the truth. Be not ashamed to confess Christ. Be bold on *His* behalf. Be strict with juniors. Be faithful in the practice of earnest Prayer. Every act of this class, which any one of you shall at any time perform, will be the thing I covet most at your hands,—the only thing I *at all* covet; and if any thing I may ever have said in your hearing shall indirectly have been the cause of such acts in any of you,—do believe me, *that* will be the most precious 'testimonial' you could possibly offer me. Tell me not in reply that 'I shall not know of this, and that therefore it will be no tribute to *me*.' I answer; *I* shall not know, true ; BUT GOD WILL! and that is more than enough for me, and ought to be quite enough for yourselves also.

"Gratefully, dear Mr. Knollys,

"Yours,

" JOHN W. BURGON."

In sending the above letter to the author, Mr. Knollys, the gentleman to whom it was addressed, adds that " after the Bishop of Lincoln" (Christopher Wordsworth), " had in vain tried to persuade Dean Burgon to reconsider his decision, a paper signed by all those anxious to join in the testimonial was sent to Mr. Burgon, who acknowledged it in the following letter :—

"Oriel, March 18, 1876.

"Dear Mr. Knollys,—The expression of kind feeling towards myself, which you have conveyed to me in your name and in the name of thirty of your friends, is most acceptable, most precious to me. I shall give your address a place of honour among the papers which I preserve, and shall rejoice greatly if I may some day have the good fortune to see some of those names emerging into honourable prominence. But there is a better thing than coming before the world. This framework of things is passing away from us,—O there is no telling how rapidly! And the names which will shine brightest all through the coming ages will be the names of those who have most effectively striven to ' keep themselves unspotted from the world.'

"Tell your friends this, with the assurance of my brotherly sympathy and affectionate goodwill. I cannot think about my departure without a kind of anguish ; cannot write about it without saying too much about self. But this I may allow myself to declare, that I owe to that body, which you so well represent, some of the happiest hours of my life, and that the memory of you will many a time gladden me, when I shall be far away.

"Asking you all for an abiding place in your prayers, I am ever,

"My dear Mr. Knollys,

"Your Friend,

"JOHN W. BURGON."

We now come to a passage in the life of Burgon creditable to himself, as showing not only the esteem which his labours at Oxford had won for him in high places, but also the equanimity with which he submitted to what must have been to one, who loved Oxford as he did, a very keen disappointment. It is to be wished that it were equally creditable to the Government of the day, who seem to have been terrified out of a most suitable appointment by a few disparaging words in Parliament, inspired no doubt by the (so-called) Liberal party in the University, who had been thwarted on more than one occasion by Burgon's stedfast and unflinching Conservatism, and by his efforts to preserve the connexion of the University with the Church. This party was for revolutionising Oxford; he for reforming it indeed, where it needed reform (had not the new Theological School been established very mainly by his influence?), but always on the old lines. On the 10th of August in the following year (1877) "the Universities of Oxford and Cambridge Act," which gave legislative powers over the Universities and the Colleges therein, to two sets of Commissioners, seven for each University, received the Royal Assent. As the names were originally drafted, when the Bill was discussed in the House of Lords, March 31, 1876, Burgon's name stood third on the Oxford List. On the 4th clause, which nominated the Commissioners, the Earl of Morley moved as an amendment to strike out the words, "The Very Reverend

John Williams (*sic*) Bargon (*sic*), Dean of Chichester[3]."
Allowing that Burgon was the only one on the proposed
Oxford List of Commissioners "who was thoroughly
acquainted with the modern phase of Oxford," Lord
Morley alleged that he was "unfortunately known there
as a most decided partisan," and that his "appointment
would be unacceptable to most of the Colleges." Lord
Salisbury most pertinently replied that "it was the
duty of Her Majesty's Government to find gentlemen
who would represent different colours of opinion," that
the Dean of Chichester's appointment "had recommended
itself to the Government on the ground that he was
well acquainted with Oxford, and that, though a
clergyman deeply attached to the Established Church,
he was not a man of extreme theological views." In
a House of 90 Members the amendment was negatived
by a majority of 30. On June 12, 1876, the University
of Oxford Bill came before the House of Commons,
Burgon's most kind friend and patron, Mr. Gathorne
Hardy (now Lord Cranbrook), whose influence had
procured for him the offer of the Deanery of Chichester,
moving the Second Reading. Mr. Osborne Morgan, in
moving his Amendment, reminded the House that the
Dean of Chichester's name had been "actually challenged, not only by a debate, but by a division 'in
another place,'" and added, "Surely, if it was necessary to place on the Commission some representative

---

[3] The words are given as Hansard gives them, and every citation is made *verbatim* from the Parliamentary Debates. [See the Third Series, vol. ccxxviii (from March 15, 1876 to May 2, 1876) Col. 933, in which Lord Morley's Speech will be found.] In the motion, which follows the speech, the name is spelt *Bagon*. Either printers were careless, or reporters made strange mistakes. In glancing over the Debates one's eye catches such comical blunders as the "Hebdominal Council," (Query *Abdominal* ?).

of Dr.[4] Burgon's school of theology, some less ostentatiously aggressive—he might almost say pugnacious—champion of that school might have been selected. Oxford men had not forgotten—they could not forget—how only a few years ago Dr. Burgon had endeavoured to exclude from the University Pulpit" (yes; this was the sore point; this was the unpardonable sin) "one of the best and ablest men who had ever adorned the English Church, or any other Church, the Dean of Westminster[5]." Mr. Lowe, following in the same debate, condescended to what one of the Ministers in a private letter called "a vulgar personality." "The Dean of Chichester's pretensions," he said (to a place upon the Commission), "were of such a nature that even the House of Lords could not stand them. He spoke with great respect of the Dean of Chichester, but he believed he had been properly described as a 'jocose fanatic'—a character he had built up for himself and maintained with such consistency during life, that if a case were put before him with the Church interest on one side, and every interest on the other, it would be impossible for him, with every effort, to give an impartial judgment[6]."

These unworthy attacks had the intended effect of excluding from the Commission the one member of it, who would have acted as a drag upon the (so-called) Liberal (that is, secularizing and revolutionary) principles of "young Oxford." In the last month of the year Burgon received an intimation through his kind friend, Mr. Gathorne Hardy, that as his continuance on the Com-

---

[4] So he calls him. But Burgon never took his Doctor's Degree, as the Statutes of Chichester Cathedral did not demand it of him, and as feeling, no doubt, that his very narrow resources might be better spent than on an expensive and somewhat empty honour.

[5] Hansard 'Parliamentary Debates,' vol. ccxxix. (From 3 May, 1876 to 16 June, 1876) Col. 1722.

[6] Hansard (as above). Col. 1744.

mission, after what had passed in Parliament about him, might embarrass the Government, they would be glad if he would allow his name to be withdrawn. The letter in which he sets Lord Salisbury free to act as he pleases in the matter (or rather so much of it as may with propriety be published) is, by the kindness of Lord Cranbrook, presented to the reader at the end of the record of this year. Part of an earlier letter (of June 22) is also given, from which it will be seen what line he would have taken in the matter of Academical Reform, had his name continued on the Commission.

The whole transaction, so damaging to the character of the Government for not having the courage of their opinions, and to that of the Liberal Party at Oxford for their unfairness and unwillingness to hear both sides, cannot be better summarised than in the following sentence of a letter to the author from one of the present Heads of Colleges;—

"There was much to recommend Burgon for a seat on the Commission; but, seeing that Mr. Gladstone had already de-Christianized the University and the Colleges by 'the Universities Tests' Act,' there is no wonder that the extreme Secularist party in the House of Commons should view the selection of him as 'reactionary' (that I believe to be their slang term); and Conservative Governments derive their name, in the old way, *à non conservando*."

In the August of this year a correspondence took place between Burgon and the Dean of Ely (Dr. Merivale), a brief reference to which may be useful, as the question on which the correspondence turned is one, which in these days of frequent Celebrations of the Holy Communion is continually recurring, and is most often settled in a manner adverse to that in which these two authorities, learned and able men both of them, and the Dean of Ely particularly remarkable for his soundness of judgment and moderation, would have had it settled. The question on which Burgon seems to have consulted his brother Dean was whether the Priest-Vicars [7] of Chichester Cathedral, having already communicated at the Early Celebration, might properly assist in the distribution of the elements at the later *without again communicating*. The Dean of Ely points out that many Clergymen, being single-handed, are *obliged* to celebrate the Holy Communion twice in the same day, sometimes even more than twice, having to communicate the sick after Church in private houses [8]; "and I do not understand," he adds,

"on what principle you should feel justified in celebrating twice, but not justified in receiving twice without celebrating...... I fear that to allow a man to assist in the distribution without receiving, is the same thing *in principle* as to allow him to attend without communicating. To this 'Non-Communicating Attendance,' or 'hearing Mass' (the same thing), I hold that Art. xxv. [9] and one of the Homilies [1] are significantly opposed, to say no more...... As to assisting without receiving, I must for my own part stand on the

---

[7] Called Minor Canons in Cathedrals of the New Foundation.

[8] It should be understood that the reception of the Sacred Elements by the Celebrant himself, before he delivers them to the people, has always been considered both in the Eastern and Western Church indispensable.

[9] "The Sacraments were not ordained of Christ *to be gazed upon*, or to be carried about, but that we should duly use them." [Art. xxv. Last paragraph.]

[1] Dean Merivale refers no doubt to Homily xv. in "The Second Tome of Homilies." *Of the worthy receiving and reverent esteeming of the Sacrament of the Body and Blood of Christ.* "Our loving Saviour hath ordained and established the remembrance of his great mercy expressed in his passion, in the institution of his heavenly supper, where everyone of us must be *guests and not gazers*, eaters *and not lookers*, feeding ourselves, and not hiring other to feed for us, that we may live by our own meat, and not perish for hunger whiles other devour all." [First paragraph.]

The Chichester Life. 141

Rubric[2] and Canon xxi.[3] ('as oft as he administereth,' &c.). In King Edward's Liturgy I think you will find it still more expressly declared that all Ministers shall receive first, in order *that they may be prepared to help the Priest in the distribution*[4]."

Burgon is sometimes thought of and talked of as if he had too good an opinion of his own judgment to consult or be guided by the more eminent and judicious of his brethren. Let this slight incident suffice to show that such an estimate of him requires at all events very considerable modification.

There are those who, while passionately vehement for truth, are by no means equally vehement for righteousness. This was not Burgon's case. In the Michaelmas of this year (when he had removed to Chichester and was just getting into his harness there) he put forth a pamphlet, "addressed to Members of Congregation; especially to the Vice-Chancellor, the Proctors, and the other Members of the Hebdomadal Council," headed thus; '*Our present Lodging-house system, immoral: and requiring Reform.*' This pamphlet being marked STRICTLY PRIVATE, no quotation can properly be made from it; but the matter which it concerns is shortly told. In Col-

---

[2] "Then shall the Minister first receive the Communion in both kinds himself, *and then proceed to deliver the same to the Bishops, Priests, and Deacons, in like manner (if any be present),*" &c., &c. [Rubric after the Prayer of Consecration.]

[3] "In every Parish-church . . . the Holy Communion shall be ministered by the Parson . . . so often, and at such times, as every parishioner may communicate at the least thrice in the year (whereof the feast of Easter to be one), ... Provided, that every *Minister, as oft as he administereth the Communion, shall first receive that Sacrament himself.*"

[4] "Then shall the Priest first receive the Communion in both kinds himself, and *next deliver it to other Ministers, if any there be present (that they may be ready to help the chief Minister*), and after to the people." [First Book of Ed. vi. 1549.] And similarly (as to the point in question) King Edward's Second Book of 1552.

leges the servants are, as a rule, male; in the Lodging-houses girls are employed. In former days, Undergraduates, on first coming up to reside in Oxford, were always provided with rooms in College; and it was not until the last term of their residence that they were liberated from the closer surveillance involved in being domesticated within the College walls, and allowed (indeed required) to take lodgings in the town. Even then, it was evident that the system must be attended with risks, and absolutely demanded that the licence of the University authorities should be given only to Lodging-house keepers of the most respectable and well-established character, and such as might be depended upon to engage none but respectable maidservants, and, when they were engaged, to keep a sharp eye upon them. But in 1868 the ancient discipline was so far relaxed (under pressure no doubt from the numbers applying for Matriculation) that Undergraduates were allowed, on first coming up, to lodge out of College. At the time of Burgon's protest he calculates that one-third of the whole number of young men *in statu pupillari* were so domiciled. His leading gravamen was that six of the licensed Lodging-house keepers (he refused to give names, as that would only have ensured the withdrawal of the licence from the parties, without any improvement of the system) had temporarily filled up vacancies for servants in their households, by applying for some of the inmates of a Penitentiary, which he and a clerical friend of his had established. The commotion made by this pamphlet was something terrific. An Indignation Meeting was held in the Council Chamber (Nov. 22), at which he was charged with cowardice (!) for "waiting until he got away, instead of setting down his foot," while he was resident in Oxford, "and telling them to their face of what was going on."

The University authorities seem to have shared in the indignation of the citizens. The Censor of Unattached Students (that is, of Students not entered at any College, but simply matriculated at the University), whose office would make him guardian of the morals of such students, is reported to have said at a private party; "The Bishop" (Dr. Mackarness) "says we have no faith; Burgon that we have no morals. How can an University live without faith or works?" In vain did Burgon explain in a published letter to the Vice-Chancellor that he had never denied for a moment that many Lodging-house keepers were of the highest respectability [5]; that he had never charged even the six guilty ones, who had resorted for servants to so questionable a source, with any evil design,—they had only erred from culpable neglect, and from the real difficulty of finding respectable maidservants; in vain did he allege, in answer to the charge of cowardice, that he had pressed upon the University authorities the viciousness of the Lodging-house system, as strongly as he was able, in the spring of 1875, before his appointment to the Deanery; but that no steps had been taken in consequence. Now therefore, he said, he was determined not to rest, till steps *were* taken. He suffered deeply, however, from

---

[5] In the midst of all the worry and annoyance which the incident must have caused him, his humour cannot help breaking out. "Some lodging-house keepers," he admits, "are even entitled to extraordinary praise. One admirable woman (Mrs. Bassett) is as solicitous about her lodger's reading as if she were his Tutor. I have *heard* the objurgation; and 'it was as good as a comedy, Sir!'—as old *Mo. Griffith* of Merton used to say, aside, of his friend Dr. Frowd of Corpus, after inviting him to dinner."

"Mo." [i. e. Moses] "Griffith," tender-hearted but obstreperous, was one of the "characters" of old Oxford. They are all gone now, those "characters," one tendency of modern (so-called) progress being to reduce all characters to a dead level, —one uniform uninteresting type.

"the indecent and offensive language" which the Oxford newspaper press freely hurled upon him, and which made him feel for a time as if he were alienated from old friends both in the City and University. Thus he writes to his last Curate, the Reverend G. H. Gwilliam, who had addressed to him a kind letter of sympathy under the foul abuse which had been heaped upon him:—

"Deanery, 20 Nov.

"My dear and kind Friend,—Pray have the comfort of knowing that your words are to me a cordial to a sick man. No one seems to have any idea what it has cost and is costing me to stand all this publicity, misrepresentation, odium, unkindness. But you enter into all, and do not fail me at a moment when I feel the want of friendship most. God bless you!

"Ever yours affectionately,
"J. W. B."

"It was a disastrous business," continues Mr. Gwilliam. "No considerable modification of the system, such as the Dean desired, was the result. And it was a terrible shock to his popularity in Oxford. I believe it was the chief cause that he was allowed to leave Oxford without any memorial of his long and faithful pastorate. It certainly cost him his seat on the Oxford Commission. Dearly as he loved his *Alma Mater*, it may be imagined what pleasure his nomination on the Commission caused him. Then came this unhappy affair: the citizens, including many of his own parishioners, were furious. He had always been an object of aversion to the Radicals both in University and general politics. Strong pressure was brought to bear on the Government. Doubtless they were moved by fear of losing a seat at the next Election. When his name was challenged in the House, they shamefully abandoned him."

There remains nothing more to be added to the record of this year beyond the letters to Mr. Gathorne Hardy

The Chichester Life.

already referred to, and five others, addressed to Miss Monier-Williams, which last will give some idea of the elasticity of spirit which buoyed him up amid very serious discomforts and annoyances, and also of the affectionate interest with which he clung to the old disciples, who owed so much to his instructions and his influence.

To Miss Monier-Williams.

"Oriel, March 9, 1876.

"My dearest little Girl,— . . . . . .

"Now I must really leave off. Fifty stupid things occur to me, to make you laugh; but I have scarcely the heart to write them. *One* is that, when I am in full dress as Dean, I am so *thin* that I am not sure you will forgive me. . . . My friends tease me by reminding me that henceforth I must give up playing with the children in the streets: but I am determined to carry on my old ways *when none of the Canons are looking*. . . . By the way, we have a capital Bishop. You would delight in him and *his cat*. He cannot breakfast until Puss is seated on a cushion at his side; and then the poor animal keeps *patting* him with his paw every few minutes for a bit of bread. Quite a pretty sight!

"'Leave off—Mr. Dean—leave off!' Not if you call me 'Mr. Dean.' My gardener calls me by that name (Yes, Mr. Dean'; 'No, Mr. Dean') two or three times a minute. I cannot forget my trouble—turn where I will. . . . . .

"Ever, my dearest Girl,

"Your loving and faithful friend,

"J. W. B."

To the Right Honourable Gathorne Hardy, M.P.

"Oxford, June 12, 1876.

"Dear Mr. Gathorne Hardy,— . . . . . .

"There will be skilful navigation needed, to get that Bill through the troubled waters of the House of

Commons, without *damage* to the Bill. I deprecate all attempts to prejudge any of the questions which the Commissioners will have to consider. If the Headships are taken from the Church[6], the one remaining safeguard will be lost. Scarcely less mischievous (though in a very different way) should I deem the *endowment* of the *unattached* system[7]; which is a mere blot,—a mere excrescence, and a confession of weakness, for which I have a triumphant remedy. Pray let us try to protect this Bill against the enemies of true religion, who are enraged at seeing the Conservatives doing what they had intended the Liberals should do instead. Their wrath against the only Clergyman on the Commission is a suggestive circumstance.

"Ever very gratefully and affectionately yours,

"JOHN W. BURGON."

To Miss MONIER-WILLIAMS.

"The Deanery, Sleepy Hollow, Aug. 10, 1876.

"My dearest little Girl,— . . . . . .

"When I was last in Oxford, I fully intended calling at Merton Lea, but simply *could* not. Then you sent me a lovely nosegay; and I went away smelling it, like a Knave of Clubs; and I was so pleased with my decoration, and with you, that I thought I was going at once to write. But somehow, here in 'Sleepy Hollow,' I run in a kind of groove, and often feel conscious that a toasting fork[8] would be a desideratum.

"What to say in reply to your allusions to S. Mary's, I know not. My heart is so much there,—so wound up with the place and the people:—moreover, in my simplicity, I had been secretly planning for myself so much

---

[6] He means, if other than Churchmen are allowed to be Heads of Colleges;—if Churchmanship is not made an essential qualification for being the Head of a College.

[7] The system of allowing persons to be members of the University, without belonging to any of the Colleges.

[8] To quicken his steps by application *a tergo*.

of increased usefulness there,—resolving to teach you all *this* thing and *that*,—that it is very difficult indeed for me to play the oracle, and speak as sagely and gravely, as I could speak, if the place were *not* S. Mary's, and if my Ella was *not* one of the Congregation.

"But I am convinced that *all* that happens here is *for our good*, if we will but accept GOD's discipline. Thus, I, for my own part, bow, as meekly as I know how, to a kind of lot I never wished for, and, finding that at least my new life gives me more leisure for study,— in spite of your sweet objurgations, I study, I confess, *very* hard, and try in this way to make my advantage out of what seems to be my discomfiture.

"For those I have left behind, I have little doubt that, if they will but do as I am doing, they will find their acquiescence attended by the like results. That which sends us back to our Prayer Book, to our Bible, to our GOD, is good,—is *best* for us. I know that it is delightful unspeakably to be the channel of blessedness to others, and that one never stops to think, nor indeed cares, how fond of *oneself* people may choose to grow. But my reason—my better reason—tells me that it is unsalutary for Pastor and people alike, when *he* is much thought of. It is sectarian. It is alien to the spirit of true Religion. It may easily become a snare for all concerned,—a snare all round.

"There!—I have told you my mind. You *see* me on the paper, so much do I mean and feel what I have been saying.

"I am ever, my dearest Girl, as you know,

"Your affectionate and loving Friend,

"J. W. B."

To MISS MONIER-WILLIAMS.

"Deanery, Chichester, October 27, 1876.

"My dearest little Girl,—. . . . . .

"I think the Cooking Class all well; but it is not knowing *how to make*—pastry for example—but knowing *how pastry should be made*, that a Lady should learn. The skilful flavouring of soups, the excellent cooking of vegetables, the *secrets* of stewing, boiling, roasting,—all these are the things to be *shown* by a first-rate Cook; and then you can *guide* a Cook yourself. You will smile to hear that I am such a *Molly*; but I really judge a Lady very much by the way her dinner is served up—*not* for a party (for *that* is a different affair), but for every day. A roast leg of mutton in a dish soiled all round the edge with gravy; *cold* French beans; *watery* spinach; mashed potatoes like pomatum (instead of being floury, pressed though a tammy); and pastry as heavy as lead,—these are the things to avoid, my dear! Presently comes an omelette, weighing a pound! I would rather a hundred times dine off bread and cheese, and a mug of honest home-made beer.

"You say you are to be in London for a fortnight from the 2nd Nov. My Lectures are on the 13th, 14th, 15th. So perhaps we might go and see something together in London. People seeing us would be sure to think that I was on a lark with my y—— w——: but we don't care for the public, do we?

"Seriously, if Mamma is good, *she* shall be of the party.

"Thank you heartily, dear, for the wrapper. To make, or to be, a comforter, seems natural to *you*.

"Ever, my dearest Ella, your loving Friend,
"J. W. B."

To Miss Monier-Williams.
"Deanery, Dec. 12, 1876.

"Dearest Ella,—If a young man (what are you laughing at?) cannot send a line to his young woman (what *are* you laughing at?)—on her birthday. . . . . Well, I declare this laughter is unbearable! I'll write to your Papa,—and I'll do it in Sanskrit[9]. so that you will never know what I have said about you.

"('No'—says the saucy Girl,—'nor *he* either.')

---

[9] Sir Monier Monier-Williams was then, as he is now, Professor of Sanskrit in the University of Oxford.

"But, as I was saying when you interrupted me,—on your dear Birthday[1] I must needs send you a few loving lines. And so, with nothing to send you but my love, and nothing to say, except that I wish you whatever good things are best for you, here I am! Long may you be spared to those who love you; and they to you! And as you grow older, may you grow holier—wiser—better (dearer and sweeter you cannot be): and may you know as little of sorrow as is necessary for your perfection; and with the sorrow may there always come that blessed inward peace, which verily the world can neither give nor take away.

"I would tell you of something to entertain you,—if I had it to tell. My mind is just now full of my birds. There are some old jackdaws floating about the Cathedral, who this morning thought they might as well come and take a mouthful as not. So they came to reconnoitre—and at last looked in at my window. Would you believe it? They were so disgusted at my appearance that away they flew at once; and to judge from the expression on their countenances they do not mean to come near me any more.

"Ever, my dearest little Girl,
  "Your affectionate J. W. B."

To the Right Honourable Gathorne Hardy, M.P.

"Deanery, Chichester, Dec. 12, 1876.

"Dear Mr. Gathorne Hardy,—I should be unworthy of your friendship, if I could hesitate to return any answer but one to your kind communication, this instant received. I unconditionally set Lord Salisbury free to act in any way he pleases. I write the words, be assured, without one particle of bitterness; and yet with my eyes wide open to all the bearings of the case. My connexion with Oxford as a resident had been severed four months, when Lord Salisbury was so good as to write to me (10th March, 1876) as follows: ' o one

---

[1] The letter was to *reach* the young lady on her Birthday, which was the 13th; and had to be posted therefore on the 12th.

knows Oxford better than you do; and the interests of Theological study and Religious teaching in the University require to be well looked after. I hope therefore that your engagements will permit you to undertake this useful work.'

"Perfectly well aware was I, when I accepted this flattering proposal, that Lord Salisbury had made the very appointment which the enemies of 'Theological study and Religious teaching in the University' would most hate. I knew very well that the presence on the Commission of one who would indeed represent the Church would prove gall and wormwood to the large and powerful party in and out of Oxford, whose *one idea* is to injure the Church,—whose one object at this time is to sever the connexion which has subsisted from the beginning between the Church and the University. It is *me*, whether resident or non-resident,—*me* that the enemy has been all along straining every nerve to get rid of. I learn that they have succeeded. . . . . . I rely on your known fairness and friendship for taking care that every word I have written shall be submitted to the Chancellor [2], when you let him know how facile you have found me. I shall then have discharged my duty, as faithfully as I know how,—towards God as well as towards man: towards the University of Oxford, whose unworthy but devoted son I shall ever remain, as well as towards Lord Salisbury, and I will add towards yourself. Far be it from *me* to embarrass my party, or to hesitate about jumping overboard, in order ever so little to lighten the ship. I again assure you that I do it without a particle of bitterness,— or indeed of concern,—except for Oxford and for the Church.

"I am ever, my dear Mr. Gathorne Hardy,
"Affectionately and faithfully yours,
"JOHN W. BURGON.

"*P.S.*—I do not mark my letter *Private*, only because I really care not who sees it."

---

[2] He means Lord Salisbury, the Chancellor of the University.

THE CHICHESTER LIFE.

To Miss Monier-Williams.

"Deanery, Dec. 13, 1876.

"My dearest little Girl,— . . . . .

"But it is getting late, and I must leave off. I forgot to tell you that I give my birds an expensive kind of rape and canary on Sundays and Saints' Days, by way of creating in them a regard for the Prayer Book. *To-day*[3] they had a dose. I daresay they will think there is a 'Saint Ella.' they might make a greater mistake than that!

"Don't call me '*Mr.*' Dean, whatever you do. I shall think you mean to cut me, if you introduce '*mistery*' into so plain a matter as our friendship.

"Ever your affectionate,

"J. W. B."

1877.

In this year appeared the threefold pamphlet, entitled '*The New Lectionary examined, with reasons for its amendment at the present time,*' in which Burgon wrote the last paper, expanding and pursuing into particulars the objections to the New Lectionary, which he had already advanced in his Sermon on the last Sunday of 1871. In speaking of that Sermon [see *sup.* p. 59 *et sequent.*] we anticipated all that needs to be said on the subject of that pamphlet, and may now pass on.

Several interesting letters belong to this year, excerpts from which are here subjoined. They record his dissatisfaction with the scanty and unsatisfactory ministerial work which he found at Chichester; the devotion of all his leisure to the indispensable preparation of his great work on Textual Criticism; his intense love and longing for Oxford, revived by a recent visit there; and his high estimation of the influence exercised by the works of Sir Walter Scott. The final letter, addressed

---

[3] Miss Williams's Birthday.

to one of the young men who had attended his Bible Class at Oriel, not only shows his lively and abiding interest in those whom he had instructed in the Scriptures, but contains much valuable advice for all who contemplate taking Holy Orders.

To Miss Washbourne.
"The Deanery, Chichester,
"Easter Monday, 1877.

"My dear Secretary,—It was very kind of you to send me an Easter greeting. I *thought* of you, though I did not write. There cannot be a greater desire *for me* on the part of those whose presence in Church used to be the happiness of my life, than there is in my bosom *for them*. My *ministerial* work *here* is a kind of unreal shadow;—a lesson read—an occasional sermon preached—I don't know to whom. That is all! And I can follow up no teaching—have no classes—have no disciples of any sort: so that my influence as a Teacher seems at an end. Of course, I remind myself that GOD has ordered it for me; and so I acquiesce, and throw myself *with my whole heart* into my great work; and I make visible progress. Well I may;—for I *never* take a walk—rise early—retire late—and give it every minute of my time: *much to the discomfiture of all my other duties*.

"So really, Miss, if you ever have to smart for your raillery, by finding that there is a good deal more of the work than you wish for, I shall remind you that it serves you right. Another Secretary I have not found,—could not find if I were to try,—and I would not employ her if I could.

"But the history of my silence, or rather of my *not sending you things to copy*, is just this. I feel more and more that I had better,—before I set about deliberately writing my Book,—accumulate all my materials, as well as finish the fashioning of all my *tools*. Indeed, until *all this is done*, I can make no real progress. So knowing that you *have* a great job in hand, I have thought it best not to interrupt you in it by asking you to copy *what is not pressing.*

"Between ourselves, Dean G., Lord A. C., as Chairman of the Revision Committee, and your humble Servant, are to breakfast with the good Bp. of L. on the 26th April, during Convocation[4].

"Talking of Convocation, and all such things, I almost sigh to see quiet Lent over, and to know that the frivolity of dining out is to begin again. The only pleasant invitation I have had for a long time is one from *the Royal Academy* on the first Saturday in May. What with Gresham Lectures and so on, I shall not get on so fast with my book, I fear, as I desire. But it is a satisfaction to me the days lengthening out, and to know that even my interruptions must come to an end at last.

"I mean to bring you a lot of volumes of pamphlets, which sadly want indexing; by way of giving you a little variety of work.

"Ever yours very gratefully,
"J. W. B."

To Miss Monier-Williams.

"Deanery, Whit-Tuesday [May 22], 1877.

"My dearest Girl,— . . . . .
"Yes—Oxford does indeed look lovely just now. I think she put on her sweetest smile the day I was there, in order to break her old lover's heart,—which was unkind. But I forgave her,—she did smile so very sweetly. Moreover she whispered, as she passed me,—'Am very fond of you, remember!'"—and put her lips so close to my ear I was obliged in self-defence to turn round and kiss them.

---

[4] The object of this meeting was to take into consideration whether anything could be done to improve the New Lectionary before the use of it became obligatory upon the clergy. It was indispensable, therefore, that Lord Alwyne Compton, as Chairman of the Committee of Convocation for the Revision of the Lectionary, should be present, and hear the objections of persons who had written against it.

"What rubbish I am writing! but it is 'all along of Oxford.'

"Ever, my dearest Girl,—*and longing to have you here*,

"Your affectionate friend,

"J. W. B."

To an attached Member of one of his Oxford Bible Classes.

"Turvey Abbey, Bedford,
"Sept. 13, 1877.

". . . . For my own part, I am trying to make Chichester my home indeed. But it is wondrous hard,—impossible rather is it,—to uproot oneself effectually from Oxford, the happy, thrice happy home of 34 years of active life. I never catch a glimpse of those towers and spires—of *one* spire especially—without feeling my eyelids moistened, and my heart beating inconveniently fast.

"I was there lately. Oxford is a changed place—the same eternally; yet changed entirely to one who leaves it for a few years: changed, I mean, in respect of the disappearance of old faces, and those minor notes of identity which make you feel that you are *at home*. But it is still as yesterday that I was there; and the flowers and shrubs round St. Mary's were bright as ever. And I went in and out exactly as of yore. And I felt like one in a dream.

"Ever, my dear Girl,
"Yours faithfully,
"J. W. B."

To a Candidate for Holy Orders, who had attended his Bible Class at Oriel.

"Sept. 21, 1877.

"To speak of something far more important,—yourself and your coming Ordination.

"I will not fail to remember you (D. V.). I trust that a

blessing will indeed attend your dedication of yourself to God's service. *He* is the best of masters, and there is no service like His. But He will have an undivided heart. You will do well to bethink yourself at this time of the probable meaning of valid Ordination, as explained by our Lord Himself in St. John. (Christ the *door* through which, or rather through Whom, you will have to enter.) You should also give considerable attention to the Pastoral Epistles. Of all the many topics that present themselves, I am sincerely at a loss to know which to select for a few words of counsel. But I will offer you two hints; 1. The first,—Be more attentive than ever to the reading of Scripture. You will find Dr. Mill's work simply invaluable. Begin with his volume of sermons (the cost 10/- or 12/-). I suppose you have read his Sermons on the Temptation? Also be sure you are thoroughly familiar with Pearson on the Creed. These books are good commentaries and helps to the meaning of Scripture.

" 2. Beware of joining any party in the Church. *Stand on the P. B.* The Church Union is detestable,—as bad in its way almost as the Church Association. Join neither; avoid all singularities, and tricks, and party names, and the like. Be a simple *English* clergyman.

" I will add a third hint.

" 3. In preparing a sermon, do this: always write your sermons. Never exceed 20 minutes. Take easy subjects, and treat them naturally (as the fifth Commandment or the fourth); or take an easy Parable or Miracle, or a character which you think you understand. Let every sermon leave a definite impression,—express one particular truth or duty. Be sure you know what you mean to say, and take care to say it. Go to the point *at once*; never beat round the bush, and waste your time with preface, &c., &c., &c. As soon as you have said what you want to say, *leave off*. Write *fast*;—always on one side of the paper. Correct at leisure, next day, on the blank page opposite, pruning away all redundancies of thought or expression.

" And take care to be *natural*, and try to get rid of

self-consciousness, and think only of God and the preciousness of the souls you are addressing.

"Adieu, my dear Knollys!

"Ever affectionately yours,

"J. W. Burgon.

"What need to speak of the indispensable nature of private prayer, and a life *above the world*?"

To the Right Honourable Gathorne Hardy, M.P.

"The Deanery, Chichester,
"St. Thomas' Day, 1877.

"Dear Mr. Gathorne Hardy,— . . . . .

"I read your speech at Edinburgh with much interest and satisfaction. Specially congenial to me was your tribute to Sir Walter Scott, to whom I suspect tens of thousands of English gentlemen owe not a little of their chivalry of sentiment and early influences for good. He taught us *loyalty to womankind*, and many a precious lesson, which while this heart beats it never can forget.

"And now farewell; and may all blessings attend you and all yours this Christmastide and for ever! I assure myself that they who have gone before us, keep these seasons after some blessed fashion, in the place of their mysterious sojourn, remember us faithfully,—at Christmas especially,—and pray for us with love unutterable; yes, and with powers too, passing speech.

"Ever, my dear Mr. Hardy,

"Most faithfully and affectionately yours,

"J. W. Burgon."

1878.

The Regius Professorship of Divinity at Oxford, to which a Canonry of Christ Church is annexed, having become vacant by the death of Dr. J. B. Mozley, it was thought and hoped by many of Burgon's friends that he might be appointed to a post so thoroughly congenial to his tastes, and for which his studies, and the deep interest he had shown in the younger men at Oxford, had so pre-eminently and abundantly qualified him. That the Prime Minister, in case of Burgon's appointment and acceptance of the office, would have a Deanery at his disposal, seemed to be an inducement, independent of Burgon's fitness for the position, which might carry weight with it. But this very circumstance was alleged as fatal to the proposed arrangement. "It would be against all precedent, whatever might be Mr. Burgon's wishes on the subject, that Her Majesty should transport a Clergyman from a higher to a lower preferment."

The following short letter to Miss Monier-Williams shows that, while Burgon was disappointed (for indeed of all positions in the Church of England this was the one which he most coveted, from the influence it would have given him with candidates for Holy Orders), he had prepared himself, as a devout Christian knows how, for a result adverse to his wishes.

"The Deanery, Feb. 21, 1878.

"My little Dear,—. . . . . .

"This morning's '*Times*'" [announcing the appointment of Dr. Ince, a man in every way qualified for the post, to the Regius Professorship] "dashed all my hopes; but I have insisted on feeling cheerful all day. My prayer has been all through that GOD will send the man to that post *who will serve Him best*. Would it not be wrong to doubt that I behold in Ince the answer to my prayer? My own private opinion on the subject is *clearly* not the question. But we will *talk* of all this!

"I am ever, my dearest Ella,
"Your affectionate Friend,
"J. W. B."

The author well remembers that when he next visited

Burgon at Chichester, and expressed the vexation felt by many of his friends at his disappointment, he replied with the greatest calmness ;—

"But *I* am not vexed. I prayed so often and so earnestly that the Prime Minister might be led to make such an appointment as might be the best for the Church, that I cannot doubt that what has been done *is* for the best."

The Lent of this year was marked by the publication of some short Sermons on '*The Servants of Scripture*[5],' "addressed in the first instance to the afternoon Congregation of St. Mary-the-Virgin's, Oxford (1871–1875), because it was perceived that domestic servants of either sex largely frequented the Church" at the afternoon Service. This is certainly not the least attractive of Burgon's many works. The scantiness of the record of a servant mentioned in Scripture does not deter him from seeking, and does not prevent his finding, an instructive and edifying lesson in his or her history, as in the case of Phurah, and as in the case of Rhoda. In the Sermon on Deborah, a character which offered rather more ample materials, the soul of the preacher is evidently in its pleasant places, and his task is thoroughly congenial to him.

"Deborah ends her days," he tells his hearers, "with Jacob and his family. Of course she does. She dies; and he writes the tale of his sorrow,—the record of his own tears and of the lamentation of his household,—on the place of the aged woman's burial. 'She was buried beneath Bethel under an oak: and the name of it was called Allon-bachuth,' that is, 'the oak

---

[5] The little volume was published under the direction of the Tract Committee of the S.P.C.K., and may be had at any of the Society's Repositories (*price*, 1s. 4d.) The Dedication is to his "Brother-in-law and love," the late Mr. Higgins of Turvey Abbey, and the Motto,"Ourselves your servants, for JESUS' sake."

of weeping.' *That* must have been no common sorrow, *that* must have been no ordinary lamentation, which imposed a name on a hitherto unknown locality; a name which carries with it to this hour the memory of a Patriarch's tears and the mourning of his mighty household! .... Ah, ye who read the Bible fast, and do not care for the little details of the story,— ye who think scorn of the humbler characters, and perhaps have never taken the trouble to gather up the first and the last link in the story of such an one as Deborah the aged, and to clasp them together, and to recognise the exquisite beauty, the tender outline of a long life of faithful service, personal devotion, reciprocated love,—ye are at least invited to note that, in the annals of the chosen family, second only to the burial of Jacob himself, is the burial of his mother's nurse,—in respect of the particular record of the mourning which attended it."

In urging his hearers to try to keep their places, and explaining to them how it might easily come to pass that they might not " better themselves " by a change of masters, even if they should succeed in getting better wages, he argues thus:—

"If a servant stays with me and serves me faithfully for thirty years—aye, or for less—I cannot any longer forsake that servant. I myself may become poor; but that faithful old servant has a real claim on me, which I should be a wretch if I were not eagerly to acknowledge. He or she must at least have a room in my house,—food and raiment,—sympathy and kindness,—medical aid in time of sickness,—an honourable grave after I have closed his or her eyes in death.— Now the giddy and the restless ones, every time they change their place, make such a claim as I have been describing less and less *possible*, even though they may get a slight increase of wages."

This was no mere outburst of fine sentiment. *He actually did what he said he would be "a wretch" not to do.*—and did it with all the sympathy and generosity of his intensely sympathetic and generous heart. A very old servant of his family, who had nursed him through the Jerusalem fever, under which he was suffering on his return to England in the July of 1862. found an asylum in the Deanery of Chichester when she was able to work no longer; and when she became blind, *an additional servant was kept*, his own straitened circumstances notwithstanding, whose special charge was to wait upon her.

In a letter of Mr. Livingstone to '*The Irish Ecclesiastical Gazette*,' dated Sept. 5. 1888, we are told of Bishop Christopher Wordsworth's appreciation of '*The Servants of Scripture*.'

"Dean Burgon sent a copy of the little book, when it first appeared, to the late Bishop of Lincoln. I saw the Bishop's letter acknowledging the gift. He told the author that he was so interested that he read the whole volume through at a sitting. And then I remember he added the half reproachful question, ' But why did you not give us a Sermon on the servants of Boaz?' "

In the July of this year passed away Hugh James Rose (the eldest son of Burgon's eldest sister), at the age of 38. It will be remembered that at the time of the family troubles, Burgon and Professor Corrie had stood sponsors for this nephew of his at Houghton Conquest [see Vol. I. p. 91],—a gleam of sunshine at a dreary time.

"His end," he writes to Dr. Corrie, now Master of Jesus College in Cambridge, "was so truly Christian that it has been an unspeakable comfort to us to recall it ever since. Often before a little unsettled in his notions, and accustomed to talk of Divine things as if they were not eternal verities, resting on an immutable

The Chichester Life.

basis of authority, he showed at last plainly enough *where* his hopes were anchored, and on *whose* merits and mercies alone he relied. Truly penitent and truly resigned, he expired in the presence of us all, who were kneeling about his bed.

"We carried him down into Bedfordshire," [Mr. Rose died at Guildford] "and in the Churchyard of his native village laid him by the side of his loved father, amid the tears of the villagers, who remembered and loved him from his childhood. Truly he was a most affectionate fellow: a most chivalrous spirit; a truly engaging and attractive companion. With abilities of a high order, he should have done better than he did."

On the 13th of October, at the recommencement of the Academical Year (an opportunity of addressing the Undergraduates of Oxford, which he was glad to avail himself of), Burgon preached before the University his Sermon on '*Nehemiah, a Pattern to Builders*[6].' The Dedication to the Bishop of Chichester bears testimony to "the cordial and (to me) delightful relation which has subsisted between us from the first hour when I crossed your hospitable threshold," and also to "the entire similarity of sentiment which (as I rejoiced to be reminded when I listened to your recent Charge) we entertain on a certain burning question of the day." The "burning question" was the revival of Mediævalism in the Church of England by the Ritualists, their distortion of the proportions of the Faith by exclusively dwelling upon the doctrine of the Holy Eucharist, "as if it were the sum and substance of all Divinity," and their industrious advocacy of the "*Romish* doctrine of Con-

---

[6] "Nehemiah, a Pattern to Builders: Counsels on the Recommencement of the Academical Year. A Sermon preached before the University of Oxford, at St. Mary-the-Virgin's, on the Seventeenth Sunday after Trinity (October 13th, 1878), by John William Burgon, B.D., Dean of Chichester. Published by request. Oxford and London: James Parker and Co., 1878."

fession." As to the "lighted candles, and incense, and birettas, and the use of the chasuble,"—Burgon "cannot away with" them;—"the masculine vigour which the severe study of Scripture imparts to a well-trained mind must produce a recoil from all such trumpery, an utter revulsion of mind." It was the old, old story which he had so often told before,—that the Bible, studied as a whole, furnishes the sufficient refutation of all religious error, whether Ritualistic or Rationalistic. The Sermon, while somewhat loosely strung together, and not sufficiently pervaded by unity of idea, is interesting as revealing one of the deepest secrets of the preacher's character, his strong tendency, wherever he felt he was right, to act alone and independently of others, without asking advice from them, or seeking co-operation with them. Nehemiah "*consulted with himself*," he tells his hearers, in coping with the manifold evils which beset him in the execution of his enterprise.

"He had become profoundly sensible that the present was precisely one of those moments in his life when consultation with others is useless. Such moments are apt to occur in most lives; and further, when they do occur, a man's wisdom is to act as Nehemiah acted. It is an unreasonable, a craven, a cowardly thing at such moments, to have recourse to friends. You *know* what you ought to do. What is the use of trying by counsel to thrust off upon another a burden of responsibility which ought to be entirely your own?"

But supposing you do *not* know what you ought to do,—that you are honestly, and without any perverse leaning of the will, doubtful what is the right and wise course to pursue? This was a state of mind which Burgon could hardly realise. He was always perfectly assured of the rectitude of his impulses, and of the truth of the conclusions at which he had arrived.

The Chichester Life.

He had only to follow those impulses, and speak out those conclusions bravely, let who would hear or forbear. Hence he never could or did co-operate with others, inasmuch as all co-operation implies to a certain extent compromise and mutual concession. He was only enabled to work with his own Chapter by the experience of the bitterness of domestic feuds. As he himself confessed, he had no following in the Convocation of the Church, as a man of his genius and learning might be expected to have, and made no mark there. Wonderfully gifted for the instruction and guidance of inferiors,—and in touch also with his superiors, from his reverence for those who were set over him, and his general social acceptability,—he had no gift for carrying his equals with him.

"Burgon" (writes Mr. Deane) "had no party at Oxford among the Fellows of Colleges. He was respected by all, but was no leader. He never could have become a leader of men, because he was so thoroughly impressed with the truth of his own view of any question, that he would not admit any compromise. Burgon was Burgon. He was an 'identity,' so to say, and not an 'equation.' He influenced his friends by his love and by his varied learning; but his influence offered few votes, if any, in Congregation [7]. Had he done so, he could not have been Burgon."

Excerpts from three letters of this year to Miss Monier-Williams are here subjoined, which will show how Burgon, in memory of his old pursuits, pricked up his ears at any reminder of Art, as an old hunter does at the sound of the huntsman's horn, and with what good sense, and worldly as well as spiritual wisdom, he

---

[7] The Oxford Congregation, part of the legislative Body of the University, consisting of the Resident Masters of Arts, who are for the most part College Tutors or Professors.

counselled the young disciples who in former days had hung on his lips.—Miss Williams is about to start for Munich shortly.

"Turvey Abbey, Bedford,
"Sept. 3, 1878.

"My dearest Girl,—I must not delay my thanks for your charming letter, or you will be in Munich first.

"How you will enjoy your visit! I never saw a more *royal* City. The new part is so very stately. But oh! commend you and me to the old town for *fun*. I am reminded of the Scotchman, who, after visiting all the capitals in the world, remarked that they were 'a' vara weel,—but Peebles for *play*sure!'

"Seriously. Spend some hours in the Glyptothek, or Sculpture Gallery. I will tell you the story—(a *most* interesting one) of the Egina Marbles some day when I am by your side. For the moment, all you will require to know is that they exhibit the earliest phase of Greek Art—dating about 550 years B.C.,—in other words, being about a hundred years older than the Elgin (or Athenian) Marbles in the British Museum. They were found all just under the surface of the earth—having been toppled out of their places in the pediment of the Temple of Jupiter by an earthquake. They are truly exquisite. [He gives here a rough sketch of the pediment.]

"So is the Picture Gallery. Study it carefully. Such a sweet Raphael!

"Then go and poke about old 'Munchen.' You will find the *Hotel des Quatre Saisons* the best. *We* were there!

"Inspect their *Cemetery* too,—and take Papa a drive to some romantic lake in the neighbourhood, which I *should* have gone to see *but* for my MSS.[8],—which sucked out my life's blood.

"I am here for my holiday: which means that I am

---

[8] In the autumn of 1872 he had been with his nephew (Rev. W. F. Rose) at Munich, collating MSS. He was then, as he had been in 1871, collecting materials for the series of 21 letters to Dr. Scrivener which appeared in the 'Guardian' of 1873, 1874.

working all day long. I brought so many books with me, that my butler fairly laughed at the spectacle. I wake early—rise at 5—and get such a delicious time of it—being spoiled, fairly *killed*, with kindness: and all is *so* quiet! so tranquil and happy! My heart flows over with gratitude to the Giver of all good.

"In about a month, I must return to Chichester. All looked very pretty when I came away,—viz. on the 28th August. I have just built myself a little greenhouse—for £15—which I tell myself is done for economy. Yes; I shall save the cost in four or five years, if I live so long. And certainly it will afford us all a *deal* of pleasure.

"I am glad you can see Chichester Cathedral from your downs. I wish I could see *you*.

"With love to you all,
"Ever, my dearest Ella,
"Your loving,
"J. W. B."

"The Deanery, Oct. 7, 1878.
"My dearest little Girl,—. . . . . .

"You were not at all wrong in sending the poor girl a German Bible. But I question much the wisdom of trying to proselytize in a R. Catholic country. I will tell you some day the story of the maid-servant in my lodgings at Rome. I am more and more struck with the precept in S. Matthew x. 16" ['Be ye wise as serpents'], "as I grow older . . . . . ."

"The Deanery, Dec. 18, 1878.
"My dearest little Girl,— . . . . .

"All quite right about *the butcher*. Believe me, it is RELIGION to keep the weekly accounts low: and I can tell you (though I am no 'Molly') that it is astonishing—if there be knowledge and prudence—how *well* all may fare, and how *small* a sum will be required. I often think with tears,—yes, *with tears*—of my own loved mother's housekeeping. She was large-hearted as a Queen, and there was always a very liberal well-spread table. But—

she knew that it was a duty to keep the expenses down,—and she once told me some details which convinced me that she fulfilled that duty, as she did every other, *in perfection*.

"Your loving friend,
"J. W. B."

1879.

Impressed, as any one must be, who is called to preach the University Sermon, with the immense importance of the congregation,—"the flower of England's youth" and "the earnest of England's greatness," as he had called them in his "Nehemiah" Sermon of 1878,—Burgon contrived in some way or other to be never very long absent from that most influential pulpit. Early in the May of this year we find him preaching before the University on Types, a subject in which he was deeply versed, from having given much thought and study to it, and which happily furnished no occasion for one of his polemical outbursts. The discourse is extremely valuable, and it is greatly to be regretted that it was never published (as so many of his Sermons were) in a separate form, and is now accessible only in the Reports given of it in the 'Oxford University Herald' of the 10th of May. He is "not particularly fond," he says, "of the expression 'a type,'" and proposes to "substitute for it a different phrase—the typical structure of Holy Writ." His view, very briefly summarised, is that the entire volume of the Bible—its narrative, as well as its expressly predictive parts—is prophetical, and that since "the testimony of Jesus is the spirit of prophecy" (a text which singularly enough he never quotes), the Holy Ghost not only framed all the institutions of the Ceremonial Law, so as to make them shadows of Christ and His Church, but selected with the same reference the characters and incidents which should be recorded. Accordingly he would have us fasten our attention not so much on the characters or incidents themselves as on what the Scripture says (or leaves unsaid) about them. Of course he finds Melchizedek very apposite to his argument. Melchizedek was born, and died, and had a line of ancestry like other men; but the Apostle to the Hebrews finds his "likeness unto the Son of God" not only in the significance of his name and title, but also in the fact that, contrary to the usual rule observed in recording the more eminent Scripture characters, *nothing is recorded of his birth, death, or parentage*. The Holy Spirit had Christ full in view, when He directed Moses to pass over these particulars, and so to make *the inspired record of Melchizedek*,—rather than Melchizedek himself,—predictive or prefigurative of Christ. This is the key to Burgon's whole doctrine of types. "The Divine Mind is found to have been so full of the great object for which He caused all Holy Scriptures to be written, that as if unconsciously, yet evidently with profoundest as well as most persistent purpose, it so constructs its stories, so handles the utterances which it preserves, that they shall foreshadow,—shall be evidently intended to foreshadow,—the Person and the Mediatorial work of Christ, who in this way is witnessed to as well by the historical as by the prophetical Books of Scripture."—Burgon was always urging upon his disciples the study of the Septuagint, on which he set the highest possible value, as every one must do who considers the undoubted fact that our Blessed Lord and His Apostles almost always cited the Old Testament in that Greek Translation of it, thereby giving it the sanction of their authority; and he shows in this Sermon that a student of the Septuagint will find in its phraseology sufficiently clear—nay, unmistakeable—hints that what is told us of Isaac and of Joseph is prefigurative or typical. "'He that spared not his own Son[9], but delivered him up for us all,' says St. Paul (Rom. viii. 32). When we turn to the Septuagint Version, from which St. Paul was in the habit of quoting, we find exactly the same Greek word used in the Angel's commendation of Abraham's fidelity to God; 'By myself I sware, saith the Lord, because thou didst this thing, and for my sake *didst not spare thy beloved son*[1],' &c. — Again; in the Parable of the Wicked Husbandmen our Lord, according to the three first Evangelists, represents the husbandmen as saying when they caught sight of the heir, 'Come, let us kill him[2].' These are the identical words with which, in the Septuagint Version of Gen. xxxvii. 20, Joseph's brethren are represented as conspiring against him[3], when they saw him afar off. These are glimpses given by words[4] into the prefigurative significance of two passages of Holy Scripture," although, as Burgon adds, "the typical resemblance in these instances is so patent that it cannot be overlooked, and might have been left to vindicate itself." It should be said also that Burgon in this remarkable Sermon finds the typical structure of Holy Scripture even in the New Testament histories, which instances of typical structure he seems to think far less surprising and less impressive to the imagination than that, antecedently to our Lord's appearing, "Old Testament narratives should prove to be full of

---

[9] Ὅς γε τοῦ ἰδίου υἱοῦ οὐκ ἐφείσατο.

[1] Οὗ εἵνεκεν ἐποίησας τὸ ῥῆμα τοῦτο, καὶ οὐκ ἐφείσω τοῦ υἱοῦ σου τοῦ ἀγαπητοῦ δι' ἐμέ. Gen. xxii. 16 [LXX.].

[2] Δεῦτε, ἀποκτείνωμεν αὐτὸν, St. Matt. xxi. 38; S. Mar. xii. 7; St. Luke xx. 14.

[3] Νῦν οὖν δεῦτε ἀποκτείνωμεν αὐτὸν, καὶ ῥίψωμεν αὐτὸν εἰς ἕνα τῶν λάκκων.

[4] It will be remembered that Burgon avowed, and entertained to the end of his life, the profoundest conviction of the verbal Inspiration of Holy Scripture. See vol. i. pp. 273, 274.

THE CHICHESTER LIFE.

Him, minutely predictive of all the most concerning acts of His Ministry, His Death and Passion, His Resurrection and Ascension." As one example of symbolism in the Gospel histories, he refers to "the raising of Jairus' daughter as exactly representing the rejection and the receiving back again of God's ancient people, the Jews." An interesting Sermon of his will be found in the Appendix [C], in which he developes this particular instance of the typical structure of Holy Writ.

It would appear that the above Sermon on Types, delivered before the University in the May of 1879, had been in substance delivered previously, and was probably re-written for the University pulpit. For we find an allusion to a Sermon on the same subject in a letter to an old disciple who had attended his Bible Classes at Oriel, which bears date May 17, 1878. His correspondent had consulted him, it appears, about the best works on Types. He answers thus:—

"Strange to relate, I know of no better book on Types than one by a Presbyterian minister, William McEwen, Minister in Dundee, Edinburgh, 1768. It is called '*Grace and Truth: or, The Glory and Fulness of the Redeemer displayed*[5].' But McEWEN ON TYPES should

---

[5] McEwen's is undoubtedly an able work. He writes most devoutly; but never gives way to mere fanciful allegorizing, as some devout writers have done. But the reader who desiderates the laying down of general principles, the application of which may exclude fanciful types and include reasonable ones, such as we may suppose to have been intended by the Holy Spirit, will look in vain for such principles in McEwen. Is it perhaps impossible to lay down any such principles satisfactorily?

One might be disposed to think so, when one finds Professor Fairbairn, whose '*Typology of Scripture*' is a really valuable contribution to our Theological Literature, ruling out, by the application of one of his principles, the typical significance of Isaac's bearing the wood on which he was to be laid. This he does on the ground that Isaac's bearing the wood for the altar and Christ's bearing His cross to Calvary were "circumstances alike outward in their nature," and that thus the

find it. . . I must be allowed to say that any one reading the Sermon of mine you allude to, and then examining McEwen, may go on to the actual histories in the Old Testament, and with the aid of '*Bishop Wordsworth's Commentary*' will, I think, make out all he wants to know.

"Except a weekly Lecture, which I give to the pupils of Bishop Otter's College, I have no class here. I miss my Sunday evenings at Oriel more than anything.

"Ever yours,
"J. W. B.

"Work at your GREEK TESTAMENT. Adieu!"

In the June of this year Burgon fell a victim to serious illness (congestion of the liver, accompanied by symptoms of the "malaria fever," from which he had suffered previously in the East) which lasted a full month, and obliged him at the beginning of August to leave home, and go to his nephew's house in Somersetshire to convalesce. But before his convalescence was completed, the author received from him a letter, which shall be submitted presently to the reader,

antitype does not "involve any rise to a higher sphere of truth" than the type. But, even granting the Professor's principle that the antitype must move in a higher sphere of truth than the type, is it certain that the carrying of the Cross does not rise into a higher sphere than the carrying of the wood? Ought we not, in interpreting this type, to reckon with the text of St. Peter, which seems to raise the carrying of the Cross into a higher significance than the carrying of the wood,— "Who his own self bare our sins in his own body on the tree" (or "carried them up to the tree," *Marg.* of R.V.)? Thus McEwen puts it tersely and beautifully;—

"Ask you the manner of His death? Behold it in this lively type. For as Isaac carried the wood, so the beloved Son of God carried His Cross. O ye children of men, your iniquities were the heavy load He bore in His own body on the tree. These, like the wood that was intended to reduce Isaac to ashes, rendered Him combustible to the fire of divine wrath."—In truth the bearing of the Cross was itself emblematical of the bearing of the sins. [See Fairbairn's '*Typology of Holy Scripture,*' vol. i. p. 199 (5th Ed.); McEwen's '*Grace and Truth,*' p. 35 (Edinburgh: 1827).]

showing wonderful energy of mind in a man still invalided, and the turning of his thoughts to a difficult subject on which he contemplated preaching at Oxford in October. This subject was, "Our Saviour's knowledge of the day of Judgment," and the true interpretation of the passage in St. Mark (xiii. 32), which seems at first sight to assert His ignorance of it. It was an Assize Sermon[6]; but no other connexion with the Assize is found in it than that the subject and text both direct the mind to the day of Judgment. Burgon, with St. Basil, whom he refers to as having received the explanation by tradition from his fathers, finds the solution of the difficulty presented by the text in the doctrine of the Eternal Generation of the Son of God, according to which the Godhead, with all its faculties, powers, attributes,—omniscience among the rest—*is derived from the First Person to the Second.*

"*All things whatsoever the Father hath, are mine*, saith Christ; because in Him is the same fulness of the Godhead, and more than that the Father cannot have: but yet in that perfect and absolute equality there is notwithstanding this disparity, that the Father hath the Godhead not from the Son, nor any other, whereas the Son hath it from the Father; Christ is the true God and eternal life; but that he is so, is from the Father: *for as the Father hath life in himself, so hath he given to the Son to have life in himself,* not by participation, but by communication." [Pearson on the Creed, Art. ii. vol. i. pp. 242, 3, Oxford, MDCCCXXXIII.]

"Accordingly," says Burgon, "our Saviour does not deny that the knowledge of that day and hour dwells in fullest measure with the Son, but He mysteriously intimates (in conformity with what is found to have been

---

[6] This Sermon also was never published in a separate form. The author has before him two reports of it, one given in 'The Oxford and Cambridge Undergraduates' Journal' of Oct. 30; another in the 'Oxford University Herald' of Nov. 1.

His practice on many other occasions), that the Son Himself does but know because of His oneness with the Father, the Fountain-head of all knowledge and of all being, who had reserved that secret from the holy angels themselves. He knows because the Father knows. He would not know, if not (εἰ μὴ) [7] the Father knew."

The "only" in the parallel passage of St. Matthew [8], which does not appear in the passage of St. Mark, is of course appealed to in corroboration of their mode of explaining the passage. The "only" excludes the "angels," —indicates that the knowledge is not entrusted even to the highest creature, but reserved exclusively for GOD. But the verse of St. Mark has no "only," and is to be rendered (freely) thus, if St. Basil's and Burgon's solution of the difficulty be the right one ;—

"But of that day and that hour knoweth no man, no, not the angels which are in heaven, nor indeed doth the Son know, except by communication to Him of the Father's Omniscience, as of all the other attributes of Godhead."

Here is the letter to the author referred to above :—

TO THE VERY REVEREND THE DEAN, NORWICH.

"The Deanery, Chichester,
"July 12, 1879.

"My dear Friend,—I have to thank you (as I have

---

[7] This sense of εἰ μὴ (or ἐὰν μὴ) might be paralleled by other passages. Thus we have in the Alexandrine Greek [Exod. iii. 19]; Ἐγὼ δὲ οἶδα ὅτι οὐ προήσεται ὑμᾶς Φαραὼ πορευθῆναι, ἐὰν μὴ μετὰ χειρὸς κραταιᾶς—"I know that Pharaoh will not let you go but by a mighty hand,"—not denying that he would let them go eventually, but asserting that, if it were not for the display of God's mighty hand, he would not have done so.

St. Matt. xxiv. 36.
But of that day and hour knoweth no *man*, no, not the angels of heaven [a], but my Father only.

[a] οἱ ἄγγελοι τῶν οὐρανῶν.

St. Mark xiii. 32.
But of that day and *that* hour knoweth no man, no, not the angels which are in heaven [b], neither the Son, but the Father.

[b] οἱ ἄγγελοι οἱ ἐν οὐρανῷ.

often had to thank you before) for a very kind and considerate letter, received when I was still very, very ill. I am at last what the Doctor calls 'convalescent.' If lying on a chair with many a moan—a wondrous loss of brain power—inability to do anything but eat (which seems to have become the one business of the day)—and a curious sense of despondency mingled with the clearest Christian confidence in GOD, and (what tries to be) entirest resignation:—if *this* be convalescence, I am convalescent indeed.

"Intending to write to you these few lines, and determined that they should be worth the reading, I just now (to my niece's astonishment) announced to her that 'I was going down into my Library.' She threw up her needlework, gave me her arm, and down the stairs I stalked—pulled out (to her amusement) the third volume of Basil, and made a memorandum of p. 360 *top*—362. Read that letter, dear friend, when you are quite fresh, beginning at the beginning; and towards the end of p. 362 you can leave off—with the subject.

"But if it teaches you—and convinces you—of what you may have perhaps at times suspected, but never saw clearly laid down by competent authority before,—then let it make you think gratefully of

"Your affectionate Friend,

"J. W. B."

The Epistle of St. Basil's referred to is numbered ccxxxvi. in the Benedictine Edition, and is in the Second Class of his Epistles, containing those which were written from A.D. 370 to A.D. 378. Burgon's Sermon is little more than a setting forth of Basil's explanation of the passage, (as against the Anomœans or Arians, called Anomœans from their maintaining the dissimilarity of essence—$ἀνομοιότης$—between the First and Second Persons of the Blessed Trinity), and of the arguments by which Basil supports it[9]. This he prefaces by a notice of other

---

[9] With the exception of an argument drawn from St. Matt. xxiv. 6; "All these things must come to pass; but *the end is not yet.*" "To say

explanations given by the orthodox, which he considers unsatisfactory, and rejects.

1880.

In the early part of this year Burgon's attention seems to have been called to a work put forth by the Christian Evidence Committee of the Society for Promoting Christian Knowledge[1], which had appeared as far back as 1877, and had then made considerable stir in the Church, the late Lord Shaftesbury having withdrawn his name from the subscribers to the venerable Society, on account of its having authorised a publication considered by him to be so objectionable. Burgon himself gives no other account than the following, of his replying to this work in a Sermon preached before the University[2] so long afterwards :—

"For a long time I hoped that some other person would have been found to come forward and do battle for the Truth: but this is the third year since '*The Argument from Prophecy*' made its appearance, and the book still remains without rebuke[3]."

'the end is not yet' sounds," says Basil, "not like the affirmation of one who has any doubt as to the time, but rather of one who has none."

[1] THE ARGUMENT FROM PROPHECY.—By the Rev. Brownlow Maitland, M.A., author of '*Scepticism and Faith*,' &c. [London: 1877].

[2] PROPHECY,—NOT "FORECAST," BUT (IN THE WORDS OF BISHOP BUTLER) "THE HISTORY OF EVENTS BEFORE THEY COME TO PASS." A Sermon preached before the University of Oxford, at St. Mary-the-Virgin's, on the First Sunday in Lent (February 15th, 1880). With Introductory Remarks: Being a Reply to the Rev. Brownlow Maitland's '*Argument from Prophecy*,' by John William Burgon, B.D., Dean of Chichester. Oxford and London : James Parker and Co., 1880.

[3] Introductory Remarks, p. 17. In presenting a copy of the Sermon to Lord Cranbrook, he writes (May 17, 1880); " I found it impossible to repress my desire to remove the stain which a recent book on Prophecy will leave (if it is suffered to go unanswered) on the Church."

It is possible that the finding that other writers were not only allowing without remonstrance, but adopting, the new terminology which this book had introduced into one great department of Christian Evidence, may have induced Burgon to enter a protest against the new term, before it should establish itself in general usage. At all events, in the year 1879, there appeared a tractate on the predictions put forth by our Lord and His Apostles as to the future of the Christian Church, entitled, '*The Divine Forecast of the Corruption of Christianity, a miraculous evidence of its truth*[4],' which possibly may have met Burgon's eye, and have given an impulse to his ever-ready controversial pen. It is in the word "Forecast," as applied to Inspired predictions by the writer of '*The Argument from Prophecy*,' that he finds the fundamental error which runs through the Book.

"The last-invented method of dealing with this department of sacred evidence" (Prophecy), "the newest device for unfaithfully handling this portion of the Deposit . . . may be described in a single sentence. It consists in resolving 'Prophecy' into *Forecast*. By proposing (I mean) to substitute the word 'Forecast' for the word 'Prophecy,' modern Unbelief ignores the

[4] By the Rev. Edward Huntingford, D.C.L., author of '*A Practical Interpretation of the Revelation of St. John*,' &c. [London: Bickers and Son, 1 Leicester Square.] It is only fair to Dr. Huntingford to say that except in calling "Prophecy" by the name of "Forecast," he does not in the smallest degree seem to sympathize with the writer of '*The Argument from Prophecy*.' He takes the old-fashioned view of Prophecy as containing many very remarkable explicit and specific predictions, though veiled for the most part in symbolical and figurative language. —But what is the meaning of a "Divine Forecast"? Do not the two terms destroy one another? God cannot possibly *conjecture*. He foresees all things in the remote future with the most entire accuracy. And thus foreseeing, He predicts. Burgon reasonably quarrels with the term "Forecast," as applied to Inspired Prophecy. It imports into the Divine Mind the anticipations and conjectures which characterize human speculation on the future.

predictive element; tacitly assumes that what GOD and man have in every age called 'Prophecy' is nothing more than a shrewd guess."

Whether or not '*The Argument from Prophecy*,' a well-written and plausible book by one bearing a justly venerated name, might not have escaped censure, if it had been given to the world on the sole responsibility of its author, a clergyman now no longer holding any position in the Church; and whether or not Burgon, in his burning zeal for the honour of God's Word, has handled all parts of it with perfect fairness [5], few persons who look into the matter will be disposed to acquit the Christian Evidence Committee of the S.P.C.K. of a grave want of judgment, or even something worse, in allowing such a book to go forth with their "general approval," qualified though that approval is by the announcement that "the Committee does not hold itself responsible for every statement or every line of the argument." It is desirable that the Church of England should have some organization which may give a passport for soundness to such religious and devotional works as are designed (like '*The Argument from Prophecy*') for general currency. Such a passport it has always been understood that publication by the S.P.C.K. gives (the religious books put forth by it being subjected to a sifting examination, first by a Committee of leading and influential Clergymen, and afterwards by certain trustworthy Episcopal referees), upon the guarantee of which examination hundreds of Clergymen, who could not possibly find leisure to read

---

[5] The author does not deny, but rather asserts, the necessity of miraculous foresight to certain large outlines of Prophecy. Thus he says in respect of the predictions of a *personal* Redeemer, "This was a forecast to which neither human sagacity, nor the unassisted theistic instinct, would naturally give birth. The victory of good over evil might easily have been expected to be wrought otherwise; by a gradual annihilation, by 'a stream of tendency,'" &c., &c.

every religious work which they give, or lend, or recommend, circulate the publications of the Society without hesitation, as being assured of their soundness. But what confidence can any longer be placed in the Society, if its authorities affix their *imprimatur* to a work on Christian Evidence which, to say the least, presents Inspired Prophecy in a new and strange light; draws off attention from the supernatural element in it by giving it the new name of " Forecast "; heads several consecutive pages with the words PROPHECY NOT PREDICTION [6]; throws suspicion on the received interpretation of Daniel's prophecy of the Seventy Weeks, as possibly " not referring, in its original, to the Christ of God [7] "; warns its readers against " confounding the grand prophetical spirit . . . with a narrow prescience of specific and isolated events [8]," and at the very outset announces that " the tendency of modern critical research" (*for* " critical" *read* " rationalistic ") " has been in the direction of reducing the proportion of the definitely predictive element, and raising doubts about the evidence of it generally [9]." Burgon in his Sermon impinges exclusively upon the contents of the book. He might have directed some of his strong words against the Committee, which had given it a " general approval," and thus helped it to a currency which it never could have obtained as the expression of individual opinion. The inevitable inference from such an authorisation of such a work was that the *imprimatur* of the Society was no safeguard at all (as up to that time it had been) against unsound religious teaching, or, not to put the matter too strongly, teaching of a highly questionable character. The opening of Burgon's Reply, in which he traces up Prophecy to its first

[6] Pp. 31–37.
[7] Pp. 102, 103.
[8] P. 36.
[9] Preface, pp. iii. iv.

comprehensive outline of the whole future in the sentence upon the Serpent, and shows how Satan had studied both that outline, and the particulars with which, as the ages rolled out, it had been filled in, is well worth reading, independently of the controversial argument. And his collection of many minute and specific predictions as to our Lord's career (pp. 38–42) as well as his remarks on the entire satisfaction which the Evangelists and Apostles, and persons of that time, seem to have felt with the application to Christ of certain Old Testament passages, as in their view altogether cogent and conclusive[1], are valuable and serviceable.

The University of Oxford, like its sister University of Cambridge, has undergone a revolution in our days, the unhappy result of which has been to dissever the connexion, which formerly subsisted between the Church and the higher education of the country. "Your University Tests' Bill," wrote Dean Mansel to Mr. (now Lord Chief Justice) Coleridge, "is but one of a series of assaults destined to effect *an entire separation between the University and the Church.*" And Dr. Chase, the Principal of St. Mary's Hall, said of this Bill that, should it pass into an Act, "its effect would be nothing less than the de-Christianizing of the Colleges of Oxford[2]." This secularizing Bill became Law in 1871, after having been rejected by the Lords, though read a second time in the Commons, in 1867. The Tests which it abolished

---

[1] "I submit," says Burgon, "that the defect must reside rather in *us*, than in the instrument of proof, if there should seem to us,—men singularly unlearned in the Scriptures,—a want of cogency in the prophetic words cited," p. 43.

[2] See Burgon's Sermon on "The Disestablishment of Religion in Oxford, the betrayal of a sacred trust," preached before the University of Oxford, Nov. 21st, 1880,—from which the words of Dean Mansel and Principal Chase here cited are taken, (*see* p. 54, end of Appendix E).

THE CHICHESTER LIFE. 179

were the subscription to the Thirty-nine Articles, and the avowal thereby of membership in the Church of England, which hitherto every one, on presenting himself for a degree, had been most properly required to make. This subscription was now required no longer, except in the case of degrees in the Faculty of Divinity. The divorce between the University and the Church, however, was not quite complete, so long as Heads of Colleges, and a certain number of Fellows in each College, were required to be in Holy Orders, and so long as certain Colleges had as their Visitors Bishops, who might naturally be expected to watch over the interests of the Church in the Societies which they were bound periodically to inspect, with the view of seeing that the Statutes of the Foundation were observed. But the *animus* of University Legislation hitherto had been greatly to loosen the ties which under the old system bound the Universities to the Church[3];

---

[3] It may be convenient here to exhibit the several measures affecting the Universities, taken either by the Crown or by Parliament. These have been furnished to the author by the kindness of Archdeacon Palmer.

i. A Royal Commission of Inquiry (under the Premiership of Lord John Russell) into the State, Discipline, Studies, and Revenues of the University and Colleges of Oxford, was issued August 31, 1850.

ii. This Commission reported, April 27, 1852. [Lord Derby was then Premier, with Mr. Disraeli as Chancellor of the Exchequer].

iii. On the 7th August, 1854, an Act " to make further provision for the good government and extension of the University of Oxford, and of the College of St. Mary's, Winchester," received the Royal Assent. [The Coalition Ministry of Lord Aberdeen was then in power; Mr. Gladstone Chancellor of the Exchequer; Lord John Russell Foreign Secretary. It was the year of the Crimean war.] Lord John Russell, who had charge of the Oxford University Bill, acknowledged the assistance he had received from Mr. Gladstone in drafting it. It was this Act which remodelled the constitution of the University, and entrusted seven Commissioners with power to make Ordinances and Regulations for the Colleges. These Commissioners finished the bulk of their work in 1858, and reported

and it was no secret that the (so-called) Liberal party in Oxford itself aimed at nothing less than what one of

June 10th of that year. But St. John's College having kept them at bay, a short Act was passed May 25, 1860, referring their proposed Ordinances for that College to the Queen in Council, who finally confirmed the Commissioner's Ordinances on June 26, 1861.—This concluded the 1st Act of Oxford University Reform.

iv. A Royal Commission of "Inquiry into the property and income belonging to, administered or enjoyed by, the Universities of Oxford and Cambridge, and their Colleges and Halls," was issued on the 5th January, 1872. This is known at Oxford as "The Duke of Cleveland's Commission," that Duke having been its Chairman.

v. This Commission reported in 1874.

vi. An Act was passed (40 and 41 Vict. c. 48) which received the Queen's Assent on the 10th of August, 1877, "to make further provision respecting the Universities of Oxford and Cambridge, and the Colleges therein," which gave legislative powers, subject to the Queen in Council, to two sets of Commissioners (seven in each set) for the two Universities. The Statutes made under this Act by the Oxford Commissioners for the University and the Colleges, were finally approved by the Queen in Council, May 3, 1882.

This concluded the Second (and so far last) Act of University Reform.—Thus far Archdeacon Palmer.

It cannot be said, in view of this summary of the steps of the (so called) Reform, that the changes were made hastily, or without careful and even laborious enquiry. Nor will any right-minded man have any sentiment but one of sympathy with a sifting enquiry on the part of the State as to how Institutions of such vast importance as the Universities are working and administering their large finances. It is the solemn obligation of the State to see that all trustees (and especially trustees of the highest education) do their duty, and benefit the body politic in the way their Founders contemplated. But to divert from the Church of the country funds expressly meant and bequeathed by old Founders to give her a stronger hold and a wider influence; to appropriate endowments, designed for the education of poor scholars, to the erection of Professorships, or simply to make these endowments prizes for the cleverest competitor, disregarding the preferential claims of poverty; to reduce to a minimum—sometimes to reduce to zero—the number of College authorities officially connected with the Church of England, and as regards the remainder, to strike away every guarantee for their even being Christians, this is not the reformation of abuses, which in long lapse of time have grown up around an old Institution, but the remodelling of the Education of the country on the wholly new principle that Education and Religion are things apart, having no essential connexion with one another.

them had expressly called " the Disestablishment of Religion in the University[4]." It needs not to be said how with the old *alumni* of Oxford, who had regarded it as a Citadel of the Faith, and had learned there the claims which the Church of their Baptism had upon them, this subversion of all that they had loved and venerated was a real grievance, and seemed to estrange their sympathies from their *Alma Mater*. But those of them who in after life were separated, as Burgon now was, from the University, and had found pursuits and interests elsewhere, readily consoled themselves for the most part by dismissing the subject from their thoughts. Nothing called them back to their University, unless it were an invitation now and then to come up and vote as Members of Convocation, which could easily be declined; why should they vex their righteous souls in their snug retreat, whether Parsonage or Deanery, or amid the new interests which absorbed them, whether political or professional, in thinking of, much less in struggling against, a catastrophe which they could do nothing to avert,—a catastrophe, branded indeed, and, as they believed, justly branded, with the ugly names of Secularization, Godless Education, Sacrilegious confiscation,—worse than all,

---

[4] In the Appendix (B) of Burgon's Sermon now under review, we are informed that, a Statute being proposed in Congregation beginning thus, " Also it is enacted that no Professor or Public Prælector shall either directly or indirectly teach, or assert dogmatically, anything which is in any wise contrary to the Catholic Faith, or to good morals," " an Amendment to leave out the words *to the Catholic Faith or* was proposed by the Rev. E. Hatch, M.A., Vice-Principal of St. Mary's Hall, and seconded by J. R. Thursfield, Esq., M.A., Tutor and Dean of Jesus College. Mr. Hatch, in moving the Amendment, remarked that '*the time was come for* THE DISESTABLISHMENT OF RELIGION IN THE UNIVERSITY.'" See the whole Appendix [pp. 40-43] on the EFFORTS OF THE SECULARISTS TO DISESTABLISH RELIGION IN OXFORD. It should be observed that it is not only the Church, but *Religion*, which the Secularists avowedly aim at disestablishing.

De-Christianization [5],—but which would work itself out in mischief to certain noble Institutions anyhow, do what right-minded individuals might to block it? The reader who has accompanied this Biography up to this point will not need to be told that John William Burgon was not one of those who would let objectionable measures, spe-

---

[5] This is not Burgon's term, though he adopted and uses it. In 1869, when Mr. (now Lord Chief Justice) Coleridge's Tests Bill was impending, Dr. Chase, the present Principal of St. Mary's Hall, had written an able letter to The 'Standard,' headed "The De-Christianizing of the Colleges of Oxford," which was afterwards published in a separate form. "I wish to ask all Christian men in England," says the Principal,—"first, whether they wish our Colleges to be Christian? next, whether they think the Christian training of their sons will be safe so soon as the bodies of men, to whom that training must be committed, may by law consist of persons of whose belief they can know nothing?" That these apprehensions of good and learned men, like Principal Chase and Dean Burgon, as to the effects of the Academical Revolution at Oxford, are not chimerical, was shown to the author several years ago by a piece of his own experience, which may be here appropriately recounted. He desired an Oxford Undergraduate, in whom he was deeply interested, and who was seeking to take Honours in the Law School, to enquire for the best private tutor in that subject who was to be had, and to engage him. The tutor most highly spoken of belonged to one of quite the first colleges, of which he was certainly a Fellow, if not a College Tutor. When next the author met the young man, he enquired naturally how he was getting on under his private tutor. The answer was, "Pretty well, I hope; but he" (the tutor) "is an odd man." "In what way odd, do you mean?" "Why, when I went to engage him, he asked me whether I believed in the Bible; and on my telling him that of course I did, he said, 'Surely you cannot believe in those silly stories about the Flood, and the Ark, and Balaam's ass speaking, and Jonah's being preserved alive in the fish. Nobody believes them now: they are all given up.'" "Well; and what did you answer?" "I told him that I came to him to learn Law, not Divinity; that I believed what I had read in my Bible; but had not knowledge enough to argue about it; and that I must beg him not to talk upon such subjects. This stopped him." This shows that Oxford (so called) tuition at that time (now more than twenty years ago) offered serious dangers to the faith of the young. And query whether the changes, which the University has undergone since that time, have done anything to arrest the process of "De-Christianization," whether they have not done something to accelerate it? Only last year it

cially when they concerned his much-loved University, go by the board. The clergy, and specially the dignified clergy, were in his view the guardians of the Christian Faith, and of all Institutions founded for the support and propagation of the Faith. In the new Statutes and Ordinances which the Commission (from which he had been excluded by a little rude blustering language in Parliament) were about to make, he desiderated,—and had he sat on the Commission, he would have fought valiantly for,—some "guarantee that the cause of Theological Study and Religious Teaching in the University would be upheld," amid all the changes that were to be expected. "The last ray of hope" for so desirable a consummation "vanished," he tells Lord Salisbury, "when Lord Selborne" (known as a cordial friend, not only of Religion, but the Church) "resigned the other day his Chairmanship of the Commission[6]." His withdrawal was probably necessitated by his acceptance of the office of Lord Chancellor in Mr. Gladstone's Government, the duties attaching to which office would prevent his giving attendance at the Commission. But the mischief which Lord Selborne, while he remained, had served to hold in check, as well as the general *animus* of the Commission, became apparent as soon as his back was turned. Immediately after his retirement, and the appointment of a new Commissioner in his place, the draft of the new Statutes for Magdalen College, which was actually in

---

was the author's misfortune to hear from the pulpit of Christ Church Cathedral a sermon from one of the Canons which, without denying the edifying moral use that might be made of the story, threw doubt upon the historical character of the miracle recorded in the Book of Jonah, though to simple people it certainly seems as if our Divine Lord had set His seal to that miracle in a very emphatic manner.

[6] See the Prefatory Letter to the Sermon now under Review, p. 5, with Appendix A, p. 39.

print, and which secured to the College at least five Clerical Fellows, was recalled, and the number of Clerical Fellows was (by a majority of one) reduced to *two* [7]. Burgon was instantly up in arms. He had been appointed to preach the "Pride Sermon" before the University (as in 1876 he had preached the "Humility Sermon" on the same Foundation,—see *sup.* pp. 9, 10); and he made this Sermon the vehicle of his righteous indignation against the proposed and impending Academical changes, calling it '*The Disestablishment of Religion in Oxford, the betrayal of a Sacred Trust: Words of Warning to the University* [8].' Starting from the old-fashioned principle that the foundations of all education worthy of the name must be laid in the knowledge of God, and having pointed to the Board Schools, High Schools for Girls, and Ladies' Colleges, as having discarded all distinctive religious teaching, he then opens fire upon

"the recent, as well as the pending Legislation for this loved place, which may be described as a determined effort to 'disestablish Religion in the University.' To abolish Clerical Fellowships :—to abolish Clerical Headships :—to introduce the 'lay' teaching of Theology" (Professor Bryce at a meeting of the Liberation Society had already advocated the making a vigorous effort to *liberate the Chairs of Hebrew and Ecclesiastical History from clerical restriction*, that is, to place "learned and judicious" laymen in them) [9] :—" to substitute Lay for Episcopal Visitors : — these, which (I learn) are the changes chiefly aimed at by the dominant party, amount

---

[7] See Appendix A to the Sermon now under Review, p. 39.

[8] "A Sermon preached before the University of Oxford, at St. Mary-the-Virgin's, on the Sunday next before Advent (Nov. 21st, 1880), by John William Burgon, B.D., Dean of Chichester, late Fellow of Oriel College. Second Edition. Parker and Co., Oxford, and 6 Southampton Street, Strand, London."

[9] See Appendix C to the Sermon—" PROFESSOR BRYCE, M.P., AND THE LIBERATION SOCIETY," p. 44. Two last paragraphs.

to nothing else but a scheme for confiscating endowments expressly set apart for the encouragement of Sacred Learning;—a scheme for secularizing Institutions essentially religious in their character, which for half a thousand years have exercised over Society an unmingled influence for good, by providing for the Christian training of the youth of England, no matter *what* their subsequent destination in life[1]."

Not the least valuable part of this Sermon is that in which he protests against the system of recognising Unattached Students. The number of these, he says, was (at the time of his writing) 417. A very small minority of these were men of fortune, who simply disliked the restraints of College discipline, (a gross abuse of the system, doubtless, which was set on foot purely for those who were too poor to bear the expenses of life in a College, but still coveted the advantages of education at the University, admission to Professor's Lectures, &c.). He points out how the necessity of receiving Unattached Students had arisen from disregard of the preferential claim to Scholarships and Fellowships, which Founders of Colleges had almost always given to the POOR Student. The preferential claim had been disregarded, and the Fellowships either thrown open without restriction as prizes to the intellectually ablest competitor, or sometimes confiscated for the endowment of University Professorships. One of his suggestions for checking the growth of the Unattached Academical population is, that "Colleges with a surplus income shall be called upon, as far as that surplus goes, to undertake that for the sum of £50 (the payment required to get through the University on the Unattached system) as many as can prove that they absolutely require it, shall be admitted as poor Scholars of the College[2]." A class of much the same kind already

---

[1] Sermon, pp. 17, 18. [2] Sermon, pp. 29-36.

existed at some of the Colleges, under the name of Bible Clerks.

In sending a copy of this Sermon to Lord Cranbrook, he says that

"it has cost me no little pain and anxiety . . . How disastrous the working of the Commission has been, you will see with regret . . . I would fain hope that it may yet be in your power, and of the other friends of Religion, to administer some check. There remains no longer any guarantee for Christian Education in the University of Oxford at any of the older Colleges."

One of the chief points of interest about this Sermon is that it indicates clearly what measures he would have advocated, and against what evils and dangers he would have striven, had his name been retained, as it ought to have been, upon the Oxford University Commission.

1881.

A movement at the beginning of this year, prompted no doubt by desire to save the Church from those legal suits on questions of Ritual, which not only harassed her peace, but exposed her weak points to her adversaries, elicited from Burgon all that was Protestant (and, despite all his staunch High Churchism, there was much that was Protestant) in his theological position. Ten dignitaries of the Church, none of them under the rank of a Canon Residentiary [3], basing their action on an invitation given by the Archbishop of Canterbury to those Clergy who felt "dissatisfied or alarmed at the present circumstances of the Church, to state what they desired in the

---

[3] The Dean of St. Paul's (Church); The Dean of Durham (Lake); The Dean of Manchester (Cowie); The Dean of Worcester (Lord A. Compton); The Dean of York (Purey Cust); The Archdeacon of Derby (Balston); The Archdeacon of Berks (Pott); The Archdeacon of Montgomery (Ffoulkes); The Archdeacon of Brecon (de Winton); and Canon Gregory.

way of remedy," put forth an address to his Grace, expressing their "desire for a distinctly avowed policy of toleration and forbearance, on the part of our ecclesiastical superiors, in dealing with questions of ritual." The strong point of the address was its alleging "the requirement of justice" that the same allowance should be given to the excessive Ritual of the High Church Clergy as was extended to the defective Ritual of the Low; that if one man were to be censured for wearing a chasuble at the celebration of the Holy Communion, his neighbour should not be allowed to escape censure, who read the Communion Office from the desk instead of at the Holy Table. Its weak point was that it suggested no answer to the question, Where is the proposed policy of toleration and forbearance to stop? or is it to stop nowhere? Is the individual Clergyman, at all events if he can succeed in carrying with him the majority of his congregation, to be allowed to bring the Communion Service of the Church of England into so close a resemblance to the Roman Mass that the eye of an ordinary observer can detect no difference? Burgon, in his Letter to the Archbishop of Canterbury, entitled '*Divergent Ritual;— Remarks on "The Address for Toleration*[4],"' was not slow to pounce upon this weak point;—

"The 'desire' they express 'for a distinctly avowed policy of toleration and forbearance' would seem to amount to a demand that henceforth individual Clergymen shall be at liberty to introduce into their Churches with impunity just whatever extravagances of Ritual they and their congregations may please ... It would

[4] [Rivingtons, Waterloo Place, London: Oxford and Cambridge, 1881]. Mr. James Parker was Burgon's usual Publisher for Sermons and theological papers; but probably Mr. Parker's sympathy (to some extent) with the Ritualistic movement would have made it awkward to offer such a Letter to him for publication.

greatly have simplified the issue which has thus been raised, if the framers of the present Memorial had been so obliging as to state *which* precisely are the concessions they expect to obtain at the hands of the Bishops. For they cannot seriously suppose that *indiscriminate license* is henceforth to become the Law of the Church; or that, simply in order to facilitate 'Ritualistic irregularities,' the Sectarian principle of mere *Congregationalism* is going to be recognised, to the prejudice of our ancient Parochial System," [pp. 4, 5].

Nor does Burgon, as to the strong point of the address, admit that an offence in the direction of defect in Ritual is of equal gravity with an offence in the direction of excess.

"Detestable as is the method of one who is 'slovenly' [in his observance of the Rubrics], *his removal from the Parish* at all events brings the mischief to an end. Not so when a Ritualist has had it all his own way in a Church for years; and where Vestments, 'Ornaments,' and Romish practices have been freely introduced and firmly established. His successor is reduced to the alternative of either continuing what his well-informed conscience entirely condemns, or else of setting the Parish in a blaze. Now, for a Clergyman to impose such a necessity on his successor, is nothing else but a *crime*" [pp. 6, 7].

Burgon adhered throughout life to the view that the Church movement, as originated by the primitive Tractarians, had nothing in common with that efflorescence of Ritual, which indeed succeeded it historically, but which he held to be merely its running to seed and degeneration. John Henry Newman, the father and founder of the movement, had been somewhat austerely plain as to vestments, paced up to the pulpit of St. Mary the Virgin's cassockless and scarfless, in the ordinary Master of Arts' black stuff gown, and preceded neither by beadle nor mace-bearing verger. Yet the Sermons which he delivered, when he reached the pulpit, were among the most powerful of the spiritual forces of the day, keen as any two-edged sword, " piercing even to the dividing asunder of soul and spirit, and discerning the thoughts and intents of the heart." And even apart from his extraordinary delivery of them, and when read thoughtfully after a long interval of time, those Sermons still search the conscience and ransack the thoughts of the heart ; and it may be said of them, as of the great Hebrew Legislator in the latest year of his life, that their "eye is not dim, nor their natural force abated."

But his Letter to the Archbishop was only the precursor of a much lengthier and more substantial protest, which later in this same year Burgon made against the introduction into the Church of England of a florid Ritual, utterly unauthorised, as he thought, by the Book of Common Prayer, or rather condemned by it, when fairly and reasonably interpreted, and the tendency and effect of which was to assimilate the Service of the Holy Communion as closely as possible to the Roman Mass. This protest he makes in his '*Letter of Friendly Remonstrance to Canon Robert Gregory* [5].' The letter was addressed to Canon Gregory rather than to any of the other nine dignitaries, who with him had signed the address for toleration, partly (in all probability) because Burgon's experience of the Lower House of the Convocation of Canterbury, in which he sate officially as Dean of Chichester, had shown him that the Canon, in virtue of his strong sense, general fairness, and pronounced, but not extreme, High Church views, exercised greater in-

---

[5] [CANON ROBERT GREGORY : A letter of friendly remonstrance. By John William Burgon, B.D., Dean of Chichester. "Is there any Communion in Christendom in which more true liberty is enjoyed than in the Church of England?" BISHOP OF LINCOLN (1881). *Second and Corrected Edition*. London : Longmans, Green and Co., 1881.]

fluence in that assembly than almost any other single member, "enjoyed a considerable following, and obtained very much his own way [6]," and also because Burgon entertained personally kind and friendly feelings for the Canon, and was sincerely grieved to see him (as he thought) lending the shelter of his patronage to that Romanising party in the Church of England, to whom the Protestant ingredient in its formularies and Articles is undisguisedly and avowedly an offence and a disfigurement, which they would be only too glad to obliterate [7]. '*The Address for Toleration*' had the effect in Burgon's view, even if it were not so intended, of backing up this traitorous, disloyal, and un-English party; it pleaded for a licence for them to introduce, without restraint from authority, any extravagance of ceremonial, to which they could induce the bulk of their congregations to accede. The policy of "Live and let live" as regards all parties in the Church, which had been insinuated in the Address, and was more explicitly avowed in the *Gravamen* on the same subject presented by Canon Gregory to Convocation [8], fair and reasonable

[6] P. 1.

[7] There can be no manner of doubt as to the feelings of regard and respect which Burgon entertained for Canon [now Dean] Gregory. He calls him "a man of candour and trained understanding" [p. 20], "so prominent and respected a member of the Synod as yourself" [p. 39]; says of him, "I cannot so much as imagine what you have in common with the 'Ritualistic' section of the Clergy" [p. 69]; says that he has known him throughout his whole ministerial career, and that "You used to be no 'Ritualist,'—no Romaniser,—no novelty-monger, no leader of a lawless faction. Not you."—True; there is a grotesqueness in the form in which he shows his regard for the Canon,—by administering to him a scolding for the support lent by him to the Ritualists; but the utter simplicity and sincerity of John William Burgon's character entirely preclude the notion that his affection for the Canon was simulated.

[8] This "Gravamen" is printed at length in Appendix II. to Burgon's '*Letter of Friendly Remonstrance*,' pp. 77-79.

as it seems on the first statement of it, and propounded, as doubtless it was, by all the signataries of the Address with a sincere desire to bring about peace and mutual forbearance, has no doubt a side on which it is assailable. And Burgon struck it, with all the impetuosity and passionate vehemence characteristic of him, on its assailable side.

" Do you mean that a Clergyman ought to be at liberty to violate the Law, provided only that *his Congregation will go along with him in his lawlessness*? A more immoral doctrine, or one more destructive of Ecclesiastical order, it has seldom been my lot to hear gravely propounded ... *Sectarianism*, pure and simple, must be the inevitable product. The principle you plead for is the merest *Congregationalism*. Strange, that the 'Ritualistic' method should be so closely allied to that of the Nonconformists! And yet, not strange either: seeing that it is purely *Sectarian* in its spirit, nature, origin" [p. 23].

Of course his argument leads him to the discussion of the so-called "Ornaments Rubric" (Sec. xviii. p. 49 *et sequent.*), by an appeal to which, in its *primâ facie* sense, it was sought to justify all the Ritual extravagances of which he complains. The reader may see for himself how he deals with the intricate and difficult question as to the meaning of this famous Paragraph (Rubric he will not call it; but gives it the probably more correct appellation of a "Rubrical Note"), and as to the probable reasons for its retention at the last Revision of the Prayer Book in 1662. Suffice it to say that starting from the "unassailable fact" that "*never* in this Church and Realm, *nowhere*, and *by none*, since the Rubrical 'Note' in question first appeared, have the Ornaments" [in question] "been employed by the Clergy of the Church of England" [p. 51], he infers from hence that "it must have been perfectly well understood from the first that the meaning of the 'Ornaments Rubric' is not what" [the Ritualists] "assure us it is, and has all along been" [p. 52]. Whatever conclusion may be come to on this vexed question (and we are concerned now simply to exhibit Burgon's conclusion), certain it is that he was perfectly right in insisting that the "Rubrical ote" in question must take its interpretation from its history and surroundings, cannot be fairly viewed as an isolated direction, independent of other directions given elsewhere, and of the uniform practice of the Church for upwards of 300 years.

It was probably about this time that Burgon, finding that, as he states in the first page of his *'Letter of Friendly Remonstrance,'* he had no following in Convocation, and never obtained his own way there, discontinued his attendance, thereby, no doubt, securing not only much valuable time for his studies, but also an immunity from periodical friction and exasperation.

The author, who, as living at a great distance from London, and feeling that he could obtain from the published Reports all that was valuable in the debates of Convocation, seldom or never attended, remembers well receiving a solemn remonstrance from Burgon on his *lâches* in this respect; "It was the duty of every member, official as well as elected, to attend and contribute to the discussion; those who simply sit at home and read the Reports do not acquit themselves of their duties as members of a Church Synod," &c. Three or four years elapsed; and then the author, being on a visit at Chichester Deanery, and nothing having reached him lately as to Burgon's proceedings in Convocation, asked him somewhat archly, and with a suspicion as to the real state of the case, what had been going forward there of late. "Oh! I gave up attending some time ago," he replied, "and have found my account in doing so. You were right in what you used to say about it; attendance is a waste of good time." What he said further was to the effect that he had been so often thwarted in a somewhat unmannerly way, that, finding that he could not carry his point, he had made up his mind to withdraw for good. Such was his own account of the matter; and the author, never having been present, cannot either confirm or contradict the statement. But it seems fair, under such circumstances, to give the impressions of some who were present, as to the reason for his being thwarted, and generally for his failure as a debater. Here then are the impressions which three dignitaries of the Church, who happened to sit with Burgon in Convocation, formed of his demeanour. The last passage is from the pen of the late Dean of St. Paul's, whose natural irritation at the conduct he describes does not however seem to suppress his moderation and fairness of mind,—as what could suppress either justice or gentleness with a spirit like his?

"I took the opportunity of asking——" (naming a leading member of the Lower House of Convocation) "what was in his opinion the cause of Burgon's failure in Convocation? He said; 'Chiefly this; Burgon could not or would not speak to the question before the House, and was, in consequence, constantly called to order; and in the end the House would not hear him. Instead of speaking to the question, he would air some pet grievance.—He was, besides, not a good speaker.'"

"What I should say," writes another dignitary, "about Burgon in Convocation would be, that it was not the sphere in which he was at all calculated to move. He was in no sense a power there; for he was *constitutionally unfitted for discussion with equals.*"

And thus the late Dean Church, in the course of a letter to the author (under date Aug. 23, 1889);—

"...... You ask me about Burgon in Convocation. As far as I remember, it was not the place for him. He had a kind of lecturing and sometimes scolding way, which does not suit a popular assembly; and he was not in touch with it. I don't remember his ever making any great effort to carry some policy of his own; and though he made some speeches, he generally confined himself to short criticisms. He brought with him strongly his dislike to that 'thing called Ritualism.' I remember one occasion, on which he pointed with a distinctness which could not be mistaken, to our encouraging Romanising practices (I forget the exact words) in St. Paul's, and while he was speaking, fixing his eyes upon me from the other end of the room, glowering sourly and steadily, like a schoolmaster at a naughty boy, whose demerits were held up to the Class without naming him. With all his many and excellent gifts of mind and character, Burgon somehow had more of the τὸ ὑβριστικόν" [vituperative vein?] " in his composition than any so good a man whom I ever came across. It was a great pity."

In another of his letters to the author about the same period, Dean Church, smarting probably under one of the "scoldings," of which he gives a specimen above, calls Burgon, "that dear old learned Professor of Billingsgate,"—allowing his affection for the man's person, as well as the respect which he entertained for his learning, to peep through his censure of "Billingsgate" phraseology.

Yes; it must not be concealed that, with all his loveable, generous, and chivalrous traits of character, "he had a lecturing and a scolding way [9]" (it comes out, and

---

[9] No doubt the scolding way chafed himself as well as the persons scolded; and it must have been a real relief to him when he retired from Convocation to the seclusion of his study at Chichester. Not but that he was naturally controversial, and loved crossing swords with a

somewhat comically, in the '*Letter of Earnest Remonstrance to Canon Robert Gregory*'), and that so far from mollifying, the lecture and the scolding acted as an irritant on those to whom they were addressed. Scolding seldom answers even in the pulpit, where however the pastor is set over his audience, and where he is bound (with discretion and tact) to "reprove and rebuke," as well as to "exhort." How much less is it likely to succeed in a deliberative assembly, the members of which having equal rights and equal votes, are not likely to tolerate any assumption of a magisterial position?

There was wisdom in Burgon's retirement from a sphere for which he must have felt himself disqualified, and in his devoting himself to that exposure of the faults of the Revised Version of the New Testament[1], for which he possessed such ample resources, and on which he expended such indefatigable research,— resources and research which made him second to none but Dr. Scrivener as a Textual Critic. In the October of this year was published in the *Quarterly Review* his first Article on "The Revision Revised," which fairly inserted the wedge into the New Version. It needed only a few more blows of the hammer to cleave it right asunder. All who read that Article carefully felt (to say the least) their confidence in the New Version to be shaken.

But that, amid the fire and fury of controversy, he was

theological adversary; he did so more or less up to the last year of his life ; but it is the tendency of increasing years to make a man sigh for repose.

[1] In the letter to Lord Cranbrook, given at the end of the record of the next year he says that the Revised Version *appeared* May 17, 1881. The Preface to it is dated 11th November, 1880. Shrewdly surmising the erroneous principles (as he considered them) which would underlie the treatment of the Received Text by the Revisers, Burgon had been long previously engaged in collecting materials for the vindication of that Text in its great features.

still the same affectionate and wise counsellor to those disciples who had sat at his feet at Oxford, let the following letter testify. "The Ella" of the Oxford Bible Class had now become Mrs. Samuel Bickersteth; and this is the advice he tenders her in her new circumstances, as the wife of a devoted young clergyman about to enter on the duties of his first Curacy.

To Mrs. Samuel Bickersteth.

"The Deanery, Chichester, Mar. 15, 1881.
"My dearest Ella,—.....

"I trust the Curacy at (or near) Lancaster Gate may prove all your fancy paints. I feel as if I could scarcely help you at all in a sphere of work of which I know nothing—and in a style of Parish with which I never have had any practical acquaintance. But my heart tells me what *ought* to be done—and what will be the thing most to be *aimed at*—viz., to avoid secularity as much as possible,—and gather one's self up, as much and as often as possible, with GOD.

"Do not undertake too many things; nor encourage Sam to begin what he will be unable to carry on for many months together. And certainly do not fritter yourselves away on things which may be done by others. *He* should take great pains with his *Sermons*—and resolve (GOD helping him) to make them really *useful*. *You* may consider how far it may be possible to have a Class of girls,—especially of that kind which abounds in London—shop girls, and *employées* of all sorts, who are practically without friends and alone in the midst of the crowd.

"Ever, my dearest Girl,
"Your affectionate
"J. W. B."

1882.

This year the Cathedral Body at Chichester received an accession, which gave Burgon a thoroughly cordial and congenial colleague, between whom and himself no shadow of misunderstanding ever interposed, and whose friendship lighted up with quite a golden ray the six last years of his life at Chichester. On March 15 the Reverend Thomas Francis Crosse, D.C.L., was installed as Canon Residentiary of Chichester, and five months afterwards (Aug. 16) the Precentorship (one of the four "dignities" of a Cathedral of the old Foundation) was conferred upon him by the Bishop. Dr. Crosse was not only a man of considerable parts and cultivation, but he possessed that invaluable social gift of tact,—that intuitive knowledge of character, and dexterity in applying the knowledge, which often enables a man to direct others, while appearing to do no more than concur with them. Dr. Crosse had been a barrister before he became a Clergyman, and there was something of legal training as well as of natural qualification in his calm judicial habit of mind, and in his careful survey of a subject on all its sides. These qualifications made him an invaluable adviser in Capitular business, and supplied an useful corrective to the Dean's impulsiveness of natural character. Having himself charge of a large flock at Hastings (Parish of Holy Trinity), which he tended with great zeal and much acceptance, he was in full sympathy with the Pastor's heart, which was so marked an element of the Dean's character. And there was another gift which Burgon shared with Crosse,—the power of wielding the pencil and the brush. The Canon had executed some beautiful paintings in water-colour; and the great number of sketches, coloured or otherwise, which the Dean has left behind him,—many of them dashed off in a few minutes while waiting for a change of horses or for a train,—abundantly show what genius he had in this direction, and how he might have made his mark in drawing and painting, if he had followed Art as his vocation.

In the summer of this year Burgon found time to resume his letters in the '*Guardian*' to Prebendary Scrivener on Cursive Manuscripts of the Gospels, a series of which had already appeared in that journal in 1873, 1874 [see *sup.* pp. 82, 83], Dr. Scrivener having "encouraged him to believe" that any additional information he had collected on the subject since that time would be of use to him in preparing the third edition of his '*Introduction to the Criticism of the New Testament.*' "Since I became a Dean," says Burgon in the first of these letters, "it has ceased to be in my power to visit foreign libraries, in furtherance of our favourite study—yours and mine." It is therefore "primarily of our insular resources" [in the way of manuscripts] "that I am about to speak"; nevertheless "one may have something interesting to communicate concerning manuscripts deposited in Libraries which yet one has never been able to visit in person." This Series of Ten Letters [2], as also a Series of Five Letters which followed it in 1884, is headed *Sacred Greek Codices at Home and Abroad*, the earlier Series of Twenty-One Letters in 1873–4, having been entitled *Manuscript Evangelia in Foreign Libraries.* Like the earlier one, it denotes not only the industry and laboriousness of his research, but his critical acumen. Witness his identification of the manuscript indicated as "*Em.*" and "*Usser.* 2." in Letter II.,—a manuscript exhibiting a certain reading of St. John viii. 8, which always, according to Burgon, "in-

---

[2] These Ten Letters are dated, I. June 14, 1882; II. June 23rd, 1882; III. June 30, 1882; IV. July 6th, 1882; V. 13th July, 1882; VI. July 20, 1882; VII. July 28, 1882; VIII. August 3, 1882; IX. August 9, 1882; X. August 17, 1882, —all from "Deanery, Chichester."

dicates a copy with an unusual text,"—"He stooped down and wrote upon the ground *the sins of each one of them.*" The question having occurred to almost every Bible reader what it was that our Divine Lord wrote, on the only recorded instance of His having written anything,—the reading, whatever it may have to say for itself, and quite independently of its being accepted as genuine, is surely full of interest.—In the Seventh Letter (dated July 28, 1882) he relieves his communications to Dr. Scrivener, "hitherto insufferably dull," with the account of the visit paid by him to the Library of the Convent of St. Catharine on Mount Sinai in the course of his Eastern Tour (March 28, 1862), from which an excerpt may be given;—

"It was idle appealing to the monks for guidance. They knew absolutely nothing at all about the matter. At last I spied a row labelled Εὐαγγέλιον, and mounted the ladder. It was amusing as well as annoying to see how astonished and suspicious the monks looked when they perceived that I had at last subsided upon the object of my search. Most of the volumes proved to be Evangelisteria" (copies of the *Liturgical* Gospels read in the Communion Service); "but many were copies of the Gospels proper. So I pulled these down, carried them to a table before the window, and tried to puzzle them out. While thus engaged, the monks kept tapping me on the shoulder:—'Who are you?'—'What are you?'—'Where do you come from?' and so on. I assured them, on my honour, that I was nothing and nobody; and that they would not know the place I came from, even if I were to tell them. A fresh tap on the shoulder:—'But say where you come from.' 'Oxford,'—(without looking up from my book). It was like throwing a hard nut into a cage of monkeys. 'Horks?' 'Auk?' 'Hoc?' Suddenly one exclaimed, 'Ah! then do you perhaps know a little gentleman on crutches?' and he proceeded to imitate the lameness of the dear fellow he referred to. 'What?

Philip Pusey? Yes: one of my dearest friends.' whole party were at no pains to disguise their astonishment. That admirable and enterprising scholar had visited their library, and testified the same interest and curiosity which they witnessed in your present correspondent."

In Letter VIII (dated August 3, 1882) he gives a very interesting and detailed account of the great treasure of the Library of the Convent of St. Catharine, "the Golden Evangelisterium," "a most sumptuous volume truly, written in large and very beautiful gold uncials," at the beginning of which

"are seven truly exquisite illuminations of Saints, &c., on a gold ground, with their names inserted. .... The patience of the old Sacristan (*Vitale*), with whom I was left alone to inspect this codex, was exemplary. I gave him five francs. In return he gave me some sugar-plums, and wanted me to drink some eau-de-vie of the Convent out of his own private bottle. He wrote his name for me in my book,—σκευωφύλαξ Βιτάλιος [?] Σιναΐτης."

The last Letter but one, No. IX (dated August 9, 1882), ends characteristically and beautifully;—

"I am sorry that my communications should have been so wondrous dry. But it has been inevitable. I am reminded of what takes place in the cultivation of a garden. The preliminary steps (some of them at all events) are of the most unpromising—I might say, the most repulsive description. The ultimate issue is unmingled delight: blossoms of unimagined beauty: the flowers and fruits of Paradise. .... But the truest illustration is furnished by the progress of a building. We must dig deep, and lay our foundations wondrous broad and strong, if we intend that our edifice shall last for ever. And *this* edifice, be it remembered, is nothing else but THE PALACE OF THE GREAT KING."

The following letters,—the one giving an account to

Lord Cranbrook of the sensation produced by his Article in the 'Quarterly' on the Revised Version (in the October of 1881), and of a Royal visit to Chichester, at which it devolved upon him to do the honours; the other to Precentor Crosse, showing how a devout and pious mind finds matter for solemn thoughts in the ordinary incidents of life,—will be read with interest.

To Viscount Cranbrook.

"Deanery, Chichester,

"Jan. 27, 1882.

"My dear Lord Cranbrook,— ......

"Do you remember my telling you a year or two ago that I was giving all my time to the study of the Textual Criticism of the New Testament? The appearance (17 May, 1881) of the Revision exercised me much; for I found that the Greek text had been remodelled on what I consider entirely mistaken principles. Mr. Murray was willing to admit an Article upon the subject; and accordingly in the October number appeared the fruit of not a little labour. Let me request you, if you have not yet seen that number of the 'Quarterly,' to give what you will find there a patient hearing. My performance seems to have fallen like a shell into the enemy's position. It sold the 'Quarterly,' and another edition is called for. A shower of letters from every quarter convinced me that I had been passing the long summer days not unprofitably. Not least surprised was I to learn from Murray that Mr. Gladstone had driven to his door, and sat with him to discuss the merits of Burgon's Article (for the authorship of it, in spite of all my endeavours, transpired instantly), with which he said he agreed entirely.

"I then turned from the new Greek Text to the new English Version, and I only finished my task on the 14th of this month; working at least for fifteen hours a day. It broke my health, and I have felt ill ever since; but it comforts me to know the arrow has found its mark.

The Bishop of Lincoln writes to me in terms which I am ashamed to transcribe. And so much for my recent occupations.

"A visitor of more than usual respectability honoured this dwelling in the course of last autumn,—the Princess Imperial of Germany. The Bishop being away, the Station-master entreated me to receive the Princess, which I did as well as I knew how at an hour's notice; and very gracious and charming she was. The first thing was to send word to the Canons; the next to collect the Cathedral servants and explain. They rose to the occasion. A moth-eaten old red plush chair was to be a kind of chair of state; a mouldy strip of red cloth was spread beneath it; and all were to be on the *qui vive*. The special train was delayed considerably; but at last we drove to the Cathedral, which was very crowded. Every one behaved exceedingly well, falling back whichever way the Royal lady moved. Each of our body in turn did the honours; and one of the servants told her R.H. of what Prince Albert had said, when he visited the Cathedral. Then we inspected the Palace, which interested her greatly, particularly the historical initials (of Catherine of Arragon) on the ceiling of the dining-room. She then said she was anxious to get back to her children; but she readily promised to come to the Deanery for some coffee. My ladies had everything ready of course, and the Princess was all affability; she really seemed pleased and happy; one of her *suite* remarked to one of my nieces, 'Somehow we always seem to fall on our legs.' The weather was superb. I asked whether she would do us the honour of coming into the garden. '*That* she would'; and she noticed everything. An old mulberry tree was freely shedding its fruit. 'Mulberries!' exclaimed the Princess, stooping down and picking some up. Of course I chose a few nice ones for her. She ate them; and turning to me, remarked confidentially, 'They make one's teeth so black, don't they?' On the whole it was a delightful incident. She again and again told me how pleased she had been with her visit; but *how* she did puzzle me with her questions! I sent her a keepsake; and in return she wrote me a very graceful letter, not by any means formal and conventional, but full of womanly kindness. She seemed to me truly charming. The whole way from the station to our door was lined with spectators.

"You are, I think I have heard, sharing in our own extraordinary winter,—" [Lord Cranbrook was at Biarritz] "which is not winter in the least. The hedges are full of primroses; and in the cottage gardens I see wallflowers, stocks, marigolds, and such like—in bloom. I only hope the winter is not to come by-and-by; for the vegetation will not be able to stand it.

". [in Parliament] "will recommence. O to have Lord Beaconsfield, or rather Benjamin Disraeli, Esq., M.P., in his place for a week, to get up when Mr. Gladstone sits down! But I trust there will be found some equal to the occasion."

The remainder of the letter is occupied with the troubles of the smaller Irish landlords, as reported to him by a friend in that country, who adds,—

"One of the incidental results of Mr. Gladstone's policy seems likely to be the establishment of the Roman Catholic domination over three-fourths of Ireland!"

Whereupon Burgon remarks to Lord Cranbrook;

"I am reminded of your exclamation, when Mr. G. proposed the disestablishment of the Church in Ireland,—viz. that the Act of Union should be produced and read,—which provided (with far-sighted wisdom) that the maintenance of the Church in Ireland shall be regarded as an integral part of the Union.

"I am ashamed of this long letter. I only meant to send you all my love, and beg to do so now. Let me be most kindly remembered, pray, to and by all.

"Ever, my dear Lord Cranbrook,
"Gratefully and affectionately yours,
"JOHN W. BURGON."

To the Reverend Precentor Crosse.

"The Deanery, Chichester,
"Aug. 30, 1882.

"Dear Precentor,—This is my last night in Chichester. My sister vanished on Monday; the two dear girls to-day; the servants go to-morrow morning: and Payne" [the Dean's Verger, who acted also as butler at the Deanery] "will be supreme in Creation when I shall have gone the way of all flesh early in the afternoon. I have been virtuously employed for two days,—viz. clearing up every arrear, epistolary or otherwise; sorting and putting away papers,—or else tearing them asunder, and so making a clearance. . . . . . Such acts always strike me as *a rehearsal* of a more solemn departure. I cannot say what *a homily* I keep on preaching to myself all day long, and how low my spirits are at this instant.

"Not in order to inflict any portion of my heaviness upon *you*, am I addressing you; but simply because your letter to Awdry has been before me for a week, and it deserves a word or two." [It appears that Canon Awdry had consulted the Dean about the propriety of reading the Prayer for Parliament at the Daily Office in the Cathedral, during the period of the two months' suspension of the Parliamentary Session, from the middle of August to the middle of October. The Dean thinks there are considerations both *pro* and *con*, and recommends a reference to the Precentor.] "And so I took refuge in a reference to your thoughtful self.—We are already looking forward with pleasure to having you both again for our neighbours.

"Ever affectionately yours,
"and Mrs. Crosse's,
"J. W. B."

1883.

Late in the March of this year Burgon paid a visit to his old and attached friend and *quondam* disciple, Mrs. Samuel Bickersteth, to see her first-born son, Monier, then six months old. Here are the very characteristic few lines in which he accepts her invitation "to come and see the little wonder."

To Mrs. Samuel Bickersteth.
"The Deanery, Chichester,
"March 20, 1883.

"My dearest Ella,—Will you forgive a hasty scratch in reply to your charming letter?

"I shall be delighted to come and see *the little wonder*, and to breakfast with you: and I will come *either* on Wednesday or Thursday—as you may prefer. It is all one to me.

"But—MIND!—on the condition that we have NO FISH[3] —nor anything of the kind. When alone, my breakfast is a cup of coffee and a slice of bread and butter.

"Give me *that*, and I'll come to the little wonder— Sam—and you. Ever, my dearest Girl,
"Your—his—and *its*
"Affectionate Friend,
"J. W. B."

The Bill for legalizing Marriage with a deceased Wife's Sister having passed the Commons this year and been sent up to the House of Lords, Burgon put forth a short paper, dated June 9, 1883, and signed Decanus, which he "respectfully submits to the consideration of those with whom a very solemn Legislative responsibility will shortly rest." What would be his view upon that very important social question can easily be guessed.

"Undeniable it is, that when our Saviour re-syllabled the primeval decree concerning Marriage ('They twain shall be one flesh'),—besides republishing what was said

---

[3] "I did provide some fish for his breakfast," writes Mrs. Bickersteth to the author, "knowing he had come some distance that morning— from Gresham College to the West End. He was persuaded to eat some; and when he had finished, he took all the fish bones from his own plate, and slily laid them on mine, saying, 'May my bones lie beside your bones.'"

'in the beginning,' He added this solemn sanction of His own ;—'*Wherefore they are no more twain, but one flesh.*' It follows, from the relation thus declared to subsist between Man and Wife, that the Wife's Sister is her Husband's Sister also; and therefore, that a Man may no more marry His Wife's Sister than his own Sister. Accordingly, such marriages are prohibited by the Laws of this Church and Realm."

His arguments against the legalization of such marriages drawn from their unhappy social effects are such as have often been advanced before. He concludes ;—

"It shall only be added that the eyes of England are at this instant—(not for the first time!)—fastened anxiously, hopefully, trustfully, on the House of Lords. The prayer of this Church and Nation has gone up that they may have the constancy, the wisdom, the courage given them to defeat the proposed legislation by a large majority."

The paper was sent to every member of the House of Lords. The Duke of Richmond and Lord Cranbrook would hardly need to be told who DECANUS was.

The Postscript to the Preface of the Third Edition of Dr. Scrivener's great work ['*A Plain Introduction to the Criticism of the New Testament for the Use of Biblical Students*'] shows one of the many forms which Burgon's indefatigable industry had been taking in the earlier part of this year ;—

"POSTSCRIPT (July 5, 1883). When the last sheets of this volume were about to go to press, I most unexpectedly received from Dean Burgon a catalogue of about three hundred additional manuscripts of the New Testament or portions thereof, deposited in European libraries, but hitherto unknown to scholars, which must be hereafter examined and collated by competent persons" [in Burgon's letter to Lord Cranbrook, given below, asking leave to dedicate to him '*The Revision Revised*,' he himself puts the number of new MSS., which his inquiries had brought to light, at 366]. "The catalogue is compiled from replies to inquiries made of the several custodians by Dean Burgon, who has most liberally placed at my disposal the results of his pains and energy. Our chief obligations are due to the Papal Librarian, the Abbate Cozza-Luzi, who set three assistants on the search, and has contributed to the list no less than 179 separate Codices in the Vatican, unaccountably overlooked by Birch and Scholz, the only critics who have had tolerable access to these treasures.

"I had said [p. 246] that 'the sum of extant copies must be considerably greater than we know of,' without in the least anticipating so sudden an accession of fresh materials. Now that the Vatican Library is administered in a free spirit, it is hard to conjecture what light its contents may throw ere long upon this and other branches of sacred learning." [Preface, pp. ix. x.]

The letter to Lord Cranbrook (dated July 16, 1883) in which he asks permission to inscribe to him '*The Revision Revised*,' will be found among those appended to this year. —The letter to the Reverend John P. Hobson, written from Turvey in his autumnal holiday, Sept. 21, 1883, which also will be found at the close of the year's record, is a good specimen of the interest which Burgon took in the minuter points of Greek Testament phraseology, and of the promptitude and pertinence with which he answered enquiries on that subject. It also shows the confidence which was reposed in him by those who, without any closer connexion with him, had simply been attendants at his ministry at St. Mary the Virgin's.—
The letter of Oct. 5, 1883, to Precentor Crosse, has reference in its earlier part to the New Statutes which the Cathedral Commission required the Chapter of each Cathedral to propose for their own future government

(subject of course to the supervision and correction of the Commissioners), and shows the perfectly good and amicable terms on which Burgon was at this time with the members of his Chapter. In the latter part, the illness of Mrs. Crosse elicits from him the tender sympathy (it was a quasi-pastoral sympathy), of which his heart was always so full, and which was ever ready to respond to the troubles with which his friends were visited.

In the October number of the '*Quarterly Review*' for this year appeared Burgon's Memoir of the late Provost Hawkins, which, together with his Memoirs of Bishop Wilberforce, President Routh, and other biographical sketches, written subsequently, was to be published (after the writer's death, alas!) as one of '*The Lives of Twelve Good Men.*' Of this Memoir it is needless to say more than that, in a very interesting and popular way, it has done justice to the memory of one whose great talents, strong character, and exemplary piety, might otherwise have lapsed into oblivion, like those of some other of the " Twelve Good Men," because the sphere in which they shone was the Academy,—not (as in the case of Bishop Wilberforce) the world. But, as the letter to the Rev. W. Foxley Norris appended to this year's record shows, Burgon had another motive in writing this Article, besides that of doing honour to the memory of one whom he both venerated and loved, and whom he calls "The Great Provost." The works which stand at the head of the Article are the Provost's Dissertation on " The Use and Importance of Unauthoritative Tradition, as an Introduction to the Christian Doctrines "—quite a standard Sermon of English Theology (it was preached originally as a University Sermon on May 31, 1818); and "the Memorandum respectfully submitted by the Provost of

Oriel to Her Majesty's Commissioners under *The Universities of Oxford and Cambridge Act*, 1877, with reference to a New Code of Statutes framed by the College." The sending in of this Memorial (March 5, 1879) was the venerable Provost's latest public act. It was his solemn protest against the diversion of the great Institution, over which he had presided with so much efficiency and dignity for nearly half a century, from the avowed design of its Founder,—a piece of sacrilegious iniquity. "It" [Oriel College] "was to be *Ecclesiastical: a School of Divinity*; not for Education generally, but *specially for Theology*, and the training up of *Christian Ministers.*" It is especially on this that Provost Hawkins founds his protest; as well as on the manifest injustice and inexpediency of the proposed revolutionary changes. eedless to say that Burgon finds (as he assures Mr. Foxley Norris) "a peculiar solace and satisfaction" in once again rehearsing in the ears of the Church and the World the mischiefs and wrongs done to his *Alma Mater* by the Universities Tests' Act, and the Oxford University Commission,—mischiefs and wrongs against which he had already protested in his Sermon of 1880 on '*The Disestablishment of Religion in Oxford, the betrayal of a Sacred Trust.*' Six pages of the Review on Provost Hawkins [pp. 344–348] are given to a recapitulation of these grievances, in connexion with the "Great Provost's" Memorandum.

At the end of this year there appeared (the Preface is dated All Saints' Day, 1883) '*The Revision Revised,*' one of the three great works—the other two being '*Inspiration and Interpretation,*' and '*The Last Twelve Verses of St. Mark,*'—by which Burgon has established a claim upon the gratitude of all who are jealous for the honour and integrity of GOD'S written Word, and which, we may confidently predict, will find for themselves a permanent place, all rationalistic cavils notwithstanding, in the standard theological literature of the Church of England. 'The Revision Revised' is a reprint in a separate form of the three Articles which had already appeared in the 'Quarterly,' the first of them (on "The New Greek Text") in the October number of 1881, the second and third (on "The New English Version," and "Westcott and Hort's New Textual Theory") in the January and April numbers respectively of 1882. To this is appended '*A Reply to Bishop Ellicott's Pamphlet in defence of the Revisers and their Greek Text of the New Testament, including a vindication of the traditional reading of* 1 Tim. iii. 16,' ("*God* was manifest in the flesh," which the Revisers have altered into "*He who* was manifested in the flesh," asserting in their margin that "the word *God* . . . . . rests on no sufficient ancient evidence.") Without entering into the controversy between Burgon and those Textual Critics, under whose advice, as experts, the majority of the Revisers acted, and whose Textual Theory is represented in the Revised Version, this may safely be said, that the Convocation of Canterbury made a fundamental mistake in giving instructions to the Revisers for any alteration of the text whatever [4], and this *because such alterations were premature.*

---

[4] In occasionally adopting a Greek text diff　　　　　that which the translators of 1611 had employed, the Revisers did not exceed their Commission. For the fourth of the Instructions issued to them by the Committee was, "That the Text to be adopted be that for which the evidence is decidedly preponderating." The Revisers might fairly assume, as they do in their Preface, that this "was in effect an instruction to follow the authority of documentary evidence without deference to any printed text of modern times, and therefore to employ the best resources of criticism for estimating the value of evidence." The resources of criticism, which as a fact they employed, were no doubt "the

Textual Criticism is a science of comparatively recent date, whose materials—Manuscripts, Fathers, early Versions—have not yet been worked out, nay, have by no means yet been all brought to light [5]; and, pending new researches and new discoveries, it was surely a fatal

best" in the eyes of those Textual experts whose lead they followed, while in the eyes of Burgon, and the opposite school of Textual Critics, they were the worst. Why should Convocation have opened the door for them to meddle with the Text at all, under the circumstances of the wide disagreement of learned men as to the true text, and as to the right method of arriving at it?

[5] How much has yet to be done in Textual Criticism before finality is reached in this comparatively new Science, we may learn from Burgon himself ('*Revision Revised*,' p. 125). "*The fundamental principles* of the Science of Textual Criticism are not yet apprehended . . . . Let a generation of students give themselves entirely up to this neglected branch of sacred science. Let 500 more COPIES of the Gospels, Acts, and Epistles, be diligently collated. Let at least 100 of the ancient *Lectionaries* be very exactly collated also. Let the most important VERSIONS be edited afresh, and let the languages in which these are written be for the first time really *mastered* by Englishmen. *Above all, let the Fathers be called upon to give up their precious secrets*. Let their writings be ransacked and indexed, and (where needful) let the MSS. of their works be diligently inspected, in order that we may know what actually *is* the evidence which they afford. Only so will it ever be possible to obtain a Greek Text on which absolute reliance may be placed, and which may serve as the basis for a satisfactory Revision of our Authorized Version."—The Rev. Edward Miller, in his invaluable '*Guide to the Textual Criticism of the New Testament*,' distinguishes four ' Periods in the history of Textual Criticism, so far as it has yet been evolved,—Infancy, Childhood, Impetuous Youth, and Incipient Maturity" (p. 7). The Childhood, according to Mr. Miller's division of the Periods, terminated with Griesbach, who died early in the present Century. Under the period of "Impetuous Youth" he places Lachmann, Tregelles, and Tischendorf (the discoverer of the Codex Sinaiticus), whose principles, more fully expounded and developed, have been applied by our Revisers in their dealings with the Greek Text. In the labours of Prebendary Scrivener, Dean Burgon, and Canon Cook he recognises the "Signs of coming Maturity." But there must be a vast deal more labour, according to Burgon, before anything approaching to maturity is attained. And beyond question, the Science is not yet in such a condition that a new Greek Text, materially different from the traditional one, can safely be constructed

blunder to allow any alterations of the text which King James's Translators had used. Tischendorf and Lachmann and Hort, on the one hand, may be right in the results at which they arrive ; or, on the other, Scrivener, and Burgon, and Cook (who in the main are agreed as to their methods and conclusions) may have the best of the argument ; but while new Manuscripts are still being discovered, while new researches into the early Fathers and the early Versions are still in progress, and there is no saying what new lights may be thrown upon various readings, and while thus *adhuc sub judice lis est*, it was surely the height of temerity (to use no stronger word) for the Sacred Synod of the Church to give a commission for the alteration of the Traditional Text in any particular. And this, first on account of the very grave issues at stake ; and next, because it was very well known that, on the most important parts of the Traditional Text which had been called in question, there were two opinions among Divines who had given themselves to the study of Textual Criticism, the one party as stoutly defending the genuineness of the readings questioned, as the other party vigorously assailed it. Is not the throwing of doubt upon the account of the strengthening Angel, the Agony and bloody Sweat, as the Revisers have done, by telling us in the margin that "Many ancient authorities omit" it, totally unjustifiable, while yet the battle for and against the genuineness of St. Luke xxii. 43, 44 has not been fought out,—while yet there is a possibility, not to say a great probability, that those verses really formed part of the Evangelist's sacred autograph ? And meanwhile the Revisers, by the surmise which they inject into the minds of Christians, and which is dismissed as groundless by men quite as learned and able, and as well furnished in critical lore, as themselves, make our voices falter, and our hearts to have misgivings, while we pray in words which the Church has put into our mouths;—"By thine Agony and bloody Sweat, Good Lord, deliver us."—And these Revisers inject suspicion also into the minds of believers as to the first of the Seven Sayings upon the Cross,—"Father, forgive them, for they know not what they do,"—the one palmary illustration, by our LORD's example, of His precept that we should "pray for them which despitefully use us, and persecute" us. Nay; they will not allow us even to say the Lord's Prayer in its full form, without confronting us with mental scruples as to whether the LORD did give the doxology appended to it (which they banish into their margin), and as to whether two of the petitions, in one of the forms in which our LORD gave the Prayer, ought not to be eliminated altogether. Are not these three passages alone,—the record of the Agony, the record of the first Saying on the Cross, and the Doxology of the Lord's Prayer,—passages of such value as to make it wrong and cruel to shake the faith of ordinary Bible readers in them, so long as they are maintained by men quite as learned as those who dispute their genuineness, so long as Textual Criticism has by no means as yet said its last word, or even come to full maturity as a Science? And these three passages are only specimens of several others, which the Revisers have challenged and called in question, not in a Treatise addressed to Textual Critics, and which only Textual Critics would read, but in a New Testament to be placed in the hands of every English Bible reader, as the volume from which he is daily to derive the precepts, hopes, solaces of the spiritual life.

But it is not only the value and importance of the passages upon whose genuineness doubt might be cast, if the Revisers were permitted to meddle with the Text, but also the perfect knowledge, which the members of the Sacred Synod must have possessed, that, as to all the main passages called in question, there were two opinions among Divines, advocated with at least equal learning and ability. Take as a single instance of this the last Twelve Verses of St. Mark, the genuineness of which Burgon himself had so elaborately vindicated in 1871. There is perfect justice (although one could wish that it had been said by another for him rather than by himself), in what he says on this point to Lord Cranbrook in the Epistle Dedicatory of his work.

"As Critics they have had abundant warning. Twelve years ago (1871) a volume appeared on '*The Last Twelve Verses of the Gospel according to St. Mark*,' —of which the declared object was to vindicate those Verses against certain critical objectors, and to establish them by an exhaustive argumentative process. Up to this hour no answer to that volume has been attempted. And yet, at the end of ten years (1881), —not only in the Revised English, but also in the volume which professes to exhibit the underlying Greek [6] (which at least is indefensible)—the Revisers are observed

---

[6] '*The New Testament in the Original Greek, according to the Text followed in the Authorized Version, together with the variations adopted in the Revised Version.*' Edited for the Syndics of the Cambridge University Press, by F. H. A. Scrivener, M.A., D.C.L., LL.D., Prebendary of Exeter and Vicar of Hendon, Cambridge, 1881.

'Η ΚΑΙΝΗ ΔΙΑΘΗΚΗ. *The Greek Testament, with the readings adopted by the Revisers of the Authorized Version.*' [Edited by the Ven. Archdeacon Palmer, D.D.] Oxford, 1881.

By the fourth rule agreed to by the Committee of Convocation, the Revisers were instructed, when the Text adopted by them differed from that from which the Authorized Version was made, to indicate the alteration in the margin. This recording of the variations in the margin, they tell us in their Preface, had been found inconvenient. "A better mode, however, of giving them publicity has been found, as the University Presses have undertaken to print them in connexion with complete Greek Texts of the New Testament." This undertaking resulted in the two volumes, the titles of which are given above.

to separate off those Twelve precious Verses from their context, in token that they are no part of the genuine Gospel."

The author ventures to differ from Burgon as to what was the "indefensible" part of the conduct of the Revisers. Not having been convinced by his work of the genuineness of the verses in question, they might surely have indicated their own doubtfulness about them, by leaving an hiatus *in their new Greek Text* between verses 8 and 9 of S. Mark xvi. But to exhibit, as they have done, *an hiatus in the English Version*, and to inform the English Bible-reader that "the two oldest Greek manuscripts and some other ancient authorities omit from v. 9 to the end," was certainly, when cause had been shown so ably, so learnedly, so exhaustively, for believing the verses to be perfectly genuine, "indefensible." The least that can be said for Burgon's book is, that it makes out A VERY STRONG CASE INDEED for the "last Twelve Verses." This being so, it was certainly quite unjustifiable to impose upon the general Bible-reading public their own conclusion, that the verses are questionable. And independently of the wrong done to the public, it was an unjust slight upon Mr. Burgon's labours. And an unjust slight is sure to awaken a spirit of retaliation and defiance. Powerful as is '*The Revision Revised*,' and successful as it has been in checking the demand for the Revised Version, it must be confessed that, had its language been milder, and more respectful to the acknowledged great learning and critical ability of his opponents, this extremely able and really grand work would have gained in persuasiveness, while it would have lost nothing in power. "You will be amused to hear," writes Prebendary Powles to the author, "that when I suggested a softer tone of criticism in some of '*The Revision Revised*' passages, Burgon said to me; "Ah! I see you're like my Quaker friend, who, in thanking me for my Gresham Lectures, said, 'But Oh! if thee wouldst but dip thy foot in oil.'"

It must be added that, even as to the Translation, Convocation, judging from what the result has been, gave to the Revisers far too free a hand. It is true that their first instruction was "to introduce *as few alterations as possible* into the Text of the Authorised Version" (pity that the word "Text" was used here, as a confusion is thereby hazarded with the *Greek* Text, which is the subject of the fourth instruction) "consistently with faithfulness," and their second, "to limit, as far as possible, the expression of such alterations to the language of the Authorised and earlier English Versions,"—restrictions, which, as Burgon triumphantly shows ['*Revision Revised*,' p. 127], they have utterly set at defiance. It is easy to be wise after the event; and it could not have been expected beforehand that from so really eminent a body of learned Divines and Greek scholars (the ablest in the country), a version so pedantic, so unidiomatic, so unrhythmical (to bring no graver charges against it) should have issued; but such being the result, the course which ought to have been pursued has now become obvious. "We do not contemplate," said the Convocation of Canterbury in the third of their fundamental Resolutions, "any new translation of the Bible, or *any alteration of the language, except where in the judgment of the most competent scholars such change is necessary.*" Be it so; but then let sufficient securities be taken for the strict observance of this Resolution. Let it be ruled that no alteration whatever should be made, except in passages where, by common consent of the best Greek scholars in the country, there was a manifest error in the Authorised Version. (Textual Critics, *as* Textual Critics, need not have been admitted to the Revising Company at all, if it had been resolved not to interfere with the Greek Text which King James's Translators had employed.) A score of the most eminent scholars,—several of them, it might have been provided, specialists in the Alexandrine Greek,—would have been abundantly sufficient. Let their instructions be, to report to a Committee of Convocation such passages of the Authorised Version of the New Testament as, in the unanimous judgment of the whole body of them, contained "clear and plain errors" of translation, requiring amendment. And let them at the same time submit to the Committee the renderings of those passages which they proposed to substitute for the Authorised Version. Let the Committee, in considering their Report, have the power, not of questioning the decision of the experts as to the necessity of alteration in those particular passages, or as to the true meaning of them, but of objecting to and altering the language in which the meaning had been expressed, so as to make it more idiomatic, more smooth, more "happy" (to use the Revisers' own language) in its "turn of expression, in the music of its cadence, and the felicity of its rhythm[7]." When the Committee had agreed upon any modification of the language,

---

[7] It is wonderful how utterly defective the Revised Version is in "turns of expression, music of cadence, and felicity of rhythm." The late Archbishop Magee used to say "that it would have been very much better if John Bright" (a master of pure English style) "had been one of the Revisers; and that at all events they ought to have had some colleague like him, who did not know Greek, but would judge the translation solely from the stand-point of pure English."

See Dean Macdonnell's paper on ARCHBISHOP MAGEE in the Aug. 1891 number of '*Good Words,*' p. 552.

which in any passage might seem advisable, let the passages, with the proposed emendations of them, be laid before the Upper and Lower Houses, and let each alteration separately be put to the vote either for acceptance or rejection. And let no alteration stand eventually, which had not been accepted by both Houses. Some plan of this kind would have been unenterprising indeed, and unambitious, and when the result had been achieved, it could not have been ushered into the world with a flourish of trumpets, and with "great swelling words" about modern theories of Textual Criticism; but it would have been useful, generally accepted by the Church, and welcomed by Christians of all Communions, and last, not least, would have given rise to no angry words or mutual recriminations. And the Sacred Synod of the Church of England would not have laid itself open, as it already had done in the Revision of the Lectionary, to the charge of *doing a great deal more than there was any necessity for, and making a great many very questionable alterations.*

We part from 'The Revision Revised,' probably the second work of our age and country on the Textual Criticism of the New Testament,—the first being by unanimous consent Prebendary Scrivener's '*Introduction to the Criticism of the New Testament*' [Cambridge, Deighton and Bell]—with an expression of deep regret that Burgon was not permitted to complete that methodical treatise [8] on the Principles of Textual Criticism, which he regarded

---

[8] "I deplore more heartily than I am able to express," he says in the Preface of '*The Revision Revised*' [p. ix.] "the injustice done to the cause of Truth by handling the subject in this fragmentary way, and by exhibiting the evidence for what is most certainly true, in such a very incomplete form. *A systematic Treatise is the indispensable condition for securing cordial assent to the view for which I mainly contend.*" It is satisfactory to know that he has left this Treatise in a state so far advanced, that in the hands of a skilful and learned Editor its leading principles may be exhibited to the world.

as the *magnum opus* of his life, and for which he has collected such ample materials [9]. If anything can mitigate this regret, and compensate for "the last touch of a vanished hand," it is the welcome information that so highly accomplished a Textual Critic as the Rev. Edward Miller has, after a thorough examination of the papers which Dean Burgon has left behind, undertaken to edit them, and is now engaged in that very laborious but useful task. Of the materials upon which this gentleman has to operate, he writes to Dean Burgon's representative thus;—

" . . . . . . I will only add a renewed opinion of the extreme value of the MSS. through which I have gone a first time, of the unrivalled acquaintance with the *entire* history of the sacred Text, the marvellously acute intuition, and the breadth of sound system hitherto unequalled, which they evince."

It may confidently be predicted that this work, when it appears, will mark a new era in Textual Criticism.

A letter from the late Sir Stafford Northcote, afterwards Lord Iddesleigh, acknowledging a copy of '*The Revision Revised*,' and giving his own view of the unsatisfactoriness of the Revised Version, as also a letter from Prebendary Scrivener to the author, expressing his general agreement with Burgon's principles of Textual Criticism, will be found at the close of this year's record.

At the Reading Church Congress, held in the October of this year, Mr. Le Gros Clark, F.R.S., a very old family friend of Burgon, who had been intimate with him in early life [1], read an able paper on '*Recent Advances in*

---

[9] Mr. Miller reckons up 2400 papers in the huge portfolios, containing the late Dean's "studies" in the Greek Text of the New Testament. The pile of these portfolios figures pathetically, as will be seen, among the incidents of his death.

[1] In a hasty note to this gentleman (13th Feb. 1885) he writes: "Be sure that *I* too recollect the

Natural Science in their relation to the Christian Faith;—in which a qualified assent was given to the doctrine of Evolution. Burgon's reply to him, showing both his affectionate feeling to his friends of *Auld Lang Syne*, and his abhorrence of the Darwinian theory, will be found among the letters appended to this year.

At the end of a year which must have exhausted him by its intensely hard work, and agitated him by its somewhat acrid controversies, it is pleasant to find Burgon in a sportive and frolicsome vein; but there was at all times a buoyant elasticity in him which relieved his graver moods. An antique signet, once belonging, as appeared by the legend encircling the effigy[2], to John de Maydenhithe, Dean of Chichester from A.D. 1400 to 1407, was dug up in the garden of the Bishop's Palace. The Bishop, knowing that Burgon had received some early training in numismatic lore, sent it to him to see whether he could throw any light upon it, and Burgon lost no time in bringing the curiosity under the notice of the head of the Numismatic Department at the British Museum. Having ascertained all that could be ascertained on the subject of the gem, he remitted it again to the Bishop, after weaving (entirely out of his own head of course) a pretty little "local tradition," to give point and significance to the curiosity. The *jeu d'esprit*, in addition to its playfulness, is a pleasing incidental token of the perfect amity which always subsisted, even at the

old Brunswick Square days very vividly, very faithfully. *Your* dear family is inextricably bound up with my earliest memories and all that pleasant time." On the death of Archdeacon Clark, Rector of Tenby, (Dec. 11, 1874), the brother of Mr. Le Gros Clark, Burgon wrote a touching *In Memoriam* of him for '*The Guardian.*'

[2] The effigy is a winged animal, with a dragon's tail, and front legs like those of a horse in full gallop,— representing probably the fabulous *hippocampus*.

time of serious dissensions with his Chapter, between him and his Bishop. It should be borne in mind that cordial friendship between a Bishop and the Dean of his Cathedral Church is supposed to be a somewhat rare phenomenon. There is to be seen on one of the monuments in Hereford Cathedral a reference to such a cordial friendship, as something which from its extreme infrequency deserved to be commemorated on the tomb of one of the parties.

To the Lord Bishop of Chichester.

"The Deanery, Chichester,

"Nov. 10, 1883.

"My dear Friend,—This interesting object belongs to a known class, of which specimens are to be seen in the British Museum. An antique engraved stone—set in silver (or gold)—and used as a signet. The setting is of the 14th century. I have cleaned it with my nail-brush and a little soap. You would have been surprised to see how much dirt was in it.

"The chief point of interest consists in its fitting in so exactly with the local Tradition. Dean John de Maydenhithe [1400-7] and Bishop Robert Reade [1396-1417] were firm friends. Walking round your garden, the Bishop said to the Dean,—'I wonder, John, if ever there will be a Bishop and a Dean so friendly as thou and I are?'— 'Marry, my lord,' (quoth the Dean), 'never until this seal of mine be found, will the thing come to pass.' So saying, he flung the jewel as far as he could—and it disappeared among the Episcopal cabbages. 'Ah! John' (said the Bishop)—''twill take 1000 years to recover thy lost jewel.' 'Not so' (replied the Dean), '*within half a thousand* years my seal will come back to thy successor—provided always that *my* successor's name be *John*, as mine is.'

"You find this legend in so many of the old books that I need hardly specify one of the places.

"The interesting thing is that *thou* hast found the seal—and *my* name is *John*—and at the end of exactly 480 years the lost jewel has been recovered; and it bears (as you see) the name of Dean John Maydenhithe—though the engraver has spelt it Medenit.

"Ever affec^{ly} y^{rs}
"& Mrs. D's.

JOHANNIS✠MEDENIT✠   "J. W. B."

On the 13th December of this year, it was proposed in the Oxford Convocation that the Rev. R. F. Horton, a Dissenting Minister, should be one of the Examiners appointed to examine Undergraduates " in the Rudiments of Faith and Religion," i. e. in the Thirty-nine Articles of the Church of England. How an appointment so unsuitable (to say the least) on the face of it came to be accepted by Congregation (that is, by the body of Resident Masters, most of them Tutors of Colleges) seems almost inexplicable; but so it was; Mr. Horton's name was carried in that assembly by a majority of nine. No need to say that, when the Non-Resident Masters were called up to accept or reject the nomination, the Dean of Chichester appeared among them. The Vice-Chancellor (Professor Jowett, Master of Balliol), in proposing Mr. Horton's name in the usual Latin formula, inadvertently made a slip of the tongue, and coupled a neuter substantive with a masculine participle; "Nomen vobis approban-*dus*." Unaware probably of the mistake, and perhaps nettled by the laughter with which it was greeted, he said words to this effect; "Perhaps, however, as many of you may not understand Latin" (a skit at the assumed ignorance of the country clergy), "it may be well to propose the name in English,"—but before he could complete the sentence, a perfect roar of laughter drowned the last words. The country clergy, if they did not know Latin, knew perfectly well that one not in communion with the Church of England, however highly qualified in other respects, was an unsuitable person to examine in her standards; and the result was to administer to Congregation a stinging rebuff;—*Placets*, 155, *Non Placets*, 576; majority against the nomination, 421. The Dean of Chichester, and those who felt with him on the degeneracy of " Young Oxford," went to their homes happier than they had been wont to do of late after contests in Convocation, and in ' *T Times* ' of Dec. 15 appeared this epigram from Burgon's pen ;—

PROFESSORIAL LATIN, Dec. 13, 1883.

"Nomen," quoth Jowett, " vobis approbandus,—
But p'rhaps in Latin you'll not understand us,—
So, in plain English "—all that followed after
Was lost (*quid mirum?*) in a roar of laughter.

J. W. B.

To VISCOUNT CRANBROOK.

"The Deanery, Chichester,

"July 16, 1883.

"Dear Lord Cranbrook,—I have been engaged for full nine months carrying through the Press a reprint, with considerable additions, of my three articles in the ' *Quarterly*.' It is quite inexplicable to myself, and seems incredible, how such a task can have kept me closely occupied so long; but dates are stubborn things.

" *Six* of the months, I ought to explain, have been consumed in writing a reply (of 150 pages) to a pamphlet of Bishop Ellicott's; chiefly in defence of my general principles; but in the main as a vindication of the commonly received text of a famous controverted place (1 Tim. iii. 16), which I have tried to establish for ever.

" This has led me into a correspondence with the principal Librarians of Europe, and has resulted in several new facts, and a vast accession of knowledge. I have communicated it all in outline to Dr. Scrivener, (366 new

MSS.), whose book will be out in a week or two. This makes my volume 520 pages long.

"But I am travelling wide of the only purpose I have in taking up my pen, which was, to ask leave to inscribe my book to yourself. Will you also forgive the simplicity of the inquiry; but will you kindly either destroy the enclosed scrap, if it be perfectly right, or else return it to me corrected, if there be *any thing* in it you would like to see added or altered? I always feel nervous when I am meddling with another man's good name. Whether Murray will decide to wait till the autumn for publication, or not, I cannot tell; but I wish to have done with the job, which has taxed me greatly. And one is not 'out of the wood,' until 'Title and Dedication,' 'Preface,' and 'Indices,' are all fully achieved and in the printer's hands.

"I beg to be most kindly remembered to all your dear party. Pray believe me ever, my dear Lord Cranbrook,
"Most gratefully and affectionately yours,
"JOHN W. BURGON."

FROM THE REVEREND J. P. HOBSON, VICAR OF STANSTEAD ABBOTTS,
TO THE VERY REVEREND DR. GOULBURN.

"The Vicarage,
"Stanstead Abbotts, Herts, Aug. 3rd, 1889.

"Dear Sir,—Hearing you are engaged in writing the life of the late Dean Burgon, I venture to send you a copy of a characteristic letter received from him, in case you might like to insert it. The circumstances of its reception are as follows. Having read in his treatise on the '*Pastoral Office*' the following sentence, 'Has it ever been noticed that when the Paralytic, borne of four, was healed by our Saviour, his bed ($\kappa\lambda\acute{\iota}\nu\eta$) *was left on the house-top, not* let down into the house?' I wrote to ask him if the explanation was the difference between the $\kappa\lambda\acute{\iota}\nu\eta$ and the $\kappa\rho\acute{\alpha}\beta\beta\alpha\tau\sigma\varsigma$ or $\kappa\lambda\iota\nu\acute{\iota}\delta\iota\sigma\nu$? I mentioned also

The Chichester Life.

the pleasure and profit it had been to me to hear him on Sunday evenings at Oxford. I asked also, as his book on the Pastoral Office was published in 1864, whether there were any other new commentaries he would recommend in addition to, or instead of, those mentioned in that book. The following was the reply;—

'Turvey Abbey, Bedford,

'Sept. 21, 1883.

'Dear Sir,—It is very pleasant to be reminded of those blessed days, which I seem to myself to have made so little use of. *Domine, miserere.* You have exactly seized my meaning, or rather the meaning of the Evangelist. The *grabátum* was a pallet,—often a very sorry one. St. Luke calls it by a peculiar name, κλινίδιον (v. 19, 24),—the thing ἐφ' ᾧ κατέκειτο (v. 25). The κλίνη was a bed, often raised from the ground (for consider St. Mark iv. 21); the κράββατος was the mat which lay upon it. St. Luke distinguishes the two in Acts v. 15. They were not *necessarily* connected, but in order to carry a man upstairs, it is more convenient of course to lay him on *a stretcher* (which is all that is meant by κλίνη in this case) than in any other way. St. Matthew, writing first, is not careful to distinguish the words (for see St. Matt. ix. 6). But that they are to be distinguished, and in the way I mention, is plain from the subsequent narrative, and indeed from other parts of Scripture (see St. John v. 8, 9, 10, 11, 12). All languages use words in a vague way. If I speak of a "bed," it is not plain whether I mean a fourposter with curtains and a canopy, or whether I mean the mattress (or feather bed) which lies upon it. The ancient church did not understand this. They represent a boy struggling to carry off a sofa, thus:

'In reply to your other question;—Pusey on Daniel all should read. It is invaluable,—*the* Book of the Age, so to speak. Wordsworth's Commentary on the whole Bible, is on the whole the best extant. Alford I have spoken rather too hastily of; he is valuable as a help, but not as a guide. Scott I have also spoken too strongly of; his Commentary is really useful, though deficient in learning. I do not see that I have mentioned "*Hall's Contemplations*." They are most valuable. "*Kay on the Psalms*" is also excellent for reference.

'Yours faithfully,
'JOHN W. BURGON.'

"I remain, dear Sir,
"Yours very faithfully,
"J. P. HOBSON."

TO THE REVEREND PRECENTOR CROSSE.

[*On the New Statutes, which the Cathedrals Commission had required the several Cathedrals to draw up and lay before them.*]

"Turvey Abbey, Bedford, Oct. 5, 1883.

"My dear Precentor,—I was intending to send you a few words of acknowledgment of your kind and acceptable letter, when the enclosed (as mercantile people say) 'comes to hand.' I have sent the Secretary a line in reply, promising to attend: and I daresay you have done the like. Will you, in the meanwhile, bring your own proposals to a definite issue—and let me have them *to study* for a few days —any time after the 16th, on which day I expect to be leaving this dear place and returning to the mill? —I wish the necessity had not arisen. I am quite content to live on with such men as yourselves—like a family — *without* a code of laws. But since we must absolutely have new Statutes, what need to add—εὐβουλίας δεῖ?" [we must take good counsel.]

"You mention your dear wife's continued affliction. It must of course be so. We were made what we are, with design: and these loving, anxious, sorrowing hearts of ours are, I suppose, the very kernel of our being. Religion is not intended to unmake what God made 'in the beginning,' and pronounced 'very good'; but only to sanctify and to bless,—to elevate,—to purify,—and to guide 'into the way of peace.'

"Invite the dear woman to ponder over the words—
'What I do'—
'Thou knowest not now'—
'But thou shalt know'—
'Hereafter'—
clause by clause.

"And then point out to her the comfort of the expression (found elsewhere) 'according to *the counsel* of His will' [Eph. i. 11].

"We—(you, she, I)—would willingly submit ourselves to His will—*because* it is His will; and because absolute, unconditional submission is as clearly our wisdom as our duty. But Oh, when I am assured that His will is *with counsel* (κατὰ τὴν βουλὴν τοῦ θελήματος αὐτοῦ)—then I gather myself up into a different attitude. Instead of crouching trembling at His feet, I lay my head on His bosom. It is no longer blind submission. It is trustful love. Tell the dear woman *that*.

"Ever affectionately yours,

"J. W. BURGON."

To THE REVEREND W. FOXLEY NORRIS, RECTOR OF WITNEY, OXON.

"The Deanery, Chichester, 22 Nov., 1883.

"My dear Foxley Norris,—It is very agreeable to me to see your handwriting again, and in any way to be reminded of you. Yes; of course the Article" [on Provost Hawkins in the '*Quarterly*'] "was mine, and has been recognised as such by a surprising number of persons. I am glad I wrote it, for it seems to have gratified many. I must add that *I* found a peculiar solace and satisfaction in placing on record the iniquitous history of Oxford during these few last years. I have not *done with the rogues yet*.

"Oh! how they hate me!

"You are a poet indeed, if you can tag rhymes while suffering tooth-ache. Thank you much for your verses. I send them on to Turvey, where they will be as much appreciated as here.

"I trust you are well and thriving? My ladies join me —I suppose I may say—in *love* to you!

"Ever, dear Norris,

"Yours affectionately,

"J. W. B."

FROM SIR STAFFORD H. NORTHCOTE, M.P., TO THE VERY REVEREND THE DEAN OF CHICHESTER.

"Pynes, Exeter, Dec. 22, 1883.

"My dear Dean of Chichester,—I have been keeping your letter in the hope of being able to give a little time to the Revision question before answering it; but the waves of to-day succeed the waves of yesterday with such pitiless persistency, that I go to bed every night *re infectâ*, and meantime my conscience threatens to become seared. So I must no longer delay to thank you both for the book, and for the very kind letter which accompanied it; and which I warmly appreciated. My general idea of the Revision is, that, while some amendments and corrections were undoubtedly necessary, the travestie of the whole text of the Scripture destroys far more than it can possibly give in exchange. What becomes of all the associations, with which from early childhood we had learned to surround the old text? How would Keble have felt, when he was writing the lines on the Catechism, had he foreseen that the 'sacred air'[3] was one day to be *un*learnt, and a new setting adopted?

"With best Xmas wishes, I remain, faithfully yours,
"STAFFORD H. NORTHCOTE."

[3] "O say not, dream not, heavenly notes
To childish ears are vain,
That the young mind at random floats,
And cannot reach the strain.
Dim or unheard, the words may fall,
And yet the heaven-taught mind
May learn the sacred air, and all
The harmony unwind."

From the Reverend Dr. Scrivener to the Very Reverend Dr. Goulburn.

"Hendon Vicarage, Nov. 18, 1889.

"Dear Mr. Dean,—I am much pleased that you have undertaken my valued friend's life. I do not know how to express in a few lines my literary obligations to Burgon. He often says I was first in the field; but by reason of the difficulties of life, I was soon left far behind.

"If you have before you the 3rd edition of my '*Plain Introduction to the Criticism of the N. T.*' (1883), the Index II (Burgon, J. W.) will show you how much I owe to him, and with what gratitude I have acknowledged his help.

"In principle I fully agree with him in believing that all existing materials of every kind ought to be known, before the text can be regarded as permanently fixed. But as a result of my own studies I do not expect so much help from the later copies of manuscripts, as from a thorough examination of the ante-Nicene Fathers (begun, not completed, by him). I reject Dr. Hort's baseless theories as earnestly as he does, and am glad to see they are not gaining ground. On the other hand, I think Burgon's wholesale disparagement of Cod. Vaticanus as 'the most corrupt of all copies,' quite unreasonable. On this head we have held many a conflict, without either of us yielding an inch. You will see that I stand midway between the two schools, inclining much more to Burgon than to Hort.

"I am sorry that I can do no more for you. I am lingering 'superfluous like a veteran on the stage.' Yet all resigned, I trust, to the Divine Hand, which has bestowed on me in life so many good things.

"I am, Mr. Dean,
"Yours very respectfully,
"F. H. A. Scrivener."

To F. Le Gros Clark, Esq., F.R.S.

"The Deanery, Chichester, 22 Nov., 1883.

"My dear 'Fred,'—We are getting old boys, but must keep up the ancient appellations.

"I am grateful to you for your two little productions, which I instantly read through with great interest—the address to the Hospital students with entire agreement. I particularly like the counsel given at p. 8 (lower half).

"In the other paper you are not so happy. Physical science, when it is *unscientific*, makes itself ridiculous, when it runs foul of Revealed Truth. Thus Evolution, when it sets about accounting for the existence of man, is a dream pure and simple,—and not a very pure dream either. The Creation of man and of woman is a matter of *express* Revelation, to the truth of which the *Creator Himself*, —the *Incarnate Word*,—JEHOVAH—pledges Himself. It is mere chaff and draff for the Scientist to approach such a matter with a weak theory, unproved and unprovable. He prates of what he knows nothing. Let him keep to his *well ascertained facts*, and we listen to him with pleasure. But he ventures on what is to him confessedly *terra incognita*, when he pretends to account for the Origin of Man. I fasten on *one definite point*, you see.

"I believe you would grant all this, if pressed. But from your paper, one would suppose you were on the side of Darwin, or at least of Darwinism.

"I trust you are all well?

"Ever affectionately yours,

"J. W. B."

"In my reply to this criticism," says Mr. Le Gros Clark, in a memorandum on the subject of Burgon with which he has kindly favoured the author, "I ventured to remind him that God speaks to us by His Works as well as in His Word, and that if the two revelations appear to be at variance, it was more probable that we had misinterpreted the Word, than that the works should have misled us. I was anxious for his answer to this suggestion, but it did not come. I think this was the nearest approach to a disagreement that we ever had."

Mr. Le Gros Clark, like all who knew Burgon intimately, was drawn towards him by his affectionateness

The Chichester Life.

and transparency of character. In a letter to the author dated Sept. 2, 1890, he says;—

"I think I have never known a character so simple, so childlike, so pure. His fondness for children was remarkable; and to women he was uniformly most courteous, and evidently took much pleasure in their society. I do not believe he was sensible of the pain he inflicted in his polemical writings; for such consciousness would have been inconsistent with his tender and loving nature. Indeed these characteristics must seem irreconcilable to those who do not know that his strong convictions—were they not prejudices?—overwhelmed all other considerations."

1884.

In the January and February of this year Burgon published in the columns of the 'Guardian' another series of five letters[4] to Dr. Scrivener on copies of the

---

[4] The dates on which the five letters were written are I. Jan. 2, 1884; II. Jan. 10, 1884; III. Jan. 17, 1884; IV. Jan. 29, 1884; V. Feb. 6, 1884 (all from "Deanery, Chichester").

It may be convenient here to present a list of all Burgon's Letters to the 'Guardian' on the subject of Codices of the New Testament, as they are given in a Memorandum in his own handwriting, found among his papers.

"Memorandum.

2 Letters in the 'Guardian,' which are reprinted in my 'Letters from Rome' (on Cod. B.).

21 Letters, which also appeared in the 'Guardian' (i-xv. in 1873: xvi-xxi. in 1874), entitled 'Manuscript Evangelia in Foreign Libraries.'

10 Letters, which also appeared in the 'Guardian' (21 June to 23 Aug. 1882), entitled 'Sacred Greek Codices at home and abroad.'

5 Letters, which also appeared in the 'Guardian' (Jan. and Feb., 1884) under the same title.

38 Letters in all are the sum of what has appeared in this way."

It would appear from what he says in the last Letter of the last Series that he contemplated continuing these Letters: "The Editor of the Guardian' warns me that at this place, these long letters must,

New Testament, which had been brought to light by inquiries made in the early part of 1883.

"A burning wish, let me be allowed to call it a fixed determination, to settle—if possible for ever—the vexed question of the true reading of 1 Tim. iii. 16, set me on obtaining from the custodians of the chief Continental libraries the reading of such copies of St. Paul as were known to be under their respective charges. Not a few interesting discoveries (as might have been foreseen) were the consequence."

Dr. Ceriani, his learned friend at Milan, gave him "references to several MSS. unknown to me before," and sentiments of *Auld lang syne*, always so easily quickened in his heart, must have sprung up in him, when the acquaintance of his early life, Dr. Lepsius, the head-librarian at Berlin, "a friend of more than forty years' standing," promoted his wishes [see Vol. I. pp. 24, 25, and 103, 104]. But the Abbate Cozza-Luzi, the Papal Librarian, gave him greater assistance than any other foreign Librarian. "On being made acquainted with the nature of my researches, this learned man set three of his assistants to work on my behalf in the several libraries of Rome," and the result was the discovery of "a considerable number of sacred Codices which had hitherto escaped the attention of the critics,"—so considerable as to "show an increase of no less than *three hundred and seventy-four* upon the number known to us in the first half of 1883." [Letter I.]

for the present, be discontinued. I venture to hope that, when they are resumed, I shall have something to communicate which will interest those who care for the Textual Criticism of the New Testament. To all others, I am painfully conscious that my letters must be simply unreadable."

But, whatever his intention, the Letters never were resumed.

This is as much as needs to be said on this series of five letters, in the course of which Burgon, both in the second and fourth Letters gives its just meed of praise to Mr. Berriman's '*Dissertation upon* 1 Tim. iii. 16[5],' in which he had preceded Burgon by 140 years in his attempt to "settle—if possible for ever—the vexed question of the true reading" of that text.

"Berriman claims on his title-page to have 'proved' that the common reading of 1 Tim. iii. 16 ('GOD *was manifested in the flesh*') is the true one. I venture to assert that he has fully established his claim. As a critic, he was greatly beyond his age. The 140 years which have since rolled out have supplied us with a vast succession of evidence of which he would have rejoiced to avail himself." [Letter IV.]

Burgon's high estimation of the value of *Copies*, as shown in the first Letter of this Series (Dr. Scrivener, as

---

[5] The Title Page of this Book is as follows:—

"ΘΕΟ'Σ ἐφανερώθη ἐν σαρκί. OR, A CRITICAL DISSERTATION UPON 1 TIM. iii. 16. WHEREIN RULES are laid down to distinguish, in *various* Readings, which is *genuine*; An ACCOUNT is given of above a hundred GREEK MANUSCRIPTS of St. *Paul's Epistles*; (many of them not heretofore collated;) The Writings of the GREEK and LATIN FATHERS, and the ANCIENT VERSIONS are examin'd; and the *common* Reading of that Text, GOD *was manifest in the Flesh*, is prov'd to be the *true* One. Being the Substance of *Eight Sermons* preach'd at the Lady MOYER's Lecture, in the Cathedral Church of St. *Paul*, LONDON, in the Years 1737, and 1738. By JOHN BERRIMAN, M.A., Curate of St. *Swithin*, and Lecturer of St. *Mary Aldermary. We can do nothing* against *the Truth, but* for *the Truth* — 2 Cor. xiii. 8. LONDON: Printed for W. INNYS at the West-End of St. *Paul's*, and J. NOURSE, at the *Lamb* without *Temple-bar*. M.DCC. XLI"

Berriman's Treatise, though not long, is one of those solid and exhaustive ones, which are quite out of date in these superficial days.

At p. 432, n. 1, of Burgon's '*Revision Revised*,' he tells us that in the British Museum copy of this Dissertation there are MS. notes by the Author, and that another annotated copy is in the Bodleian Library.

will be seen from his letter to the author given above [p. 229], does not estimate Copies quite so highly) may just be glanced at, before we pass on ;—

"I am thoroughly persuaded that the Copies will eventually be recognized as our most precious helps in determining the text of the New Testament Scriptures. These—only because they happen to exist in 'Cursive' writing, instead of the 'Uncial' character, have, for nearly a hundred years, laboured under great and undeserved neglect. Griesbach [1774-96] began the mischief,—which Lachmann [1831-42] perfected: but it was Tischendorf's discovery (in 1844) of the 'Codex Sinaiticus' which, more than anything else, gave an impulse to the weak superstition which now prevails (*because* written in uncials, *therefore* oracular), and helped to divert public attention from the younger witnesses to the truth of the letter of Scripture."

Burgon's heart, to which Oxford at all times lay so near, was again to be saddened in the spring of this year by another proof of the degeneracy of his beloved University. On April 29, 1884, the admission of women to University Examinations was carried in Convocation by a majority of 143 [*Placets* 464, *Non-Placets* 321]. Under such an abandonment (as he and the many who thought with him regarded it) of all true delicacy of feeling, and all sound principles of Education, Burgon could not possibly be silent, if an opportunity were given him to speak. And shortly afterwards an opportunity was given him, and in a way which may be regarded as a personal compliment, inasmuch as the Trinity Sunday Sermon, which he was appointed to preach before the University, was to be in New College Chapel; and, on occasion of the transfer of the University Sermon from St. Mary's to a College Chapel, it was usual to appoint a member of the College to preach.

Why Burgon, whose whole attitude towards the modern changes in the Academical system was one of uncompromising resistance, was chosen so often as he was in his latter days to occupy the University Pulpit, requires some explanation. If indeed the nominators of the University Preachers in the main agreed with his views, that fact, without going further, furnishes the explanation. But, on the contrary hypothesis, it may perhaps have been the case that in those nominators who differed materially from him, a feeling of fairness operated, especially if they themselves were not altogether satisfied with the Academical changes;—" Let us at all events hear, as we are sure to do from Burgon, the strongest things that can be said against what has been recently done."—Or was it that his hard hitting, and occasional grotesqueness of manner and phraseology, were regarded as an amusing relief from the general dulness and dryness of University Sermons,—" Call for Samson, that he may make us sport?"—Anyhow, such was the fact, that every facility was given him of fulminating against the modern movements, which he held to be so fraught with mischief. And on June 8, 1884, Trinity Sunday, he preached in New College Chapel (it seems to have been his last appearance in the University Pulpit) his Sermon on this thesis,—' *To educate Young Women like Young Men and with Young Men,—a thing inexpedient and immodest.*' He is careful to explain that his censure does not touch the Halls already established for young Ladies in Oxford ("Lady Margaret Hall" and "Somerville Hall").

" The Halls were essentially private dwelling-houses. They existed quite independently of the University system. Many of us viewed them with sympathy,—(I avow myself of the number),—because they seemed to provide the safeguard of a pious home for just a very few young gentlewomen, who coveted access to some of the educational advantages of this place. Presided over by those whose names carry with them the savour of whatever is most admirable in Woman, the system pursued at the two Halls commended itself to our Christian chivalry, and won our confidence. But already has the object of the Halls become a thing of the vanished past. A new system of things has been set up," &c., &c. (p. 25).

In his Postscript he endeavours to explain[6] the very mistaken step to which the University had recently committed itself, by

"the attractiveness of the inmates of the two Halls which had been already opened in Oxford, and which (it was said) would be extinguished, unless the University would legislate in favour of Women, and practically change its own constitution. In other words,—the admirable Ladies who preside over 'LADY MARGARET' and 'SOMERVILLE' Halls, and the charming specimens of young womankind who had made those Halls their temporary home,—proved irresistible as an argument. The men succumbed. I remember once reading of something similar in an old Book. The Man was very sorry for it afterwards. So was the Woman."

The Allocution to Women, which occupies the latter part of the Sermon, is characteristic of the preacher in a high degree. Through the lecture which he reads them, and the rebuffs which he gives to their aspirations for equality with Man, ("Inferior to us GOD made you: and our inferiors to the end of time you will remain" [p. 29]; "If you set about becoming Man's rival, or

---

[6] Some explanation was necessary of how it came to pass that the majority in favour of the admission of women to the University Examinations was so large, and not only so, but composed in great part of persons usually found on the right side— "our natural friends," as Canon Liddon calls them in the letter in which he thanks Burgon for his Sermon. [See below.]

rather if you try to be, what you never can become, Man's equal.... you have in a manner unsexed yourselves, and must needs put up with the bitter consequence" [p. 30]), there struggles forth, almost at every other line, that intense susceptibility to the charms of women, and that chivalrous deference to them, which formed so strong an element in his character;—

"Yours are not a few of the precious qualities which have been entirely withheld from us.... You are the prime ornament of GOD's creation; and we men are, to speak plainly, *just what you make us*" [p. 29]; "Woman is the one great solace of Man's life, his chiefest earthly joy" [p. 30], &c., &c.

If it were desirable to show that it was in the interests of women themselves that it was sought to exclude them from competition with men, John William Burgon was an entirely suitable advocate of such exclusion, than whom, though unmarried, a more devoted and chivalrous admirer of the softer sex never existed. Whatever judgment may be formed of his Sermon, it at least relieved the University from the grave charge of so objectionable a measure having been passed into law without any public and official[7] protest being made against it. And this he tells us was his object in delivering and publishing the Sermon:—

"That it may not be said in after years that when the University (29th April, 1884) passed a Statute to enable young women to come up to Oxford and undergo the same Examinations as young men,—none of her sons remonstrated with her on the dangerous course to which

---

[7] Canon Liddon wrote a powerful letter to the '*Guardian*,' dissuading members of Convocation from voting for the measure; but this was before it passed, and can hardly be called "official," as a Sermon before the University, preached by appointment of certain Academical functionaries, may be called.

she was thereby committing herself;—the ensuing pages have been sorrowfully written, and are now published."

After all, the measure in question was only a symptom,—as Burgon, Canon Liddon, Bishop Christopher Wordsworth, and other devout and spiritually-minded men deeply felt,—of the malady which has been long working among us, by Woman's invasion of the position and functions of Man, by her abandoning the position of a helpmate, which is her true province, and taking up the position of a rival. That our Transatlantic brethren repudiate, as earnestly as any one of us in the mother country can do, this dislocation of the Divinely constituted order of Society, and discern as clearly as ourselves the frightful social mischiefs which must accrue, may be seen from that very valuable series of Lectures by Dr. Morgan Dix, on the '*Calling of a Christian Woman*[8],' which has already obtained a considerable circulation in this country, and which it were to be hoped might be in the hands of every young woman of promise, and every mother of a family.

This last University Sermon of Burgon's elicited from the late Canon Liddon (whose communication to the '*Guardian*' of April 23, 1884, is quoted in the Sermon), the following Letter;—

---

[8] '*Lectures on the Calling of a Christian Woman, and her training to fulfil it.*' Delivered during the Season of Lent, A.D. 1883. By Morgan Dix, S.T.D., Rector of Trinity Church, New York. Fifth Edition. New York: D. Appleton and Company, 1, 3, and 5, Bond Street, 1884.

The subjects of the Lectures are, I. The place of Woman in this world; II. The Degradation of Woman by Paganism, and her Restoration by Christianity; III. The Education of Woman for her Work; IV. The Sins of Woman against her Vocation; V. Divorce; VI. A Mission for Woman.

To the Very Reverend The Dean of Chichester.

"3 Amen Court, E.C., June 20, 1884.

"My dear Dean,—Let me thank you for your kindness in sending me a copy of your Sermon preached at Oxford on Trinity Sunday. If, as I fear, there is no chance of our undoing the fatal mistake of April 29, such earnest expressions of opinion as yours will delay, and perhaps will help to defeat, the next move, *viz.*, the demand for a B.A. Degree.

"The sad thing about the matter is that so many of our natural friends helped to pass a measure, which is really at issue with all they have most sincerely at heart.

"Let me once more thank you, and remain,

"Ever very truly yours,
"H. P. Liddon."

Before the time at which we have now arrived, Burgon, having found that mode of instruction to be very successful in his ministry at Oxford, had instituted Bible Classes at Chichester. A lady residing in the city put her drawing-room at his disposal for this purpose; and, as at Oxford, so here also, those who joined the class highly valued the instruction given them (none the less edifying on account of some grotesque ways and phrases), and conceived a sincere esteem and affection for him who conducted it. An account of this Bible Class, by a Lady who attended it, with a copy of some notes taken by another member of it on Nov. 28 and Dec. 6 in this year, will be found at the end of the Biography. But the Chichester Bible Class was not his only effort of this kind. He offered himself to give Sunday Evening Lectures to the pupils of Bishop Otter's College, about half a mile distant from Chichester; and immediately after the Afternoon Service at the Cathedral, at all seasons, summer or winter, and in all weathers, he started on foot on this self-imposed mission to those who were being prepared to instruct others, and whose own careful instruction therefore in the "wondrous things" of God's "Law" he regarded as of peculiar interest and importance. In the end of the year, it would be nearly dark when he set forth, and quite dark when he returned; but, while he was in residence at Chichester, nothing short of serious illness would prevent his fulfilling this engagement. How greatly his instructions were prized by those to whom they were addressed, will be seen by the accounts of them given at the end of the Biography, which have been kindly furnished to the author by two Ladies, formerly Students at the College.

1885.

On Jan. 23rd of this year Burgon lost his remaining Brother-in-law, to whom he was so tenderly attached, and whose house had been, since the death of Archdeacon Rose, the home where he spent what must be called (for want of a better word) his vacations—that is, his annual retirements for two months' change of scene. Of Mr. Higgins's death he has himself given an account in the '*Lives of Twelve Good Men.*' Some of the letters of this year, which will be found at the end of the year's record, show how deeply he felt it, and what devout reflexions and aspirations the sad event stirred in him.

It may perhaps be chronicled also that on April the 8th, 1885, there appeared a letter from him in the '*Guardian*,' which elicited assent from many quarters, advocating the publication separately, and at a reasonable price, of the Revised Version of the Old Testament, unencumbered with that of the New. Needless to say that he takes occasion in this letter, and in another

THE CHICHESTER LIFE.

which followed it, to reiterate the charges brought against the latter in his '*Revision Revised.*'

"Pray let us have the Revised Old Testament by itself. It ought to contain a great deal well deserving of study, if the Revisers have only adhered to their instructions — namely, to remove none but '*plain and clear errors,*' and '*to introduce as few changes as possible* into the text of the Authorised Version': above all, if they have not been guilty of the incredible folly of tinkering the *Hebrew* text."

It was in the Easter of this year that, at the urgent request of friends, he put forth a small volume, containing some of his fugitive poetical pieces[9], headed by his Oxford Prize Poem "PETRA." The Preface glances at his recent bereavement ;—" By this time so many loved ones have vanished from the scene, who would have given to these Poems (such as they are) a loving greeting, that scarcely does it any longer seem to myself of the least importance what becomes of them" ; while in the inscription to his sister, Mrs. Higgins, of Turvey Abbey, he "invites her to regard the present Volume as one more wreath sent to adorn the grave of her sainted husband."

It only remains to say that Mrs. ———— ————, to whom most of the subjoined letters are addressed, was a lady residing in Chichester, with whom he was on intimate terms, and who from his faithful ministrations, both in the Cathedral Pulpit and in his Bible Classes, had conceived the most cordial esteem for him.

[9] POEMS (1840 to 1878). By JOHN WILLIAM BURGON, B.D., Dean of Chichester. London : MACMILLAN AND CO. 1885.

VOL. II.   R

LIFE OF DEAN BURGON.

To Mrs. ———— ————

"Turvey Abbey, April 18, 1885.

"It is a strange sensation to be in this house without *him*,—and even my dearest Helen in bed. I can hardly believe that he will not enter the room at any instant. His things are all left in his study, exactly as he left them,—the very hat and stick placed as if he had set them down an instant ago. And thus it comes to pass that one moves about like a man in a dream,—and the strangest speculations present themselves as to his whereabouts and occupations. I do but know that he is supremely happy; and I am sure that he is thinking perpetually of the place he has left for ever. . . . . . ."

To Viscount Cranbrook.

"The Deanery, Chichester,

"Ap. 20, 1885.

"My dear Lord Cranbrook,—Thank GOD that you are back, safe and well! I have felt the *miss* of you greatly: I mean, the sense of your being so many ugly leagues away from your dear ones and from me. It is a real comfort to me to have it under your hand and seal that you are returned feeling well. I choose to assume (what I have been in part assured of) that the voyage has been productive of the like blessed result to your son and his wife.

"You return to find us in a rare *kettle of fish*. Oh! if Beaconsfield could but have drawn his 'scientific frontier,' when he was advocating and explaining it, we should have been spared present humiliation and future danger. That same *imperial policy* which he sketched in his last Manifesto, while in power, would have made us great all the world over by this time. I verily believe that we should have had *a Canal of our own*, and have enjoyed the absolute control of Egypt. . . . . I do not profess to be a politician; but I watch public events daily, and for the last year or two it has been with a sense of *dismay*, for which I find no words.

"You have found dear Lord Cairns gone,—a grievous loss, on personal and private, as well as on public grounds. I am feeling greatly the loss of the Bishop of Lincoln. We were *one* in theological sentiments, and I believe in everything else.

"Your reminiscence of Mansel (send me more, if you have them) reminds me of Eden's advice to a man who asked him how he was to study the Thirty-nine Articles. 'Oh, buy Tomline—and *Burnett*' [burn it]. In return for your joke, I will tell you one in which you will recognise a true bit of Mansel. He was driving out into the country with a party of friends. A child in the carriage remarked of a donkey by the roadside that 'it had got its head into a basket, and could not get it out.' Mansel murmured, '*a case of ass-fix-ia*' [asphyxia].

"With love to all your party, I am ever (with fresh welcomes back), my dear Lord Cranbrook,

"Affectionately yours,

"JOHN W. BURGON."

To MRS.

"Turvey Abbey, Sept. 6, 1885.

"Yesterday was a sad, sad day with me,—the anniversary (the 31st) of my loved Mother's departure. I live in the past to an extraordinary extent. I seemed with her—or rather felt as if she had been with me—all day.

"This is also a sad house to be in. Every thing in every room is bound up with his loved memory—and (naturally enough) nothing is moved: so that one fancies he will enter the room at any time. I rejoice to be here all the same; but cannot deny that the sense of depression is strong upon me, and is perpetual.

"In the meantime I sit at the accustomed window, and work on,—as incessantly as if my life depended on my exertions."

To Mrs. ——— ———

"Turvey Abbey, Sept. 9th, 1885.

"I do not know what may have been the result of your own thoughtful heart's ponderings,—but the result with me—(a remark which I do not by any means now make for the first time)—is, that happiness is very evenly distributed, and that God is very good to all His creatures. There are drawbacks everywhere; but everywhere there are also privileges and blessings. The best alchemy is that which insists on turning *every thing* into gold: the transmutation may be made without a miracle, except indeed it be a miracle of grace.

"Another of my sage remarks is, that our happiness has been entrusted to a surprising extent, to our own personal keeping. And further, that happiness is to a great extent a *habit of the soul:* a thing we may acquire and cultivate, or neglect and lose, as we are of a grateful and appreciative turn of mind, or the contrary.

"Shall I go on? I am also inclined to believe that there is a great deal more of goodness—(as well as of *naughtiness*)—in the world than people commonly imagine. And I hold it to be very wrong to think—and far more to speak—evil of one another, unless we are actually constrained to do so. Even then we should (I think) cherish a secret suspicion that folks may not be nearly so bad as they seem. . . . . "

To Mrs.

"Turvey Abbey, Sept. 23, 1885.

"I am concerned to hear of the death of Mrs. . . Those young daughters of hers will feel the want of a mother sadly. Nothing can make up for it on earth: absolutely nothing. 'I feel,' said the poet Gray, when his mother died, 'that a man can only have one mother.' I often think of his words. I think lovingly, mournfully, of *mine* every day; and sometimes often in the course of the day. I must not forget my dear father also, when I thus speak. I recall his strong, wholly unselfish love and *concern* for me, with great tenderness and gratitude. Those who have never married are apt, I suspect, thus to live in the past. But in the case of young girls, oh! how grave and irreparable is the loss of a mother!

I hope (to recur for a moment to your own recent sorrow [1]) that you will learn to cherish the thought that the *Past* is at least your imperishable *possession*. Surely, it is not fanciful so to speak. It is surely, in a true sense, the only thing which is unalterably one's own. No doubt, where there has been subsequent unkindness, the memory of antecedent tenderness becomes in a manner cancelled. But where—as in your own happy case—the love has gone on unbroken until the spirit went to God, *that* love is a thing to fall back upon in memory, and to cherish, and to feed upon, and to *console one's self withal*,—to the end of one's own life. . . . the *miss* of the loved object, I am far from denying, occasions many a pang: but the other thought brings a healing balm with it, and may always be recurred to with secret gratitude and joy.

"I am busy with the life of the dear brother" [Mr. Higgins] "to whom—(it seems but yesterday)—everything I see *belonged*. Scarcely credible is it that one who went out, and came in, from these familiar portals, for eight and seventy years, should never, never, more—so much as once—be seen, or heard, or felt,—no, not for an instant. The swallows twitter, and the wood pigeons coo, and the squirrels play,—as they used exactly. The harvest time has come and gone, exactly as of old, and Ruth has not forgot to go a-gleaning, and lay down the ears she has gathered at her cottage door. The bells ring out on Sundays—and the congregations gather—and the services of God's house are conducted—exactly as of yore. All seems unchanged—the sunshine and the shade, and the dewy lawn at early morning,—and the cattle feeding on the upland,—every shrub and every tree,—but he, the loved one,—he who made the place so interesting—*he, he*—is not!

"It must be so. Ere long, the same will be said of

---

[1] His correspondent had recently lost her husband.

myself. It is right also that the coming ones should be made way for; and that all should be reminded that we are but pilgrims here below, at best. . . . . . ."

To Mrs.

"Deanery, Nov. 24, 1885.

"I cordially subscribe to your view that where Death has set its seal on the life, the doom is unchangeable. We are *quite* agreed, believe me.

"But *that* is no reason why they who wish,—and find comfort in the practice,—should not bless God for their sainted ones departed, and thank God for them *by name*. Prayer for the Dead, *in the sense of a Prayer that their ultimate doom, for weal or for woe, may be reversed—or even mitigated*—is 'a fond conceit,' finding countenance neither in Scripture nor in Antiquity. I condemn it entirely."

1886.

Burgon's pen, employed so much at all times in expressing sympathy and giving friendly counsel, was never allowed to rest long from controversy. An Article by Professor Pritchard, Savilian Professor of Astronomy at Oxford, which appeared in '*The Guardian*' of Feb. 10, 1886, and was entitled "The Creation Proem of Genesis," elicited from him a fortnight later (Feb. 24) a spirited reply, afterwards printed in a separate form. The Professor, while asserting his "full conviction of a superhuman element running through" [the account of the Creation in Genesis] "from its beginning to its end," conceived the account to be unhistorical. It was the record of a sublime and God-inspired dream, he thought, full of precious teaching no doubt, but not intended to be taken as a narrative of facts. The dreamer, whoever he was, "recounted the wonderful dream," when he awoke from it; and the tale, "after the manner of the East, sped its rapid way from city to city, until at length the vision lost its name and became a tradition." This was just the sort of theory to elicit Burgon's strenuous opposition. And he meets with considerable power the Professor's objections to the literal and ordinary view of a Great Creative Week. In reply to the difficulty raised by "the existence of waters before the appearance of the sun," and by the "clothing of the earth with " vegetation "before the creation of the sun," he points out that Moses speaks phenomenally in recording the creation of the luminaries on the fourth day,—that what we are meant to understand by the fiat of that day (" Let there be lights in the firmament of the heaven to divide the day from the night; and let them be for signs, and for seasons, and for days, and years "), is "*the summoning into view* of the two great luminaries," whose orbs had been hitherto obscured by the aqueous vapour which enwrapped the earth, and *the assigning new functions to them* in connexion with man. As to the difficulty of supposing "the successive stages of Creation to occupy each one single day," Burgon has nothing to reply but what reduces itself to this (and the author holds the reply to be amply sufficient), "Why not, if Almighty GOD willed it? And in this case He tells us by pure Revelation (pure in recording what there had been no human witness of) that He *did* will it."

As for the account of the Creative Week being the story of a vision, he takes up strong ground when he points out (p. 16) that "although to His prophets GOD did sometimes make Himself known in a vision, or spoke to them in a dream, He 'spake unto Moses face to face, *as a man speaketh unto his friend*'" (Exod. xxxiii. 11; Num. xii. 6, 7, 8), and that Moses's authorship of the Pentateuch is vouched for by our LORD Himself (St. John v. 46, 47). And thus [p. 12],—

"I insist on taking everything in this Chapter of Genesis *quite literally*. I cannot even suffer it to be called a poem or a psalm. It is neither. The Book of Job claims the former title, to be sure; the 104th Psalm is 'a Psalm of Creation' indeed. But Genesis i. is very severe, very unadorned prose. It purports to be, and it undoubtedly is, history in the strictest sense: *revealed* history, and therefore *true* history. It claims to be, and it certainly is, the history of six ordinary *Days*."

Professor Pritchard had not denied the Days to be ordinary days. Nay, one of the objections which he alleged proceeded (as we have seen) on the assumption that they *were* ordinary days. But "not a few eminent persons holding a widely different opinion, and choosing to assume that in this place 'Six Days' must mean six indefinitely long periods of time," Burgon deals with this assumption in the Postscript to his '*Reply*, May 11th, 1886, nearly three months after the Reply itself, which is dated Feb. 13. While not denying that "the word Day is sometimes employed in Scripture (as in the familiar speech of mankind) with metaphorical license," he points out that the understanding of the days literally is necessitated by our being informed 1. that GOD called the light *Day*, and the Darkness *Night*, 2. by the fact that each one of these Days (except the Seventh) "comes before us furnished with its own evening and morning"; and 3. by the reason assigned in the Fourth Commandment for the sanctification of the Sabbath. In the remainder of the Postscript, he leaves the pre-historic period—that is, the period prior to "the Creative Week which happened nearly 6000 years ago"—to the Geologist and Palæontologist. "The Natural Philosopher is the historian of prehistoric time, the interpreter of its obscure records" [p. 21], and when he is in his own sphere, Burgon is

ready to "listen to his teaching with the profoundest interest, and receive his lawful decrees with the most submissive deference.' "Scripture reveals nothing concerning the universe during the prehistoric period, except the fact that GOD was its Creator."
showing how completely the doctrine of man's being the product of EVOLUTION is put out of court by the Revelation of the Great Creative Week.

It must have been in the October or November of this year (1886) that the incident occurred which Mr. Herman C. Hoskier mentions in the first sentence of the Preface to his very valuable '*Full and Collation of the Greek Cursive Codex Evangelium* 604' [David Nutt, 270 Strand, MDCCCXC].

"Three and a half years ago I was in Dean Burgon' study at Chichester. It was midnight, dark and cold without; he had just extinguished the lights, and it was dark, and getting cold within. We mounted the stairs to retire to rest, and his last words of that night have often rung in my ears since: 'As surely as it is dark now, and as certainly as the sun will rise to-morrow morning, so surely will the traditional text be vindicated, and the views I have striven to express be accepted. I may not live to see it. Most likely I shall not. But it will come.' . . . . .

"Dean Burgon has passed away," continues Mr. Hoskier, "out and beyond the region and sphere of imperfection. His *Magnum Opus*, had he lived to edit it, would have for ever vindicated his reputation, his views, his methods, nay, the very manner of expressing himself, if by a too decided front he had made himself enemies, and curtailed the extent of his hearing for a time. A misjudged man by many, as hard a worker as any, as generous and true a heart as any brother could desire, his name, his efforts, his labours will still be revered. And in the near future shall we not blame ourselves for being so blind and so prejudiced, so narrow and so human, as not to be able truly in an even balance to weigh real merits and demerits, real work against mere speculation, sincere investigation against imperfect and hasty conclusions? '*It will come.*'"

Mr. Hoskier's valuable contribution to Textual Criticism is inscribed to Dean Burgon's memory.

The correspondence subjoined to this year's record between Burgon and Mr. Arrowsmith of Fillongley, shows how the question of the Days being long periods of time of indefinite length had been brought under his notice. The letter, in which Lord Selborne acknowledges his pamphlet on the First Chapter of Genesis, indicates decided disagreement with him as to the necessity of understanding the Days literally. The author is grateful for the permission to publish this letter (which is granted to him with the assurance that Lord Selborne has " not at all changed the opinions expressed in it"), not only on account of the eminence of the writer, and his well-known character for sound and well-balanced judgment and for orthodoxy, but also because the publication is an act of justice to those who take a different view from that of Burgon, with whom the author entirely concurs.

The Holy Scriptures, whether in their interpretation, or in the criticism of the text, were Burgon's favourite and, towards the end of his life, his absorbing and all-engrossing study and field of labour; but he had paid much attention to the Prayer Book also; and he put forth in the course of this year two Sermons (preached at Chichester Cathedral on the two Sundays preceding the Advent of 1885) on "The Structure and Method of the Book of Common Prayer." In the first of these he points out how the structure of the Book is determined by "the course and order of the Christian seasons," and again how this course and order had been outlined beforehand by the Three Great Festivals of the Jewish Church. In the second he points out how the daily Morning and Evening Offices are framed upon the model of the Lord's Prayer,—Praise in the first section of them, Prayer in the second (the penitential introduction in both of them being merely the porch of entrance to the Service itself), and what is the theory of the sequence of the Psalms, Lessons, Canticles, Creed, and the significance of each of these constituents of the Office. The Tract containing these two Sermons was published under the direction of the Tract Committee of the S.P.C.K.

TO MRS. CHARLES PAGE EDEN ON THE DEATH OF HER HUSBAND.

"The Deanery, Chichester,
"Feb. 23, 1886.

"My dear Mrs. Eden,—I will not delay to thank you for your nice letter, every word of which seems to me to go straight from your heart to mine. I see the Rectory in the red light of that last frosty dawn,—and know well the *tightness* about the chest—and the mist of tears—and the strange sorrow,—and the confused images,—sweet, sad, tender: and the sense that a landmark has been passed—and that a fresh beginning has to be made. . . . Read carefully over Numbers ix. 15–23, and believe that the cloud which led you forth on that day, will prove a cheerful flame of fire to you by night.

"It was because I divined that you must be on the wing that I did not write to you before. I am off to London (to give four Lectures), and shall not be back till

Saturday. But immediately after my return, I will send you back the Sermon and something else I have had prepared for you. Be quite at your ease about the 4 volumes. *They are as safe as they can be*, and to make *any* use of them, I must have them by me for a few weeks. I am very busy, and can only spare the odd moments of my time.

"You are right about your dear husband's Sermons. *About* 30 (not more than 50) should be carefully selected from the mass—and published within a year, if possible, of his death. Call the volume '*Aberford Sermons*'; (it will distinguish it from the legion of volumes put forth under similar circumstances); and if you are afraid of the expense, publish by subscription. . . . I respectfully advise you to begin by jotting down *from memory* the name, text, times (or by whatever other way you can identify a Sermon) of *every Sermon which struck yourself most*, or which friends *have told you of*, as having affected them. The rest must be done by a careful (who must also be a competent) editor. Every Sermon should have a title. The Sermon you sent me to read, for example, should be entitled, 'THE FAITHFUL DEPARTED, AT REST.'

"I could not undertake to help in the selection; but I would undertake (if wished) to read over the proof sheets, and indicate the title for the Sermon.

"*Do not let this matter sleep.* It is now or never. We live so fast that 5 years hence (if any of us are alive so long) there will be little curiosity and no enthusiasm.

"Thank you for your kind expressions about the little Memoir[2]. You will be far better pleased with it, if God spares his servant till the close of the year. I beg to be remembered to Alice, and am ever,

"My dear Mrs. Eden,

"Affectionately yours,

"J. W. B."

---

[2] The Memoir of the Rev. Charles Page Eden in '*The Guardian*,' afterwards revised and enlarged, and published as one of '*The Lives of Twelve Good Men.*'

FROM THE REVEREND ROBERT ARROWSMITH, OF FILLONG-
LEY, NEAR COVENTRY, TO THE VERY REVEREND THE
DEAN OF CHICHESTER.

"The Moor House, Fillongley, near Coventry,

"Feb. 27, 1886.

"My dear Sir,—As an old Oriel man, I may perhaps be excused if I take the liberty of writing to you and conveying to you my thanks for your admirable notice in '*The Guardian*' of the late Mr. Eden, which has revived so many pleasant reminiscences;—nor are thanks less due to you for your protest against that extraordinary view of the Creation, which has been aired by Professor Pritchard in the same newspaper, and which in one of the Periodicals of the day has been described as 'so beautiful.' It is high time that some one spoke out on the other side. But may I venture to ask a question? You consider the six days of the Creation to have been natural days—from sunrise (or sunset) to sunrise: —Are we bound to understand the word 'day' in that sense? To me it seems that whatever meaning is attached to the word 'day' in Gen. ii. 2—'God rested on the seventh day'—the same meaning must attach to the word in the preceding Chapter. Can this meaning be that God's resting day continued twenty-four hours and no longer? My own long-cherished opinion has been that God's Seventh Day commenced after man had been made in His image, and is still going on, and will continue to the end of time. When His noblest work was done—when the crown was put on the arch—He ceased to create: and thenceforth nothing remained but for the work itself to develope and multiply according to the law of its being, and for God to superintend and regulate the whole. Nor does this interpretation turn the narrative into a poem. The word 'day' is used frequently in Holy Scripture, and in our ordinary conversation, with very considerable latitude. For instance, our Lord says that Abraham desired to see 'His Day'; and we often speak of the 'day' of adversity,—which is not seldom prolonged in God's wisdom to a very considerable length,—sometimes a lifetime. If, then, it is allowable to understand the word 'day' in this larger signification, and if God's Sabbath is an extended period, then it seems necessary to hold that the other six days are extended periods. And perhaps, as there is symmetry in all God's works and ways, we may be permitted to believe that the seven days are equal periods of immense duration, and that when the seventh has reached the limit of each of the other six, then the end will come. But Dr. Reville, I see, affirms that if the days of creation were periods of vast length, they could not support an argument that men should work for six days and rest on the seventh. It is on the supposition, he says, that the days were similar to our own that the commandment about the Sabbath is based. I fail to recognise the force of the reasoning. I can see no flaw in my contention,—nothing at variance with common sense,—in saying that as God worked during six periods (each of which had an 'evening' or close), and rested on the seventh (which as yet has had no evening), so He required man to labour during six (natural) days, and to rest for a seventh of his time. . . . . . . I am afraid you will think me somewhat presumptuous in writing to so eminent a scholar, the minnow to the dolphin; but perhaps my Oriel connexion may cover my presumption. . . . . .

"With best wishes, I remain,
"Yours faithfully,
"ROBERT ARROWSMITH."

TO THE REVEREND ROBERT ARROWSMITH.

"The Deanery, Chichester, 1886.

"Dear Arrowsmith,—After thanking you for your kind letter, I will at once—(though *very* busy)—answer your questions. If Pritchard's doubts had been yours, I should not have turned aside to notice them. Those who think that they can receive Gen. i. faithfully—as the work of the Holy Ghost—the very word of God—

and yet explain the days of Creation as long tracts of Time,—may do so, for aught that I care. I think them illogical—mistaken—queer—what you will. I will never accept their view—nor suffer them to deliver it in my presence, without protest. But I will not pursue them with argument, nor go out of my way to condemn their teaching.

"Since however you ask me, I will tell you *why* I cannot for an instant admit your explanation of Gen. i.

"And it is enough that I should show *you* why 'the meaning attached to the word "day"'' in Gen. ii. 2, is NOT 'the meaning attached to the word in the preceding chapter.'

"*The seventh day is described differently from the preceding six days.* The plain facts of the case are that six days—each consisting of 'evening' and 'morning'—are discoursed of. Each has its *work* described. They come to an end at last. The seventh day arrives, and the work of Creation is discontinued. God RESTS therefore—rests from His creative labours. Man, accordingly, when *his* seventh day comes, must rest from *his* work and his labours. In twenty-four hours *another week begins for man*; and therefore a renewed obligation.

"But with the Eternal God it is not so. *The necessity of the case* has introduced, with regard to *Him*, a prolonged period (if one may say such things without profanity of God!) of cessation from creative agency.

"But this discovery is not to invalidate the antecedent narrative. True it is, that *perforce* the 'seventh day' spoken of in Gen. ii. 2 was a day of twenty-four hours like any other—that is, the earth revolved once on its axis, as on each of the preceding six days, but what *then*? By *significantly withdrawing the mention of 'evening' and 'morning*,' the author of Scripture intimates that the Divine rest is NOT *a rest of twenty-four hours*. Now do you understand?   "Yours,
    "JOHN W. BURGON.

"Note that ἀπολείπεται σαββατισμὸς τῷ λαῷ τοῦ Θεοῦ.

"I do not know who you mean by 'Dr. Reville.' But he is quite right."

LIFE OF DEAN BURGON.

TO THE VERY REVEREND THE DEAN OF NORWICH.

"The Deanery, Chichester,
"Easter Eve, 1886.

" My very dear Friend,—I must break through what I feel to be a galling bondage, on this blessed day, in order that the best of all days may bring you a few affectionate lines from me. How it has happened that I have maintained silence so long, I cannot explain, seeing that I have been a letter, if not two letters, in your debt throughout.

'But how the silence *began*, I well remember. It was because your letter about childhood and children touched me so deeply that I felt it deserved an extraordinary reply. I was at that very instant *extraordinarily busy*; and you can divine the rest. To-morrow promised to repair the omission; but to-morrow never came. *Then* I grew ashamed—and sorry; and at last I am quite perplexed at myself; and nothing but a deep conviction of your Christian nature would encourage me to believe confidently that you will forgive me, when I have explained that I know I am very guilty, and that I am very sorry to possess that knowledge.

"Very little to the purpose is it to explain that I have had a constant pressure of work throughout. The pressure of work does not prevent one, for weeks together, from writing a letter to a dear friend.

"To begin then, I must acknowledge with a full heart that I never knew *any* one who more fully felt with *me*, on the subject of children and childhood.

" And next, I must say how greatly gratified I am—or rather we all are—by your appreciation of our darling little chap[3]. Truly he seems to me well worthy of being loved and cared for. A more original child I never knew, or a more endearing one. He lives in a world of his own; corresponds with all the crowned heads of Europe; regulates provinces; quells outbreaks; threatens

---

[3] The son of the Rev. Hugh James Rose, Jun., Burgon's nephew, who had died July 6, 1878. (See the record of that year.) The "little chap," therefore, was Burgon's great nephew.

and punishes insurgents in every part of the world. But, what is not least absurd, after giving the Emperor of Russia his orders, he leaves the document on the drawing-room table, and is carried off to bed. When he was with us in the winter, I found the enclosed strange *State Paper* one night, after the house was quiet, and was so tickled that I remember putting it among my papers for you.

"Willy, who dotes upon him and is teaching him Latin, often sends us his '*last*.' The enclosed exercises will make you smile......

"Well,—there! I have scribbled off the letter I have been so long wishing to write, and only regret that it has been a scribble. But I wish it to reach you on Easter Day, and the post will soon be going. With love to your better half,

"Ever your very affectionate friend,
"JOHN W. BURGON."

To MRS. ——— ———

"Turvey Abbey, May 2, 1886.

"Now for your question. I do not say that liberality and covetousness go hand in hand—or anything of the sort. Such a position would be utterly false. I do but say that lavish expenditure is *quite consistent with*—often is accompanied by—inordinate greed.

"A Latin writer says of a bad man—that he was 'alieni appetens, sui profusus,' which hits off the character in 4 words;—covetous of what was his neighbour's—lavish in squandering away his own.* . . . . The very *supply* is obtained by such an one for his own wasteful expenditure—by grasping at anything which comes in his way, and to which he has no lawful claim. Have I made myself clear?

"I spent all yesterday at Hendon, and saw my friend Scrivener, and a whole host of new faces. I also found myself recognised strangely by old Oxford men and others, and was reminded of several remarks I have often had occasion to make before;—as, (1) How much kindness there is in the world; and (2) how much graceful hospitality;—(3) how agreeable womankind is everywhere;—then (4) how there seems to be a perpetual succession of graceful forms, and enchanting features, and sweet voices. Well then, (5) what a strong family likeness there is among mankind, so that the same types are everywhere discoverable. And next, (6) that the world is after all a very small place, and that every one —somehow—seems to know everybody. Further, (7) that folks are *pious at bottom*—all the world over. And then, (8) that children are always enchanting. You would have laughed to see my departure from Hendon. One little girl (eight years old) would see me off; so she went with me alone — stood on the bench till the train came up, with *her arm round my neck*. And the last words were, 'You will let me have a letter from you on Monday—won't you?' 'Well, we'll see.' 'No; promise!' 'Very well then; I *will* write to you.' 'And about once a fortnight afterwards?' 'Oh! no, no, you little flea! nothing of the sort! so good-bye!!' There was something so ridiculous in the transaction—faint shadows of things that happened 100 years ago [4]—that I was greatly tickled, and said to myself on reviewing the whole day,—'Life does but reproduce itself! the child is father to the man!'"

To HIS SISTER, MRS. HIGGINS [*on the first anniversary of her birthday after her husband's death*].

"The Deanery, Chichester,
"May 27, 1886.

"My darling * * * *"—[a family *sobriquet* for Mrs. Higgins],—"I am down before the world; have opened my shutters, and planted myself at my desk; and *before I do anything else*, I will send you a few words of loving kindness on the return of a day which, as long as I can remember, has been precious to us all. I trust it may be a

[4] Probably he means reminiscences of his little sister Kitty in his early days, and her way of behaving to him.

The Chichester Life.

day of peace and joy to you : a day of sunshine also; for we have been sitting under weeping skies till I declare I feel the effect upon my spirits. There is every reason why the day *should* be thus peaceful and joyous to you; for the memory of the past and the prospect of the future, are alike full of blessedness, through God's mercies to us in Christ. Remembered in the place of peace, you are *sure* to be to-morrow; for I will never believe that the memories of earth are sponged out *there*. Rather will I believe that they are quickened as well as sanctified, and result in ministrations of love to ourselves, not unfrequently. Certain at all events it is (and it is best to keep separate what one *hopes* and what one *knows*), certain, I say, it is that he, dear sainted spirit, is in the enjoyment of rare felicity and the blissful anticipation of yet greater accessions of joy. It is delightful to think of such a one as he, translated into the fruition of his faithful hope, and in the society of the saints gone before, in whose footsteps he trod, and whose examples he cherished, and with whom he longed so devoutly to be. God bless you *both*; for the bond is not severed by death, though the hearts are parted for a while.

"I am glad you have been able to look over the dear fellow's letters and papers. It is a sacred duty,—too often neglected or performed in a senseless hurried way......

"You must have had quite a plague of waters for the brook to have overflowed its banks,—a very unusual thing 'surely' in May!......

"I congratulate you upon your lodger's[5] having come back. I much wish the birds would take up their quarters more freely with me. They come to be fed freely enough, but where they go for their lodgings, I have no idea. I am indeed just now too busy even to speculate, being ankle-deep in my Memoir of Hugh James Rose. I devoutly long to get all done, and to see the volume out, and to be able to turn to my proper work, which is Scripture. In a day or two I will send you, D.V., a pamphlet of mine on Genesis i., and wish I

---

[5] A swallow building in the porch at Turvey Abbey.

could send it as a *symbol* of a birthday offering. But I have nothing to send you that you would care to accept, except my love, to-day.

"Believe me ever, my Darling,

"Your loving Brother,

"J. W. B."

To Mrs.

"The Deanery, Chichester,

"June 2, 1886.

"My dear kind Friend,—Surely, Ascension Day should bring you a letter from me; for a more glorious Day is not to be found in the Church's year, and with it shall come a copy of the Pamphlet[6] which has occupied a great deal of my time and thought of late. Read it from end to end—at twice; and tell me if you quite understand and like it. I live a wondrous quiet life as you know; and as I *see nothing* scarcely of periodical literature, and converse with scarcely anybody, I cannot be said to *know* what the world is thinking, feeling, believing. But whenever a throb of the great human pulse reaches me, I am shocked to find in how many respects the body politic seems to be in an unhealthy state. To mention only two matters—I find *unbelief* rampant; and I find a *Romanising* sentiment on the increase. The latter I feel I must tackle with soon. With the former I have tackled in these thirty pages.

"In the meantime I am getting on with my Memoir of Hugh James Rose, and reading through Cardinal Newman's letters, written in 1833-4-5 and so on. O how I long to be at *Scripture* again—and to be free to work on steadily at it!

"You give me a most graphic picture of your past as well as of your present. Yes, the contrast of feeling

---

[6] His Reply to Professor Pritchard's '*Creation Proem of Genesis*,' which appeared first in the '*Guardian*,' but was afterwards reprinted in a separate form.

which old scenes set before the memory and the imagination is saddening—exceedingly: especially as it is ever attended by the consciousness that all who made up those ancient *tableaux* are in the unseen world—severed from us by an impassable barrier. Then, there invariably supervenes the thought of one's *own* immortality—and so the lonely walk becomes a very lonely business indeed.

"But I incline to the belief that such meditations are salutary: and there really does supervene a sense of resignation, which is rather to be called a conviction, that it is best to be growing—or *grown*—old, and to be moving off the scene. May we not also both say with truth that the predominating thought is one of gratitude for the goodness which has watched over one so lovingly, repaired so many of the losses in a very lovely way—and reserved to one the enjoyment of so many of Heaven's best gifts, as, health of mind and body—a living faith,—the society of very sweet and dear beings—but how can I enumerate them all? the time would fail me. I am sure I carry about with me a *very* thankful heart. And so, I know, do you. Moreover *you* know one of *my* best Friends—and *I* know one of *yours*.

"Be assured, that if life is spared to me, and the sad necessity should arise, I shall not be wanting to you. I am concerned to think that you should have been made so *very* uncomfortable... Last Sunday seemed hardly Sabbatical without *you* .....

"The garden does really begin to look very lovely. We are *potted out* in every direction—possible and impossible. Colour is showing in every quarter. And this heavy rain and warmth is causing everything to grow visibly—and to grow wondrous green.

"You will think of us at 5 o'clock on Sunday, I know, but in fact we think and talk of you every day......

"Believe me, ever your most affectionate,

"J. W. B."

LIFE OF DEAN BURGON.

FROM THE EARL OF SELBORNE TO THE VERY REV. THE DEAN OF CHICHESTER.

"Blackmoor, Petersfield,

"August 17, 1886.

" Dear Dean Burgon,—I am afraid I have been ungrateful in not sooner thanking you for your thoughts on the first chapter of Genesis.

"In what you say about the Sun and Moon [7], I must entirely agree. But why you should object, on the same principle, to understand *days*, and 'evenings' and 'mornings,' of periodic times of any length whatever (which must each have had their opening and their close), I do *not* understand. To me, the facts of Geology appear to point in that direction, as, to both of us, the facts of Astronomy exclude Professor Pritchard's too narrow literalism about the Fourth Day's work. Nor do I find any difficulty in supposing three long periods, before the vapoury covering of the earth was dissipated sufficiently to enable the heavenly bodies to be *seen*. We have, even under the present conditions of our atmosphere, many days and nights when they are quite invisible, though *light* still reaches us.

"Even less than as to the other days, do I see any difficulty as to the *seventh*,—representing the period after the work was done, which is not said to have had 'evening' or 'morning'; and of which the sanctification of every seventh ordinary day of twelve hours is the Memorial and *quasi*-Sacrament to us.

"The *manner* of the Revelation of that order of Creation which, as it preceded man, could only be known to man by Revelation, is *not* itself revealed; and, as it is certain that *some* of the Divine revelations to man have been by *visions*, it has always seemed to me (since I read a Christian book on Geology, which suggested it), that it is most probable that this was so. And, on that suppo-

---

[7] That what we are to understand by "God made two great lights" [Gen. i. 16] is, not that the lights were *created*, but that they were *caused to appear*, on the Fourth Day.

sition, there can be nothing more likely or more congruous (however long the periods of time), than the description of what was seen, under such language as we have in the Chapter, 'days,' 'evenings,' and 'mornings.' The question with me always is, not whether the words of Scripture-Revelations are true, but *what do they mean?* And to insist upon literalism is, often, the very most unlikely way of arriving at their true meaning....

"Believe me ever, my dear Dean,
"Yours truly,
"SELBORNE."

To MRS. ——————

"Deanery, Aug. 29, 1886.

"Yesterday was the 50th anniversary (is it possible?) of a death of which I shall now certainly carry the scar to my grave—a beloved little sister—the first death in the family!

"How deep some sorrows seem to lie!—the sweetness of that little one passes speech. She was also most tenderly attached to *me*—and her departure when seven-and-a-half years old, left a gap in our circle which nothing could make up for—or enable us to speak of, one to another, with resignation: 'I shall go to her—but she will not return to me.' I still keep her little toys in a drawer!"

To MRS. —————— ——

"Turvey Abbey, Sept. 16, 1886.

"Yesterday was an *event* with us. And what do you suppose the event consisted of? Walking over the fields (and losing our way) in order to repair to the Reformatory—some two miles off—to witness the yearly distribution of prizes. It has always been a very cheerful day in these parts,—bringing together the neighbouring gentry and clergy—and culminating in rustic games and a pleasant tea-party—where everything but the tea and sugar have been contributed by the boys. They farm many acres of spade-husbandry, have annual crops,—and produce a loaf of the first fruits which would fill a wheelbarrow . . . . . The moral pleasure is of course the charm.

"There are fifty boys, who would else be in gaol, or on their way thither, *earning* their bread (for the Reformatory is *self-supporting*)—learning husbandry, cared for and loved,—in excellent health (for the Reformatory stands on a breezy eminence) and a blessing to their kind. About twenty money prizes have been instituted—(for skill on the farm—kindness to animals—punctuality in going errands—reading Scripture, and learning it by heart—reaping, baking, cooking, &c., &c.) money is all put to their account. A general *good conduct* prize is attainable by any one. On going out the money is given them in a lump sum—and they begin the world—or *can* begin it—with some pounds in hand . . . . . Finding every kind of virtue and praise pre-occupied, *I* instituted a poetry recitation prize, and it has become the most (indeed the *only*) entertaining feature of the performance. Yesterday we had 'The Burial of Sir John Moore,' and 'The Dog and the Water Lily.' . . . . Of course, I go up and rehearse the boys, alone, the day before; but of a truth, the cleverness with which they seized the points—imitated my manner—and tried to copy my tones—was admirable. The ladies rewarded them with applause enough to turn an actor's brain.

"Yes, you are quite right. A very singular note it is of God's goodness, power, wisdom in creation that with the ability—he should withdraw from us the strong desire—to do what we once did. I grow more and more thoughtful, as I grow older—and am more and more struck with God's goodness in Creation,—wisdom in Providence—mysteriousness in all His ways. But above all, the mysteriousness of *His Word* strikes me. I like to think that it strikes *you* likewise. And here one has the great consolation of knowing that all one fails to fathom in this life, will—by His great mercy and undeserved favour—be revealed to us fully in the next."

To Mrs. ——— ———
"Turvey Abbey,
"St. Matthew's Day, 1886.

"How strange, by the way, it is that little children should have such a marvellous knack of entwining their little selves around one's heart—and not only so, but (in a manner) of prolonging our interest in life! a most Divine provision truly it is: for else we should be indifferent to the future, whereas,—for their sakes—we look forward anxiously to it,—and are willing to make what provision we can *for* it. I suppose it is all the outcome of a longing for immortality; whereby we bear unconscious witness to our own indestructibility. But oh! if the next 50 years are to be as prolific in discoveries and inventions as the last, what a different place this world will be in 1950! I suspect that intercourse between distant countries will be conducted by the telephone;—that the Queen will hear the debates in the House, or listen to a song at the Opera, as she pleases. Bed-ridden Christians will hear the Sermon in Church by a tube fastened to the bed-post; and luxurious folks in the country will listen to a play without undergoing the trouble of a journey to London, and a visit to the theatre. . . . . locomotion will also be by electricity, and the town will be lighted up by a device for which science has not yet invented a name.

"Pleasant it is—to you and to me—to think that when all these wonders take place, the Church Catechism will still contain the whole sum of faith and practice, and the blessed Book of Books will be the selfsame unfathomed well, from which men will draw the Water of Life for the sustentation of their souls throughout the days of their pilgrimage, and for their support under affliction, and for their comfort in the hour of death."

1887.

Professor Pritchard had, as we have seen, opened the question as to the historical character of the Mosaic record of the days of Creation. Other thoughtful and able divines were not slow to follow in the path of speculation on that First Chapter of Genesis. In the 'Contemporary Review' of October, 1886, there appeared an Article on "The Week of Seven Days," from the pen of an eminent Prelate of the Northern Province, affirming—in a much less conjectural tone than Professor Pritchard had assumed,—that "the literal theory" (the understanding, that is, of the narrative as a literal record of facts) "*must be simply and completely given up*, as in the very nature of things impossible." The impossibility (or one chief impossibility) of the literal theory resided, according to the writer of the Article, in the necessary inadequacy of the faculties of a newly created man to "comprehend so refined and comparatively complicated an arrangement as the division of time by weeks, and the keeping of a Sabbath." As to the ground alleged for the observance of the Sabbath in the *Exodus* Version of the Fourth Commandment, he called attention to the absence of that clause from the *Deuteronomy* Version of the same precept (v. 14, 15), and seemed to incline to the hypothesis of Ewald, that the clause had formed no part of the original commandment. And as to the real origin of the week of Seven Days, he supposed that, "so far from being of Divine institution, it took its rise from the physical fact that seven planetary bodies are visible to the naked eye," and thought it probable that the Israelites derived the knowledge of the seven day week from the Egyptians, by whom he inferred from a passage in Dion Cassius that such a week was recognised. At all events the Babylonians appear very early to have had a seven day week, and thus the Jews might have been led to adopt such a week in the Babylonian Captivity.—Of course speculations like these drew out Burgon's strenuous and uncompromising opposition. In two Articles in the '*Guardian*,' which appeared respectively Jan. 5 and Jan. 12, 1887, though written in the November and December of the preceding year, he, after waiting a few weeks to see whether some more qualified champion would not come into the field, replied to the argument which had appeared in the '*Contemporary Review*.' As to Adam's incapacity to have comprehended, immediately after his creation, the sevenfold division of time, and the sacredness of the Sabbath, which was bound up with that sevenfold division, he takes the ground with which Holy Scripture furnishes him, and which therefore is unassailable, that Adam having given names (characteristic ones no doubt) to the lower creatures, and having, after the creation of Eve, spoken under Inspiration the words by which Matrimony was ordained, must have been created both a Philosopher and a Prophet, and have been fully competent therefore to comprehend the Revelation made to him as to the divisions of Time and the sacredness of the Seventh Day. On referring to an expert in Egyptology, he learned that the Egyptians, at the early date of the Exodus, had no knowledge of seven day weeks at all, but only of months of thirty days, divided into three decades. And on referring to persons learned in Babylonian and Assyrian lore, he was apprised of three essential differences between the seven day week of the Babylonians and that of the Hebrews, making it improbable that the latter was borrowed from the former.—But the objection having been insinuated that, if the week of seven days and the institution of the

Sabbath were in truth (as the Book of Genesis represents them to have been) co-eval with the very beginning of human history, they must have been familiar to the Antediluvian Patriarchs, and that there is no conclusive evidence that they were so familiar,—in a second Article in the '*Guardian*,' which appeared Jan. 12 of this year, Burgon addressed himself to this objection, and from a close study of the sacred narrative of the Deluge (Gen. vii. 4 *to* viii. 14), with its many notes of time, so evidently studied and meant to be emphasized, drew out a Calendar of the Flood, from which he thinks that "no one of fair mind will hesitate to admit that a case has been at last made out for the Sabbath as a recognised institution in the days of Noah." While it may be freely admitted to have been an intellectual weakness of Burgon's, of which we have seen several previous instances, that the strength of his convictions on a particular subject always outran the premises on which his conclusion was formed, it is certain that in this last paper, for which he claims originality, he has made out a very strong case indeed for the acquaintance of the Antediluvians with the seven day week and the Sabbath. It is thought best to submit the whole paper to the reader *in extenso* in the Appendix [see Appendix D], only adding here the testimony of the Rev. John Forbes. D.D., Emeritus Professor of Oriental Languages in the University of Aberdeen, appended to his recent '*Commentary on The Servant of the Lord in Isaiah* xl. *to* lxvi.— *reclaiming that passage to Isaiah as its author from Argument, Structure, and Date.*' [T. and T. Clark: Edinburgh.]

"I cannot refrain here from drawing attention to a most remarkable discovery made by my friend the late Dean Burgon, which he communicated in two papers to the '*Guardian*,' the first dated Jan. 5 and the second Jan.

12th, 1887. I wrote to him immediately to say that I hoped he would put his discovery in a more permanent form before the public, as it had an importance immeasurably greater than he seemed aware of, as not merely proving his point against the Bishop of Carlisle,—the Divine Origin of the Week of Seven Days,—but demonstratively proving the Divine origin of the entire narrative of the Deluge, and refuting the most plausible of the objections that have been adduced against the truth and genuineness of the Pentateuchal legends, as they have been styled. The objections against the Deluge narrative have been paraded as furnishing demonstrative evidence of its absurdity and inconsistency. It has been represented as made up of two independent and contradictory accounts, an Elohistic and a Jehovistic document, the first of which represents the Flood to have lasted about 54 days, and the other 150. Dean Burgon in a Calendar of the Deluge shows that all the important events, Noah's entering and leaving the Ark, the commencement and abatement of the flood of waters, the resting of the Ark on the mountains of Ararat, the various sendings out of the birds, &c.,—nine events in all,—took place on one and the same day of the week, which could have been effected by Divine appointment alone, and that the time Noah was in the Ark amounted to exactly 365 days [8].

"The Deluge narrative (vi. 9 *to* ix. 20) which (after the introductory fundamental ordination of the Sabbath in Chap. i. ii. 3, claiming and consecrating man and his six days' work for the worship of his Creator) forms the third and central member of the beautifully and symmetrically arranged 10 documents, beginning each, 'These are the generations of,' which constitute Genesis, and illustrates remarkably the distinctive use of the two names Elohim and Jehovah.

---

[8] There is a slight deviation here from the calculations in Burgon's paper. What he points out is, that "*from the commencement of the Flood* until the day when Noah left the Ark, was a period of exactly 365 days." But Noah had been in the Ark (though not yet "shut in") seven days before the Flood commenced, as he also shows.

"Bishop Colenso has unwittingly done great service by the analysis he gives of the Elohistic and Jehovistic passages in Genesis, in Part V. of his '*Pentateuch*.' He has brought out the remarkable fact that Jehovah is the Name (never Elohim) uniformly employed where *sin* is the subject, e.g. the Fall, Cain killing Abel, &c., and secondly, wherever an altar or sacrificial offering is in question. This, though Colenso failed to draw the logical inference from the premisses, proves that Elohim refers to God's natural attributes alone (Power, Wisdom), whereas Jehovah (while not excluding the other) refers more specially to his moral attributes (Righteousness, Mercy, Retributive Judgments) as the God of Redemption.

"This, as I have said, furnishes at once the rule for the use of the two Names throughout Genesis, and explains their interchange in the Noachic document. Elohim, as the Giver and Disposer of Life, is the prevailing Name. Jehovah takes its place where, as the Covenant God of Noah, 'Jehovah shuts him in' [vii. 16]. It is Elohim who commands to take of the animals '*two* of every sort' [vi. 19, 20]; but Jehovah, when sacrifice is in view, commands to take of the 'clean beasts and fowls by sevens' (vii. 1 *to* 3), and so when he offers them in sacrifice (viii. 20). The contrast too is very marked in ix. 26, 'Blessed be Jehovah, the God of Shem'; but 'Elohim shall enlarge Japheth.'"

We must not omit to add that in a third paper, which appeared in the '*Guardian*' of Feb. 9, 1887, Burgon "disposed of certain critical objections" which his two previous "essays had elicited."

From the two short letters to the Rev. H. M. Ingram of Southover, near Lewes, which are appended to the record of this year, it will be seen that his two articles in the '*Guardian*' awakened not only hostile criticism in certain quarters, but cordial sympathy in others, and that he entertained a design (never unhappily carried into effect) of enlarging them, and publishing them as a pamphlet in a separate form.

We now approach the last of Burgon's many controversial publications; and vividly does the author recall the occasion on which he first became aware that such a publication was about to be made. Being in London on one of the last Sundays in the Lent of 1887, and seeing that Burgon was advertised to preach at the Chapel Royal, Whitehall, he attended the service there, and at the close of it went into the vestry to greet the preacher, and found him, as ever, enthusiastically responsive to words of friendship and affection. Passing out of the Chapel we came upon a lady, who had belonged to one of his Bible Classes in Oxford, had come a long way to hear him, and was waiting with her husband for a few kind words of recognition from him, which he gave her effusively, showing that he remembered every particular about her. This interview, to which he seemed to give his whole mind for the moment, concluded, the author accompanied him to St. Martin's Rectory, where he was staying for the night; but scarcely had he done with his reminiscences, and enquiries, and adieux to the lady, than in a tone grotesquely contrasted with that in which he had been speaking hitherto, he burst in full cry upon the very objectionable paper by Canon Fremantle, which had recently appeared in the '*Fortnightly Review*,' and which he said the Editor had invited him to answer. He had already written his answer, though it had not yet appeared, and the scandal caused to the Church by the appearance of such a paper from the pen of a dignitary, and the necessity of protesting loud and long against the (so-called) New Reformation, which the "changed conditions of Theology" were (according to the writer of the paper) bringing about, so strongly excited him in the course of that short walk, that the author sought and found an opportunity to divert him from this burning question to another and calmer topic. Striking and sudden was the contrast between Burgon in the affectionateness of old reminiscences, and Burgon in his rabid controversial vein,—so striking that he who witnessed it can never forget it. As to his "Reply to Canon Fremantle," which appeared in the *Fortnightly Review* shortly afterwards [9], while it must be admitted that his usual controversial faults of passionateness and scolding are exaggerated in it (the intensely hard work of concluding, amidst so many other engagements, the *Lives of Twelve Good Men*,' had evidently told upon him, lowered his physique, and weakened his power of self-control), it should also be borne in mind that the greatest possible provocation had been given in the *Fortnightly* Article to all who loved and clung to the old Faith, as taught in the Bible and Prayer Book, and that Burgon exhibited in his Reply a crowning specimen of that burning zeal for GOD's truth, and that splendid uncompromising intrepidity and outspokenness, which characterized all his controversial efforts. It was the blood of the old Austrian grandfather, who stood single-handed in the porch of St. Polycarp's Church, and told Osman Digma, at the head of his Turkish soldiers, that, if he passed into the sacred precincts, it should be over his own dead body. Who is there among us in these degenerate days, when the religious opinions of people are held to be a matter of such supreme indifference, that is

---

[9] THE NEW REFORMATION.—"Theology under its changed conditions:"—A Reply to Canon Fremantle. The Paper is dated, "Deanery, Chichester, *March* 24th, 1887"; but bears no name of Printer or Publisher.

The Chichester Life.

animated by such zeal for truth and righteousness as John William Burgon consistently exhibited,—a zeal, be it granted, which cannot tolerate those who deprave the truth or lower the moral standard,—nay, which desires the extermination of all such ;—" I would they were even cut off that trouble you"? Such zeal however met in the olden time with high encomium and high reward ;—

"Phinehas, the son of Eleazar, the son of Aaron the priest, hath turned my wrath away from the children of Israel, while he was zealous for my sake among them, that I consumed not the children of Israel in my jealousy. Wherefore say, BEHOLD, I GIVE UNTO HIM MY COVENANT OF PEACE: AND HE SHALL HAVE IT, AND HIS SEED AFTER HIM, *even* THE COVENANT OF AN EVERLASTING PRIESTHOOD; BECAUSE HE WAS ZEALOUS FOR HIS GOD."

Burgon was present at the great Jubilee Service in Westminster Abbey, which was held in the Midsummer of this year, as it was right that one should be, so brimming over with loyal and patriotic feeling, and so full of poetic sentiment. A letter of his to Miss Washbourne referring to the occasion will be found at the end of this year's record.

Here is a picture of "Dean Burgon in his study," kindly transmitted to the author by one who visited him there in August 16 of this year.

"We found the Dean just returned from the Cathedral, and in his study. In his long black cassock he moved or flashed about, tall and lithe, sparkling with unexpected turns of thought and quick varying expressions of face and tone. A marvellous study lined with books; even a shelf over the door laden with Jerome's works, in six great folio volumes. Quaint rubbings and slightly framed pencil sketches hung or placed in every possible nook, a head of Dean Church, sketched by Dean Burgon himself; another delightful pencil head by Haydon. Over the mantelpiece a photograph of Leonardo da Vinci's original crayon drawing for the head of our Lord in the Last Supper; below a chromo-lithograph of the new Raphael. He pointed to the line of immense volumes containing the wonderful work, which had occupied him for fifteen years, and told how he came to begin it. 'In '72 I was at Oxford. I was leaving the Schools one evening, when a nobleman accosted me (a nobleman in the present Cabinet, President of the Council). He began talking about the book I had written on the last twelve verses of St. Mark, proving their genuineness. He said he had been very much interested in it. I did not believe he had understood it. I began to catechize him. Yes; he had understood it. He said that by my book he had been enabled to prove the genuineness of those verses to the Archbishop.

"'The thought flashed across me—Why shouldn't I do for the whole New Testament what I have done for those twelve verses of St. Mark? Why shouldn't I? I walked home. The street was dark, but it was all luminous within.—I got home.—I said to myself—It will take you a long time.—I know it. The rest of your life.—I know it. It will cost a great deal of money.—I know it. And you will never finish it.—No; I know it. No one will ever appreciate it.—I know it. I will do it. I have been fifteen years over it. Oh, and a great deal more than that! See, here is one of the Indexes. Isn't that an unearthly-looking thing?' It was indeed unearthly-looking, small squares of paper of all the colours of the rainbow, each numbered,—the colour representing the author (some particular Father), and the number representing the volume and the page of his work, in which the text in question was referred to.

"'This you see,' unfolding a long page in the beginning, 'shows the number of times St. Chrysostom quotes from St. Matthew,—178; how many times from St. Mark, and so on; and each reference is given in the Index.

"'A number of ladies help me. Very good help.

Little bits of genius sometimes. Here's a letter from a young lady, received this morning; does her great credit, great credit.'

" Then he showed us his coins, pointing out minutest beauties and peculiarities of line and balance. 'The coins are such a help in studying history. You should take some period of history, and study it in connexion with its literature, its architecture, its paintings, its seals and coins.'

" And besides all this accumulation of learning, and these absorbing antiquities, upon the table a box of hemp-seed—for the birds—scattered to them each morning at his whistle. 'He says it is the happiest moment in the day when they come fluttering down to him,' Mrs. Crosse told me afterwards.

" He stood at the door waving his hand and his handkerchief, till we turned out of the gate. Mrs. Crosse said; 'That's what is so pretty in the Dean, he always does that to his friends.'"

And here another incident of the same year, narrated by Mrs. Crosse, which will be read with interest, not only as showing the reflective and deeply serious turn of mind, which was habitual with him and interlaced with his sprightly moods, but also from the melancholy presage it seemed to give of what was to come so soon after.

" During the Goodwood week at Chichester in 1887 we met the Dean near the gate at the entrance of Canon Lane, and we stood still for a short time, watching the gay company passing to the Station. When we moved on, walking back to the Deanery, the Dean began to meditate aloud, and said,—

"'I often think, and think increasingly, of the wonderful surroundings to which our eyes will one day open. The vail of flesh now hides them from us; but in a moment we may find that close to us, and about us, a great company may be present.

LIFE OF DEAN BURGON.

"'I often think too that we have the germs of great future powers within us. Our sense of beauty, harmony, &c., are all comparatively undeveloped here;—they are not *fulfilled*; they will be by and by.'

"During the Goodwood week of the following year, the Dean was dying, and the vail *was* removed."

In the October of this year he attended, as he usually did, the Diocesan Conference (held on this occasion at St. Leonard's), and manifested there his interest in the religious welfare of young men. Youth in either sex, —and not only in the adolescent stage, but in childhood and even babyhood,—always powerfully attracted his sympathies. Thus writes the Rev. William S. Carter, the Clerical Organizing Secretary to the Young Men's Friendly Society, to the author (July 6, 1889);—

"Dean Burgon's letters to me were always full of the kindest expressions of his sympathy in my work for young men in connexion with this Society. I shall never forget the kindness with which he placed the Cathedral Pulpit at Chichester at my disposal at a very early stage of my work, and in the interviews which I had with him subsequently he, over and over again, told me that one of the greatest dreams of his life had been to see the Church of England take up definite and united work for young men.

"To me, personally, he was for the last two years of his life a warm-hearted and most valued counsellor, for on more than one occasion I took advantage of his kind offer to look over some of my proposed addresses, and to give me any information he could.

"At the Chichester Diocesan Conference held at St. Leonard's in October, 1887, at which I was invited to move one of the resolutions, he came up to me, and (knowing that it was the *first* time I had been asked to undertake such a task) thinking that I should be nervous, he chatted most pleasantly; and in order to set me at my ease, said he would support the Resolution himself, which he did in a most kind and generous speech.'

To the Right Honourable Viscount Cranbrook,
G.C.B., &c., &c.

"Deanery, Chichester, Feb. 21, 1887.

"My dear Friend,—I hasten to reply to your kind letter. Ever since 1831, the Text of the N.T. has been like a storm-tossed barque, drifting along without captain, chart, or compass. At the end of 50 years, things reached their climax—viz., in 1881, when the maximum of damage was sustained. Dr. Scrivener, the best critic living, says of the latest editors of the Greek Text;—'*splendidum peccatum*, non κτῆμα ἐς ἀεὶ, in lucem emiserunt.'

"Ever since 1866 or 7, I had had my eye fastened on this danger. It was a conversation *with yourself*, by lamplight, in Christ Church quadrangle (I suppose in 1871 or 2) that finally determined me to make it the business of my life (Christo duce!) *to try to secure the deposit*:—to recal men to their senses,—to vindicate the Truth of Scripture, and to establish it on a scientific basis.

"It was a gigantic undertaking: but I was confident of success—full of hope and full of spirits. I cannot say how hard I worked. Besides visiting the principal libraries of Europe, in order to familiarise myself with MSS., I collated the most famous of them for myself. I formed a Library of Fathers, and *began to index them*. At the end of 1875, the Deanery was offered me, and I gratefully accepted it, chiefly in order to be able to devote myself without distraction to my self-imposed task. . . . . I toiled on unremittingly—in spite of every discouragement,—and with such success that, in the autumn of 1881, I was able to pour such a broadside into the (so-called) Revised Greek Text, which had appeared in the spring of the same year, that it was declared on all hands to be no longer sea-worthy.

"It was a tremendous effort; but I repeated the broadside in January, 1882, and again in April. These three articles in the '*Quarterly Review*' I greatly enlarged, and republished in 1883. I dedicated the '*Revision Revised*' to yourself.

"I have been at work ever since;—the danger has not been overcome. It has only been checked and retarded, but it will reappear,—inevitably. I have nothing on my side, scarcely, but *the Truth*. Crippled as I was last year, I resolved to strengthen my defences, to gather allies, and to make one more systematic advance against the enemy. So I have had my Indexes of the Fathers increased,—have carried down my inquiries to the viiith and ixth century,—and in less than two months from this date, shall have my ponderous tomes back from all my white negroes; and (D.V.) shall be resuming seriously my great work.

"You will understand then that—in brief—my object is to vindicate the Traditional Text of the N. T. against all its past and present assailants, and to establish it on such a basis of security, *that it may be incapable of being effectually disturbed any more*. I propose to myself to lay down logical principles, and to *demonstrate* that men have been going wrong for the last 50 years; to explain how this has come to pass in every instance; and to get them to admit their error. At least, I will convince every fair person that the truth is what I say it is—viz., that in nine cases out of ten, the *commonly received text* is the true one. What *you* are bent on doing for the Imperial interests of Great Britain, *I* am seeking to do for the Word of GOD. And *when* (you ask) do I expect to have done this? The labour is so great, that I hardly dare to forecast. A *single text* has, before now, occupied me *all day long* for many weeks. A crucial place (1 Tim. iii. 16) taxed my energies for six months. (I corresponded with every great Library in Europe.) But, to come to the point—I *believe* that in four or five years (at furthest) from this time, I shall be able to give to the world the result of my 23 or 24 years of toil; that is, if God grants me a continuance of health.

"In the meantime (as I ventured to tell you) the struggle I have had to make against insufficiency of income, which has long been embarrassing me, is at last entirely disheartening, or rather paralysing me. My health seems at last to be giving way—I can bear it no longer. The secret of my success hitherto has been my unbroken sleep. I no longer sleep soundly. I wake early, and distress myself with the gloomy forecast.

"Anxieties preying upon me, night and morning, effectually hinder my working—and will end by embittering hopelessly my life and ruining the prospects of those whom God has given me. I fear I have wearied you—but I have tried to answer your question as succinctly as I can, without being unintelligible.

"Ever yours affectionately and gratefully,

"J. W. BURGON."

To the Reverend Henry M. Ingram, Southover, Lewes.

[In explanation of the occasion of the following two letters, Mr. Ingram writes to the author, July 3rd, 1889;—

"They were written in acknowledgment of certain remarks of mine on the 'Sunday question,' arising out of Dean Burgon's two printed Essays on the subject, which had appeared in the '*Guardian*' newspaper of Jan. 5 and 12, 1887. If I remember right, my main purpose in writing to the Dean was to urge upon him the fuller investigation of the passages alluding to the subject in the Epistle to the Hebrews, in the belief that that wonderful Epistle has not yet received anything approaching to its deserts (so to speak) of patient study and elucidation, on all subjects connected with the sudden and impending 'passing away' (at the destruction of Jerusalem) of the ancient Judaic ritual and worship, and the necessary establishment in its room of the 'better' rites and ordinances of the Catholick Church. It was owing to the putting on paper of some crude thoughts on this subject, that the Dean wrote back with his characteristic warmth of kindness. I fear that, from the inevitable break in our correspondence, I was not successful in satisfying him with the fuller thoughts he asked for on 'the transference of the religious obligations of the Seventh Day (the Primæval Sabbath) to the First Day of the week, the Christian Sunday or LORD's Day.'"]

"Gresham Coll., London,

"Feb. 16, 1887.

"My dear Sir,—I am anxious to thank you for your interesting letter of the 14th instant. I acknowledged it yesterday in a hurry—intending to return to the subject from London to-day.

In reply to your question—(whether I will publish those two Essays in a pamphlet form,)—I answer that I will do what will be better (D.V.), viz. enlarge them, and leave out the (unavoidable) personalities in them, and incorporate with them the question you touch upon so eloquently—and (in my judgment) so admirably,—I mean, the supplanting of the Jewish Sabbath by the Christian Sunday.

"Few things have surprised me more than the discovery that this is made a difficulty by many of the Clergy. To *me* (and, I rejoice to see, *to you*)—it seems one of the most beautifully clear things in the whole range of unrevealed [1] Truth.

"If anything occurs to you in illustration of the subject, pray let me hear from you again. Certainly my own views *on the entire subject* have been wonderfully enlarged and rendered more precise by the inquiries into which I have been led by the perverseness of my opponents. It

---

[1] He means probably that the transfer of the religious obligation from the Seventh to the First Day, however it may approve itself to the Christian conscience as suitable and right, does not rest on express revelation.

is, in truth, a large and a curious question—*when* and *where* the custom arose of *calling the week-days by their present names.*
"Very truly yours,
 "JOHN W BURGON."

"The Deanery, Chichester,

"1 March, 1887.

"My dear Sir,—I will not go from home for three, or rather four, days—without first thanking you for your two interesting and valuable letters. The second I was especially glad to receive: though indeed in neither did I find what I most wished for your thoughts on—viz. *on the transference of the religious obligation of the 7th day to the first day of the week*—a point on which I find many persons are troubled,—and on which, in your first letter of all, you spoke eloquently, and (as I felt) satisfactorily. It quite *refreshed* me to find any one so sound and strong on the subject.

"I do not mean that I am *disappointed* in not hearing more on that special point; for I am not. But it is perhaps *the* point which most stands in need of elucidation.

"I propose—GOD helping me—to try to methodize, and perhaps to put into the shape of a pamphlet of 16 or 32 pages, what I have to say on the entire subject. It has never—that I know of,—been nicely handled yet.

"I understand the Sabbath to be an emblem from the first of man's everlasting beatific rest ($\sigma\alpha\beta\beta\alpha\tau\iota\sigma\mu\acute{o}s$): for which reason (there being 'no night there') no mention is made of 'the evening and the morning.'

"The republication (for it was nothing more) of the Sabbath at the Exodus is best explained by the 215 years of practical neglect it must have experienced during the age of the Egyptian bondage. I was much struck just now in Church by the xxvth of Leviticus, which reminded me of the extent to which the original enactment was there by its Divine Author expanded as well as enforced.

"The notices in the prophets *also* well deserve special attention. They are not many, but they are very striking.

"One or more of these you have yourself touched, and indeed I only take up my pen to thank you for your valuable remarks.

"Your obliged,
"JOHN W. BURGON.

"I find no mention of *months* till Gen. vii. 11."

TO MISS WASHBOURNE.
"The Deanery, Chichester, June 28, 1887.

"Yes,—I went (as *Dean*) to Westminster, with my wife (Tan[2]),—and a very glorious sight it was. The Queen was immediately before us, and not further off than the length of St. Mary's nave. But we were obliged to sleep in London over night, bribe a cab, and get to the Abbey by 8. Doors (or rather windows, for we went in by a window) not open till 9. At 12.30 the Queen appeared. Her embracing her forty children and grandchildren who sat round her was a beautiful and affecting sight."

TO MRS. CROSSE.
"Turvey Abbey, 26 Aug., 1887.

"Already have I subsided into my bad ways in this dear place—up to my eyes in ink. The quiet and repose is most congenial to me: but I am bound to confess that I work nowhere *better* than in my den. I question whether there is a happier Dean—or a pleasanter den—in Great Britain."

TO MRS. ———— ————
"Turvey Abbey, Bedford,
"Aug. 30, 1887.

"My very dear Friend,—It is high time that I should thank you for your few loving lines, and assure you how much we missed you on Sunday Evenings" [his correspondent was a lady resident in Chichester, who, like one

---

[2] His niece, Miss Anna Rose.

THE CHICHESTER LIFE.

or two other intimate friends, used to resort to the Deanery on Sunday Evenings], "and send you a brief report of myself.

"All here is unchanged. Long may this be the case! The sameness of the scene in country houses is very striking. Within, books and furniture abide in their places; and the punctuality of Nature without is (like its Author) unchangeable. But I still miss, and shall long miss our loved Charles. Some persons there are who, more—far more—than others, make themselves an integral part of the house they once occupied. Of no one could this be more truly said than of the master of this house till the hour of his departure.

"You ask for some 'good words to-morrow.' the morrow I could not write them. I was called upon suddenly to preach two Sermons, and, as you know, I was very tired when I left Chichester;—there was such a deal to be done before I could get away. Whether I can offer them now is doubtful, but I will try.

"It is remarkable—and deserves to be remarked—to what an extent God has provided us, in this world of ours, with *reminders* and *rehearsals*. There is no rehearsal like that of leaving home for a time. O the many unfinished, unanswered—unattempted—unremembered things! O the many reproaches, regrets, and faint resolves! I take it that these are *intended* by Him who contrived the curious network of our existence—intended for our health, and growth, and improvement. The pang of parting is a faint shadow of the latest pang of all: the unpreparedness is intended to warn us: the reproaches of conscience are meant to save us from more serious reproofs. Need I go on? You will see that I mean to call your attention to the Providential character of this part of our experience. The love concealed under the pain we feel, when we have to say 'Good bye.'

"Ever believe me,
"Your affectionate and faithful friend,

"JOHN W. BURGON.'

LIFE OF DEAN BURGON.

To Mrs. ——— ———

"Turvey Abbey, Bedford,
"Sept. 12, 1887.

"My very dear Friend,— . . . . . .

"I am suffering from a tremendous cold,—*how* caught I know not,—which almost keeps me sneezing, barking, and doing other graceful things all day. . . . . . . This seizure is the more unlucky because I have made several engagements for the present week. Thus, on Thursday, I am to conduct the Reformatory Boys' recitation of John Gilpin—and I must rehearse them for the last time to-day: and this requires spirit and the free use of one's voice.

"When I tell you that dearest Helen has manufactured *a wig* for John Gilpin (which I will exhibit in a foot-note),—to say nothing of a scarlet cloak—a boddice—and two bottles with curling ears—you will understand how busy we have both been. The wig is of *tow*. The

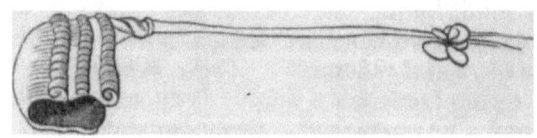

difficulty is to make these articles absurd enough. I am obliged to direct Mrs. Gilpin's cap in person—thus:

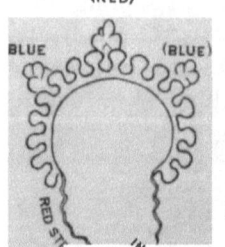

But seriously—it is really affecting to see how the boys enter into the fun of the thing. For I make *one* talk in a squeaky woman's voice (for Mrs. G.); *another* has to show how the horse behaved; and when it comes to 'the dogs did bark'—you would suppose you were in a kennel. My humble object is that they may see that there is a *silver edge* to the cloud of life, and that the more gifted of their spirits may reach out into the—unseen. O, how I feel for human kind! How sincerely I love it! How faithfully my heart beats with it, and responds to it! ....

".... Such a letter as that which I enclose .... makes me desire to throw over the '*Twelve Lives,*' and charge the infidels. But how can I do more than one thing at a time? or do *that* thing more vigorously than by rising at 5—or soon after— every morning, and working all day? On Friday and Saturday I think I worked for 12 or 14 hours—and was not tired!

"Believe me ever your affectionate Friend,

"JOHN W. BURGON."

To MRS..

"Turvey Abbey, 16 Sept. 1887.

"My very dear *Father-in-Law*[3] (ahem!),—You will be glad to hear that John Gilpin reached his journey's end in safety—and that his wig gave universal satisfaction. Mrs. G.'s cap was a general diversion to the ladies. One of the smallest boys did so well,
Mrs. Gilpin) 'pulled out half a crown,' and made the urchin happy. You never saw a queerer exhibition. And now I am wondering what is to be the programme for 1888, the life of Moses is to be prolonged till then.

"The auditory yesterday were the neighbouring clergy and gentry; the distribution of prizes is in a tent. Almost twenty prizes. amounting in money to £10 or more. are distributed—and placed to each boy's account: so that he begins life with a balance at his banker's in hi favour —(which, by the way, is not the way I hall *end* life!)
".... the races—scrambling for gingerbread-nuts, &c., &c., , &c.—are most grote que. The whole party then adjourned to the Building, where a grand tea is provided—and a loaf *too big to carry* is cut up: ALL the work of the boys, who are supposed to be first rate farmers,

---

[3] The Editor of these letters cannot profess to interpret all the grotesque names by which Burgon addressed his intimate friends,—indications all of them, however obscure to the uninitiated, of playful affection.

nurses, dairymen, cooks, and even *Gilpinians.* It was touching to see how they looked out for *my* departure—and gave the carriage chase,—vociferating until I was out of sight. I like the poor fellows much. . . . . . On Saturday week I have promised to go to my friend, Dr. Scrivener, at Hendon, and to preach his Harvest Sermon. Can you not fancy how *dry* we shall be?

"And now all blessings attend my very dear Father, and her party,—so says her faithful and affectionate Friend,

"JOHN W. BURGON."

Of the Reformatory Festival and the preparations for it, described in the two last letters, Mrs. Higgins (his sister) writes thus;—

"That merry meeting at the Reformatory Harvest Festival in 1887 was the last my Brother attended. How heartily he entered into the costume, which I prepared (under his direction) for Mrs. Gilpin, I shall never forget, —he constantly rising from the table in the window, where he was slaving morning, noon, and night, over the '*Lives,*' to suggest something which would make Mrs. Gilpin's cap more grotesque,—finally running into the garden and returning with a huge sun-flower and red dahlia, which I was to fasten on either side of the cap! Alas! how little I thought that summer of 1887 was to be the last summer he was to spend in this house,—the last summer he was to comfort and cheer me by his tenderness and ever sympathizing companionship."

TO THE REVEREND PRECENTOR CROSSE.

"Turvey Abbey, Sept. 17, 1887.

[*This letter was occasioned by the announcement of the death of a former Canon Residentiary, to whose house Canon Crosse had succeeded, and who had been on bad terms with the Dean. It shows, even in the comical incident with which it ends, that every particle of resentment was obliterated from Burgon's mind.*]

"Optime Præcentorum,—I feel Dr. ———'s death. I have written to Raper to telegraph to me the time and place of interment. I should wish to attend; not merely for form's sake by any means. I do not bear him the slightest ill will.

"I think *one or two pages* about him from the Cathedral pulpit would be most graceful and reasonable. You will be well in time for this *to-morrow week*; though Read should play the Dead March in Saul after the afternoon service *to-morrow*. And perhaps *also* on the Octave as well.

"I sympathize profoundly with you in your feelings. There is a reality in the house—the rooms—of a man's occupancy, which nothing can obliterate.

"By the way, do you know Mrs. ———? a most dear creature! One day, in Chapter, after a kind of row, I remember Dr. ——— saying, in a meditative voice,—'I am told you say our wives are much better than we are.' . . . . . 'Yes, I think each of the wives of you four Canons worth any half dozen of you,' and so I did—and *do*.

"Ever affectionately yours,
"J. W. BURGON."

FROM DEAN BURGON TO A FRIEND.

"Tuesday night, Oct. 11, 1887.

"Your complaint about the lifelessness of your prayers is one which I can deeply sympathize with. All are more or less either prone to, or at least have had some sad experience of, the same infirmity; but it is to be wrestled with, and by God's help to be surmounted. Remember that GOD is a *Person*; and that the one Person of our Lord Jesus Christ consists of two distinct natures inseparably united. Address yourself to Him; or, addressing the Eternal Father, address Him through the Son; and set before yourself your Saviour as receiving your prayers, and as it were presenting them. Do whatever you can to make your prayers real. Besides direct prayer, there is the habit of devout communing with GOD. It is to be done at all times, by meditation on His perfection, and power, and goodness, and so on. If you lie awake, think of Him, and dart up your soul to Him by repeated efforts of love, and gratitude, and admiration. In travel, during the intervals throughout the day, and during the lulls of conversation, you may, if you will, always steal away in thought to Him, as you would to a stronghold or a fortress.

"I recommend you to send for C. Marriott's '*Hints on Private Devotion.*' This will be a prodigious help to you. Read a chapter in this little book daily, or every second day, and try to act on his advice. You will be very grateful to me for telling you of this book."

1888.

We approach the end. The last year had been marked by much controversy; and controversy, with a nature like Burgon's, ardent for the Truth, though it had never any touch of personal animosity, could not fail to be somewhat fiery. But the only trace of controversy in the records of this last year is to be found in letters addressed to him by two able and learned divines, occupying both of them very high positions in the Church, who found themselves hopelessly at variance with him as to the literal character of the Creation narrative in the Book of Genesis. Here is an excerpt from one of these letters, the writer of which, though differing from him materially, writes with Christian kindness and courtesy. Many probably will be found to agree with him; but the author is not of the number;—

"March 25, 1888.

"You will let me say that I am one of those who have not been able to see that anything essentially Christian, or even essentially religious, is lost or jeopardized by the acceptance of the theory of evolution. It is a curious thing,—I wish I could verify my reference; but I think with time and leisure I could recover it.—that a book was written last century, which in commenting upon the story of Creation, suggested a sort of evolution as its mode, and that *merely on the strength of the sacred story and language.* ...... I have felt that the saying, 'The Bible was given us, not to teach us how the heavens go, but how to go to heaven,' might cover much of the present controversy."

One would be curious to see how the theory that Evolution was the mode of Creation could be maintained on "the strength of the sacred story and language," when that language seems so emphatically to affirm the distinctness of species both vegetable and animal [see Gen. i. 11, 12, 21, 24, 25]. The two letters above referred to,—one of them three or four weeks later in date than that from which the above excerpt is made, —are the only documents of 1888 (entrusted to the author) in which any vestige of controversy is discoverable.

Quite at the beginning of the year (Jan. 5, 1888) he had written to his attached friend and former Curate, Rev. R. G. Livingstone, a long letter, from parts of which it appears that he still hoped for the best, both as regards the prospects of his beloved University, and as to the continuance of his own life until his great work upon the principles of the Textual Criticism should have seen the light ;—

"Your news about Oxford is the only news I have had; and, thank God, it is cheering. Do you know I have a deep inveterate feeling that the prayers, and tears, and substantial sacrifices, with which, four, five, and six hundred years ago, our Founders built and endowed our Colleges, are not forgotten before GOD, and, although He has suffered the Secularists for a while to have their brief day, He will yet remember His ancient servants, and bring back a better day to Oxford in due time? I can never think of certain Headships without indignation and abhorrence."

Then after dwelling upon the growing inadequacy of his income to meet the claims upon him, and the need for retrenchment in his domestic expenses, and after describing the almost incredible labour which ' *The Lives of Twelve Good Men* ' had given and were giving him, he proceeds thus ;—

" But I desire to assure you that I am surrounded by countless blessings, carry a joyful heart *in spite of everything*, and only want to get to the end of ' *The Lives*,' in order to take in hand my great work (so intended to be) on the Text of the N.T. . . . I shall not lie quiet in the grave (so at least I feel) unless I may be allowed first to do *that*. My object is to establish the question on a footing which shall never more admit of disturbance. The subject occupies my mind incessantly, and fills up every vacant moment ; e.g. while I am dressing in the morning, and falling asleep at night."

In the early spring of this year he was sufficiently strong to administer for the last time the Holy Sacrament of Baptism on an occasion of peculiar interest, which must have called out all the sensibility of his loving and tender heart,—the infant whom he was summoned to baptize being a child of his old attached friend and disciple, Mrs. Samuel Bickersteth,—and named after himself, " John Burgon."

Soon after came the beginning of the end. It was on the 26th of April that the author, being in the neighbourhood of Chichester, went over to see Burgon, little thinking that this was the last time he should ever look upon him, and that the next visit would be not to himself, but to his study as he had left it. He was looking very ill, —" peaked," to use a word now somewhat antiquated,— with a thin high note in his voice not usual to him, and wizened. He was in the lowest spirits about his own health, and said he felt that he should die in two or three days ;—that this was the result of over strain and nervous exhaustion, brought on by the intense application which his last work ('*The Lives of Twelve Good Men*') had exacted from him, but which work he rejoiced to think was then finished, and (as far as the composition of it went) out of hand. "The Book is to appear," he said, "in October; but Murray does not think it will have any great run." In his then state of extreme dejection, everything was clad to him in the most sombre hues. He then turned to spiritual subjects, and said, "Dear friend, I daresay you think I have led a most reputable Christian life; but I assure you that, in looking back upon it, my past life yields nothing that is satisfactory to me, and that I have no hope but in the Blood and Grace of our Divine Lord." "One thing, however," he continued after a short pause, "is a consolatory reflexion, that I have been enabled to crush the Revised Version of the New Testament, so that I believe it will never lift up its head again."—It was wonderful how during luncheon (for, although so ill, he was dressed and downstairs) he seemed to revive, and there came now and again a gleam of the old fire and fun. The exertion, however, seemed to exhaust him, and, before we parted in the late afternoon, the depression in which I had found him closed round him again. The complaint ran its course, and assumed in a short time a most alarming aspect.

On the 5th of May he writes again (from a couch, and dictating the letter to his nephew) to Mr. Livingstone, speaking of his illness as "the saddest and strangest of breakdowns,—a very serious, and, I daresay, well-needed reminder of my own mortality and frailness." The purport of the letter is to send a word of sympathy to an old friend (the Reverend John Rigaud, fellow of Magdalen College) to whom he was strongly attached, and of whom he had been informed that he was in a dying state (he pre-deceased Burgon by eight days);—

"I am sure you will have caught my meaning, which is to convey a message of kindness to a dying friend. Tide what tide, you will be so kind (if the chance is allowed you) as to say from me to dear J. R. somewhat as follows:—

'Farewell, dearest fellow, until, GOD grant it! we meet in another world, not hemmed in by the shadows of Time, but introduced to some of the realities of Eternity. *Do not forget Whom you have trusted*, and Who has said, *I will never leave thee nor forsake thee*. Repeat to yourself again and again the Comfortable Words in the Communion Service, and the grand close of the Service for the Visitation of the Sick (*O Saviour of the world, who by thy cross*, &c.). Be assured we shall often think, often talk about you.'"

But with that wonderful vitality and recuperative power, which he had displayed on previous occasions, he rallied; and in the following letter to the late Dr. Bloxam, of Beeding, an eminent Oxonian, who had kindly off him assistance in the shape of a manuscript memoir of one of his '*Twelve Good Men*,' he seems to have almost regained his usual tone of spirits.

"The Deanery, Chichester,
(*Not in his own hand*.) "May 17th, 1888.

"Dear old Friend,—I have been in the very jaws of death; but by GOD's mercy am recovering, and am this day pronounced convalescent. But I have not yet left my bed-room, and to dictate a letter is as much as I am fit for. I have, as you justly suppose, greatly overtaxed my powers. I had no idea that I had brought myself so very low.

"The '*Lives of Twelve Good Men*' have been in type for some weeks. But John Murray requires that their publication shall be delayed till October, or the sale will be hopelessly damaged. I submit of course.

"Charles Marriott's Life will interest you greatly. I have taken exceeding pains with it, and have been largely helped by the family. But I can add nothing to it now. I had better therefore for every reason repress my curiosity to read the memoir you speak of, until my health shall return, and I am able calmly to consider what use might be made of so important a contribution to the family history. Thank you gratefully all the same for your kind offer.

"One of the first copies of my book, D.V., shall be sent to you, to whom it is so largely indebted.

"Ever affectionately yours,

"JOHN W. BURGON.

"The Rev. Dr. Bloxam." (*With his own hand.*)

Here is another letter, of a rather later date, addressed to the Rev. William Valentine, Vicar of Whixley, York, who had known Burgon's family, and to whom afterwards at Oxford he had shown kindness. It shows that at this date Burgon thought he might be spared, and enabled to do more work for the Divine Master.

"The Deanery, Chichester,

"26 May, 1888.

"My faithful Vally,—Though still very weak and ill— (I have not yet in fact been allowed to enter my library, though I have been downstairs twice, and have tottered the length of the garden). I must yet trace a few lines of gratitude and affection to you for your friendly and very acceptable letter. You summon up many a slumbering image, be sure, when you refer to the Osnaburgh Street days, and that loved, sainted one" [his mother], "who I *know* has been for 34 years with CHRIST.

"Yes; I must take more care of my health; for I seem to have still a great work to do; and the night cometh wherein no man can work. I was very near the portals of the other world on Sunday the 29th April,— very near indeed. I have ever since been slowly recovering, slowly gaining strength,—but *so* slowly that I am half in despair. And now they order me to repair to Folkestone, and declare that sea air is necessary for my re-establishment. I shrink from all that is before me— the expense included: for my income has fallen, and I have been trying hard to diminish my yearly expenditure.

"It is an unspeakable comfort to me, in my affliction, to *know* that I am being dealt with by Almighty God, 'according to the *counsel* of his will,' and that none of these things are by chance; but on the contrary are all wisely, lovingly, graciously ordered for one's own truest good.

"I cordially congratulate you on your boys' distinctions. May GOD preserve their heads in the day of battle!

"Ever, my dear Vally,
"Your affectionate old Friend,
"JOHN W. BURGON."

Burgon had a warm friend in the caretaker of Gresham College, to whose children he had shown much kindness, giving them small gifts and playing with them, as was his wont with all children who crossed his path. His kindness was most deeply felt by Mrs. Skeet; and his last visit to Gresham College lives, and will ever live, in her memory.

"He wished particularly to see my children every time he came," she writes, "and Norah he always gave a sixpence to, and in his kind and comical way, said, 'Now

you are to get seven Bath buns in a bag for sixpence :'" [the envelope of the last sixpence is enclosed, with the inscription in his own hand, " For the little old girl."]
" . . . . . I shall never forget his dear, kind, affectionate ways to us all; and Norah to the last he would kiss with the affection of a father. My heart, so to speak, seems to melt, when I think of the wonderful friend he was to us all, and that *we have lost him*. . . He was all goodness to everybody he had to do with, which I have felt should be made known. . . . . . He felt every one's trouble so from his heart. I shall never forget the last shake of the hand, as he was going into the cab, and the tears rolling down his dear cheeks. His heart was too full, and he was too feeble for words ; but his look told me he was thinking it was the last time we should meet on earth."

To this worthy person, in reply to her enquiry about his health, Burgon wrote thus, just before leaving home for Folkestone.

"May 30, 1888.

"Dear Mrs. Skeet,—I was greatly touched by your kind letter of inquiry concerning my health, and am thankful to be able to assure you that, by God's goodness, I am sufficiently recovered to go away to the seaside [Folkestone]—with a view to my complete restoration. I am still of course very weak, and incapable of exertion—whether of mind or body: but I am assured that sea air will speedily bring me round—and restore me to my duties and to my friends. So may it prove! for I feel that there is still a great deal I should like to do before I die.

"I often think of you and of your anxieties for your family. Let me invite you to learn by heart the beautiful words in St. Paul's Epistle to the Philippians iv. 6, 7 ; yes, and that saying of St. Peter (1 St. Peter v. 7), 'Casting all your care upon *Him*—for He careth for *you*.'

"We must learn to *trust* our heavenly Father, and to believe that He loves us. His very chastisements He has taught us to regard as tokens of His love.—You remember the words I mean; they are found in Hebrews xii. 5, 6, and many other places. Some words seem made for you, as for example, that beautiful declaration of the Psalmist,—' I have been young, and now am old; yet never saw I the righteous forsaken,— nor his seed begging their bread.'

"True it is that none are really and truly 'righteous': but God is merciful, and accepts of our small measure of faith, and accounts it righteousness for Jesus CHRIST's sake.

"I am ever—with my love to you all, dear Mrs. Skeet,
"Your friend,

"JOHN W. BURGON."

Before finally quitting the Deanery for Folkestone[4], he wrote and lithographed the following circular letter of acknowledgment for the many enquiries which had been made about his health;—

"Deanery, Chichester, May 30, 1888.

"Recommended to go to the sea-side with a view to my complete restoration to health, I cannot cross the threshold of my home until, out of a full heart, I have traced these few lines.

"No ordinary card of acknowledgment for 'kind inquiries' would express how deeply I have been touched by the many proofs which at first hourly reached me of the solicitude of friends and neighbours on my behalf,— the many unmistakeable tokens which still come to me every day, of personal affi   individual anxiety for my recovery.

"I will only say that I am deeply grateful for all this; and that the response on my side throughout has been the warmest possible;—not unmixed, now at last, with

---

[4] He left it on Thursday, May 31, and returned, after an absence of just three weeks, on Friday, June 22. On the afternoon of the succeeding day, June 23, he installed Archdeacon Sutton in the course of the Service.

profound anxiety that the life which has now been so mercifully spared may be permitted to bear clear evidence that it was prolonged for a gracious and beneficent purpose.

"I trust to be back and in my place very soon."

At Folkestone he recovered sufficiently for his medical attendants to permit his return to Chichester, where he again undertook his duties at the Cathedral, the earliest of them being the installation of the Reverend Robert Sutton, Vicar of Pevensey, into the Archdeaconry of Lewes, which had become vacant by the death of Archdeacon Hannah. But although, when he first returned, both he and his family thought they saw a gleam of hope that he might be perfectly re-established, the ground he had gained at Folkestone was not maintained, and he gradually lapsed again into the condition described above, in which the author had found him on the 26th of April.

"About three weeks before his death," writes Mrs. Crosse, (that would be about July 14,) "I met the Dean coming out of his private gate, following his verger to the Cathedral. He was then becoming very feeble, and had already been to one Service. On my remonstrating with him for attempting to go again, he answered; 'To what better place can I go than to the house of God?' And he went on until almost quite the last. It made our hearts ache to see each day his growing weakness. . . . . . . On his last Sunday [July 29] he was at the Cathedral; and when he could hardly stand from exhaustion, he insisted on reading the Prayer at the close in the Vestry, dismissing the Choir with 'God bless you all! I am very ill'; and then leaning on the arm of his verger, he left the building, never to re-enter it alive.

"It was his custom to ask his particular friends to come into the Deanery for five o'clock tea on Sunday afternoon. On this occasion, knowing how ill he was, we had not intended going; but he turned to Canon Crosse, and reminded him to be sure to come in, as usual. We found him seated in his chair, gasping for breath; but he struggled to his feet to give us his usual greeting, and again, when we shortly after left, he rose, saying 'God bless you' in an unusually solemn manner, and even trying to accompany us, as usual, to the door, when fortunately the arrival of another friend arrested him. His gatherings of this kind were always interesting. He used to bring out some old book or curiosity, and discourse upon it; and his bright quick eye took in at a glance the real or the pretended listener; and there were quaint little outbursts of fun to enliven all. The Dean had, as you know, considerable dramatic powers; and in telling a story, he would surprise his audience with an illustration as clever as it was unexpected. . . .

"Three weeks before he died, an old friend of ours, Bishop Quintard of Tennessee, came down to pay us a brief visit; and the Dean came in to see him. He was then extremely weak; but he brightened up, as the Bishop stepping forward took him by both hands, and blessed him, pinning a rose-bud in his coat, and telling him his name was a household word in the American Church, and adding that he had that morning been out to buy the largest photograph of him he could get in Chichester, and that he must now write his name beneath it. At luncheon some of the old fire returned, and he was full of anecdote and story, carrying the Bishop away with him afterwards, to show him his beloved garden, and sending him back laden with roses, and a large branch of his favourite syringa.—A few days after this, the Choral Festival brought to him as his guest another American Bishop, Dr. Cleveland Coxe of Western New York, a valued friend of his, and we met for the last time round the hospitable Deanery table. But it was a sad gathering. It was evident to us all that the Dean was fast failing; and though he struggled with his weakness, and even brightened up to tell some College stories, it was an effort to him to recall the points, and at one moment he paused and said, 'I want something to stir up my memory.'"

Mrs. Higgins, of Turvey Abbey, one of his two surviving

sisters, alarmed by the account she had received of her brother's state, had arrived at the Deanery. She found him occasionally in great suffering. On July 25, throwing his arm over the back of a chair in an agony of pain, he said: "Nothing but 'the everlasting arms' can support me now!" "On the 27th July at 8 a.m., in much suffering and distress from want of breath, he said to me, 'Read the Psalms for the day;—it's the 27th.' I read them; and he repeated the *Gloria Patri* after each Psalm. When finished, he pointed out in his Prayer Book, from which I had read, some pencil *memoranda*, which he had made when in the Holy Land, and spoke of his journey there. He said: 'I ought not to have gone, but staid at home, and taken St. Mary's.' I said: 'Do not reproach yourself for going; you went to see the places you knew so well by reading the Bible,—a sort of *pilgrimage*,—and pilgrimages have been made from the earliest times.' 'Yes,' he said, '*Elijah was the first pilgrim,—to Sinai;—it was a forty days' journey from Beer-sheba where he dwelt under a juniper tree.*' He added; 'I was punished for going; for I was laid up for nearly two years on my return.'"

The account of quite the closing scenes shall be given in the words of one of his nieces, both of whom had watched over him during his illness with tender and unceasing solicitude, and who felt that they had lost in him, not so much an uncle as a second father, their wisest counsellor, their truest friend.

"On Sunday, July 29" (his last Sunday; he died on the following Saturday, Aug. 4) "he was so very much worse that it was not thought he would last throughout the day; and very early in the morning, about 5.30 a.m., he wished to have the Holy Communion celebrated. He told me exactly where to find everything in his Library, his own private set of Holy Vessels, and a special Prayer Book. He wished us all, of course, and the servants also, to receive the Holy Communion with him. Before the Service he was very much exhausted,—unable to lie down on account of the terrible difficulty of breathing; but as the Service went on, he seemed to gain strength. My brother" [Rev. W. F Rose, Vicar of Worle] "officiated,— I think it was about 6.30 a.m. My Aunt " [Mrs Higgins] " Gertrude and I, and all our servants were kneeling round him. As the Service ended, he signed that he would give the Blessing; and to our astonishment and comfort he stood up, and gave it clearly, distinctly, and *beautifully*, putting his hands, as he did so, on Gertie's and my heads, as we were kneeling next to him.—He was very ill all through Sunday, but rather rallied for a day or two. On Wednesday he became worse again.

"A letter from Bishop King of Lincoln pleased him greatly three days before the end. He was too ill then for letters to be brought to him. But we recognising the hand-writing, and guessing what it would be, I took it upstairs. He wished it read to him, and expressed great pleasure in it, short as it was. It ran thus; 'My dear Dean,—This is only to assure you of my gratitude, my love, and my prayers.—I am, as of old in Oriel[5], Your affectionate E. LINCOLN.' I think this was *quite* the last letter he was able to hear,—the last message which reached him from the outer world."

About two days before the end he looked wistfully at another bed in the room, besides that which he was himself occupying, and expressed a wish to have the great portfolios, containing the notes for his work on Textual Criticism, on which he had spent so many laborious days and nights, brought upstairs and placed upon it where he could see them. Some slight resistance was at first made to this by members of the family, who apprehended that

---

[5] The Bishop had been in former days an Undergraduate of Oriel, where he had rooms on the same staircase with Mr. Burgon.

the excitement of seeing what had interested him so much might be prejudicial to him. He gave way, as was uniformly his wont, when crossed in any thing by those who loved him; but seemed afterwards so much to hanker after the indulgence which had been denied, that it was thought best to humour him. Accordingly the portfolios were carried up to his room and laid where he had desired.

"His face of satisfaction and pleasure," writes his niece, "was a sufficient reward; and he said, 'I won't read them, or open them;—I only want to look at them. You know, when a man is dying, he wants to kiss and to say Good-bye to his favourite child:—he may have been a naughty boy; but his father wants to see him and to say Good-bye, all the same."

The papers contained in those huge portfolios were the children of his brain; he had lived among them and loved them with a parental love,—fondly, perhaps over-indulgently. But why were they "*naughty* boys"? Doubtless the thought crossed him that the labour bestowed upon them had shortened his days.

"I remember how often during the last week or fortnight he liked us to read over to him the 'Comfortable Words' in the Communion Service; and once he said to me of the first sentence; 'Ah! the words don't go down to the end of the Chapter'; and then went on to say, 'How wonderful! the one place in Holy Scripture where the Creator Himself, the Lord of heaven and earth, deigns' (or 'condescends'—I don't remember which of the two words he used) 'to explain—if we may so call it—His own character!' ['I am meek and lowly in heart.'] . . . .

"The night before his death, hardly able to speak, he kept repeating, '*Two words*,' and then over and over again; 'THY Cross. THY Cross. THY Blood. THY Blood.' . . . . .

"About five minutes before his death, he said to me, 'Give me a pencil.' I gave it. '*And now S. Mark.*' I held the New Testament before him, and was turning the page to find which passage he wanted, when quite suddenly the breathing changed, and the end came immediately."

The cause of death was certified by the physician in attendance as having been, first, "nervous strain resulting from prolonged mental work," and, as produced by this, "exhaustion of the organic nervous system." We resume Mrs. Crosse's narrative which concludes thus;—

"The day after the Dean's death we saw him once more, lying in the familiar cassock, stole, surplice, surrounded by his books, his unfinished work" [on the Principles of Textual Criticism] "upon his writing table, and his favourite flowers. Everything the same outwardly, and yet so finally altered. The look of peace upon his face, and the thought that he had but gone to the presence of the Master whom he had loved and served in life, remained to console those whose lives were changed and their home broken up by his withdrawal.

"The Dean once told me that, when a young man, he had a great idea of the happiness of married life; but that he and another young man (now an eminent Bishop of the Church) had agreed that it was not fair to ask a woman to undertake the cares of a home, until they could surround her with its comforts. In his case, as we know, when that time came, he had made a home for his widowed sister and her daughters, so that he never married. He was rewarded by the care and love of his nieces until the end came."

It scarcely needs to be said that Burgon himself had chosen Oxford and the Holywell Cemetery,—where were already lying the remains of his father, mother, brother, and two sisters—as his own last resting-place. "Dean Burgon's last home was at Chichester," says the *In Memoriam* which appeared in the '*Guardian*' Newspaper of August 15, and which is understood to have been from the

THE CHICHESTER LIFE. 303

pen of the late Dean Church; "but Oxford, which had been to him the scene of so much happiness, and of so much suffering, had never ceased to be the home of his heart; and he was fittingly laid to rest in an Oxford graveyard . . . . . . no more suitable place for his grave could be chosen than the quiet Holywell Cemetery." On the day after his death (Sunday, Aug. 5), the venerable Bishop of Chichester, who had been on terms of cordial intimacy with Burgon during the twelve years of his Decanate, delivered in the Cathedral a Sermon on his character, in which all its points are faithfully touched upon, and yet which perhaps is the most highly appreciative of all the many notices of him which appeared at the time of his death,—a very model of what Sermons on such occasions ought to be [6]. And in the Episcopal Charge of July 1890, nearly two years afterwards, the Dean, who had passed away since the last Visitation, was the first topic touched upon.—his delight in, and punctual attendance upon, the daily Services of the Cathedral, his devotion to the study of God's Word and of " such studies as help to the knowledge of the same," the influence he had gained over many Clergy all over England, who in time past had sat at his feet, his deep erudition, his rare poetical gifts, his conversancy alike with the Fathers of the ancient Church and of our own. " Less than this could not be said of one, whom the Cathedral of Chichester must ever count among the most remarkable in its long catalogue of

---

[6] This Sermon, or rather that portion of it which has reference to Dean Burgon, will be found in Appendix E. The Bishop has most kindly permitted the author to make a copy of it from the original manuscript.

It is thought also that the volume may appropriately close with one of Burgon's own Sermons, containing his views on the State of the Faithful Departed. It appeared originally (after his death) in the *Parish Magazine*, from which a reprint was made of it, by the kind permission of the Editor, for circulation among the late Dean's Friends. See Appendix F.

Deans, but whose fame and influence extend far beyond the narrow bounds of a single Diocese."

The body of Dean Burgon was borne into the Cathedral for the last time on Friday Aug. 10, where the first part of the Order for the Burial of the Dead was chorally rendered over it, after which, covered with wreaths and floral offerings, it was conveyed to Oxford, where it arrived about 8 p.m. and was deposited for the night by his own express wish in the Chapel of Holywell Cemetery. At noon on Saturday the Principal of St. Mary's Hall (the Reverend Dr. Chase), the Dean's kind friend, and who had both preceded and succeeded him in the charge of the Parish of St. Mary's, committed the body to the grave with the Church's words of supplication, hope, consolation, and benediction. There were present, besides the relatives and many of the personal friends of the deceased, Canons Awdry and Teulon and Prebendary Bennett, representing the Dean and Chapter of Chichester; the Bishop of Western New York (Dr. Cleveland Coxe), an intimate friend and correspondent, who, as we have seen, had visited Burgon shortly before his death,—and four Heads of Colleges, the Provost of Oriel, the Provost of Worcester, the Warden of All Souls, the Rector of Lincoln, with several other persons of distinction, Professor Max Müller, Sir John Stainer, the Vicar of Brighton (Rev. Prebendary Hannah), the Rev. C. Gore of the Pusey House, Father Benson of Cowley, and (what need to add?), the Rev. R. G. Livingstone and the Rev. G. H. Gwilliam, who had formerly been, as we have seen, his Curates at St. Mary's, and whom he had there, in an intercourse with them, which with many Vicars would have been purely official, "grappled to his soul with hoops of steel." The gathering was fairly representative of several different schools of thought, as might have been expected; for while Burgon had declaimed furiously against controversial opponents, he had somehow made it felt that he was quite free from personal rancour, that it was the tenet, and not its maintainer, against which he declaimed; and it may be doubted whether those whom he hit hardest could find it in their hearts to owe him a grudge. And it should be added that the American Church testified on this occasion to her sense of the irreparable loss, which she, no less than the English, had sustained by his death, one of her most eminent Bishops being among the mourners gathered round the grave, and one of the Professors in Hobart College, Western New York, having sent a request to his son, then happening to be in England, to represent him at the funeral.

The Biography of John William Burgon may appropriately be closed by Lord Cranbrook's beautiful poetical tribute to his friend, so truly appreciative and at the same time so faithful, which shall be followed by another piece from the same pen, written when '*The Lives of Twelve Good Men*,' Burgon's posthumous work, reached him with the inscription "from the Author."

To John William Burgon, Dean of Chichester.
Buried at Oxford, August 11th, 1888.

I.

At rest—beside the walls thou lov'dst so well,
Near the "dear Worcester" of thine early lays[7],
Within the Oxford, where, in later days,
With ever new affection thou didst dwell.
Teacher and preacher bold the truth to tell;
Friend of the poor, well versed in childhood's ways,
Thyself as children guileless, to them dear,
Trusted and trusting with a soul sincere.

[7] See lines to Worcester College, Burgon's Poems, p. 81.

To those, who knew thee only by thy pen,
Counted impetuous, bitter, almost fierce ;
Yet was thy heart filled full of love to men,
Even when thy weapons keenest seemed to pierce,
Eager and earnest, yet from malice free,
With old world quaintness and simplicity.

II.

The Church will miss thy learning and thy zeal,
Unwearying her bulwarks to defend :
Hastening by over-toil the journey's end,
More precious to thee than thine own her weal.
To arm thyself for her from head to heel,
Thou didst to deepest stores thy search extend,
Still keeping sword and shield and armour bright,
Watching by them in prayer, as a true knight.
So hast thou filled thy course, a champion pure,
So hope we that thy guerdon thou hast won ;
Small faults forgotten—thy good works endure ;
A faithful servant greeted with "well done."
The Church's sons pay honour to thy bier,
The friend would lay this humble tribute there.

LINES WRITTEN ON RECEIVING FROM THE PUBLISHER A COPY OF '*The Lives of Twelve Good Men*,' SENT BY DESIRE OF THE AUTHOR BEFORE HIS DEATH.

Books "from the Author," and he speaks to me
  From the unseen, as in his living tone:
  I seem to watch him in his study lone
By his Cathedral's spire of symmetry,
  Calling the friends he valued, one by one,
To group them in this goodly company,
As he had known them here: now he can see
And share the home of that fraternity.
While with enfeebled hand he did not cease
To enrol the good who had the dearest been,
He knew his nearness to th' abode of peace,

THE CHICHESTER LIFE.

And calmly chose the resting-place foreseen [8];
Yet not unmindful of friends left behind,
To them by name these last words he consigned [9].

A notice of the monuments raised to Dean Burgon's memory in three several places,—in the Cemetery where he rests; in the Church of St. Mary-the-Virgin's at Oxford, in connexion with which the active part of his work was done; and in Chichester Cathedral, under whose sacred shadow he pursued the theological studies preparatory to his great work in vindication of the Traditional Text of the New Testament,—will be found at the end of this Chapter.

Meanwhile, however, certain monographs must be presented to the reader, one of them recording several authentic stories (all the stories are by no means authentic) of his extraordinary love of children and power of attracting them, the others turning on subjects, which during his life at Chichester, occupied much of the good Dean's time and mind, and which brought him into connexion with different classes of persons, over many of whom he gained a salutary and permanent influence, not more by the direct instruction conveyed to them, than by the always affectionate, and sometimes quaint and pungent, manner in which it was conveyed. The first of these subjects is the Lectures which he delivered as Gresham Professor of Divinity, a post which he held for nearly twenty-one years, having been appointed to it, as we have seen, at the end of 1867.—The second is the

---

[8] See vol. i. of First Edition. Preface, p. xxviii. "He" (Mr. Golightly) "sleeps where I shall soon myself be sleeping,—in Holywell Cemetery."

[9] "One of his last acts before his death was to dictate to his nephew a list of the friends to whom he desired a copy should be sent." Letter from Mr. Murray to Lord Cranbrook, Oct. 11, 1888.

Chichester Bible Class, at which, just as at his Oxford Bible Classes, an attached group of disciples gathered round him, one or more of whom have kindly furnished the author with accounts of what passed on those occasions.—The third is the weekly instruction given by him, when in residence at Chichester, to the pupils of Bishop Otter's Memorial College, whither he regularly repaired on foot, whatever the weather might be, after the afternoon Service of the Cathedral, to hold a Class there. This College had been originally founded in 1851 in memory of Bp. Otter (consecrated Bp. of Chichester, Oct. 2, 1836, died Aug. 20, 1840) *as a Theological College*. That scheme however failing, and the Education Act of 1870 leading to an increased demand for Teachers, the College was re-opened in 1873 as a Training College under Government Inspection for the purpose of training Ladies as Schoolmistresses for Elementary Schools, in the principles of the Church of England. The Dean of Chichester is an ex-officio Member of the General Committee; but the religious instructions given at the College by Dean Burgon were perfectly gratuitous, not in any way a part of the duties of his position. He felt no doubt the need for his own mind of some corrective in the shape of practical work, so much of his time being absorbed in theological research and the daily Offices of the Cathedral; and he dearly loved to train the young in the knowledge of GOD's Word, and to make the study of studies attractive and interesting to them. He commenced his visits to Otter College in 1877, the year after his settlement at Chichester, and continued them till 1887, the year before his death.—Nor must the helping hand which he held out to Candidates for the Ministry, whose means, without some help from others, would not have enabled them to procure an Academical Education, go without distinct record from the pen of one or more of those who feel that they owe their present position (in one case at least a distinguished one) to the interest and sympathy which in their early days he showed to them.

I. HIS LOVE OF CHILDREN AND POWER OF ATTRACTING THEM.

1. *Mrs. Crosse.*—" No Dean ever loved his Cathedral more, and few indeed have ever been so constant in their attendance at the Services. Day by day, a few moments before the bell ceased, the little garden door of the private walk leading from his study used to open, and the quaint, tall, bent figure clothed in cassock, surplice, hood, stole, and college-cap, preceded by his Verger (himself a character) would pass out, crossing St. Richard's walk to the cloistered entrance of the Cathedral. He was generally intercepted by a perambulator, and a small group of children drawn up with a sure hope of being noticed. The Dean would never pass a child without a word; and generally some small fun passed between them, no matter how short the time remaining before the stopping of the bell. Or if a lady was on her way to the Service, the Dean would stand cap in hand until she had first passed through the entrance door, his courtesy never failing. . . . . . .

"His love for children was perfectly unbounded, and the quiet of Canon Lane was often broken by the merry sound of children's laughter from the Deanery Garden. I remember on one occasion of a children's party, which was going on without him, a small girl of three years old, almost hidden in the depths of a white sun-bonnet, feeling the gathering was incomplete, took upon herself to walk to the Dean's study, where he sat immersed in his books, and asked him to come out and dance with her; and accordingly, in a shorter time than it takes to tell it, she returned in triumph, hand in hand with the Dean in cassock and college cap; and he was soon within the weeling circle, enjoying it as much as the youngest present, the life and centre of the fun."

2. *One of his nieces.*—"There are so many stories of his love for children, that I need hardly add any more; but one rather pretty story comes to my mind, which we may not have told you. One of his great pets was a little girl of three, who responded most prettily to his affection. During Lent their mother told the elder children that, if they had no sugar in their milk at breakfast and tea, at Easter they should have the sum which would have been spent in sugar, to buy flowers with for the Church. Lily participated in the self-denial; but when Easter Even came, and the flowers were about to be taken to the Church, the child was in a state of great distress. She came to her mother,—'No, no! Deanie, Deanie,' and could not be pacified until her mother allowed her to choose some flowers, and to bring them *herself* into his Library. This was evidently her idea of an offering *to the Church*! I mention the story only to show how fully children understood him and returned his love for them.

"Do you know the story of his calling one day at the Palace, I think to take a walk with the Bishop, when Mrs. Richard Durnford brought her baby into the room for him to admire? Its hair, of a light golden colour, was somewhat in disorder; and so, delighted with the mother's admiration of her child, he thought he would tease her in his humorous way by fixing upon the one feature which he *could* quiz. In the evening he sent her a sketch of the baby (so pretty, and yet a sufficient caricature), with these lines;—

Mrs. R. D. sings.
Attend, all ye lasses!
My Baby surpasses
All Babies that ever were known,
With the eyes of Mamma,
And the nose of Papa,
And his periwig wholly his own!

She was delighted, and called the representation of the hair 'his glory';—it did look something like a golden halo.

"One more story of children I think you asked me to let you have. I ought to say that these children were two of the shyest and most nervous little ones we ever knew; but my uncle never rested until he had at last made him no longer afraid of him. I shall never forget his look of triumph the first time he had induced the eldest little fellow to take hold of his finger, and come with him through the iron gates and up to the Deanery door (it was done, as he said, by the encouraging word 'Cakie' repeated at each step); but beyond the door no power on earth would persuade the little creature to venture. The mother wrote to me in Jan. 1889, five months after my uncle's death, as follows :—' I am pleased that my little boys retain a most vivid picture of him in their minds. Only last week one of them said (the child was ill); '*Spect me be deaded 'fore next Kissmas: then me go to God: me see Deanie! Is Deanie waiting for me, mother?*'"

3. *Rev. John F. Kitto, Vicar of St. Martin's, Charing Cross.*— "On one Sunday, when Dean Burgon was staying at this Vicarage, and had been preaching (I think at Whitehall Chapel) in the morning, he went up into the drawing-room after dinner, to rest until the evening service, when he had promised to preach for me at St. Martin's. By and by two little girls of four and five years of age came down, ready to go to the afternoon children's Service. 'Ain't you going to Church with us?' was their appeal. To the Dean, tired though he was, it was irresistible. He at once got up, a willing captive to his two playmates, and with a hand stretched down to each, he took them to the Service."

II. THE GRESHAM DIVINITY LECTURES.

Here is a specimen of some of the latest topics chosen by him for these Lectures, furnished to the author by the kindness of the Reverend Edward Collett, M.A., who laboured long and faithfully in two most important parishes of the City of London (St. Botolph's, Aldersgate, and St. Botolph's, Bishopsgate), and gave constant attendance at the Gresham Lectures.

"*Lent*, 1887. I. On the Unbelief of the Age. II. The Unbelief with regard to Holy Scripture, which calls itself scientific. III. The Analogy between God's Word and God's work,—a plea on behalf of Bible difficulties.

"*Easter*, 1887. I. Popular Unbelief,—in relation to Miracles. II. Popular Unbelief,—in relation to Prophecy. III. Popular Unbelief,—in respect of the general scheme of Redemption. IV. Practical counsels to those who are not disinclined to be believers.

"*Michaelmas*, 1887. I. God, the Creator of the Universe, an axiom of the reason. Man, the great mystery of this lower world. II. The Bible, professing to be a Revelation from God, furnishes a sufficient solution of the mystery of man's being. III. The Divine Origin of the Bible argued from its supernatural structure. IV. The prophetic texture of Holy Writ, a proof that the Bible is what it professes to be, namely, a Revelation to man from God."

The very last Series of Gresham Lectures given by him, partly in the Lent, partly in the Easter-tide of 1888 (Easter fell that year on April 1) was on the Epistles to the Seven Churches in the Book of the Revelation, the eighth and concluding Lecture being on "The Doctrine of the Millennium explained." Rev. xx. 4, 5.

"Many of the answers," says Mr. Collett, "given by the late Dean to questions put to him by those who attended his Lectures, were as useful as the Lectures themselves. Many of the questions put from time to time were irrelevant and impertinent. Nevertheless he always displayed the greatest patience and forbearance in dealing with them."

Here is the greater part of the Gresham Lecture given by him on April 5, 1883 (it was the Thursday after Low Sunday, Easter having fallen that year on Lady Day, March 25). It is in fact an expository Lecture on the Journey to Emmaus, and is a good specimen both of his lively and interesting style of exegesis, and of the way in which he sought to give a practical turn to his instructions in Divinity at Gresham College.

The Chichester Life.

The paper was written out from notes made at the time by one of his hearers, and was procured for the author by the kindness of Mrs. Ashworth of 42 Canonbury Park, in North London.

St. Luke xxiv. 13 *to* 50.

"We now go on with what has been revealed to us of the events of the day of the Resurrection. We admit that none of the Lord's appearances on that day posses the same dewy fragrance, or Divine sweetness, as those in the early morning. The later ones however are not wanting in variety and tender beauty; and (if I may be allowed to make such a personal allusion) I would rather have been an eye-witness of one of these appearances of our Lord in the evening of that day. We saw that St. Mary Magdalene was not permitted to touch her risen Lord, because the touch of faith would be more *real* than that of sense [St. John xx. 17]. ext followed His appearance to the company of women as they went to tell the disciples. Jesus met them, and bade them go and tell His brethren that they should see Him in Galilee [St. Matt. xxviii. 9, 10]. We notice how differently he dealt with different persons; to one severe; to another indulgent; and yet the severity may be the greater kindness. How does this message declare His human heart to be overflowing with human love! Much might be gained in the study of Scripture if we would only acquire the habit of tracing *reverently*, with chastened imagination, outlines given us, and try to recognise in them that of which they are the anti-type. We are reminded of the words, 'I am Joseph, your brother' [Gen. xlv. 4]. Here again in the Gospel is the same tender 'my brethren';— the true Joseph comes out! You may ask, 'What is the use of all this?' I answer, 'A thousand different uses': not the least of them being, that we are in this way convinced of the oneness of Holy Scripture,—that it is woven out of one piece.

"The next recorded appearance was that to St. Peter; we do not know for certain whether it was first to St. Peter, or first to the two disciples, as they walked to

Emmaus. There is something secret and pathetic in this appearance to the Apostle, who had three times denied Him!—But we pass on from the *unknown* to the *known*! St. Luke was divinely guided to pass by the Saviour's appearing to St. Mary Magdalene; he beginning his narrative of Easter morning like the rest; and then passing on at once to the evening of the day. 'And, behold, two of them went that same day to a village called Emmaus, which was from Jerusalem about threescore furlongs,'—or seven miles; 'And they talked together of all these things which had happened.' These two were Cleopas, and probably St. Luke himself. I say, *probably*; because if any one should say, 'You can't prove it,' there is certainly but shadowy evidence to go upon. It seems not unreasonable, however, to suppose that, as St. Mark records one thing about himself [xiv. 51], St. Luke may have done the same also. Well might they talk despondingly of the events that had happened. To us the incidents of the Resurrection are a matter of course; but how different to His earliest followers! To them it was a thing incredible. But had He not foretold it? Yes! but they had 'questioned one with another what the rising from the dead should mean' [St. Mark ix. 10]. Thus what *we* look on as a matter of course, *they* considered a sheer impossibility. All this, and more, was the case with these two. The whole was a story to them of some wild dream. 'And it came to pass that, while they communed together and reasoned, Jesus Himself drew near, and went with them. But their eyes were holden that they should not know Him.' I confess that the remark that first occurs to one here is one which experience has caused us all to make,—that we are prone to overlook our choicest blessings, though nearest to us. The hearts of these two were full. A stranger draws near to them. It is the *Saviour* Himself; but they overlook the fact, and pour into His ear what they have been speaking of. St. Mark says, 'He appeared in another form unto two of them' [xvi. 12]. Here it is, 'their eyes were holden.' The two statements convey the same thing,—that He was not known. The difference was not so much in *Him* as in *them*. Not all of us know Him now. Some but dimly; some indeed never recognise our ascended Lord at all; for a veil is on their hearts. The above are but two ways of saying the same thing. From the earthly side, it was that our Saviour took a different form. From the heavenly side, it was that 'their eyes were holden, that they should not know Him.' 'And He said unto them, What manner of communications are these that ye have one to another, as ye walk, and are sad?' There must have been a marked sadness in their voices, a deep earnest tone of debate, to draw forth such an inquiry as this. 'And Cleopas answering said unto Him, Thou art the only one sojourning amongst us who doth not know these things. And He said unto them, What things?' You notice how completely, by this remark, He lulls all thoughts of Himself to sleep. That our Saviour was to rise again no one understood. And an inquiry why they were so sad must have seemed to them to sever the inquirer from themselves completely. It shows how overwhelmingly important the things of those days must have been—the preternatural malice—the madness of the people—the darkness over the land—the portents that followed—the vague rumours of a rising again! All these combined made up such a cluster of marvels, that for two to walk together and not talk about it was simply impossible. 'They said unto Him, Concerning Jesus of Nazareth, which was a prophet, mighty in deed and word before GOD and all the people. And how the chief priests and our rulers delivered Him to be condemned to death, and have crucified Him. But we trusted that it had been He which should have redeemed Israel: and beside all this, to-day is the third day since these things were done.' This last saying is very remarkable; it means more than that this was the third day after the Crucifixion, and that nothing as yet had taken place. We have this mention of the third day which had come, and was almost over, because of its setting forth one more ground of perplexity. It was a veteran form of belief among the Jews that the third day was set apart for some special relief, for a gracious display of unexpected mercy, and hitherto they had buoyed themselves up by the hope that some such refreshment as had been extended in the cases of Joseph's brethren [Gen. xlii. 18], Esther [Est. iv. 16], Jonah [Jonah i. 17], and others, would be granted them; but behold! they say, no such refreshment has come! 'Yea, and certain women also of our company made us astonished, which were early at the sepulchre; and when they found not His body they came, saying, that they had also seen a vision of angels, which said that He was alive. And certain of them which were with us went to the sepulchre, and found it even so as the women had said: but Him they saw not.' The fulness of their narrative is a particular very surprising. Notice that it is *not* related so much in detail, because St. Luke was the other disciple, but that Luke was the companion of Cleopas, because these events needed to be closely recorded. It is because we are meant to have full details concerning other incidents[1] that Peter was present. He was made to be there. And this extraordinary fulness here is precisely one of the things that strikes you as remarkable. You see this was an unusually solemn event, when on the evening of Easter day, there was *no incident* which more occupied their thoughts. Thus these two disciples uttered what was in their mind. 'Then He said unto them, O fools' (wanting in intelligence), 'and slow of heart to believe all that the prophets have spoken: Ought not Christ to have suffered these things, and to enter into His glory? And beginning at Moses and all the prophets, He expounded unto them in all the

---

[1] He means the incident, recorded in v. 12, of St. Peter's having run to the sepulchre, and looked in, and seen the grave-cloths, and returned to report his experiences to his brother Apostles. He had been accompanied by St. John (as we know from St. John xx. 3); but in St. Luke's own narrative of the Resurrection St. John's having been with St. Peter is not noticed. In reporting the incident, however, to our Lord, Cleopas and the other disciple *use the plural*, showing that more than one disciple had visited the sepulchre, to ascertain the correctness of the women's testimony;— "Certain of them that were with us" [ἀπῆλθόν τινες τῶν σὺν ἡμῖν] "went to the sepulchre, and found *it* even so as the women had said," v. 24.

scriptures the things concerning Himself.' Oh! beyond all earthly things to have been permitted to *listen* to *that* discourse! You will notice in the margin of your Bibles that but six places of Scripture are given you here as references: four in Genesis, one in umbers, one in Deuteronomy [Gen. iii. 15; xxii. 18; xxvi 4; xlix. 10; um. xxi. 9; Deut. xviii. 15]. But do you suppose such a meagre set of references sufficient? Could these few texts possibly give any notion whatever of the discourse of our Lord to the two disciples? He spoke to them of things undreamed of. How Christ was the second Adam. How, 'by man came death, by man came also the resurrection of the dead' [1 Cor. xv. 21]. This passage, which is now part of our Easter anthem, must have found a place in this discourse. He spoke to them of the new heaven and the new earth [Isaiah lxv. 17; Rev. xxi. 1], and showed that He claimed to be the Head of the whole human family!—that He, Christ, was the true Abel, and Cain the unnatural people who compassed His death. He spoke of Noah, Melchizedek, Isaac and Jacob, and when He came to the story of Joseph, hated by his brethren, sold by Judah, tempted, imprisoned, lifted up, made second only to Pharaoh, how amazed the two sorrowing men must have been! Then followed the typical teaching of the Passover, with the singular grafting in of the Lord's Supper; then the crossing of the Red Sea, the manna, the crossing to Canaan, until they must have felt as some traveller crossing an Alpine mountain might feel, that, at first, *all* is *veiled* in *mist*; but as this rolls away, one beautiful peak after another comes in sight. The valleys are seen, and the rivers carrying verdure as they flow, until the pilgrim knows where he is going, and his soul overflows with rapture! Not less wondrously than the five barley loaves did these five books of Moses, when so divinely handled, suffice for the needs of a dying world! It was a theme for angels to come down to listen to! *Such* a commentary *never* has been, and *never will be* again! Yet not only was the Divine Speaker's form unrecognised, but his voice also! They knew Him not while they gazed on Him! Yet the method of handling the Scripture; the aptness, the skill, to elicit the most enchanting harmonies —all this filled them with wonder! How natural that their hearts should have burned within them! 'And they drew nigh unto the village whither they went: and he made as though he would have gone further. But they constrained him, saying, Abide with us, for it is toward evening, and the day is far spent. And he went in to tarry with them.' By the time they reached the village, what strange emotions must have filled the minds of Cleopas and his companion! A stranger, who had heard all they had to say, had then turned round on them with upbraiding, and then showed that He knew so much more about the matter! When He seemed about to leave them, well might they exclaim, 'Abide with us!' Notice here a parable in action. This was not the only occasion when our Lord acted in this manner. The three angels who came to Abraham were pressed to remain [Gen. xviii. 3, 4]. The mysterious Person who wrestled with Jacob was detained till He blessed him [Gen. xxxii. 26]. Our Saviour, when He came to His disciples walking on the sea, as they toiled in rowing, would have passed by them [St. Mark vi. 48]. And here again, 'He made as though He would have gone further.' Depend upon it, we have here a great practical lesson, that some conscious effort, on man's part, is required for keeping the Saviour's presence in the soul. No doubt they laid their hands gently on His, and shewed the pain His leaving would give them.

" I wish you to observe expressly that this lesson is needed when, as now, Easter is far spent. *Abide with us!* ' should be the language of our hearts. Has He not been with us in His agony? in His humiliation? in His crucifixion? in His entombment? in His rising again? If any good lessons have been learned, if one good intention has been solemnly formed (as you will notice the Collect for Easter Day implies), shall we not, at this time, make the prayer of this verse our own? You must surely have been struck by the curious phenomenon of the Collect giving expression to this thought.

The Chichester Life.

"'*Abide with us!*' The young should say it, because they need His guidance. The middle-aged, because they have to bear the burden and heat of the day, and because it is hard, or rather impossible, to grapple with the cares of life *alone*. The aged, because their walk to Emmaus is nearly done. What makes life at its close truly dreary and solitary, or rather inexpressibly sad, is that a man's or a woman's experience should be that of Saul; 'I am sore distressed; for the Philistines make war against me, and GOD is departed from me, and answereth me no more' [1 Sam. xxviii. 15]. '*Abide with us*' is an echo which never should leave the heart; and the answer comes back to us, '*Fear not!* for I am with thee' [Isaiah xli. 10; xliii. 5]. 'If GOD be *for* us, *who can* be *against* us?' [Rom. viii. 31]; 'Lo, I am with you alway' [St. Matt. xxviii. 20]. What else would we have as the sum of *all* promises? '*Abide with me!*' It is the earnest cry of some aged one who finds the need of the Saviour's presence. I am growing old and feeble. '*Abide with me!*' My dearest ones have gone on before. '*Abide with me!*' This dimmed eye, these tottering feet, all speak of a life which is passing away. '*Abide with me!*' 'Leave me not, neither forsake me, O GOD of my salvation!'"

III. The Chichester Bible Class.

(From one of those who attended it.)

"This Bible Class, held successively at two private houses in the City of Chichester, was for Ladies only. Those attending came from Chichester and its neighbourhood. It always began and ended with prayer. The first subject chosen was the Acts of the Apostles. Afterwards the Dean took up the Old Testament History; and, when he died, he was in the middle of the Book of Joshua. At special Church Seasons however, such as Holy Week, he would take some subject connected with the Passion of our 'Divine LORD' (as he always called Him) and go minutely into all the details of the history. His usual plan was to read the passage himself (in the case of the New Testament, translating rapidly from the original); then he would explain it, refer to the parallel passages noted either in the margin of our English Bibles, or in his own Greek Testament, and would often read extracts explanatory of the passage, either from his own works or those of others. 'That dear fellow, Charles Marriott,' was often quoted. Often too he would remark on the opinions of those with whom he did not agree, *e.g.* Dean Stanley. Then he would ask questions and say, 'Have you any remarks to offer?' But it was very seldom that the remarks approved themselves to him. What *he* was driving at was something quite unexpected, and anything but commonplace.

"He was very peculiar in his method, and at times most eccentric ; but the lessons he taught impressed themselves on the minds of his hearers ; and those who attended the Class owe a deep debt of gratitude to him for opening out to them the meaning of the Sacred Writings in a manner (to say the least of it) very unusual.

"The teaching of the Types was always strongly enforced. One of his favourite types was the passage of the Red Sea, and the destruction of Pharaoh's host. He would refer to it as 'the Exode,' and connect it typically with our Blessed LORD'S 'decease[2]' and descent into Hell. As the Egyptians lay dead upon the seashore, so the hosts of Satan were vanquished by our LORD'S 'decease,' or exodus from the body.

"Joseph also was a favourite type with him. He used to compare the butler and the baker, one of whom was forgiven, and the other condemned, to the thieves upon the cross.

"One of his ideas was that the field purchased by Boaz from Ruth [Ruth iv. 3, 5, 9] was that in which the shepherds kept their flocks at the time of the Nativity [St. Luke ii. 8]; another that the offerings of

---

[2] See St. Luke ix. 31. "They" [Moses and Elias appearing in glory] "spake of his *decease* which he should accomplish at Jerusalem." The reader of the English Bible needs to be informed that the Greek word translated "decease" is τὴν ἔξοδον, "his Exodus." St. Peter uses the same word in speaking of his own death [2 Pet. i. 15]; μετὰ τὴν ἐμὴν ἔξοδον, "after my decease."

the wise men [St. Matt. ii. 11] furnished the means for the flight of the Holy Family into Egypt.

"He used to draw a very interesting parallel between St. Peter and St. Paul, showing that both had the power of working miracles; that the miracles were much of the same kind [3]; and that the presence of each had a miraculous effect [4].

"Being on one occasion asked what was the use of the Book of Canticles in the Bible, Dean Burgon replied, 'In the human body there is an organ called the spleen. No one knows its use; still it is necessary. So with the Canticles. Being a part of GOD'S Word, we may be sure that the book is necessary, and has its function to discharge, though what the use and function are may not be known.'

"He had no respect for legendary lore as compared with the sure and infallible teachings of GOD'S Word, telling us that legends were to the Word of GOD what liver, lights, &c., are to good meat,—a sort of spiritual garbage. Yet no one had a livelier appreciation than he of the poetry and beauty which there is in certain legendary tales. I remember his reading out to us a poem about a (supposed) child of Lydia, the purple-seller of Thyatira. The poem showed how Lydia's belief in the Resurrection had given her hope and comfort in thinking of her child. He recited it with great pathos, and was himself deeply affected while doing so."

Notes taken by one of his nieces of the Chichester Bible Class Lectures given Nov. 28, Dec. 6, Dec. 14, 1884.

"There are three different aspects of Holy Scripture, the Historical, the Moral, and the Spiritual.

---

[3] Compare the cure of the lame man at the Beautiful gate of the temple [Acts iii. 2, 7, 8] with the healing of the "cripple from his mother's womb" at Lystra [Acts xiv. 8, 9, 10]. Also the raising to life of Tabitha [Acts ix. 40, 41] with the raising to life of Eutychus [Acts xx. 9, 10].

[4] He alluded no doubt to the miracles wrought by St. Peter's shadow [Acts v. 15], and those wrought by the "handkerchiefs and aprons" which had touched St. Paul's body [Acts xix. 12].

"Under the Historical aspect falls whatever lies on the surface of the passage. The date; the manners and customs; the products of the country; whatever belongs to the geography, or chronology of the passage; when incidents are mentioned, whatever details of them are discoverable by a careful reader; the peculiar words employed, the modes of expression, and in fact whatever grows out of an attentive study of the place. In a word, everything that belongs to the passage, except the teaching derivable from it, or the spiritual inferences to be drawn from it.

"The Moral use of the passage consists in the lessons which it is designed to bring home to every one's conscience and heart. In the history of Joseph and his brethren, for example, how their sin found them out; how the sense of retribution was brought home to them [Gen. xlii. 21], and so forth. We may moralise thus on this narrative, that, though God's sentences sometimes seem harsh, the design of them is a loving one, to bring to our remembrance our violation of His laws. It shows too His intimate personal knowledge of each one of us. Joseph knew each of his brethren intimately and so God knows each one of us. Observe the story of Joseph's dealing with his brethren; and think of the dealing of the true Joseph with each one of *His* brethren; for in the one may be seen, as in a glass darkly, the image of the other. The lessons of piety and wisdom which Holy Scripture teaches may be declared to be its moral aspect. Whatever belongs to guidance, help, comfort, comes under this head. Holy Scripture, as it is a lantern unto our feet and a light unto our paths, a help, a consolation, a guide, an instrument of reproof, and rebuke, may be said to be Holy Scripture in its *moral aspect*."

The spiritual aspect and meaning of Holy Scripture.

"It is one thing to be fanciful in our explanation of Holy Scripture, and quite another to see that there is much more of mystery and mystical meaning in its records, than appears on the surface. If it be a book, which, while narrating past events, is so written that it not only gives a history of those events, but also, in narrating the past, shadows forth the future, it must be a book, like no other book in the world.—Illustration. There are some materials so woven, that looked at in one light, they appear to be of one colour, looked at in another light, of a different one. So too with the gilded edges of certain books. Looked at from one point of view, the edges are merely gilt; turn them a little, and you see red; turn them further, you see different colours, and sometimes even figures or views are seen in certain lights. The colours, the views, &c., are all there, but, except when they are placed in certain lights, they are invisible.

"The structure and tissue of Holy Scripture is throughout typical and prophetical. It is interwoven with typical foreshadowings. It reads like a simple story, but looked at in a different light, it is a divine prediction. No human device could achieve this. One remarkable point in this method of procedure is, that the revelation is thus extended further than it could have been by direct and express statement; another that Holy Scripture becomes a part of human probation, the Divine Author of it thus revealing to the quick ear and attentive eye of faith, mysteries which it would have been impossible to describe, and which in fact could not have been so well set forth in any other way, as by this suggestive method.

"The whole structure of the New Testament no less than of the Old is thus prophetical. In the parable of the Good Samaritan, for example, our Lord sets before us a prophetical picture of the whole human race, and of Himself as man's Saviour, when the Law, represented by the Priest and Levite who passed by on the other side, had done nothing to relieve the sufferer."

IV. THE BIBLE CLASS AT THE BISHOP OTTER MEMORIAL COLLEGE.

[*From two Ladies, both of whom were pupils at the College.*]

(1)

" I shall always remember with gratitude and pleasure

Dean Burgon's teaching. He used to come to the College on Sunday Evenings for about an hour, or perhaps longer, and take with us some part of the Bible. I think he generally asked us which Book we should like to read; and if the wish for a particular one was fairly universal, then that one was decided upon. During my two years at the College we did the Book of Genesis; and, when that was finished, we began St. John's Gospel. He used to ask each of us to read a verse in turn; sometimes he would hear two or three verses before he made a remark; but usually after each verse he would stop us and make comments upon it, or he would ask us first what we had to say about such and such a verse (he was fond of this way of questioning; he would put no definite question, but would simply ask for our opinion on some expression or incident in a verse). His own comments were the most beautiful and thoughtful I have ever heard. I think what struck one perhaps most of all was (at least so it seemed to me) his originality; one felt all the time that he had not got up his lesson for us from any commentary or other book, but that he was simply telling us what he had found out for himself from a constant reverent study of the Bible. Indeed he would sometimes say; 'This is only what *I* think about it'; and it seemed to us that this remark generally followed an unusually beautiful idea. He certainly taught us to read the Bible as few of us probably had read it before. I for one have never done such thorough work with any other teacher, either before or since. I have never seen any one with such an intense and loving reverence for GOD's Word as he possessed; his intimate acquaintance with it always struck me as something remarkable.

"He was always pleased when any of us asked him questions. This we used to do either in writing (in which case the paper was laid on the table before he came) or orally during the lesson. He answered the questions publicly, saying, 'I have been asked,' &c., but never mentioning the name of the questioner. I ought perhaps to have mentioned before his invariable habit of beginning each lesson with the words, 'Open thou mine eyes, that I may behold the wondrous things of thy law.'

"His manner in teaching was singularly attractive and winning. He carried us away with him, and *made* us feel in sympathy with him. He was full of little anecdotes, which often called forth peals of laughter. He had a characteristic way of saying; 'Now, do you agree with me? Say, Yes'   answer of 'Yes' was feeble, he would say in a louder and more emphatic tone, 'Say, *Yes*.' All old Bp. Otter students will remember this, I am sure. His courtesy towards us all was never failing. He constantly said what a great pleasure it was to him to come to the College, and how much he enjoyed those Sunday evenings. On one occasion, when he was called away into Somersetshire for a Sunday, he wrote, 'If it is a disappointment to any of yourselves, believe me it is a greater disappointment to *me*. It is the only thing, to say the truth, which makes me unwilling to be away from Chichester on Sunday' . . . . . . I will only add in conclusion that I shall ever be grateful for the privilege of having been taught by him. I think many of us felt, when we heard of his death, that we had indeed lost a friend, and that we should never see his like again."

(2)

"Many of us enjoyed the Dean's Lectures more than anything else at College. Our one grievance was that he sometimes got so much interested in his subject that he forgot to leave off; and when we heard the supper bell ring, we used to begin to get fidgetty. He rarely came punctually; but we used to be on the look out for him, and hurry into our seats as soon as he appeared. A chair was put for him, and he used to turn it round and sit down on the back of it for a few moments; but he spent most of the time walking up and down with a thin quarto volume in his hands. I should think it probably contained his own manuscript notes; anyhow it was difficult to read, and had to be carried to the window or to the gas according to the time of year.

. . . .

"One of the chief results of his teaching was that he showed us how very much there was in the Bible which we had never noticed or thought about. Sometimes we read only a few verses; but the Dean taught us all about them so very thoroughly that he made us feel how superficially we must have read them before.

"He used the black board a good deal, and drew with wonderful facility. I have in my note-book an illustration of one of the sheaves doing obeisance to Joseph's sheaf. With a few touches he drew the sheaf; and a very few more touches turned it into the figure of a woman leaning forward.

"But the black board was occasionally used for another purpose. GEESE would appear on it in large letters, when no one could answer what the Dean considered to be an easy question; and I have also seen GOOSE written there, because one of the students had forgotten whether Jacob guided his hands wittingly or unwittingly, when he laid them on the heads of Joseph's sons. Fortunately the Dean did not mind how much we laughed; and we often laughed a good deal.

"He used to tell us to read with expression; but there were some verses, especially in the history of Jacob, which only he could read to his own satisfaction. Jacob's reply to Judah [Gen. xliii. 6] begins with a long reproachful groan before he says, 'Wherefore dealt ye *so* ill with me, *as* to tell the man whether ye had yet a brother?'

"He told us he had once puzzled some boys by asking them how they would tell Jacob from Esau, if they saw them walking by, each covered from head to foot in a sheet? *Answer*: They would have seen one of them limp;—'Jacob halted upon his thigh.'

"At last he would stop,—reluctantly. We took it in turns to hand him his coat and hat, and we watched him go through the garden. He always turned round and took off his hat two or three times before he got to the gate; and the last we saw of him was his handkerchief waved over the top of it. The very worst weather never kept him away, though it was twenty minutes' walk, and the College Lane was often one mass of mud.

"He drew up a little Book of Private Prayers for us, and we valued it very much; but he always told us that the Book of Common Prayer was the best Manual of Devotion we could use."

V. THE HELP GIVEN BY HIM TO CANDIDATES FOR THE MINISTRY, AND HIS SUBSEQUENT INTEREST IN THEIR CAREER.

(*From two Clergymen of the Church of England.*)

(1)

"My first introduction to the late Dean of Chichester took place in the year 1855. I had been up to Oxford to compete for a Scholarship at Oriel, which I did not succeed in obtaining. The Provost, Dr. Hawkins, had asked me to breakfast, and at the breakfast-table I met Burgon. I was not introduced to him, but my attention was attracted to him; and I suppose it was scarcely possible to be in his company for any length of time, without his strongly marked personality making itself felt.

"The same afternoon, as I was leaving Oxford by train, I met Burgon at the station, and was introduced to him by a friend who was with me. Burgon at once proposed that we should travel to London together, and during the journey he elicited from me information with regard to my circumstances, my difficulties, and my hopes. My father, a well-known author, had been dead about a year, and, as he had left behind him no provision for his family, I was at that time acting as assistant-master in a school, and so earning my own living, with but little prospect of ever being able to save enough to enable me to proceed to the University. As I sat by Mr. Burgon's side and answered his enquiries, and assisted in the demolition of the large piece of plum-cake which he produced from his travelling bag, his eye glistened with tender sympathy, and his hand was often stretched out to grasp my own in the expression of it. When we parted, Burgon spoke a few kindly words of hope and encouragement, such as many a man might have used, without intending any particular value or importance to be attached to them. But Burgon's sympathy was true and strong; and he was not content with words. It must have been about six months afterwards when I received from him a brief note, telling me to come up to Oxford at a given date, to matriculate at ——— Hall. From that day forward until my University career was ended, I had no anxiety nor even thought about the payment of my ordinary expenses. Burgon made himself entirely responsible, and amongst his friends collected whatever amount was needed. To this day I know nothing whatever of the arrangements which were made. I only know that I owe my University education entirely to the sympathy and generous assistance of one who was at that time a complete stranger."

(2)

"When the Dean of Chichester died, I lost the best and dearest friend that a man ever had on earth. It was mainly through his disinterested kindness that I was enabled to fulfil the one great desire of my life in taking Holy Orders.

"I was first brought under his notice three or four years before he left Oxford for Chichester. I used generally to see him once a week in his rooms at Oriel. He was always hard at work when I called; but with his characteristic kindness, he would always spare me a few minutes for guidance in my reading. What a privilege it was to be able to consult him in one's difficulties!

"When he went to Chichester, he still kept up his interest in me, and allowed me to write to him whenever I wanted guidance in any matter.

"During his short visits to Oxford, after he had left it, I generally saw him for a short time. I used to meet him at St. Mary's before the early morning Service. It was on one of these occasions that he made known to me the joyful news that, through his own liberality and kind interest, I should be enabled to take Holy Orders. I shall never forget that time. It was a beautiful morning in early October. The Virginia creepers, which he himself had planted, hung down in festoons gloriously russeted about the beautiful porch of St. Mary' The Church door was locked. We stood within the porch. He took my hand and said, 'Let us pray.' After a short silence he said the Lord's Prayer aloud. When he had finished he said, 'Now don't thank me. Thank God for the blessing, and be sure you prove yourself worthy and faithful.' My heart was too full. I could only return the pressure of his dear hand in silence.

"When I went to my Curacy, I found a letter awaiting me in which he welcomed me as a Brother Clergyman into the Ministry.

"A few weeks after my Ordination the greatest calamity which can happen to a man befell me. My mother died. The letter which the Dean wrote to me in my sorrow now lies before me. The comfort it gave me has never left me."

[Excerpts from this and other letters of the Dean to this Clergyman, valuable for their own sakes as well as tending to show his continued interest in his friend, are here subjoined.]

a. Advice to an Undergraduate not to indulge in versification.

"Deanery, Nov. 5, 1880 . . . . The verses are *slight*, but very pretty;—remarkable rather for the beauty of the sentiment than for the skill of the execution. But this is in fact giving the verses a very good character. Keep a copy of them (and of everything else you write) by all means.

"Once when I discouraged you from writing poetry, my meaning was *not*, of course, to check you from giving utterance to a thought in your heart longing for poetical expression; but only to remind you to abstain from cultivating the habit, and trying to improve in the art, of writing English verses. And this, for no other reason but the obvious one, *viz.*, that you cannot *at present* AFFORD THE TIME. *That* will come, please GOD, by and by. . . . .

"P. S.—Remember the frequent prayer, and the pure life, and the habitual thought of GOD! GOD bless you!"

β. *Popular amusements not to be over-indulged in by Clergymen.*

"Deanery, Chichester, 1886. . . . . Your letter is a great comfort to me. Yes; be *very sparing in Lawn Tennis engagements*. Take my advice. You will be more RESPECTED AND MORE LISTENED TO ON SUNDAY by frequent requests to be excused (on the plea of parochial engagements), than you will be POPULAR by frequent compliances with every silly solicitation. I KNOW WHAT I SAY."

γ. *The wisdom which may be discerned in the loss of a parent by those who look for it.*

"The Deanery, Chichester, 23 Jan. 1886. . . . . This morning I learn that the heaviest grief which can befall a son has suddenly overtaken you.

"I am extremely concerned—sincerely concerned—for your bereavement. It would have been a great solace, could she have been spared to you,—a solace to her,—a solace to you. And you will realise at this time, and for the rest of your life, that a man can only have *one* Mother.

"I am bound nevertheless to declare that the marks of a loving Providence discernible in this dispensation strike me more forcibly than it is easy to express. I will enumerate some:

"1. She has been spared to enjoy for a month the certain knowledge that her son is a Clergyman, and may well have felt her cup run over (*Nunc dimittis !*).

"2. You had been with her *to the last. Henceforth you must have been severed.* The best moment for a more effectual severance had therefore clearly *come*, having been *deferred* till now,—*deferred as long as possible.*

"3. You had dutifully resolved on her support, and arranged for it effectually. In GOD'S sight, *that* is a deed which has been *done.*"

"4. Your anxieties concerning your Mother are now ended; and you must have been anxious so long as her life was prolonged. She is now with CHRIST.

"She has already told your father all about yourself, and in the place of peace will pray for you;—they both will,—and will pray effectually.

"5. How dreadfully harassing the event would have been *at any* period of your preparation for the Schools at Oxford, or for Holy Orders! . . . . . . I am amazed at the loving skill with which" [her death] "has been delayed until now."

"6. Lastly, you have been permitted to close her eyes, and be with her at the last.

"You will, I suppose, bury her with your father. You will have to consider whether you desire some day to lie *with them.* If so, better to ask leave now to enclose (with box edging) the necessary space of ground."

δ. *Clergymen should not be absorbed in the secular concerns of their flocks, and should observe Friday as a day of abstinence.*

"Deanery, Chichester, 4 June, 1886. . . . .
Being much pressed for time, I will on this occasion give you but two hints.

"1. Beware of suffering the *secular* to trench unduly on,—much less (GOD forbid) to swallow up the spiritual claims.

"There is a great tendency in the ministerial earnestness of a young man (and of an old one too) to be drawn more and more into the temporal wants and concerns of an interesting population, like this of yours. Secure for yourself the best hours of every day *for actual study* ; and when going hither and thither have some bit of the Gospel or of St. Paul (in the Greek) in your pocket to fall back upon and think over.

"2. When you give entertainments, *carefully eschew Friday*. Teach and tell the people why. For my part I simply refuse all dinner parties and festive gatherings on that day. The Head of the Depôt here invited me to dine with him at mess on a Friday. I pointed to *my* Order Book,—and declined. Ever affectionately, yours, J. W. B."

ε. *The merits of Bishop Christopher Wordsworth's 'Holy Bible with Notes.'*

"Wordsworth is very good and useful, as you say. The great merit of his Commentary is this:—(1) That he exhibits the mind of the Church in its best and purest time;—(2) That he is a really learned and well read man, and therefore never falls into the blunders of the unlearned;—(3) That he is thoroughly *Anglican*, and may be depended upon. But his work has this further extraordinary merit, (4) That being a commentary on the *whole* Bible, and all the work of *the same hand*, you meet with none of those discordant interpretations and inconsistent methods of teaching, which are *inevitable* when you have before you the joint product of many hands."

ζ. *On the Greek substantive* αὐτάρκεια *occurring only twice in the New Testament, and translated "sufficiency" in* 2 *Cor.* ix. 8, *but "contentment" in* 1 *Tim.* vi. 6.

"Deanery, Chichester, 31 August.—I am glad to see you notice the word αὐτάρκεια. It is only by cultivating this habit that you will ever *understand* languages, and be worth powder and shot as a Clergyman.

"I have not time for many words; but I will tell you something about αὐτάρκεια. It does *not* mean *contentment*.

That virtue is of Christian growth, and has no word to denote it in classical antiquity. The substitute is ἀρκεῖσθαι, ἀρκούμενοι, as in Heb. xiii. 5, 1 Tim. vi. 8,—or as in *v.* 6. αὐτάρκεια.

"Now this, as you see. is in strictness 'self-sufficiency' (*not* in the conventional sense of the word, but in the classical meaning of being *sufficient to oneself*,—not needing external aid). The underlying notion in all these substitutes for 'contentment' is always *sufficiency*. or *the sense of sufficiency*. Take the place before us, 1 Tim. vi. 6 ; 'But godliness *is* a gainful calling, if it be combined with the sense that GOD has given us enough.'

"Ponder the matter over, and you will see that αὐτάρκεια refers to the *outward supply*, 'contentment' to the *inward feeling*. *That* says (with Esau, Gen. xxxiii. 9), 'I have enough, my brother; keep that thou hast unto thyself.' *This* says (with Jacob, Gen. xxxiii. 11.), 'Because God hath dealt graciously with me, and because I have enough, (*margin*, 'all things'). The brothers were very different. Jacob was *more* than 'content'; he was grateful to GOD. Esau had enough, and knew it: but he took Jacob's gift notwithstanding (*see* ver. 11.)

"GOD bless and keep you! Take a walk daily, while the sunshine is so glorious; and go to bed early. Rise before the lark. I was up at 5 this morning, and have been working all day, and yet it was near 1 in the morning, ere I screwed out my lamp. Your friend,

J. W. B."

The Clergyman, to whom the above letters were written, saw Burgon for the last time during his visit to Folkestone in the June of 1888, when "He was quite as kind as ever. He inquired about all my doings, and took the greatest interest in my hopes and plans for the sailors and fishermen among whom I was then working. Dear holy man, he thought of everybody except himself!—I never saw him again. Soon after his return to Chichester I heard that all hope was over. He wrote me one short note in which he said he was dying through overwork, but that he was happy, because he knew in whose hands he was. He sent me a loving message from his dying bed."—The loving message was, in the words of the Rev. W. F. Rose, who conveyed it; "Tell him I feel fully repaid."

It now only remains to give some account of the Memorials erected, or in course of being erected, to Dean Burgon in Chichester Cathedral and in Oxford.

The first of these is a Memorial window in the Lady Chapel of the Cathedral at Chichester. This is a three-light window on the North side of the Lady Chapel,—the second window from the West end. The central light represents the Flight into Egypt; and in the side lights are figures of Angels, in the Eastern of *guiding* Angels showing the way, in the Western of *guardian* Angels bringing up the rear of the procession. In the tracery above are depicted figures of the Holy Innocents glorified. This particular feature was introduced as a way of marking Dean Burgon's intense love for little children; but the general subject of the window was determined upon many years ago by the Dean and Chapter. At the base of the window runs along the following inscription;—

"*Ad gloriam Dei O. M., et in memoriam Johannis Gulielmi Burgon S.T.B., hujus ecclesiae Cathedralis Decani* [A.D. 1876–A.D. 1888] *hanc fenestram P.C. amici, confratres, maerentes. Quomodo dilexi legem tuam, Domine! tota die meditatio mea est. Psalm cxix.* 97" [the text always used by Burgon at the opening of his Bible Classes].

The cost of the window was defrayed by subscription. It was designed and executed by Messrs. Clayton and Bell.—It was solemnly dedicated April 12, 1890, with a short service, the Psalm used in which was Psalm cxix.

97-104, the Lesson, Wisdom iii. 1-6, and the Prayer of the function as follows ;—

"O LORD GOD ALMIGHTY, to Thy Honour and Glory we dedicate this window, which has been placed in this Chapel in memory of Thy servant John William Burgon. May we ever strive to walk, as he did, in Thy fear and love, making Thy Word the rule of our life ; and in the study of that Word may we ever find, as he found, our chiefest delight, through Jesus Christ our Lord. *Amen.*"

The service being finished, and a Hymn ("Let Saints on Earth in concert sing," &c.) having been sung, the Reverend Prebendary Powles, one of the Dean's oldest and warmest friends, delivered a beautiful and appropriate Address, bringing out well the leading features of his history and character, and containing the following striking anecdote ;—

" When the '*Revision Revised*' was passing through the Press, he asked me to look over the proof-sheets, and point out what I thought objectionable. I confess I undertook the task with some trepidation, and when I went with my first criticisms, I did not feel at all sure how they would be received. I had to deprecate what seemed to me certain severities of expression, and a certain redundance of sarcasm. The Dean heard me patiently, and after a little consideration said, with an amused smile, ' Well, I suppose they must go.' Without exception the offending passages were struck out. In truth, all his sensitiveness was for GOD's honour. Jealous there, he had, apart from that, no care for himself."

There were present at this Service the Bishop, the Dean, three of the four Canons Residentiary, and six of the Prebendaries.

But Chichester was not satisfied with this Memorial of one of the two most illustrious men (and very illustrious both of them were) who since the Reformation have filled its Decanal stall,—and one of them in immediate succession to the other. The second Memorial to Dean Burgon is a full length figure of him in brass, inserted in a slab of Derbyshire marble, measuring about 6ft. 2in. in length. The figure, exclusive of the base on which it stands, is 3ft. 7in. The Dean is represented in surplice, cassock, stole and hood, with the hands clasped in front of the breast. Upon the breast (below, and not in the hands) is a chalice. Across the breast is a scroll, intersected in the centre by the joined hands, bearing the legend, "Credo quod Redemptor meus vivit." There is a wide border of brass, with the symbols of the Four Evangelists at the four corners, running round the sides of the slab, and enclosing the figure. On this border is the inscription; "Johannes Gulielmus Burgon S.T.B. hujusce Ecclesiae Cathedralis per xii annos Decanus S. Scripturae Indagator indefessus Defensor strenuus. Obiit prid. Non. Sext. A. S. MDCCCLXXXVIII ætatis suae lxxv." The work was designed by Messrs. Bodley and Garner, and executed by Messrs. Barkentin and Krall of London. It should be added that the placing of this monument in the Cathedral was principally due to the munificence of Archdeacon Mount.—The brass is fixed in the pavement of the South Transept, east of the S.W. pier of the central tower, and almost immediately behind the Dean's Stall in the Choir.

The Memorials in Oxford are two, one of a private character, erected by members of the family, over the spot where Dean Burgon was interred; the other a tribute to his memory shortly to be erected in the Church of St. Mary-the-Virgin's, from his former Parishioners and from members of his Congregation, from attendants on his Oxford Bible Classes, and a still wider circle of friends indebted to him in various ways.

The Chichester Life.

The first of these Memorials is in the enclosure in Holywell Cemetery, where there sleep not only Dean Burgon himself, but also his little sister Katharine Margaret (who died April 28, 1836,—see vol. i. p. 54), his mother (who died Sept. 7, 1854,—see vol. i. p. 228), his father (who died Aug. 28, 1858,—see vol. i. pp. 244, 245, &c.), his sister Emily Mary (who died May 6, 1871. —see vol. i. pp. 392, 393), and his brother Thomas Charles (who died Feb. 14, 1872,—see vol. i. pp. 407, 408), and two intimate friends, Miss Hargreave (*d.* 1872), and Miss Mary Wintle (*d.* 1880). This memorial is a solid gabled cross of white marble. At the end of each arm of the cross, under the gabled termination, are the sacred symbolic letters ☧ and A Ω blended in a monogram. At the upper end of the cross under the gable is carved a crown; at the lower end under the gable two intersecting triangles. Round the base runs this inscription; "JOANNES WILLELMUS BURGON S.T.B., DECANUS CICESTRENSIS HAC OLIM IN URBE ECCLESIAE B.M.V. VICARIUS OBDORMIVIT IN CHRISTO DIE iv. AUGUSTI MDCCCLXXXVIII NATUS ANNOS FERE LXXV." The Tablet in the Wall immediately over this monument (a very elaborate trefoil) contains the following inscription from the pen of Archdeacon Palmer;—

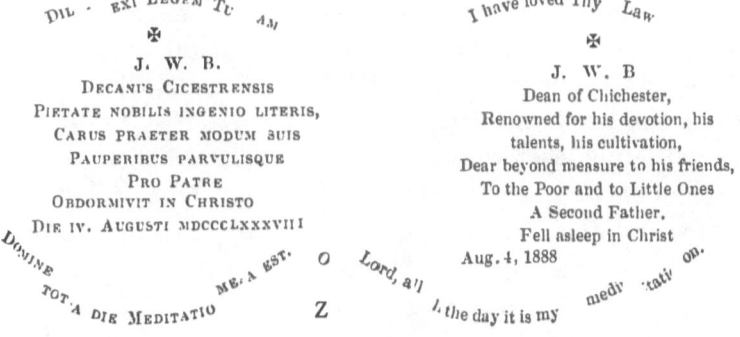

The Memorial in St. Mary the Virgin's Church, Oxford, now (June 23, 1891) in course of execution, and which will probably be in its place before these pages see the light, is the painted glass with which it is proposed to fill the great West Window of the Nave. The design for this window, which has been accepted both by the authorities of the University and by the Vicar and Vestry of the Parish, was furnished by Mr. C. E. Kempe, M.A., of Pembroke College, Oxford. The subject of the painting is a "Jesse Tree,"—the Dedication of the Church seeming to make some reference to the Incarnation appropriate. In four of the lights are inserted figures of the four Evangelists writing their histories,—an insertion suggested by an early and deservedly popular work of the Dean's, his '*Plain Commentary on the Holy Gospels.*' In the tracery of the Window are introduced figures of St. Thomas of Canterbury, St. Anne, St. Catherine, and St. Nicholas, to whom Chapels were dedicated in the old Church. The seven lower lights contain the Arms of the twenty-one existing Colleges (it will be remembered that Burgon's '*Historical Notices of the Oxford Colleges*' were written in connexion with, and as the letter-press for, Mr. Shaw's '*Arms of the Colleges*,' see vol. i. p. 239 *et sequent.*). In the tracery are the heraldic shields of King Edward II, who granted the advowson of the parish to Oriel College; of King Henry VII, in whose reign St. Mary the Virgin's Church was rebuilt; of Cardinal Morton, Archbishop of Canterbury, who issued letters of recommendation for that work; of Russell, Chancellor of the University and Bishop of Lincoln, in whose diocese Oxford was then situated; of the diocese of Oxford; of the University; of Oriel College, the patrons of the living; and of Dean Burgon himself. This Memorial window derives additional interest from a circumstance communicated to the author by the Rev. R. G. Livingstone, to whom these volumes are already so much indebted ; and who writes thus ;—

"You will be interested to hear that many years ago, when I was his Curate, the Dean mentioned to me a design which he had, viz. to fill the great West Window of the ave of St. Mary's with stained glass. He intended to apply to all the Colleges for help, and to place their armorial bearings in the Window. Now, after so many years, the design which the Dean had in view is about to be carried into effect."

Our notice of the Memorials of Dean Burgon may be appropriately closed by the mention made of him in the speech of the Public Orator (Rev. W. W. Merry, D.D., Rector of Lincoln) at the *Encænia* of the year after his death,—June 26, 1889 ;—

"Verum enimvero, quoniam in hac concione semper moris fuit eorum repetere memoriam, quos nuperrime morte abreptos moereat Academia, liceat mihi insignem pietate virum in mentes vestras revocare, qui etsi nobis longae absentiae condicione tamquam amissus, tamen et totius Universitatis, et praesertim Collegii sui Orielensis amator exstitit et castigator, unicus. Quis est cujus ex animo exciderit Joannes Burgon, Decanus Cicestrensis, vir admodum reverendus, et in critica sacra expertissimus? Qui

"Yet, as in this Oration it hath ever been the custom to commemorate those over whom the Academy mourns, as having been quite recently torn away from her by death, suffer me to recall to your minds a man of eminent piety, who, although in a manner lost to us by the circumstance of his long absence, yet ever stood forth as in an unparalleled degree the loving friend and faithful reprover of the whole University, and particularly of his own College of Oriel. Who is there that remembers not the Very Reverend John

profecto quotienscunque in controversias se injecisset, 'Impiger, iracundus, inexorabilis, acer[5]' proculdubio videbatur: idem tamen omnibus disputationibus tantum leporis immiscebat, tam suavi pervicacia sui ipsius opinionibus inhaerebat, tam sincerum acti se temporis laudatorem praestabat, ut omnium sibi indulgentiam, multorum amorem, sibi conciliaret."

Burgon, Dean of Chichester, a man profoundly versed in sacred criticism? who doubtless, whenever he threw himself into controversies, seemed to be 'Swift, passionate, uncompromising, fierce[5],' and yet with all his contentions mingled up so much that was attractive, with so pleasant a persistency adhered to his own opinions, and showed himself so sincere in his eulogy of bygone times, as to win indulgence from all, love from many."

[5] Horace's sketch of the character of Achilles, A. P. 121.

CHAPTER IV.

THE CHARACTER — INTELLECTUAL, MORAL, AND SPIRITUAL.

The writer of this Biography feels that he owes some sort of explanation to the reader of his having contravened, in Dean Burgon's case, the views which the Dean himself entertained and expressed of the proper limits of an ordinary Biography.

"I have long cherished the conviction," says the lamented author of '*The Lives of Twelve Good Men*,' "that it is to be wished that the world could be persuaded that Biography might with advantage be confined within much narrower limits than at present is customary. Very few are the men who require 500 pages all to themselves :—far fewer will bear expansion into *two* such volumes" [*Ded. Pref.* viii].

Judicious as this suggestion may be in regard to the biographies of less distinguished persons, the writer, in studying Dean Burgon's character and career, has found him to be in every way too large a man to be adequately portrayed on a very small canvass. While the names of persons of less note, who yet may have established a claim to be gratefully remembered by those who come after them, are sufficiently preserved from oblivion by a *Memoir*, there are those, surely, whose intellectual and moral pre-eminence, and whose manifoldness of gift and power, challenge a *Life*. Would anyone say that the brief Memoir of Samuel Wilberforce in 'The Lives of Twelve Good Men,' admirably as it is executed, would, if it stood alone, be an adequate tribute to the memory of one who was (probably) the greatest English Bishop of the Century? No; but before the Memoir appeared there were in existence three bulky Volumes, giving a methodical account of Bishop Wilberforce's career, from his birth to his death, and copiously illustrated by his Letters and Journals,—not more, surely, than he deserved, who in his day (and it was a day of stir and movement) was the most potent factor in the life of the English Church. His friends claim for Dean Burgon that, in regard of the variety and versatility of his intellectual powers, the intensity of his moral faculties, and that profound veneration for the Word of God which formed the chief feature both of his spiritual character and of his teaching, he showed a pre-eminence among the men of his generation, which abundantly entitles him to a Life as distinct from a Memoir. The outline of his character, now to be traced, will, it is hoped, serve to justify this claim.

I. The first character, then, in which, when his name is mentioned, John William Burgon is thought of, is that of a theologian. Theology absorbed him entirely in the later period of his life; more and more as he grew older did he, in pursuance of the charge given to him at his Ordination to the Priesthood, " apply himself wholly to this one thing, and draw all his cares and studies this way." But to say no more than this, would be to ignore the versatility of his powers and the wealth of his mental resources, and thus to give an entirely inadequate conception of his character as a whole. The century, of which the last quarter is now fast ebbing away, has seen other learned and profound theologians, some of whom possibly may have rivalled him in this single and highest department of human knowledge (though it may be doubted whether any have displayed an industry equal to his); but where shall we look to find a theologian with an equal breadth of general cultivation, and one who, while he was a devoted student, living in and for theological folios and ancient manuscripts, came down into human life, in its humblest details, so familiarly and lovingly as he, and touched all, even the humblest, whom he came across, with the tender colours of his sympathy and affection?—He had considerable knowledge of, and manifested the keenest interest in, Archæology; was a passionate admirer of ancient Art; and copied antiques with the pencil and brush of a master. This was the flavour with which the jar was first imbued, and which it retained quite to the end.— Then he had quite the genius of an artist; a genius so irrepressible that it not only led him to employ his odds and ends of time, wherever he was, in sketching his immediate surroundings (in which, by a natural aptitude for Art, he always seemed to discover something picturesque); but also burst forth in his letters, which he loved to garnish with illustrative drawings; sometimes, if corresponding with children (whom he treated as his playmates), of the most grotesque character. — Then, again, he was no inconsiderable biographer. The '*Life and Times of Sir Thomas Gresham*,' his earliest original literary effort, published at the age of twenty-six, before he had had the advantage of a University education, shows a marvellous power of historical research, and proves that he was early initiated into the secret, which since those days has been widely and generally recognised, of going to the original sources of history, and examining archives, instead of accepting and handing on the traditional accounts borrowed from comparatively modern writers. In later days, when Burgon had become a Fellow of Oriel, his great friend Patrick Fraser Tytler, who had given him "frequent good counsel and kind assistance" in the composition of Gresham's '*Life*,' was made by him the subject of a biography, which attracted much attention, was reviewed in terms of the highest commendation in the '*Quarterly*,' and rapidly attained (though the author was then comparatively unknown) a second edition. How little could it have been foreseen (and, it may be added, what a testimony is it to the immanence and indestructibility of certain aptitudes and talents) that the latest literary labour of the learned and accomplished Dean—the labour which may be said to have given the *coup de grâce* to his strength, already failing beneath the strain of undue and excessive mental application—should be what his earliest had been,—Biography! '*The Lives of Twelve Good Men*' reached a fifth edition within less than a year from the time of their publication (they have now reached a seventh); and while some portion of this success is no doubt due to the lamented removal of the author, before the work could make its appearance, and to the large crop of interesting reminiscences which sprang up in consequence of his removal, and called public attention to his career, and to the irreparable loss which the Church and the Science of Theology had sustained by his death, it is clear from the universal verdict of approval, which the work has elicited from all intelligent and discriminating readers, that what has chiefly recommended it to public favour has been its literary merit. It is seldom indeed that our great theologians have shown a proficiency like this in any department of literature distinct from and unconnected with theology.—Of his poetical powers, which were also considerable, it must be said that what he has left behind hardly gives an adequate conception of them. The little collection of fugitive pieces, which his friends " so strongly urged him to put together " in his later days (the date of the publication is Easter 1885), contains several highly pleasing little poems[6], together with two

[6] '*The Sailing of the Fleet in 1854*' is a most spirited lyrical piece, traced on the lines of Campbell's '*Battle of the Baltic*,' while the affectionate memories of his undergraduate career,—the Provost, the Tutors, his academical contemporaries, even the College Servants,—which he has enshrined in " Worcester College," have a pathos and beauty about them most characteristic of the writer. And his indomitable cheerfulness and brightness of spirit—sentiments which several of his letters also give expression to, and which had its source in the beautiful sights and sounds of Nature, and in the many blessings allowed to us all by a wise and loving Providence,—find appropriate utterance in '*L'Envoy*,' and in the verses, '*Written in a Steamboat on the Clyde*.' The volume commences with his Oxford Prize Poem on '*Petra*,' which itself rises much above the average of such compositions in poetic power. While these lines are being written, the author has received a curious testimony to the poetical merits of '*Petra*' from a passage, which has been copied out for him, in the Biography of the late Reverend Thomas Anthony Methuen, formerly Rector of All Cannings in Wiltshire. The biography was written by Mr. Methuen's eldest son, who gives this account of his father's friendship with Burgon, a friendship contracted late in life. It is right to add that the author of the present Biography, having known nothing of Mr. Methuen, cannot say what may have been his qualifications as a judge of poetry. Suffice it that a man of considerable mark, as he is assured Mr. Methuen was, was thoroughly captivated by the beauty of '*Petra*.'

" My list of friendly notables would not be complete without mention of the last, ' born as it were out of due time,' whom my father acquired. He had run beyond the span of threescore and ten years, when the feelings which receive warm impressions of others are in most men lapsing into barrenness; but in him old age was remarkably green and succulent, as the sequel will shew. It happened once upon a time that the 'Poet's Corner' of the '*Devizes Gazette*,' whither his eyes always bent first on opening the paper, contained an extract from an Oxford Prize Poem called '*Petra*.' My father was so fascinated by the lines, that he could not rest till he had got the whole poem. After he had it in his possession, his interest and pleasure knew no bounds. He

or three, such as 'The Dedication of the Temple,' 'St. Paul preaching at Athens,' and 'The Blind Minstrel's Smile,' which indicate original imaginative power in a degree that was never developed in more sustained efforts. But these are quite enough to show that he had the true spirit of poetry in him, and that it was a spirit which prompted him to sing, whenever the stress of more serious avocations was relaxed, and the result of which was to give a

never ceased his libations, till he got himself saturated, and oozed '*Petra*' at every pore. As in the case of Archdeacon Hoare's lines, I tried once or twice to put on the 'brake,' but he generally contrived to elude me, or trip me up, and get his pleasant wilful way.

"The next step was to indite a letter to the author, which being responded to in most kindly mood, an invitation to visit the Rectory followed, and thus my adventurous father, oblivious of all considerations but the sweets of poetry, and the desire to see the man who had filled his mouth with honeycomb, caught the *Rev. John William Burgon* in his artless toils, met him with the enthusiasm of a schoolboy at the Devizes Station, and carried him off in triumph to All Cannings. I really forget whether the cold-blooded sons prophesied an evil result, and cynically expected they should have to cry, 'There! I told you so'; but if they did, their prognostications were utterly wrong. A *genial Christian gentleman* and an accomplished scholar paid us a visit, not once nor twice, and always left behind a fragrant memory of his presence. This late friendship (for such it truly became) was the more remarkable,

because the two friends hailed from very different ports in respect of their Churchmanship and theological opinions; but my father's militant days were over, and whereas in his years of vigorous life and thought he would certainly have courted an encounter or two, now he carefully avoided such occasions, and his own conversation turned chiefly on the archaisms, of which his far-advanced years gave him an interesting store.

"I have been amused to see, by my father's letters which have fallen into my hands, that he was taken to task by Low Church friends on account of his new associate. He does not refuse to plead, but seems to take a lesson of the cuttle fish, and uses his ink by way of beclouding the line of attack. Or to vary the metaphor, he tries to throw his harriers off their scent by holding a garland of *Burgonia Oxoniensis* before their noses, and expatiating on the attractive qualities of the *man*.

"The following is the poetic greeting which Mr. Burgon received at All Cannings in October, 1859 :—

'Burgon, whose lyre 'mid Petra's ruins strung,
  Sounded, associate with thy tuneful tongue, &c., &c.'"

sort of ornamental fringe of song to a life of close and severe study.—And had he any gift for music,—a power which is so often denied where there is found, as there was in his case, a genius for drawing and painting? Judging from the intercourse which the writer was privileged to hold with him, and which during his tenure of the Deanery of Chichester was intimate, he should have questioned any power of Dean Burgon's in this direction were it not that one who was formerly Priest Vicar and Succentor of Chichester Cathedral[7], and therefore skilled both in the theory and practice of music, writes thus of his own mind (not in answer to any question put to him on the subject);—

"The late Dean had a fine appreciation of music, and there could not be a better listener than he when there was anything going on in the way of playing or singing. Without great musical knowledge, he seemed to know at once what was worth listening to, and what not."

In short, while of course his natural capacity for one form of Art was greater than for another, there was no form of it wholly without interest to his artistic mind. And in order to establish out of his own mouth what Mr. Brandram has here said of him, it is only necessary to cite a passage occurring in a letter to one of his sisters (Oct. 29, 1841), in which he describes very poetically the impression made upon him by the music in Magdalen College Chapel, on the first occasion of his attending Divine Service there.

"Oh! if you could see Magdalen Chapel! and hear the organ!!—oh, it is indeed seraphic. But you will

---

[7] The Rev. T. P. Brandram, Rector of Rumboldswyke, Chichester, to whom the author is indebted for much kindness, and some of whose remarks on the late Dean's Bible Classes for Undergraduates at Oriel, have already been presented to the reader.

some day see it, and feel your blood curdle with emotion. . . . We had a fine anthem and beautiful chanting; but the way the organ was managed beats everything. I don't quite know how to explain it; but it is as if,—while the full tide of music was pouring from every tube of the instrument—as if a sharp strong musical movement were taking place at the same time, —harmonizing with—contrasting with—relieving, and at the same time uniting the more powerful sound. I can only illustrate my meaning by some such fancy as that of a sweet climbing plant wreathed about the stem of an enormous oak."

He who wrote that passage must have had "a fine appreciation of music" to enable him to write it.

But indeed there was scarcely any branch of knowledge uncongenial to him, or which did not receive from him, at some time or other of his life, a measure of attention. The passion for Archæology and archæological research, which has been already adverted to, ran in his blood; it was his inheritance from his father; his earliest publication [8] testifies to it. Heraldry, with its cognate research into pedigrees, had always a strong attraction for him; 'The Arms of the Oxford Colleges,' with Historical Notices of the Colleges annexed [see vol i. pp. 239-242],—a work which he found time to put forth amid the graver studies and engrossing controversies of his Oxford life,—evinces not only a love of the subject, but a good measure of practical acquaintance with it. To Architecture he was so drawn by his natural bent, that he was wont to say that, next after Holy Orders, the vocation upon which he had set his heart from a very early period, he would have chosen the architect's profession

---

[8] 'Mémoire sur les Vases Panathénaïques, par P. O. Bröndsted. Traduit de l'Anglais, par J. W. Burgon,'—Paris, 1833. [See vol i. pp. 37, 38.]

for his pursuit in life. While his love of language and aptitude for the study of it, are shown, not only by his frequent etymological speculations, some of which will appear in the sequel, but also by the '*Glossary of Bedfordshire Words*[9]' [see vol. i. p. 214, and Appendix B], which he compiled for the local press, and which he intended to publish in a separate form, but was always diverted by more serious pursuits.

II. But I must pass from his intellectual gifts to speak of faculties of a more moral cast, in which he was equally versatile. And first as to humour. I suppose there are but few men who, while they have been immersed all their life long in the gravest and severest studies, have succeeded so perfectly as he did in retaining to the end (sobered somewhat at the *very end* by uncomfortable narrowness of means, of which he frequently complained during the two or three last years of his life, and by a constitution giving way under the strain of excessive literary toil) such a wonderful exuberance of the gaiety and light-heartedness of youth. For this was the true account of the jocose side of his character; it was not a man's cultivated and polished wit; it was not the rich humour of a matured mind; it was to the end a child's

---

[9] He has left three manuscript books, into which he has pasted the slips from the local newspaper, as they successively appeared. The blank pages and spaces of these books are copiously annotated in manuscript, with additions to the glossary, illustrative quotations, &c. In his introductory article ('*Provincialisms of Bedfordshire, No. I*'), which he dates Oriel College, Oxford, Feb. 10, 1868, he tells the reader that it was "full twenty-five years since" he "began to collect the words and phrases which form the present Glossary." So that it would have been begun in the midst of his undergraduate career, probably in one of the vacations spent by him at Houghton Conquest, when he was reading twenty chapters of Herodotus and ten of Livy daily. Excerpts from the Introductory Article and from the Glossary will be given in an Appendix. [See Appendix B.]

wild, extravagant, sometimes boisterous gaiety, which made the heart juvenile, even when old age had been attained. "I have the spirits of a boy," said he to the author one day at Norwich, when he had been keeping a room full of people in a tumultuous uproar of laughter, by narrating a comic incident with an accompaniment of the most grotesque attitudes and gestures. [See above pp. 127–130.] That was exactly the case,—"the spirits of a boy." A dignitary of the Church, who knew him well, says of him, in a letter which I am permitted to quote ;—

"He did not seem to appreciate the line which divides the humorous from the ludicrous .... his jesting, both in speech and act, passed at times into buffoonery .... sometimes his comedy passed into broad farce."

This criticism is true, and may quite be accepted by those who loved the natural frolic and sportiveness that was in the man, almost as much as they revered his profound learning, his splendid genius, his sterling worth. The spirits of childhood are naturally extravagant; and he (peculiar in this, as in many other respects) retained the spirits of childhood long after they have in ordinary men been broken in, and tamed, and chastened by the experiences of life and the monotonous routine of daily duty. In the late Dean Mansel, many of whose witty sayings are recorded in '*The Lives of Twelve Good Men*,' the fun that was in him was in harness. In Dean Burgon, if the expression may be allowed, *it was turned out to grass*;—like the fun of the old Aristophanic Comedy, it knew not how to put restraint upon itself. If, on one side of it, this must be regarded as an infirmity (for that which is disciplined and cultivated is of course *per se* preferable to that which has not been submitted to such a process), on the other side, anything which tends to keep the heart fresh amid the carking, cankering, corroding cares of life, has of itself a certain advantage, not to say a certain beauty, and helps towards the fulfilment of those sacred precepts, "Take no thought for the morrow," "Be careful for nothing [1]."

---

[1] It requires to be said that several of the grotesque stories told about Dean Burgon have, as told *of* him, no foundation at all in fact, while others which have such a foundation, have in passing through several mouths, acquired new features, which they had not originally. One story very generally told of him, to the effect that he ended a sermon very eulogistic of Bishop Jeremy Taylor and Bishop Bull with the ejaculation, "Be it mine to live the life of a Taylor (tailor?), and die the death of a Bull (bull?)," has been thoroughly sifted, and found to be untrue, as told *of* him. His nieces well remember the story having been told *to* him by a clergyman who was sitting with him at table at Oxford, and of his being greatly amused by it. They also remember his often having told it in conversation to others as a good story; and thus, as doubtless some of his pulpit utterances *were* grotesque, it came to be supposed that the connexion between the story and him was, not that he had told the anecdote with *gusto*, but that he had himself originated an *équivoque*, which, as uttered from the pulpit, would be, to say the least, of a very unseemly character. By way of showing the frequently far-back origin of many such good stories, which are groundlessly fastened, as time goes on, on any character on whom people think that they would sit suitably, the author is permitted to quote part of a letter addressed to a niece of the late Dean Burgon's by the Rev. Henry Deane, B.D., formerly Vicar of St. Giles's in Oxford,—an intimate friend of the Dean's, and one who, anxious as he is to clear him of a false charge, does not at all, as will be seen, minimise the element of the humorous which there was in his character,—and which (as in the case of South, Latimer, and other preachers similarly endowed) would occasionally peep out even in the pulpit.

"Clay Hill House,
"Gillingham, Dorset,
"March 12, 1890.

"My dear Miss Rose,—No. Your good uncle would never have said anything of the sort. In fact he never did. The story is very old. My father matriculated in 1817, that is 73 years ago, and then the story was ascribed to a Canon of Christ Church. But stories of this sort are always fathered upon some living person in a most wicked way. Even upon myself stories have been founded, which I have proved to be either fibs, or borrowed from some older story which I have been able to trace. So you may give complete contradiction to this particular story. My dear friend, your uncle, did say

But assuredly this juvenility of spirits in mature age had a deeper connexion with the subject than can at first sight be appreciated. It was essentially part and parcel of a character which, as many parts of this Biography will testify, had the strongest, the strangest, the most enthusiastic and romantic interest in children, even at the earliest age, in their pursuits, their ways, their manner of looking at things, their amusements,—an interest so constant and clinging that, busy man as he was, studious man as he was, devout man as he was, it was never out of season with him to play with children,—to make himself one of them. It is told of him, and probably with substantial accuracy, that on one occasion being missed at the week-day Office of the Cathedral, when it was known that he had habited himself for it, and had passed out of the Deanery into the Cloister, and being afterwards interrogated as to where he had been during the Service, he explained that, having found a little boy in the cloister playing with a ball, but looking very disconsolate for want of a playmate, the temptation to give the child a happy half-hour proved too much for him, and he proceeded eagerly to

funny things sometimes in his sermons (as for instance when he compared me at St. Giles', when the Organ was opened, to Jeroboam, for 'devising a feast out of my own heart,' &c., &c.), but he would never have perpetrated so miserable a joke as that about Bishops Taylor and Bull. As the story was current *at least* 73 years ago, he cannot be guilty of it—certainly, as Dean of Chichester, he would not have said such stuff. I do remember this, however. One evening in 1875 when I was hard at work on my '*Commentary on Jeremiah*,' as I was going up to Miss Wintle's for supper, I heard a voice behind me say, 'There is a strong smell of Jeremiah somewhere about here.' I turned round and saw the Dean coming up behind me, and said, 'Yes; and here are the figs.' And there they were, *in two baskets*, but as we ate them at supper we found that they were not '*naughty*.'

"With my kind regards to your sister,

"I am, very sincerely,

"H. DEANE."

throw and catch the ball, leaving the Divine Office to go on without him. Similar stories of his seizing every opportunity of participating in the amusements of children are "legion," and some of them have been recounted in our narrative. I refer to them now, only because they seem to accommodate themselves so well to what has been just said of his own juvenility of spirits. Thoroughly juvenile in heart, he was attracted by a natural sympathy towards children, even when infants, and was susceptible beyond ordinary men to the charms of their manner, their simplicity, their innocence. And thus we are led up naturally to speak of that which was indeed the very core of his character, and which supplied the interpretation of what might seem to persons, who lacked the true key to it, unamiable and repellent,—I mean the intense and altogether unusual affectionateness of his soul, and its thorough penetration with tenderness and sympathy. And here the writer is fortunate in being able to present the reader with a sketch of Dean Burgon's character from the pen of a common friend, Bishop Hobhouse, who knew him intimately (as having had charge, when the Dean was Vicar of St. Mary-the-Virgin's, Oxford, of the neighbouring parish of St. Peter's in the East) and, like all who knew him intimately, loved him cordially. The Bishop shall speak for himself; in vain would the author seek to improve upon a sketch so true, so faithful, and so discriminating.

" My intimacy with him gave me a thorough insight into his character. It enabled me to see how impossible it was for outsiders to read it aright. To many of them he made himself known by fierce utterances, and such persons cannot be prepared to hear that the key-note of the character was love. But in very truth it was so.

Whatever he had to do with habitually, whether a place, a person, a family, or an institution, he clothed it with such reverent affection, that it became sacred in his sight. To depreciate it, to alter it, to see any faults in it needing amendment, was sacrilege—to be withstood with all his might. No disparaging argument must be listened to. It was thus that his College, his University, his familiars, the Church of his Baptism, with all its standards and customs, the Version of the Bible adopted by the Church of England, were all too sacred for the touch of change to be allowed without indignant protest. Every statement that depreciated the venerated objects, he repelled as he would have repelled a slander upon his mother. His outbursts were instinctive, showing the depth from whence they came. They were not aimed at the *persons* whose utterances or policy distressed him; for with many of them he maintained unbroken friendship. Their strength gave the measure of the strength of his loving allegiance, which had been, in his view, unjustifiably provoked. His nearest friends knew the wisdom of avoiding those subjects, upon which his affections were too strong to allow the judgment to exercise its due control; but they can all testify to his utterances, though sometimes unduly disdainful, being wholly free from the venom of hatred or spite. . . . They only who knew him intimately could know the intensity of his aff⋯

While entirely concurring in the justice of the above remarks, the present writer thinks that even more might be said than Bishop Hobhouse has said, in explanation and justification of the strong and passionate utterances, with which Mr. Burgon occasionally vindicated truths or institutions, which seemed to him to be wantonly assailed. Antipathy to the opponents of what we have learned to love and honour,—antipathy passionately felt and expressed,—is generally, and not in his case only, love at its negative pole. It was the Apostle of love, who seems to have reciprocated in a peculiar manner the distinguishing affection of the Divine Master,—it was he and his brother who were for calling down fire from heaven upon Samaritans, when refusing to that Master harbour and hospitality. And although it is true that they were rebuked for this display of a carnal zeal, as seeking the destruction rather than the reformation of adversaries, and thus manifesting a spirit wholly incongruous with the genius of the New Dispensation, yet it is to be remembered that, even after the bestowal of the new heart and the new spirit at Pentecost, holy men of God, speaking as they were moved by the Holy Ghost, did use occasionally the language of anathema,—Stephen, though he died with a prayer for his murderers upon his lips, being carried away at the end of his apology by a fierce burst of indignation against the "stiffnecked and uncircumcised in heart and ears," who had been the "betrayers and murderers of the Just One," and John, in a spirit véry like that which Eusebius says that he expressed, on hearing that Cerinthus was in the bathhouse, forbidding one of his correspondents to harbour under his roof, and to bid God-speed to, those who brought not with them the doctrine of Christ. It is true, no doubt, that the inspiration of St. Stephen and St. John, at the time they so spoke and wrote, sanctions the language which it prompted, and that it does not necessarily follow that similarly strong language, proceeding from ordinary Christians, would be warrantable, even if the errors thus reprobated were as criminal as those of the unbelieving Jews, or the heretics of the Apostolic age. Still we may argue from analogy that the lower Inspiration, which all Christians share in common ("by one Spirit are we all baptized into one body, and have been all made to drink into one Spirit"), is by no means incompatible with occasional vehemence of language in censuring what is felt to be vital and soul-destroying error; and certainly, in these days of unsettled faith and spurious liberality, when men have become impatient of all definite doctrinal teaching, and prate of "large-heartedness" and "breadth of view," as releasing them from those trammels of dogma, by which their forefathers were shackled, and the free exercise of thought restrained, it may be a serious question whether an age so propense to Rationalism, has not need of one or two John William Burgons to shout defiance and anathema every now and then, as new encroachments are made upon the Faith once delivered to the Saints, and thus redress the balance. Revolutions cannot be either made or turned back by rose-water; and it is impossible to stem the tide either of unbelief or superstition by prophesying smooth things to the errorists, and using the language of compromise or conciliation.

Thus much, it is thought, may with perfect propriety and justice be pleaded by a friendly advocate in apology for those "volcanic utterances[2]" of Dean Burgon's which, looked at by themselves, apart from the rest of his peculiarly intense character, gave serious offence to many, and almost certainly alienated persons who had not the privilege of knowing him well. But the writer is quite sensible that the biographer has a duty to truth as well as to his hero, and that in exhibiting that hero to the reader, he must not play exclusively the advocate's part, but represent faithfully the weak as well as the strong points of the character. Dean Burgon himself would censure his biographer, if, while his virtues were expatiated upon, his faults were not at all events candidly admitted. For, curiously enough, a letter of his to

[2] This phrase I take leave to borrow from one of Bishop Hobhouse's letters to me on the subject of our common friend's character.

Mr. Dawson Turner (dated Feb. 1, 1840) has been preserved, in which he gives his views decidedly in favour of a biographer's portraying the faults as well as the excellences of his subject. Thus he writes;—

"I seek to act towards others, as I would be acted by. Much indeed would it grieve me to think that, when the grave had closed over me, (supposing one were to become important enough to have *any* thing said about one) some reckless person should be found willing to cast a slur upon one's name, by monstering one's nothings[3], or, if one had been betrayed into some sin, by insisting on letting all the world know all about it. But on the other hand, I should not mind having it said of me what weaknesses of character, or infirmities of temper, or other peculiar features were my bane, and prevented this excellence or that achievement: and it is this impartial statement that I desire to see in Biography. We ostentatiously put forward the energy, enthusiasm, romance, truthfulness, piety and so forth of our hero, because these were springs of high, or graceful, or good action; accordingly the imitation of these, in hopes of attaining similar results, becomes naturally inculcated.

---

[3] Burgon was very familiar with Shakspere's phraseology, and probably quotes him here without having present to his mind the way in which Shakspere uses the phrase of "having one's nothings monstered." Coriolanus, standing for the consulship, and obliged to go through the necessary forms, avows his repugnance to sit by, while his warlike exploits are recited before the Senate:—

"I had rather have one scratch
    my head i' the sun,
  When the alarum were struck,
    than idly sit
  To hear *my nothings* monstered." [II. 2, 81.]

It is clear from the context that what Coriolanus means by *monstering nothings* is *the undue exaggeration of achievements in themselves trifling*. And it is equally clear from Burgon's context that what *he* means is, *the undue exaggeration of trifling faults of character*. The *verb* "to monster" [to make monstrous, represent as monstrous] has now become obsolete. Shakspere does once again use the verb, and *in malam partem*:

"Sure, her" (Cordelia's) "offence
  Must be of such unnatural degree
  That monsters it" (as to make it outrageous, monstrous).
            'Lear' [I. i. 223].

But a love of praise, a certain degree of irresolution, a procrastinating habit, &c., &c.,—these, by being similarly dwelt upon and exhibited in Biography, would become beacons to warn us from the rock on which a goodly vessel has foundered; and therefore am I for the distinct exposure of these blemishes of character."

Be it so, then, as regards himself. The frequent want of self-control in his controversial utterances *was* a blemish, in spite of which, however, he was warmly loved and deeply venerated by all who knew him well enough to gain an insight into the secret of his character. Nor will any one who has studied the workings of his own heart, and the subterranean operation of motives in it, suppose that the fierceness of these utterances was prompted *exclusively* by love of the truth, which he supposed to be impugned. This doubtless was his *main* motive,—*the only motive of which he was at the time conscious*. But there was in him an intensely and passionately strong will, which in private life, and quite apart from theological controversy, had an autocratic bent, and could not bear thwarting, or even contradiction, unless the thwarting came from an acknowledged superior. This would break out occasionally, and lead to ruptures with colleagues and associates, especially if they stood in the position of inferiors,—which ruptures, however, were usually healed very soon by the flowing forth from him of genuine Christian love. And doubtless this despotic bent of the will, all unconsciously to himself, accentuated his controversial repugnance to those who set themselves against what he conceived to be the Truth, and in part instigated the "unduly disdainful utterances," of which Bishop Hobhouse speaks above.

Nor can it be denied that the tone of his expressions on these occasions had a deplorable effect, counteracting, as it did, the very end which he had at heart, and which he desired with all the energy of his being to subserve. Those who would have felt a genuine deference for his brilliant abilities, his profound learning, and his godly zeal, and who might have been disposed to listen to quiet and dispassionate reasoning from one so highly qualified to speak, were hardened in their errors by being set down and rated like naughty school-boys, tossed his lectures and scoldings to the winds, and said to themselves and others, 'Oh, it is only John Burgon: who cares for what *he* says?' Like many another excellent clergyman, the great and good Dean seemed to forget that the chief (if not the only) end of Christian censure is to induce the sinner or the errorist to act or to think rightly, and that therefore the censure, which is administered in such a form as to be tossed aside with indifference or even ridicule, defeats its own object.

The charge of conceit and an overweening estimate of his own abilities and attainments, which has been often brought against him by those who knew him only superficially, may be dismissed in very few words. If it means only that he was assured beyond all question that his own views and convictions,—the old familiar views in which he had been nurtured from his boyhood upward,—were the only true views and convictions, and that he was intolerant of any one who ventured to impugn them,—this has been admitted already; this conceit (if you are pleased so to call it) resolved itself partly into that "reverent affection" for all the traditions and surroundings, in the midst of which he had been born and bred, which Bishop Hobhouse has pointed out with such admirable discrimination, partly into the imperious and autocratic character of his will, which has been already commented upon, and which, as has been said, not only led to breaches of the peace between himself and his colleagues, but also, by the fiery utterances which it sometimes dictated, greatly prejudiced his influence for good.—If the charge means nothing more than that he was conscious of his own great abilities, this he had in common with every man of genius, who cannot but be conscious of his own gifts;—true humility stands, not in denial or disparagement of the gifts, but in the attribution of them to a higher source than self, ("what have I that I have not received?"), and in the recognition of a deep responsibility for the use to which they are put.—If, when examined, the charge resolves itself into this, that going to College at the age of twenty-nine,—already a biographer, an archæologist, an artist, and highly cultivated in general literature, he sometimes may have given himself airs (if it were so) among the mere striplings, of the same academical standing with himself, who had absolutely no mental furniture beyond the knowledge of Latin and Greek scholarship, which they brought with them from their Public School, (*many of whom however conceived a deep affection for him, and he for them, which lasted for life*),—well; if so it should have been, (the author has received no proof whatever that so it *was*)—there would be nothing here to excite surprise, and no serious ground surely for a charge of conceit. But proof there is, let it be added, both in his Journals and Letters, that he took in a most beautiful spirit, with expressions of thankfulness to God for any measure of success, and grateful acknowledgment of the help which his Tutors had given him, the rebuff which *Alma Mater* administered to him in refusing to him his First Class (a rebuff, which no doubt was blessed to his humiliation, and so to his

The Character.

spiritual welfare), and that his failure to win one of the highest places in the Class List, instead of disgusting and souring him, seems to have operated as a stimulus to work harder and more sanguinely than ever for the attainment of that independence, which only a Fellowship could give.

Before we pass on to sketch his theological position and views, there is a point of his character which deserves to be noticed all the more, because, from a variety of causes, the English Clergy of to-day, while often more active than their predecessors in the Ministry, have as a rule sadly deteriorated in that undefinable, but yet easily recognised qualification—*breeding*. John William Burgon was beyond all question *a high-bred gentleman*;—it was this which constituted one of the great charms of his character. His wide cultivation—for it was, as we have seen, very wide, although it consisted with very profound study of particular subjects,—gave him a refinement of mind which could not fail to transpire in social intercourse. His chivalrous devotion to the gentler sex, his courtesy (inbred and unfailing) to the whole of womankind, was another ingredient of the quality we are attempting to describe. Those who had been thrown across men of sterling worth indeed, but of coarser fibre and ruder manners, felt themselves transported into a wholly different social atmosphere, when they passed a week in his company. As a host he made this felt by all his guests, for however short a time they might be under his roof; there was that about the *ménage* in the Deanery of Chichester (due in part, no doubt, to the ladies of the family), which showed that the Dean, though the better part of his life had been spent in College rooms, thoroughly well understood how to entertain with grace, courtesy, and dignity.

The large-hearted old-fashioned hospitality which thinks nothing too good for guests, the tact which knows how to put them entirely at their ease, the vivacity of mind which knows how to draw them out and entertain them, all these transpired in his dealings with his social circle, though none of them was obtruded. This type of clergyman has hitherto never been wanting in the English Church. Often has it been met with in the retired country parsonage, where the ripe scholar, the profound student, the sound theologian, has shown himself, as occasion offered, to be also the most delightful of entertainers. Burgon was an excellent specimen of this school. It is, alas! dying off now, not only by the admission into the Ministry of men of a lower social grade, which is necessitated by the Church's exigencies, but by the pressure, restlessness, and breathless hurry, of modern life, which are partly responsible for this, as for many other very unlovely results.

III. But we have yet to speak of the uniqueness of his position as a Theologian, which even had he been a Theologian only, and nothing more, would have made him worthy of grateful commemoration by all those who regard God's written Word as the most precious treasure in the world after His Personal Word, as closely analogous to (nay, as vitally connected with) the Personal Word, being equally a Revelation of the Eternal Father; equally Divine—penetrated by Deity throughout, even as was the human nature of the Son of God;—equally human,—equally wrapping up and appealing to all beautiful human sympathies, and equally adapted to the spiritual necessities of every human soul. This Word has been insidiously assailed in our days, the assault being masked with professions of esteem and veneration, and excused by the necessity

THE CHARACTER.

of bringing it into agreement with the discoveries of Science and the progress of human knowledge; its integrity has been tampered with; and its trustworthiness called in question; in a word, the whole traditional mode of regarding and receiving the Bible, the mode in which the Universal Church has hitherto always regarded and received it, is being undermined by the subtle speculations of Rationalists, and the application to the Sacred Volume of what are called the canons of criticism. And many of the conclusions thus arrived at have been received, if not as well-established truths, yet as reasonable and worthy of consideration, not only by members, but also by ministers of our own Church, men for whose opinion on such a subject their ability and learning must needs conciliate respect. The sad traces of this sceptical *animus* are found scattered up and down throughout the pages of the Revised New Testament. In the Version of the Lord's Prayer, as given in St. Luke's Gospel, the Invocation has been mutilated and cut down to a single word, while two important petitions have been entirely expunged from the text. The Doxology is expunged from the Prayer as given in St. Matthew's Gospel,—thereby no doxology being left; for in St. Luke's Gospel the Prayer never had a doxology. English Christians then are taught by our Revisers to believe that the doxology is no genuine part of the Prayer which our Lord gave for the use of His people. And to this it must be added that the account of the descending Angel at the Pool of Bethesda, and of the troubling of the water, and the salutary effect to him that after the troubling first stepped in, has been entirely obliterated from the text of St. John's Gospel. And the passages upon which doubt is thrown by a marginal note to the effect that "many ancient authorities omit them" are of more serious import still. Misgivings are thus instilled into the mind of the reader as to the only account we have of the Agony and Bloody Sweat; as to the authenticity of the first Saying upon the Cross ("Father, forgive them"); as to the mention of the Ascension in St. Luke's Gospel; and as to far the larger part of the words of Institution of the Eucharist in the same Gospel. While still graver doubt is thrown upon the last Twelve Verses of St. Mark's Gospel by the annotation, "The two oldest Greek manuscripts, and some other authorities, omit from ver. 9 to the end," and by an ominous gap which is left in the page after the eighth verse, almost as much as if the Revisers would intimate to their readers; "If you desire to be perfectly assured that what you are reading is the Word of God, go no further than verse 8." If such excisions are made of parts of the sacred deposit of the New Testament, while other parts, of great preciousness and interest, are questioned and suspected, by a great company of learned theologians, working under a pressure from that healthy English public opinion which has prejudices (if prejudices they be) in favour of the old and familiar translation, what shall we suppose to be the views of Holy Scripture taken by critics (whether foreign or domestic) who have never been nurtured in our traditions, and who are laid under no restraint at all in what they call their free handling of the Word of God? Nor is it the text only, but the genuineness and authenticity of the Sacred Books which are assailed by these critics. While these lines are being written, the theological mind of England is still in the ferment, into which it has been thrown by the eighth Essay in '*Lux Mundi*,' which seems to admit fully that "the attribution to first founders of what is really the remoter result of their institutions" is a " process" which " has been largely at work in the Pentateuch," and that therefore " we may suppose Deuteronomy to be" (not written by Moses at all, but) "a republication of the law 'in the spirit and power' of Moses." And it has been stated to the writer, on authority which he cannot doubt, that in the course of last year an Oxford Professor avowed his conviction in a Sermon preached before the University, that Psalm cx. was of a date long posterior to David, and therefore certainly not of Davidic authorship[4], this being the Psalm, the Davidic authorship of which is absolutely essential to the validity of the argument which our Blessed Lord would lead us to draw from it as to His being both the Root and Offspring of David, both His Lord and His Son. And on the question whether "the inspiration of the recorder guarantees or not the exact historical truth of what he records," all the answer which we can extract from the Essay in '*Lux Mundi*' is that "there is nothing to prevent our believing ... that the record from Abraham downward is in substance in the strict sense historical." Most generous concession indeed! But what of the record from Abraham upward? What of the Flood and the Salvation in the Ark [5]?

---

[4] Doubtless the Sermon referred to was Dr. Cheyne's First Bampton Lecture on '*The Origin and Religious Contents of the Psalter*,' in the course of which the Lecturer concludes that Psalm cx. was originally " an encomium upon Simon" [Maccabæus] murdered by his son-in-law Ptolemæus, B.C. 135. See this sad volume of Lectures, professedly written, in conformity with the terms of Canon Bampton's will, "to confirm and establish the Christian Faith . . . . upon the divine authority of the Holy Scriptures . . . . and upon the Divinity of our Lord and Saviour Jesus Christ,"—P. 20 *et seq.*

[5] The Bishop of Manchester enables us to answer this question categorically in his (so-called) '*Teaching of Christ.*' According to the Bishop's view the patriarch Abraham, the first Polytheist, threw a Babylonian legend of the Flood, in which that calamity is spoken of as inflicted upon man by Bel in caprice, and in which the gods are

LIFE OF DEAN BURGON.

What of the events of the first five days of Creation, the recorder of which must have been, not merely assisted by Inspiration, but must have had a direct revelation made to him of every particular incident, since "the process of historical tradition" had not yet begun? The Essay seems to give us no assurance whatever that these are historical records, in the sense of being reliable narratives of matters of fact. We may accept them, if we please, as instructive myths and old-world legends, "presented from a special point of view," "in which point of view," the Essayist seems to think, "lies their inspiration." The Flood, he would probably say, is the mythical history of some great catastrophe to the human race, which "illustrates God's dealings with man—God's judgment on sin." As regards the Evangelical narratives, indeed, Mr. Gore implies that while "the Church cannot *insist upon* the historical character of the earliest records of the ancient Church in detail, *she can insist on the historical character of the Gospels and the Acts of the Apostles.*" But alas! this is cold comfort to us in our present circumstances. The authenticity of certain well-known New Testament facts was freely and openly questioned among us long before

---

represented as descending like flies upon Noah's sacrifice of thanksgiving, into such a shape that the worshippers of the one true God could accept and be edified by it. In Abraham's modification of the legend, which we have substantially in Gen. vi. vii. viii. ix., the Flood is represented as called down by the sin of the human race, and one God only is recognised as inflicting the judgment, and removing it. But there seems to be no reason for believing that the Flood ever actually occurred. The narrative of it is a heathen myth, purified from the falsehoods and follies of heathenism, by a devout worshipper of the one true God. [See Bishop Moorhouse's '*Teaching of Christ*'—Macmillan and Co. 1891—P. 5 *et sequent.*] This work probably represents the extreme limit to which rationalising criticism has as yet gone in this country. And doubtless this is but an instalment of its ultimate demands.

THE CHARACTER.

Mr. Gore's Essay made its appearance. The writer has seen a volume of sermons by an eminent clergyman of our own Church, of great repute as a preacher, and patronised in high quarters, in which our Lord's Temptation is represented as a vision rather than a real transaction, the moral teaching of the vision being that Christ was victorious over every form of temptation to which our nature is exposed, but the narrative having no basis of fact. And if the reader will only refer to that beautifully written and exceedingly popular work, Archdeacon Farrar's '*Life of Christ*,' he will find the learned and eloquent author not indeed absolutely denying "the literal reality of demoniac possession," but stating that "it is not a necessary article of the Christian Creed," and therefore it is open to us to take any view of the subject which most approves itself to our judgment. Thus he writes of the great miracle in Gergesa [vol. i. pp. 338, 9];—

"It is true that the Evangelists (as their language clearly shews) held, in all its simplicity, the belief that actual devils passed in multitudes out of the man and into the swine. But is it not allowable here to make a distinction between actual facts, and that which was the mere conjecture and inference of the spectators from whom the three Evangelists heard the tale? . . . If indeed we could be sure that Jesus directly encouraged or sanctioned in the man's mind the belief that the swine were indeed driven wild by the unclean spirits, which passed objectively from the body of the Gergesene into the bodies of these dumb beasts, then we could, without hesitation, believe as a literal truth, however incomprehensible, that so it was. But this by no means follows indisputably from what we know of the method of the Evangelists."

Indeed? These are the words in which the first Evangelist narrates the incident in question [St. Matt. viii. 28-32];—

"And when he was gone to the other side, into the country of the Gergesenes, there met him two possessed with devils, coming out of the tombs exceeding fierce, so that no man might pass by that way. And, behold, they cried out, saying, What have we to do with thee, Jesus, thou Son of God? Art thou come hither to torment us before the time? And there was a good way off from them an herd of many swine feeding. So the devils besought him, saying, If thou cast us out, suffer us to go away into the herd of swine. And he said unto them, Go. And when they were come out, they went into the herd of swine: and, behold, the whole herd of swine ran violently down a steep place into the sea, and perished in the waters. And they that kept them fled, and went their ways into the city and told everything, and what was befallen to the possessed of the devils."

If our Blessed Lord, when on being solicited by the devils He gave them permission to go away into the swine, did *not* sanction in the minds of all who heard Him the belief that the possession was transferred, under His license, from the bodies of the demoniacs into the bodies of the dumb beasts, then the Evangelists have not narrated with faithful accuracy what occurred, as it occurred; they are not trustworthy witnesses, who can be depended upon to tell the truth exactly; they have deceived the hundreds of thousands, who have received, in all its simplicity, the account which "in all its simplicity they believed"; and the only hypothesis which can explain or account for their deviation from matter of fact is their subjection to the prejudices current in their time and country, and their habit of viewing what occurred through the distorting medium of popular but groundless beliefs, and coloured and exaggerated reports, which went their rounds afterwards.—And would God have permitted the chosen witnesses of His Son's Birth,

The Character.

Death, and Resurrection, to make such misrepresentations of fact in points which really are of no small moment?

But we must add to what has been already said that not only the traditional text of Holy Scripture, and the traditional views of its genuineness and authenticity, but also its traditional interpretation, have been in these latter days assailed. When we ask for a guide in the right interpretation of Holy Scripture, the first question which arises in every reverent and rightly constituted mind is; "Does Holy Scripture itself furnish no clue to the interpretation of itself[6]?" And the answer is that it does. The Old Testament is frequently quoted or referred to by the writers of the New. And if we will but reverently and attentively study the applications of the Old Testament, which are made by the writers of the New, what a wealth of significance will they often open to us,—of meanings which lie, not upon the surface, but under it! The particular passages cited are often the last we should have looked for in that connexion; we never should have so cited them for ourselves. Take as a single example that passage of the Old Testament Scriptures, in which our Lord tells the Sadducees that the doctrine of a future life was wrapped up,—"I *am* the God of Abraham, and the God of Isaac, and the God of Jacob" [St. Matt.

It will be readily seen that in speaking here of the Interpretation of Holy Scripture, the writer is not thinking of the fundamental articles of the Catholic Faith contained in the Creeds, all of which are found in Holy Scripture, and must be proved from it before Christians are called upon to believe and receive them. These it is the province of the Church to draw forth, summarise, and present to her children for their reception. Here the Church herself is the interpreter of Holy Scripture. But what we are now thinking of and dealing with is that large mass of Old Testament Scripture, into which the Holy Spirit has been pleased to give an insight by references made to it, or direct quotations drawn from it, in the writings of the inspired Apostles and Evangelists.

B b

xxii. 32 ; St. Mark xii. 26 ; St. Luke xx. 37]. Not to find the doctrine of the Resurrection in that passage is, according to Him who is the Wisdom of God, "not to know the Scriptures," that is, not to have that deep and penetrating insight into them, which only a thoughtful revolving of every word of God, guided by the Spirit of God, can impart. Nothing less than this will our Lord allow to be "knowledge of the Scriptures." Scriptural knowledge is with Him nothing short of the mental digestion of God's Word ; He will not degrade the term by bestowing it upon the faculty of glibly rolling its sacred utterances off the tongue.

But now let us observe what is the account, which the new School of Biblical Critics are disposed to give, of that strangeness and unexpectedness of the application of passages of the Old Testament, which comes across us so frequently in the New. Mr. Gore indoctrinates us into their method of explaining such citations in a single sentence of his Essay. He has been pointing out that, as to the narratives of Holy Scripture, the Preface to St. Luke's Gospel, and other Scriptural evidence, lead us to think that the sacred historians were as much dependent on human testimony for the correctness of their information as secular writers, who had not the same assistances of the Holy Spirit. And then he adds ; —

"Nor would it appear that spiritual illumination, even in the highest degree, has any tendency to lift men out of the natural conditions of knowledge which belong to their time. *Certainly in the similar case of exegesis, it would appear that St. Paul is left to the method of his time, though he uses it with inspired insight into the function and meaning of law and prophecy as a whole.*"

We hope it is not hyper-critical to note the phrases that "St. Paul is left to the method of his time," and that

The Character.

"he has an inspired insight into the meaning of the law and prophecy *as a whole*." Let us suppose that the passage of St. Paul's writings, which Mr. Gore has in his mind, is the well-known allegorical interpretation which the Apostle gives in Gal. iv. to the Old Testament narrative of Hagar and Sarah. St. Paul had been trained at the feet of Gamaliel in Jewish Schools of Theology; and there can be no reason to deny, and probably no reasonable person will be found to deny, that this application of the narrative in Genesis was of a similar complexion with other interpretations of the Old Testament given by the Rabbies in those schools. But while freely making this admission, it is to be remembered that those Rabbinical schools were THE DIVINITY SCHOOLS OF THE ANCIENT CHURCH OF GOD; and that therefore, since God never left that Ancient Church to herself, or refused to recognise her as His witness (at all events until she had deliberately rejected the Son of His Love), more or less of Divine sanction would attach to the method of interpretation of "the Law, the Psalms, and the Prophets," traditionally handed down and taught in those Schools. But while St. Paul's allegorizing of the narrative of Sarah and Hagar may have been (and doubtless was) *in the same style* as that of the school in which he had learned his Theology, it must have been, as to the matter of it, purely new; it was the opening of a fresh vein of thought on an old passage of Scripture,—the Jewish Doctors of the day would have repudiated any such application of Genesis with horror. Whence then came this opening of a fresh vein of edifying thought in connexion with the sacred and venerable narrative? From the action of St. Paul's own mind? was it a freak of his own fancy, taking its outward shape and form from his theological training? It would be unfair to charge Mr. Gore with saying this, as he distinctly admits that the Apostle speaks "with inspired insight into the function and meaning of law and of prophecy." But why does he add, "as a whole?" Surely his words needed no such qualification. Surely this particular argument, drawn from the Law in favour of the Gospel, was suggested to the Apostle's mind by the same Spirit, under whose prompting the narrative in Genesis had been written; "an inspired insight" was vouchsafed to him, not merely into the general meaning of law and of prophecy, but into the particular Gospel significance underlying that particular narrative. Surely in this, as in so many other Old Testament references of a similar character, God the Holy Ghost Himself is interpreting for us a particular portion of His ancient oracles,—putting into our hands the key wherewith we may unlock a long concealed treasure. Away with the notion that the Apostle's fancy, trained in Jewish Schools of Exegesis, originated the allegory!

The above then are some of the noxious ideas on the subject of the Bible, which have now been for more than half a century floating about in our theological atmosphere,—germs of spiritual malady, which fasten upon weak intellectual and moral frames, and work havoc there. All of them have this point in common, that there is alike in all *a failing faith in the Bible as the Word of God, in its text, in its genuineness, in its authenticity, and in the method of interpreting it, which has become traditional in the Church of Christ.* Blessed be His name, God has not left Himself without witness amidst the various attempts which have been made to disparage and discredit His living oracles. He has raised up several honoured instruments, true and faithful, to lift up their voice in protest against any and every attempt substantially to alter or modify the usual view of the Bible, hitherto taken in this Church and nation, both by the leaders of religious thought and by their followers. But while other Divines have occupied, and occupied successfully, different parts of the field, there has been no single man who has brought such indefatigable industry, such enthusiastic zeal, such consummate and versatile ability, combined with such genuine spirituality, to the task of rehabilitating Holy Scripture in the minds of his countrymen, as JOHN WILLIAM BURGON. If the text be in question, we have already the frequent references to his most valuable assistance in Dr. Scrivener's '*Plain Introduction to the Criticism of the New Testament*' (the standard work on the subject); the fact that "to the last Edition" of this standard work, "Dean Burgon has added particulars of three hundred and seventy-four manuscripts previously unknown to the world of letters[7]"; and, last of all, '*The Revision Revised*,' a republication of certain Articles in the '*Quarterly Review*,' which exposed, and with so much point and force, the fallacy of the principles by which the Revisers were guided, that the Version itself was seriously discredited and brought into suspicion, and in consequence the demand for it materially abated. And the Church now waits for the great work, the labour of years, which was left by him unfinished, but with sufficient indications of the way in which he meant its outline to be filled up, and which is in the able editorial hands of the Rev. Edward Miller, Rector of Bucknell in Oxfordshire. Its character is to be, not destructive, like '*The Revision Revised*,' but constructive, and its design is to exhibit the true principles which should underlie the Textual Criticism of the New Testament,—a work so hallowed to its writer by his veneration

---

[7] Rev. Edward Miller's '*Guide to the Textual Criticism of the New Testament*' [Bell and Sons, York Street, 1886], p. 33.

for God's Word, so endeared to him by the thought of the many happy but laborious hours which he had spent upon it, that when death was impending, and the doctors forbade him to open a book, he implored to have the huge pile of portfolios, containing the materials of the work, placed where he could see them from his bed;—" I only want to look at them. You know, when a man is dying, he wants to kiss and to say good-bye to his favourite child."—Then as to the genuineness of Holy Scripture, it is now nearly twenty years since his '*Last Twelve Verses of the Gospel according to St. Mark, vindicated against Recent Critical Objectors, and established,*' made its appearance, of which the very least that can be said is that it makes the genuineness of the verses infinitely more probable than the contrary hypothesis. While as to the authenticity of the inspired narrative, and the true method of Scriptural interpretation, the noble stand which he made against the subtle encroachments of Rationalism (which indeed is incipient Scepticism) will be found in his Volume on '*Inspiration and Interpretation*[8],'

---

[8] The authenticity of the narratives of Holy Scripture, and specially of its miraculous narratives, is dealt with in Sermon VII., and in his observations on Professor Powell's Essay, p. xlvi; the true method of Scriptural Interpretation in Sermons V. and VI. As to the authenticity of the supernatural narratives of the Old Testament, Burgon calls attention to the fact that the most marvellous of these, and those which have most proved stumbling-blocks, are witnessed to by our Lord and His Apostles; and that therefore we, as Christians, have no need to trouble ourselves with any independent consideration of the difficulties involved in them; we take them simply on the authority of the Divine Master, who can neither deceive nor be deceived, and who is Sponsor for them. This is a line of thought which has often been pursued by others, but by none more lucidly, more convincingly, more eloquently than by Canon Liddon, in his recent Sermon on '*The Worth of the Old Testament*,' one of the greatest masterpieces of our greatest modern preacher:—" For Christians it will be enough to know that our Lord Jesus Christ set the seal of His in-

—the most popular probably of his controversial works, —containing a separate reply to each of the obnoxious Essays, together with seven magnificent Sermons preached before the University of Oxford. [See vol. i. pp. 260–274.] The above are only his larger works on questions of the text, genuineness, authenticity, and interpretation of the Holy Scriptures; to enumerate the separate Sermons, Pamphlets, letters to the '*Guardian*,' letters to Ecclesiastical Authorities, all bearing on the same subjects, which, as occasion served, he put forth, and which were sure to dart forth from his study at any new movement in the history of the Church or of the University, would be from their number almost an impossibility. It must necessarily excite surprise how

fallible sanction on the whole of the Old Testament. He found the Hebrew canon as we have it in our hands to-day, and He treated it as an authority that was above discussion. Nay, more; He went out of His way,—if we may reverently speak thus—to sanction not a few portions of it which modern scepticism rejects. When He would warn His hearers against the dangers of spiritual relapse, He bids them remember 'Lot's wife.' When He would point out how worldly engagements may blind the soul to a coming judgment, He reminds them how men ate, and drank, and married, and were given in marriage, until the day that Noah entered into the ark, and the Flood came and destroyed them all. When He would put His finger on a fact in past Jewish history, which by its admitted reality, would warrant belief in His own coming Resurrection, He points to Jonah's being three days and three nights in the whale's belly. When, standing on the Mount of Olives, with the Holy City at His feet, He would quote a prophecy the fulfilment of which would mark that its impending doom had at last arrived, He desires them to flee to the mountains, when they shall see the abomination of desolation spoken of by Daniel the prophet, standing in the holy place. ...... The trustworthiness of the Old Testament is, in fact, inseparable from the trustworthiness of our Lord Jesus Christ; and if we believe that He is the true Light of the world, we shall close our ears against suggestions impairing the credit of those Jewish Scriptures, which have received the stamp of His Divine authority."—'*The Worth of the Old Testament*, a Sermon preached in St. Paul's Cathedral on the Second Sunday in Advent, December 8, 1889,' pp. 13, 15.

time was found by him for so vast an amount of work, and this when, at certain periods of this literary activity, he had charge of private pupils, charge of outlying Parishes in the neighbourhood of Oxford, and, later, the pastoral charge of St. Mary the Virgin's in Oxford, a parish small indeed in population, but somewhat exacting in its demands, both from its immediate connexion with the University, and from the remarkable character which preceding Vicars had impressed upon it. And Burgon was ever, as has been more than once shown in our narrative, the pastor as well as the preacher, acquainting himself as far as possible with the circumstances and history of every soul committed to his charge, and giving every evidence he could of the kind and fatherly interest which he felt in it. No doubt, in this as in all other cases, God qualified His champion by peculiar gifts, and by certain surroundings, which constituted his qualifications for his life-task. No doubt, though from time to time he laboured under two or three severe illnesses, he was of an originally fine and sound constitution, which could bear the strain of excessive labour as ordinary constitutions cannot do. He could dispense with exercise without feeling the worse for it, and did dispense with it throughout his Chichester life, only taking it when some guest, or his sister or nieces, wanted him on a fine day as a companion of their walks or drives. As for sleep, it was a habit with him to sit up into the small hours of the morning, a practice which tended no doubt to shorten his life by some years, but which did not seem at the time to be attended with any painful or inconvenient results. The positions in which he was placed in the order of God's Providence, the Fellowship of Oriel and the Deanery of Chichester, both contributed materially to the great purpose of his life,—the one opening to him Libraries with unbounded stores of Theology, and the society of many learned and able Theologians, the other—a Deanery in a singularly quiet country town—furnishing the learned and devotional leisure, the atmosphere of worship and contemplation, in which alone such works as he had on hand can be brought, under God's blessing, to a successful issue. Yes! his work was appointed and indicated for him, and he was specially endowed for the prosecution of it; and quickly did he understand his mission (as God's chosen champions never fail to do), and nobly did he respond to the call, and to the needs and difficulties of the Church in his days,—if sometimes with words passionate, and wanting in self-control (such words as St. Paul once used to the high priest, and expressed regret for them afterwards), yet always without personal ill will towards those who had galled and thwarted him, and always gallantly, intrepidly, and in a spirit of enthusiastic loyalty to the Divine Master, of whose Word of Truth he was the standard-bearer in critical and dangerous times. And assuredly he has left behind him a monument more durable than any sculptured in marble, or engraved on brass, in the loving veneration of those hundreds of thousands of English Christians, who have learned to echo from their hearts God's own panegyric of His own Law;—

"The law of the Lord is an undefiled law, converting the soul:
The testimony of the Lord is sure, and giveth wisdom unto the simple.

The statutes of the Lord are right, and rejoice the heart:
The commandment of the Lord is pure, and giveth light unto the eyes.

The fear of the Lord is clean, and endureth for ever:
The judgements of the Lord are true, and righteous altogether.

More to be desired are they than gold, yea than much fine gold:
Sweeter also than honey, and the honeycomb.

Moreover, by them is thy servant taught:
And in keeping of them there is great reward."

APPENDIX (A).

[*See vol. i. pp.* 45, 46.]

A few excerpts from the Notes and Memoranda on Shakspere made by Burgon in his early life.

An example of the various headings, under which the items of information on each separate play are exhibited in Burgon's Shakspere manuscript book, is given on p. 45.

The following memoranda are interesting, as indicating his purpose of putting forth an edition of Shakspere, with Notes and a Life, and also some of the principles which he laid down for his guidance in this great literary undertaking.

"*Mem.* Not to forget in my 'Life' to mention the ungenerous saying of Milton respecting Charles the First's love of Shakspeare[9]

[9] The passage referred to in the Preface to the Catalogue "of the Royal Library" (i. e. the 7000 and odd books collected by various Kings of England from Henry VII. onward, and presented to the British Museum by George II.) is as follows:—" If King Charles I. was ever able to form a more important Library, it shared the fate of his other collections, and was dispersed; for so rancorous was the enmity which prevailed against that unfortunate Monarch, that even Milton unfeelingly and illiberally reproached him with consoling himself during his confinement in the Isle of Wight with his favourite author Shakspeare, 'the well-known closet companion of his solitude,' and that, instead of spending his time in prayer and devotion, he was studying that of dissembling, from the character of King Richard III."

The work of Milton's, in which he throws out this unfeeling and illiberal reproach, is his " Answer to *Eikon Basilike*" (Prose Works, vol. ii. p. 407. Ed. Symmons);—

"The poets, and some English . . . . . have put never more pious words in the mouth of any person than of a tyrant. I shall not

(for which see the Preface to the Catalogue of the Royal Library, vol. i. p. ii), adding, 'We cannot forgive Milton for this!'"

"*Mem.* Never, in reviewing the errors of preceding Commentators or Editors, to crow, or be, in the remotest degree, insulting. To handle their blunders delicately, if at all, and to give their assiduity a full share of praise. It is at *their* altars that each succeeding critic lights his little candle; and we must never forget the laborious nature of their researches, without which *we* should be at a loss to advance a step. It must be acknowledged that, if their controversies were sometimes petty and ridiculous, they were at least harmless; and that they were not always unproductive of good.

"Nothing is more easy than to make merry and be witty at the expense of Shakspeare's Commentators. When the gratuitous and inglorious nature of their investigations is considered, we shall feel most inclined to forgive them for having 'monstered' Shakspeare's 'nothings [1].'"

"*Mem.* In illustrating Shakspeare, 'Cette voie d'interpreter

instance an abstruse author, wherein the king might be less conversant, but one whom we well know was the closet companion of these his solitudes, William Shakspeare; who introduces the person of Richard the Third, speaking in as high a strain of piety and mortification as is uttered in any passage of this book" [*Eikon Basilike*], "and sometimes to the same sense and purpose with some words in this place; 'I intended,' saith he, 'not only to oblige my friends, but my enemies.' The like saith Richard, Act II. Scene 1:

'I do not know the Englishman alive,
With whom my soul is any jot at odds,
More than the infant that is born to-night;—
I thank my God for my humility.'
Other stuff of the same sort may be read throughout the whole Tragedy, wherein the poet used not much licence in departing from the truth of history, which delivers him [Richard III.] a deep dissembler, not of his affections only, but of religion."

[1] Here again by the Shaksperian phrase "monstering nothings" (*Coriolanus*, II. 2, 81) Burgon doubtless means the making much of trifling faults, not the unduly exalting trifling merits, which is the sense of the phrase, as Coriolanus uses it. [See above chap. iv. p. 357, footnote 3].

APPENDIX (A).

un auteur par lui-même est plus sure que tous les Commentaires.'"

"Shakspeare seems to have been so full of the ideas that struck him, that he was not solicitous about the grammatical accuracy of the words which he employed to express them. His chief object was at all times to convey HIS MEANING to his audience. Hence the *mixed metaphor* which so often occurs in his pages, and which is at variance with the spirit of accurate criticism. Hence too another curious peculiarity; he often applies *the epithet* to the word it does not belong to. Thus he would say, *thirsty weather*. A multitude of instances might be produced from his works.

"The truth is Shakspeare *thought* with amazing vigour, and force, and correctness; and when he came to clothe his purposes with words, he seized on the first which presented themselves."

"If Shakspeare had read more, he would probably have thought less."

"Shakspeare may or may not be guilty of all the puns and quibbles that are to be found in his writings. In the course of 10 or 12 years, which elapsed before several of his pieces were published §, there were abundant opportunities for interpolations and corruptions of all kinds to creep into the text. That he was sensible of the impropriety of the practice of quibbling, is, I think, pretty clear from a passage in *The Merchant of Venice* (Act iii. Sc. 5), where, when Launcelot has been punning on the word *Moor*, the following remark is put into the mouth of Lorenzo : 'How every fool can play upon the word! I think the best grace of wit will shortly turn into silence.'

"I am very strongly tempted to believe that (except perhaps in his *earliest* performances, when his judgment was as yet unformed) he disapproved of a pun, and only introduced such humble sallies of wit in compliance with the prejudice of the age he lived in.

"§ *Mem.* To observe whether the puns predominate in the

Appendix (*B*).

pieces published during his lifetime, or in those of posthumous publications."

"In the Lives of Shakspeare the critick and essayist swallow up the biographer."

"It must be confessed that there is some truth in an observation which was once made to me concerning Shakspeare's heroines, and very warmly insisted on,—viz. their want of delicacy. The warmth of Portia throughout this play" [Merchant of Venice] "offends one's ideas of a woman's delicacy; (and yet he meant Portia to be *a jewel of a woman*)."

"I always picture Shakspeare to myself a curious and inquiring man, with an ardent thirst for knowledge, and a talent for acquiring it, in whatever shape it might present itself,—I mean whether in the shape of a penny ballad, an adventure, or a book. He must have felt his inferiority (on all classical points) to the rest of his contemporaries, who, almost all, had received University educations; and he must have earnestly striven to supply from translations those deficiencies."

APPENDIX (B).

"*I have also compiled a little Glossary of the County of Beds,*"

vol. i. p. 214.

Some account of this Glossary, which appeared in the columns of a county newspaper (with the heading Provincialisms of Bedfordshire) will be found above chap. iv. p. 349 and *n*. 9. In the Introductory Article, to which reference is there made, he gives this pertinent warning to the reader;—

"Thus much it may be right to premise; viz., that the increased facilities for travelling, and the process of assimilation which is rapidly going on in consequence, seem likely in the course of a few years to obliterate many of our provincialisms,

APPENDIX (B).

and, in the end, to abolish them all. It becomes necessary therefore for those who think a record of such things worth preserving, to register their facts without more delay."

And as to the conceivable discoveries, which careful observation and research might bring to light in this field, he throws out the following ;—

"Surely it would be a curious discovery if it should be ascertained that certain words are all but unknown except within a very limited area; that a river acts like a boundary wall to certain other words; and that here and there a few terms are literally the property of one or two obscure villages,—where they maintain a precarious existence, and seem destined in the course of another generation to disappear entirely!"

From a few of the Provincialisms which appear in this Glossary the reader will be able to form an idea of its general character.

"BAVER, *n.* (pronounced *bayver*). The 'lunch' of a labouring man is so called. It is the name of the meal he partakes of at about 10 a.m. and 4 p.m., during harvest and hay-time, when he breakfasts at 6 and dines at 1. In the north of Beds these two '*bavers*' are called '*eleven o'clock*' and '*four o'clock*.' In Sussex the meal is called a 'bait;' in Somersetshire and the Isle of Wight, 'nammot.   the word had come to us from the Italian *bevere*, and implied that the refreshment taken was fluid rather than solid? In Berks I have heard the word 'beverage' used for 'baver.'"

"CANTING, *partic.* Gossiping about a neighbour's affairs; playing the busy-body. In Sussex an aged female with a taste for this occupation is called 'an old *Canterbury*.' Is the word connected with the French 'chanter?'"

"*CHURCHING[2], *n.* A going to Church on any occasion. *The* going to Church 'of women after child-birth, commonly called THE CHURCHING OF WOMEN,' has monopolized this word; which has no such restricted meaning in Bedfordshire. 'When

[2] "I prefix an asterisk to common words employed in an uncommon sense." J. W. B.

APPENDIX (B).

is your *churching?*' is the inquiry of a stranger who desires to know the hour of Morning or Evening Prayer."

"DICK-WITH-HIS-WAGGON, *n.* The constellation of the Great Bear,—'Charles's (i.e. the *Churl's*) wain, 'Charles' is evidently *Dick* in Bedfordshire."

"DILLUP, *v.* Said of the dangling legs of a person sitting on a high stool. 'Don't sit *dillupping* there!' Probably a corruption of *dewlap.*"

"FEW, *adj.* The word is constantly used in Bedfordshire (together with its correlative 'many') with reference to *liquid* measure; e.g. 'a *few* broth.' A village shopkeeper, phial to the neck with 'Godfrey's,' remarked that she had 'given a *many* for the money.'"

"FREM, *adj.* Succulent, full of sap; generally used as an epithet for vegetables which grow vigorously and look healthy, e.g., *frem* still, you maun dig them yet.'—'The time for getting *yerbs* is the spring, when all the nice *frem*'s in them.' A child growing tall and slender is metaphorically said 'to grow *frem.*'"

"'Yerbs' means such herbs as parsley, royal,—as distinguished from vegetables, which they call '*sarce.*'"

"GAWN, *v.* A person is said to *gawn after* those they gape and stare at, passer-by.—It is the same word probably as *yawn* (as 'church-*yard* is called in the northern counties 'kirk-*garth*'), denotes (like the word *gape*) open-mouthed wonder. But the meaning is very definite and peculiar, fulness and curiosity, and perhaps something more."

"GOOLABEE, *n.* A lady-bird. Evidently a corruption, query whether of *golden bee?* or of *cow-lady?* (for 'gold' was once *gould*, and a cow is often a *coo*) ..... In the north of Beds the lady-bird is thus addressed:

'Cow-lady, fly away, flee;
And tell me which way my wedding's to be.'

"*Bishop Barnabee* or *Burnabee* is the name by which this insect is known in Norfolk; and the rhyme is,

APPENDIX (B).

'Bishop, Bishop Barnabee,
Tell me when your wedding be.
If it be to-morrow day,
Take your wings, and fly away.'"

[After giving the names of the lady-bird in French, Polish, German, Spanish, &c., Burgon concludes a long article on GOOLABEE thus];

"How does it come to pass that this little insect should enjoy such singular honour in every Christian land? It is accounted a sin to kill the creature in many places."

"LIGHTER OF EGGS. *n*. The quantity of eggs laid at once by a hen. Is it the same word as *litter*?"

'Nor cast one longing, *lingering* look behind.'
The word is generally used with reference to some article of food. An old man who had lost his wife was heard to talk of 'lingering after—his *gooseberries*!'"

"MUNGY, *adj*. Said of the weather, when it is both warm and damp,—*muggy*, as we say. 'The day was so *mungy* that I sweat welly (well nigh) a pailful.' 'We can't make lace when our hands are *mungy*,' i.e. hot and moist."

"OGEE, *adj*. and *adv*. (Sometimes pronounced *wogee*.) To 'drive *ogee*,' is to drive a horse in a hay or harvest field, while the hay, corn, &c. is being carted. This operation is commonly performed by small boys,—hence called '*ogee* boys.'

"The obvious etymology would be 'wo' 'gee,'—two of the cries generally addressed to horses, and understood by them probably from one end of England to the other. But this does not appear to be the real meaning of the expression. For, besides that 'gee,' (go?) generally precedes 'wo' (wait?), (as in the well-known ballad of 'Sally Brown,'—

'Which made his woe to flow afresh
As if he'd said *gee woe*'),—

besides this consideration, I am assured by a competent informant that what the urchins are directed to cry is '*Hold ye*,' and that they address this shout not to the horse, but to the

APPENDIX (B).

men on the cart, who without such a warning might fall off, and who accordingly would flog any 'ogee boy' who omits to utter the familiar signal before setting the cart in motion. '*Ogee*' therefore is '*Hold ye.*'"

"PIMMOCK, *n.* and *v.* Dainty, delicate in appetite. 'Takes more to keep a *pimmock* than a glutton,'—is a local proverb. It is also a verb ;—'How dainty ye be, *pimmocking* !' So in Devonshire."

"SCRINGE, *v.* To cower with cold. Is it an intensive of *cringe* ; as *smelt* of *melt*, *slight* of *light*, *slender* of *lean*, *slack* of *lack* ? Compare *sweat*, *swing*, *swelter*, *smoulder*, *slash*, *stumble*.

"So SLAG, *v.* To idle ('Don't hang *slagging* behind !'), which is probably *lag* with an *s* prefixed."

When the "Bedfordshire Provincialisms" had been carried through some dozen *communiquées* in the county newspaper, it was found, from correspondence and fresh researches, that several interesting words had been omitted from their alphabetical positions. These had to be added in a Supplement, headed PART No. xiii. Of these supplementary words two instances must suffice.

"'TANDRE' CAKE, *n.* The name of a cake—consisting of little more than ·bread adorned with currants and carraway seeds— eaten on St. Andrew's day (Nov. 30), which sufficiently proves the word to be a corruption of 'St. Andrew cake.' The final *t* cleaves to the initial vowel, as in many similar instances ; e.g. Tooley Street, which is a corruption of St. Olave's ; and the epithet *tawdry* is said to be derived from the character of the wares sold at a fair held in honour of St. Etheldreda, or Audrey (June 23). Since the lace trade has been so unprofitable, the manufacture of Tandre cakes has been discontinued in some places. St. Andrew's Day is called Lacemakers' Day ; and the humble festivity here noticed is called 'keeping Tandre.'"

"SNIB, *v.* To administer correction,—as a parent to a child ; but properly, I believe, to reprove, reprimand, rebuke, and so to check and restrain. The readers of Chaucer are familiar with this good old English word. The Parson 'wolde *snibben*' 'any

Appendix (C).

person obstinate'; and 'I have my sone *snibbed*,' says the Franklin.

"'Snib' (like 'sneb') has quite disappeared from polite speech: but '*snub*' flourishes, and as used by Ray (and in the Tatler, No. 235) had no admixture of the ludicrous, as now. 'Snub' is likely to live on as a convenient designation for a peculiar form of rebuke which would else be without a name. He who '*snubs*' another may be wanting neither in dignity, courtesy, nor ceremony; but it is implied that the person 'snubbed' has been unceremoniously treated, and has experienced a certain amount of indignity,—which he deserved. All this however is quite foreign to the original signification of the word, which is retained only in the provincial speech of England."

APPENDIX (C).

"As an example of symbolism in the Gospel histories, he refers to the raising of Jairus' daughter as exactly representing the rejection and the receiving back again of God's ancient people, the Jews. An interesting Sermon of his will be found in the Appendix [C], in which he develops this particular instance of the structure of Holy Writ." See above chap. iii. p. 169.

HERE is the Sermon, preached at St. Mary's, Nov. 6, 1864, and referring, it will be seen, to one of three weeks earlier. This last it is not thought necessary to give, as it only adds to the symbolism of the narrative such spiritual and practical lessons deducible from it as might be found in any sermon on the same passage.

THE RAISING OF JAIRUS' DAUGHTER, A PROPHETIC HISTORY.

"𝔚𝔥𝔢𝔫 𝔱𝔥𝔢 𝔭𝔢𝔬𝔭𝔩𝔢 𝔴𝔢𝔯𝔢 𝔭𝔲𝔱 𝔣𝔬𝔯𝔱𝔥, 𝔥𝔢 𝔴𝔢𝔫𝔱 𝔦𝔫, 𝔞𝔫𝔡 𝔱𝔬𝔬𝔨 𝔥𝔢𝔯 𝔟𝔶 𝔱𝔥𝔢 𝔥𝔞𝔫𝔡, 𝔞𝔫𝔡 𝔱𝔥𝔢 𝔪𝔞𝔦𝔡 𝔞𝔯𝔬𝔰𝔢."—St. Matt. ix. 25.

"It will be in the recollection of some who attend the Evening Service, that three Sundays ago the Miracle, or rather

Appendix (C).

the pair of Miracles, which constitute this day's Gospel, was made the subject of a Sermon. I would fain hope that those who heard it have not forgotten a few remarks which were offered at its close, on the symbolical, or mystical, or spiritual teaching of the entire transaction. In fact, in all the Gospel history, there is scarcely to be found a more unmistakeably typical event than the raising of Jairus' daughter and the healing of the woman with the issue of blood.

"You were requested to observe, first, how singularly, in all the three Gospels, the woman's cure is thrust in, as it were,—made a kind of parenthesis in the other transaction. While our LORD was on His way to the house of Jairus, the woman pressed up to Him,—laid her hand in faith upon the hem of His garment,—and was healed. It was just so that the Gentiles apprehended CHRIST by faith, when the errand on which He came was to seek and to save His ancient people, the seed of Abraham. The maiden was 12 years old, and the woman had been for just 12 years afflicted. The life of the one corresponded exactly therefore with the period of the other's affliction; and when the one died, the other was healed. Exactly so was it with the Gentile and the Jew. The one had suffered loss exactly for as many years as the other had abounded with life; and the healing of the Gentiles was the signal for the rejection and death of the Jews. The woman 'had spent all that she had' upon many physicians, 'and was nothing bettered, but rather grew worse' [St. Mark v. 26]. Exactly so had it fared with those nations whom she represented. They had derived no benefit from the philosophers and other teachers who had undertaken their cure; but rather had grown worse, until their case was hopeless, and they betook themselves to CHRIST—pressing up to Him and snatching the blessing by force: laying the hand of faith on the garment of His humanity, and deriving to themselves healing and health from the very fountain of life and immortality. Meanwhile the daughter of Jairus died,—even as the Jewish Church died out when the Gentile Church was restored. It was shown further that the symbolic teaching of the transaction does not end here. Shall then the

APPENDIX (C).

daughter of the ruler of My people[3] lie lifeless for ever? Not so. 'Believe only, and she shall be made whole' [St. Luke viii. 50]. CHRIST entered into the ruler's house—and restored the maiden to life. And so (doubt not!) in the end it will fare with the Jewish Church. The same Divine LORD will yet take her by the hand, and she shall revive. And oh, 'if the casting away of them be the reconciling of the world, what shall the receiving of them be, but life from the dead?' [Rom. xi. 15.]

"Something like this was said on that former occasion: but it has occurred to me since, that I omitted, after all, to call your attention to what seems to be the most striking feature in the whole transaction. I will explain what I mean in a few words.

"The incident is called (and rightly) *the raising of Jairus' daughter*. It was to raise *her* from death that our SAVIOUR came forth: it was not *till* He had raised her from death that the story even makes a sensible break,—much less comes to a conclusion. The cure of the woman with the issue of blood was an incident by the way, just as the narrative of her cure is parenthetically thrust in. It forms no essential part of the story. It might be omitted, and the chief transaction would be unimpaired in its completeness,—undiminished in its interest. The tendency and application of these remarks is obvious. The part *we* Gentiles play in the history of Salvation is an incident by the way;—a very considerable incident indeed, I freely grant, but still it is no part of the main plot. It is an outgrowth,—is unmistakeably exhibited to us (so to speak) as a species of addition to the main history, a thing thrust in by way of parenthesis, not the main incident itself. Inseparable[4],

---

[3] We suppose that in this phrase Burgon had in his mind Jer. viii. 22, ("Why then is not the health of the daughter of my people recovered?") and inserted the words "the ruler of" to suit the case of Jairus, who "was a ruler of the synagogue," St. Luke viii. 41.

[4] Inseparable, he probably means, from God's plan,—bound up with it, and really a part of it; as it is written; "For as ye in times past have not believed God, yet have now obtained mercy through their unbelief: even so have these also now not believed, that through your mercy they also may obtain mercy." Rom. xi. 30, 31.

I am well aware, in the deep counsels of GOD, is the Call of the Gentiles. All Scripture shows it. But this portion of the Gospel, I contend, exhibits our share in the matter in a novel, and somewhat unexpected light. The main thing—the great transaction—is the raising of the dead Church—the conversion, or awakening, or restoring to life—*of the Jews.* CHRIST rested not, (He halted for a moment to heal, and to ask, and to bless, and to pardon, but) He rested not—*until* He had achieved His main purpose, the raising of the dead maiden to life. And you are requested to notice the prophetic light which is thus thrown on that great transaction, yet future, *the restoration of the Jews.* To achieve *this* is the great Physician's object. Till He has achieved *this*, CHRIST will not have completed His errand of mercy,—the very purpose of His coming. But when *this* act of Divine Love and Almighty Power shall have been accomplished, —the End will have come! When the daughter of the ruler of My people—the Jewish Church— is brought back to life, the whole economy of Grace, the whole scheme of Redemption, will have been completed. The miracle which forms the Gospel for the day is in fact nothing else than a prophetic history of the Church, from the days of our LORD'S Incarnation, down to the very end of the world.

"Let me invite your attention to only one more point of detail, which may have easily escaped you. As, when the typical Joseph, 'at the second time' made himself known unto his brethren [see Acts vii. 13], he caused every man to go out from him; and, behold, '*there stood no man with him, while Joseph made himself known unto his brethren*' [Gen. xlv. 1],— so was it now. It is expressly related that our SAVIOUR said, 'Give place' [St. Matt. ix. 24], and 'put them all out' [St. Mark v. 40],—and 'suffered no man to follow Him' [St. Mark v. 37],—and that it was not until the people were put forth, that He went in and took the maiden by the hand. . . . . It seems to be implied by both narratives—(prophetic histories both),—that in some marvellous privacy, which will be, in like manner, of His own Divine contriving,—the SAVIOUR of the world has decreed hereafter to recall the Jewish Church to life

Appendix (C). 391

and health and activity,—to raise up the daughter of His people from that bed of death whereon now she lies,—departed —and, to all appearance, departed for ever!

"Remarks like these, you will observe, fail to interest us deeply, because they relate to nations, not to individuals. But we are to blame, if we do not seek sometimes to look beyond the circle of ourselves, our homes, our families, our friends, our city. National prospects should interest us, no less than private and personal hopes. For national mercies we should cherish a spirit of thankfulness, to a far greater extent than seems common with the men of this generation,—with ourselves at this day. The Service which, until a few years since, was observed through the length and breadth of the land, as on Tuesday[5] last, commemorated two great national events; and all men are agreed in associating with the 5th of November a great national deliverance. We have discontinued that Service; but we need not put away the memory of the mercy, or forget to feel grateful. GOD's ancient people may well be our teachers here,—by their constant practice throughout all the days of their history. National mercies are the theme of all their inspired Hymns and Psalms,—supply the imagery of their teaching, and run into the texture of their very prayers. It is still the longsuffering of GOD in the days of Noah, and the deliverance of the sons of Jacob out of Egypt—the pillar of fire and the covering cloud—the riven rock and the heavenly Manna—the Red Sea dried up and Jordan driven back. At a later period, they rehearsed the feats of their Judges, and the faithfulness of their Prophets, and the captivity of Zion turned away by Him Who had promised with an oath unto Abraham that He would never forsake His people; 'for *His* mercy endureth for ever!'

"I will not detain you longer.—To review thankfully great national mercies, is, I repeat, a solemn duty: and, ever and

---

[5] There is some confusion here. He was preaching on Sunday, Nov. 6, 1864. "Tuesday last" therefore would be All Saints' Day (Nov. 1). But the obsolete service he is speaking of is of course that for the preceding day (Nov. 5), when the deliverance from the Gunpowder Plot, and the arrival of William of Orange, used to be commemorated in one and the same service, both events having occurred Nov. 5.

anon, to give God thanks for them on our knees is our duty too.... So likewise is it right to pray for the peace of our Zion—our public welfare—our national prosperity. Looking beyond ourselves, we should long for the reconciliation of Christendom, for the reunion especially of our own sadly divided Christian bodies here at home,—and, as far as may be, we should promote it : certainly we should pray for it. Lastly, the conversion and restoration of God's ancient people should be a frequent subject of devout anxiety with us all.... 'The maiden is not dead but sleepeth.' mourners are there, but 'the maiden is not dead.' Pale and rigid as her features confessedly are, they exhibit no token whatever that the terrible process of dissolution has begun. Above all, He who conquered death is coming ; and when He shall have reached the ruler's house, and put the people forth, and gone in where the maid is lying, He will take her by the hand, and her spirit will come again, and the maiden shall arise straightway." [St. Mark v. 42 ; St. Luke viii. 55.]

APPENDIX (D).

"*From a close study of the sacred narrative of the Deluge* [Gen. vii. 4 *to* viii. 14] *with its many notes of time, so evidently meant to be emphasized, Burgon drew out a Calendar of the Flood, from which he thinks that 'no one of fair mind will hesitate to admit that a case has been at last made out for the Sabbath as a recognised institution in the days of Noah.'*" See above *chap. iii. p.* 268.

The Week of Seven Days :—(The Calendar of the Flood).

(Reprinted from the '*Guardian*' of January 12, 1887.)

"*Nor is it at all incredible that a book which has been so long in the possession of mankind, should contain many truths as yet undiscovered.*"—Bp. Butler.

" I proceed to fulfil the promise I made at the conclusion of my former paper—viz., exhibit proof of the assertions there hazarded—(*a*) That the Antediluvian Patriarchs were demonstrably familiar with the weekly division of time; and, further, (*b*) That it may be confidently declared that '*they were acquainted with the Sabbath.*'

"Now, this task is forced upon me; because, although it is logically certain from what is related (in Exod. xvi. 22–30) with reference to the Miracle of the Manna, that the delivery of the Fourth Commandment on Mt. Sinai in the first year of the Exode (clearly a subsequent transaction), was but the republication of a law already in existence and familiarly known—objectors have, nevertheless, insinuated that no proof exists that the Hebrew race had been *for any length of time* acquainted with either the Week or the Sabbath Day. In reply to these persons, it is obvious to appeal to Genesis xxix. 27; but to this they rejoin that such a mention of a 'week' does but imply the recognition of seven days as a division of time. The same is said of Gen. l. 10, and of Judges xiv. 12. These instances (it is urged) do not 'go further than showing the custom of observing a term of seven days for any transaction of importance. They do not prove that *the whole year*, or *the whole month*, was thus divided *at all times*, and *without regard to remarkable events*[6].'

"The required proof nevertheless exists in perfection. It is to be found in the history of the Deluge—Gen. vii. 4 to viii. 14. No intelligent person ever reads that portion of Scripture without being struck by the singular particularity of the record. I will add, that no one who has made the method of the SPIRIT his study, can rise from that narrative without a profound conviction on his mind that all those chronological details must needs have been set down with some definite purpose. Let me recall them to my reader's memory; and at the same time invite his attention to the results which they spontaneously evolve. '*Years*' and '*months*' (the IInd, the VIIth, and the Xth) are freely mentioned, as things known: also, '*days of the month.*' Periods of '*seven days*' are at least

---

[6] Quoted with approval by the Bishop of Carlisle, from the '*Dictionary of the Bible,*' art. "Week," p. 1726.

three times referred to[7]. But once more, men ask,—Can it be shown that *the whole year* was divided into weeks ? Yes, I think it can. And,—Are there sufficient grounds for assuming that *one and the same day in seven* was held in special honour throughout the year ? Yes, I think there are.

"(1) I take it for granted, as all the critics have done before me, that the 'months' spoken of in Genesis vii. and viii., consisted (as they did with GOD's chosen people at a subsequent period) alternately of 30 and of 29 days. Moses states that, a solemn announcement having been made to Noah that, 'yet seven days,' and there should be 'rain upon the earth 40 days and 40 nights' (vii. 4), the Patriarch with his family entered the Ark: and that, accordingly, at the end of those 'seven days' of warning, the Flood came.

"(2) In the absence of any evidence whatever to the contrary, it is obvious to assume that the 'seven days' thus solemnly introduced to our notice indicate *a week*, of which the last day was *a Sabbath*. Not proposing, of course, to press this assumption, if it shall be found to derive no support from the chronological details which follow,—I shall, on the other hand, claim that if several striking confirmations of my hypothesis shall come to light, they are to be regarded as so many proofs that it is correct. And, at the outset, it is obvious to remark that the expression, '*yet seven days*,' clearly designates *an octave*,—which, therefore, *begins* as well as *ends* with a Sabbath-day. That *on a Sabbath* Noah should have rested from his work and his labour might even have been expected. Since, therefore, it was 'on the seventeenth day of the second month' that the flood actually began, *the 10th as well as the 17th day of the second month will* (by the hypothesis) *have been Sabbaths*. And this is the fixed point from which we proceed to construct our 'Calendar of the Flood.'

"(3) For brevity, I shall take no notice (in the table which will presently follow), after the first Week of warning, of the intermediate six days, with their notation,—a b c d e f: but, with my scheme before him, the reader may without difficulty

---

[7] Gen. vii. 4: viii. 10, 12.

construct for himself a 'Calendar of the Flood' which shall contain the days in full; and thus survey the year in its entirety and in detail. For convenience, in what follows, the Sabbaths (which are alone specified) are indicated by the letter 's,'—the more memorable Sabbaths by a blacker letter ('**S**'), to which an asterisk (*) is prefixed.

"(4) At the end of 40 days and 40 nights, a flood of waters from above and from beneath not only covers the mountains, but prevails upwards for 15 cubits. The earth continues to be thus submerged for a hundred and fifty days,—the last of which will have been the 2 th of the eighth month; and *that* day also is found to have been a Sabbath,—the *third* recorded. And now (viz., at the end of 150 days) the waters have abated (viii. 3).

"(5) But in the meantime, the Ark has rested 'upon the mountains of Ararat' in the seventh month, on the seventeenth day of the month (viii. 4). And *that* day also proves to have been a Sabbath,—the *fourth* recorded.

"(6) On the first day of the tenth month the tops of the mountains are seen (ver. 5): and at the end of a third period of 40 days, Noah opens the window of the Ark, and sends forth a raven and a dove (viii. 7, 8). This, because it coincides with the 11th day of the month, must also have been a Sabbath,—the *fifth* enumerated.

"(7) Noah 'stays yet other seven days" (viii. 10), and again sends forth the dove, which returns in the evening and in her mouth an olive leaf, plucked off. 'He stays yet other seven days and sends forth the dove,' which does not return to him (viii. 12). Thus, perforce, a *sixth* and a *seventh* consecutive Sabbath has been marked.

"(8) 'It came to pass that, in the 601st year of Noah's life, in the first month, and in the first day of the month, Noah removes the covering from the Ark' (viii. 13). This incident also coincides with a Sabbath,—the *eighth* in number.

"(9) 'And in the 2nd month, on the 27th day of the month,' the earth being now dried, Noah is commanded 'to go forth of the Ark, (viii. 14–16). And so he does, and

APPENDIX (D).

offers sacrifices. It is once more, the Sabbath day,—*the ninth Sabbath day expressly indicated* in the Calendar of the Deluge.

"(10) What precedes can only be fully understood, as well as verified step by step, by my exhibiting the CALENDAR OF THE FLOOD somewhat in detail. It follows,—having never, that I am aware, been so exhibited and explained before;—

Day. IIND MONTH (*Marchesvan*[8]): 600th YEAR OF NOAH'S LIFE (Gen. vii. 11).

*10 S   After ($3 \times 40 =$) 120 years of warning (Gen. vi. 3), [and
a   at the end of 40 days ($30+10$) from the beginning of
b   the year,] Noah is commanded to enter the Ark. It is
c   the 10th day of the IInd month. 'Yet seven days,'
d   and 40 days and nights of rain are threatened (vii. 4).
e
       f

*17 S On the 17th day [which is the 7th Sabbath
from the beginning of the year,] the Week
of Warning having expired, Noah is 'shut
in,' and the Flood begins (vii. 11) . . . . . .   1st day of
                                                     the Flood.

24 s   [1st week of the Flood ends] . . . .   8th ——

IIIRD MONTH (*Chisleu*).

2 s   [2nd week ends] . . . .   15th ——
9 s   [3rd week] . . . .   22nd ——
16 s   [4th week] . . . .   29th ——
23 s   [5th week] . . . .   36th ——
27 d   The 40 days and nights of rain end (vii. 12,
        17). [Note, that *omitting the Sabbaths,*
        this is also the 40th day since the 10th of
        IInd month, when Noah entered the ark—
        viz., $6 \times 6 = 36+4$] . . . . 40th ——
30 s   [6th week] . . . . 43rd ——

[8] Note, that *the names* of the months are introduced merely for the reader's convenience. They do not affect the argument. Neither is it to me of any importance whether the year of the Flood began with *Tisri* or with *Nisan*.

IVth Month (*Thebet*).

7 s [7th week ends]	50th day.
14 s [8th week]	57th ——
21 s [9th week]	64th ——
28 s [10th week]	71st ——

Vth Month (*Sebat*).

6 s [11th week ends]	78th ——
13 s [12th week]	85th ——
20 s [13th week]	92nd ——
27 s [14th week]	99th ——

VIth Month (*Adar*).

4 s [15th week ends]	106th ——
11 s [16th week]	113th ——
18 s [17th week]	120th ——
25 s [18th week]	127th ——

VIIth Month (*Nisan*).

3 s [19th week ends]	134th ——
10 s [20th week]	141st ——
*17 S [21st (3 × 7) week ends, and] 'the Ark rests upon the mountains of Ararat' (viii. 4) ..	148th ——
24 s [22nd week]	155th ——

VIIIth Month (*Jyar*).

1 s [23rd week ends]	162nd ——
8 s [24th week]	169th ——
15 s [25th week]	176th ——
22 s [26th week]	183rd ——
*29 S [27th week] 150 days (since the 40 days) end, and 'the waters are abated' (vii. 24 : viii. 3)	190th ——

IXth Month (*Sivan*).

	197th ——
7 s [28th week ends]	204th ——
14 s [29th week]	211th ——
21 s [30th week]	218th ——
28 s [31st week]	

APPENDIX (D).

Xth Month (*Thammuz*).

1 c	On the first day of the tenth month 'the tops of the mountains are seen' (viii. 5)..	221st day.
5 s	[32nd week ends]	225th ——
12 s	[33rd week]	232nd ——
19 s	[34th week]	239th ——
26 s	[35th week]	246th ——

XIth Month (*Ab*).

4 s	[36th week ends]	253rd ——
*11 S	[37th week] 'At the end of 40 days' from the 1st day of the Xth month (viz. 29+11), Noah sends out a raven and a dove (viii. 6–8)	260th ——
*18 S	[38th week] 'Yet other 7 days,' Noah sends out the dove (viii. 10)	267th ——
*25 S	[39th week] 'Yet other 7 days,' sends out the dove (viii. 12)	274th ——

XIIth Month (*Elul*).

2 s	[40th week ends]	281st ——
9 s	[41st week]	288th ——
16 s	[42nd week]	295th ——
23 s	[43rd week]	302nd ——

Ist Month (*Tisri*): 601st Year of Noah's Life (viii. 13).

*1 S	[44th week ends] 'The face of the ground is dry,' and 'the covering of the Ark is removed' (viii. 13)	309th ——
8 s	[45th week]	316th ——
15 s	[46th week]	323rd ——
22 s	[47th week]	330th ——
29 s	[48th week]	337th ——

IInd Month (*Marchesvan*).

6 s	[49th week ends]	344th ——
13 s	[50th week]	351st ——
20 s	[51st week]	358th ——
*27 S	[52nd week] 'The earth is dried.' Noah 'goes forth of the Ark,' and sacrifices (viii. 14–16, 18, 20)	365th ——

Appendix (D). 399

"(11) Several interesting numerical coincidences will be observed to result from the foregoing 'CALENDAR OF THE FLOOD:' as—

(a) That *three periods* of 40 days have been enumerated:
(b) That it was *on the 7th Sabbath* in the year that the Flood began:
(c) That on the 17th day of the 7th month, and at the end of the $(3 \times 7 =)$ 21st week, the Ark rested on Ararat:
(d) That from the commencement of the Flood until the day when Noah left the Ark, was a period of exactly 365 days.

"(12) More to my purpose, however, is the discovery that 53 *consecutive* weeks are distinctly recognisable in this portion of the inspired narrative.

"(13) But the only matter of real importance,—the one object I have in bringing forward this 'CALENDAR OF THE FLOOD,'—is to call attention to the undeniable (but hitherto unsuspected) fact, that it was *on the same day of the week* that—

(I.) Noah and his family entered the Ark:

(II.) The Flood of waters began:

(III.) The Ark rested on the mountains of Ararat:

(IV.) The waters ceased to prevail upon the earth:

(V.) A raven and a dove were sent forth by Noah:

(VI.) The dove was sent forth, and returned in the evening:

(VII.) The dove was again sent forth, but returned no more:

(VIII.) The ground was dry, and the covering of the Ark was removed:

(IX.) Noah and his family came forth of the Ark.

"(14) Not unaware am I that there is a sort of men who will insist that, after all, it cannot be *demonstrated* that these nine identical week-days were Sabbaths. But I do not believe that any one of fair mind will hesitate to admit that a case has been at last made out for the Sabbath as a recognised institution in the days of Noah, which may not be reasonably resisted. The reader is invited to recall what is offered above in section (2), and to note the extraordinary corroboration which has been subsequently furnished to what was at first proposed as little more than an hypothesis. Supported from behind by the primæval record of Creation, with its emphatic testimony to the fact that the weekly day of Sabbatical rest was in its origin Divine: met also in front by the narrative of the typical Redemption of the human race, into which is carefully woven, and by the very finger of God, an emphatic republication of the reason assigned in Genesis for resting on the seventh day, and for keeping the Sabbath holy; we deem it unreasonable (not to use a stronger expression), that any should refuse to discern in the 'CALENDAR OF THE FLOOD' clear evidence that the Sabbath was recognised in the days of Noah as an already existing institution. And this must suffice on the subject.

"(15) I took up my pen, in the first instance, solely to 'banish and drive away' what seemed to me 'an erroneous and strange doctrine contrary to GOD's Word[9].' It is presumed that on that former occasion I effectually demolished the wild hypothesis that it was '*the number of the planetary bodies* which settled the length of the week[1]. (By the way,—*Is* the sun a 'planetary body?' I have always been taught that *that* is precisely what the Sun is *not*!) But on the present occasion I have done something far better than refute error—viz., I have sought to establish Truth. I have made it my aim to vindicate the plain teaching of Gen. ii. 2, 3, and of Exod. xx. 11, by appealing to Gen. vii. and viii., in, as I believe, a hitherto unattempted way. Commentators have indeed discerned in the three periods of 'seven days' an evidence of the antediluvian observance of the Sabbath[2]. But I have shown that if there be so many as three Sabbaths indicated here, then there must be at least *nine*[3]: and if nine, then the consecutive Sabbaths will have been in all *fifty-four*[4].

[9] From '*The Ordering of Priests*.'

[1] Some readers of the '*Guardian*' may be grateful for a reference to Lotz's '*Quaestiones de Historiâ Sabbati*'—which is full of interesting Babylonish lore on the subject of my former letter. It was published at Leipzig in 1883.

[2] Blunt's '*Undesigned Coincidences*,' p. 21. Bishop Wordsworth (of Lincoln) on Gen. vii. 4.

[3] Cyril of Alexandria makes the sending forth of the birds occupy *four* Sabbaths.

[4] I might just as reasonably have made the three days of the sending

APPENDIX (E). 401

"(16) Whether what has been thus offered with reference to 'the Week of Seven Days' may be accepted as an illustration of Butler's striking remark concerning the Bible—'nor is it at all incredible that a book which has been so long in the possession of mankind, should contain many truths as yet undiscovered[5]'—other men must determine. Enough for me, if what I have written shall have the blessed effect of 'confirming, strengthening, settling' one doubting heart,—one anxious, wavering spirit. It is impossible to build one another up too effectually in an absolute and undoubting reliance on that Holy Word, on which we shall lean our full weight in the hour of failing nature. So employed may I be permitted to end my life, as I seek to end this present year!

"JOHN W. BURGON.

"Deanery, Chichester, St. Thomas' Day, 1886."

APPENDIX (E).

EXCERPT from a Sermon preached in Chichester Cathedral on Sunday, Aug. 5th, 1888, being the day after the death of the Very Reverend John William Burgon, B.D., Dean of Chichester, by Richard, Lord Bishop of Chichester.

2 Sam. xiv. 14. "We must needs die, and *are* as water spilt on the ground, which cannot be gathered up again."

After touching allusions to other great losses which the Chapter of Chichester had recently sustained, the Bishop continued thus:

"Again the signs of public and general grief are shown within these walls,—yea, in the very Sanctuary,—and this time for the Dean of this Cathedral Church. We miss in his accustomed

---

forth of the raven and the dove my fixed starting point, and from those two consecutive weeks—those three consecutive Sabbaths—might have worked backwards and forwards.

The result would obviously have been exactly the same.

[5] '*Analogy*,' Part II., chap. iii.,—about one-third of the chapter from the end.

place that devout and reverent figure, that earnest and solemn countenance ; we shall never more behold him in this pulpit nor hear his voice. This is no place for praise of Christ's faithful servants; and I should deem it little less than presumption to use the language of eulogy towards one better than myself, who, as I firmly believe, lived very near to God, and devoted himself, body, soul, and spirit to His honour and the good of His Church. For he was a most faithful and attached member of that branch of it, which by the signal mercy of God has been preserved and established in this land. In this respect, as indeed in the general cast of his religious belief, he was in perfect harmony with his predecessor Dean Hook, whose name and services must still be freshly remembered, not only in this city and diocese, but throughout the Church of England at home and abroad. I do not compare two men of very different gifts and qualities, but they agreed in their view of the true position of the Church of England—at once reformed and Catholic,—reformed, as purged from Roman errors and superstitions,—Catholic as adhering to the faith once delivered to the saints, and respecting the voice of Primitive Antiquity. Both held this doctrine, not as a mere matter of opinion, but as a truth for which, if need had been, they would not have feared to die.

"There could never be a doubt of Dean Burgon's sincerity. It was written in his very looks, as it found expression in his words, his writings, his actions. From the earliest days of his ministry he gave himself wholly to that great work. He prepared himself by diligent unwearied study to be a teacher of others. He had many tastes,—nay, accomplishments, which might have drawn away a less resolute man from his especial duty; but he put all aside, and was content to live for this one end, to draw all his cares to the service of the Lord, to live laborious days,—yes, and to pass laborious nights in this sacred work.

"No part of his character was more remarkable than his

Appendix (E).

reverence for the Word of God. He might take to himself David's saying, and declare with perfect truth, 'Lord, what love have I to Thy word; all the day long is my study in it.' Every jot and tittle of the Scriptures was infinitely precious to him. He treasured them not as the word of man, but the word of God, given by a real immediate inspiration, and communicated to His servants, Prophets, Evangelists, Apostles, each in his own good time. He delighted in searching out the meaning of the Word, and pondering it in his heart. He did not disdain such assistance as could be got from the old Fathers of the Church. Few men perhaps in our day have so large and profound a knowledge of the mighty teachers of the earliest Church, or have more carefully digested their manifold instruction. The great divines of our own Church he held in especial esteem, and was well content to sit at their feet. But he was no slave of commentators, as you must have observed; he often exercised an independent judgment; and whatever may be thought of his interpretations, they were always fresh and honest. Well, my dear friends; the results of his careful study of the Scriptures he gave to the world in his so-called '*Plain Commentary on the Gospels*,'—a work which later commentaries have by no means superseded. For it is no dry explanation of difficulties, though, when such exist, the Dean meets them with courage and fulness; but is a work which appeals to the heart and conscience, and embodies, as the text suggests, precious Christian counsel. In our sister Church of America, I have reason to know, Dean Burgon's commentary holds a high place in the esteem of its Bishops and Pastors, and when I lately met many of these in the great Lambeth Conference, they expressed with one accord their sense of his services to our honoured Church and their anxiety on his behalf. His reverence for the letter and the spirit of Holy Writ,—for he held that the spirit was inseparably bound up with the letter, and that both were divine,—his reverence, I say, led him to vindicate with great learning, and, as it is confessed, with great ability, the divine authority of the last verses of the Gospel according to St. Mark.

Appendix (E).

This had been attacked by a school of critics, of whom the Dean was justly suspicious; for he feared that they were subverting the authority of the revealed Word, and thus undermining the faith of many half-learned persons wise in their own conceit, and of many simple souls. For this reason he set himself to combat the conclusions as to the true text of the New Testament, which the authors of the Revised Version had adopted. 'I believed, and therefore will I speak,' might be said of him with perfect truth. It was his burning zeal for the Word of God which stirred him to come forward as a champion in a cause, which he thought was being betrayed by those who should have been its guardians. And this I think cannot be denied, that his arguments have greatly shaken the theory upon which the Revised Version is constructed, have in not a few cases exposed serious defects of omission or translation, and have retarded, if not completely barred, its general reception by our Church as supplanting the old Version, the inheritance of English-speaking people throughout the world, whatever their creed or Communion.

"But it would be a great injustice to consider Dean Burgon only or chiefly as a vigorous controversialist, a well-equipped eager defender of that Faith by which he lived;—not so did he understand his calling as 'a minister of Christ and steward of the mysteries of God.' For many years he held the Vicarage of St. Mary's in Oxford, the principal Church of that City, though the parish is small. This post had great traditions. Newman, —a name that must ever be famous in the annals of our Church, first for his services in her cause and then for his desertion of it— preached in the parish pulpit of St. Mary's the sermons which are known and read far beyond the narrow bounds of this island. And in the same Church the Dean gathered a congregation, whom he taught for many years with a faithful and true heart, and ruled them prudently with all his power. Many of the discourses which he addressed to his beloved flock he printed for their benefit, and in these 'being dead he speaketh.' They are plain, affectionate, and forcible. They reflect the real

Appendix (E).

character of the preacher, and are durable monuments of his learning and piety. He was no mere student, no recluse. If I were asked the quality which as a divine distinguished him, I should say that he was 'apt to teach,'—always ready to pour out for the instruction of others the full stores which by long toil he had accumulated. Thus in Oxford he was not content with the duties of his parish. He attracted to him many youths who sat at his feet, and learned from him how they might resist the temptations, which at that critical age, and in that place, unhappily tried alike their faith and their moral stedfastness. He taught them the way of life from the Word of life. I have known many of these his scholars who owned their deep obligations to him. And perhaps some here present may remember with gratitude his weekly lessons and expositions of the Scripture given to a chosen few in this City, and also to the students of Bishop Otter's College. Never was he happier than when he found himself in the midst of such disciples, hearing them, teaching them reverently, and asking them, and drawing out for their instruction the deep things of Holy Scripture.

"Perhaps those Oxford years were the happiest of his life. His college, like a second mother, fed and sheltered and supplied all that was necessary for his modest wants and even more; for he contrived by careful economy always to have to give to the needy and to suffering. Although a private man, he was a real power in that great University. He lived in the society of the wise and the good,—in the world, yet free from its cares and its ambitions, holding stedfastly his own course, and bearing what he believed in his conscience to be a witness to God's eternal truth.

"For his trumpet gave no uncertain sound, and on all great questions as they arose,—and there were many,—he delivered himself with courage, as one who was convinced himself and strove to convince others.

"By God's good Providence he was called to a place and dignity in the Church, which he had well earned, but never

Appendix (E).

desired, far less sought; and so called he obeyed. So you have all known him, and his constant familiar presence, and his work among you; and you have always felt that he was truly a master in Israel. Yet this profound scholar had a most tender heart. He wept with those who weep, as he rejoiced with those who joy. His love for children was always showing itself in little gifts, words of kindness, and sweet caresses; and those who were admitted to his intimacy knew the depth and sincerity of his feelings. None of us, be sure, will look upon his like again, nor perhaps in many respects on his equal. And then, in our sorrow that such a man is taken from us there is danger that we may forget that God's ways are not our ways, nor His thoughts our thoughts. He removes from their place those whom we deemed the pillars of His Church, necessary for its strength, its defence, its support,—as though to show that such judgment is not for us, that He needs no man's abilities, or zeal, or courage. Yet His servant had passed the appointed age of man; he had not done the work of the Lord negligently; he had improved the talents that were lent him; his good works follow him. His name will be honoured by this and by other generations, and when unworthy detraction shall have been long silenced, the learned defender of the faith as it is in Jesus, the thoughtful expositor and interpreter of God's Word, the jealous assertor of the literal authority of Holy Writ, will be remembered.

"Friends and Brethren, it is our comfort that God has devised means that His banished should not be expelled from Him. Surely His faithful servants, though lost awhile to our sight, are with Him, through the merits of His blessed Son, enjoying a rest which shall not be broken, a peace that shall no more be troubled. They are lost to our sight, but not to our thought. Still we behold them in mystery kneeling at our side. Still we have true communion and fellowship with them in the mystical body of our Lord Jesus Christ."

APPENDIX (F).

[*The Notes on this Sermon are by the Author.*]

Short Sermon by the late Very Rev. J. W. Burgon, B.D., Dean of Chichester.

THE STATE OF THE FAITHFUL DEPARTED.

Ἐn Παραδίσε. St. Luke xxiii. 43.

"THERE is no denying that the things after death are shrouded in mystery, difficulty, wonder. The very revelations made to us in Scripture concerning the Intermediate state—by which name we speak of the long interval between our death, and our resurrection—are themselves in a high degree perplexing. But it is by no means fair to represent this subject as shrouded in impenetrable darkness. As much as it is good for us to know concerning what will befall us after death has been sufficiently revealed. Precious hints abound, which are calculated either to comfort the heart or else to stimulate the imagination; to assist the reason, or, at least, to minister food for faith and hope to feed upon.

"1. And, first, the terms employed when 'death' is spoken of in Scripture are eminently helpful and consoling. Our Saviour calls it 'sleep' in the parable of the wise and foolish virgins (St. Matt. xxv. 5–7), and again in the case of Lazarus, His friend (St. John xi. 11–14). His design is clearly to remind men of the comfort of rest after labour; of the strength and refreshment which sleep brings to the weary; above all, of the solemn certainty that there is to be a waking up in the end, which, in the case of the departed saint, will be nothing else but a resurrection to eternal life. Elsewhere He speaks of it as a fainting or failing at the end of a race. 'When ye fail[6],' He says (St.

---

[6] Ὅταν ἐκλίπητε. In his Plain Commentary on this verse of St. Luke, Burgon points out that this word, in the Septuagint or Greek Version, is used to denote the end of Abraham, Isaac and Jacob;—of Abraham [Gen. xxv. 8], Καὶ ἐκλείπων ἀπέθανεν Ἀβραὰμ ἐν γήρᾳ καλῷ; of Isaac [xxxv. 29], Καὶ ἐκλείπων Ἰσαὰκ ἀπέθανε; finally of Jacob

APPENDIX (F).

Luke xvi. 9); whereby He hints that death is but the momentary failing of the powers of nature—to be speedily recovered from, when the race will proceed with vigour. But His tenderest image is employed with reference to the disciple He loved best. 'If I will that he tarry *till I come*[7]' (St. John xxi. 22); which shows that, in His account, the death of a saint is not so much his *going* to Christ as Christ *coming to him*; the gentlest thing imaginable, and wholly without admixture of alarm.

"Where St. Paul says that it is better '*to depart* and be with Christ' (Phil. i. 23), he uses a word which implies the weighing of the anchor, and the loosening from the shore, in the case of one who has to go a voyage. What need to remind you that this also is an image of bliss, if the journey be to some congenial clime, or destined to convey the voyager to the home of his heart's affections, and to the forms and faces of those he has been sundered from all too long? But 'to depart and' (in some mysterious way) 'to be with Christ,'—Oh! that must be a blessedness for which the tongue of man can find no adequate expression!

"Then, further, in a certain place our Saviour even says, 'He that liveth and believeth in Me *shall never die*'" (St. John xi.

[xlix. 33],—where the verb ἐκλείπω stands alone without the ἀποθνήσκω, —καὶ ἐξάρας τοὺς πόδας αὐτοῦ ἐπὶ τὴν κλίνην, ἐξέλιπε. Thus, to the ears of the Apostles who were familiar with the Septuagint Version, the word would "imply a peaceful and happy end."

[7] Burgon, with his friend Bp. Christopher Wordsworth ["Greek Testament with Notes" *in loc.*] takes Augustine's view [Serm. ccliii] of the meaning of "the coming" in this passage; "If I will that he should not *follow* Me, as thou wilt, by martyrdom on the cross, but that he should tarry for a placid consummation, and wait in expectation *till I come* to take him to Myself in peace." But while "the coming" will no doubt embrace the natural death of St. John, and indeed of every other believer, it may be questioned whether it can be restricted to this meaning,—whether the destruction of Jerusalem, the granting to St. John of the Apocalypse, and the Second Advent at the end of the world, are not comprised under it, as well as the taking of individual saints one by one to their rest. The prophetic words of the Divine Master are wonderfully comprehensive, and fulfil themselves in various ways, as the scheme of God's Providence is gradually unrolled.

APPENDIX (F).

26); by which saying He clearly abolishes death entirely, refuses to acknowledge it, will only regard it as an incident in life.

"So much for the language employed concerning 'death' in Scripture. It is reassuring, comfortable, helpful in a high degree.

"2. Next, there are not a few revelations made to us of what will befall us immediately after our departure hence. And, first, we are assured that no sooner have the eyes been closed to the affairs of this life, than the other life—without pause or interruption of any kind—begins; begins by a carrying away of the departed saint to the place where Abraham, the father of the faithful, is (St. Luke xvi. 22). Unaided reason might have divined as much. Angels minister to God's people in their lifetime. 'Are they not all ministering spirits, sent forth to minister for them who shall be heirs of salvation?' (Heb. i. 14). And is it credible that their good offices shall suddenly come to an end, when the need thereof is most urgently felt? How shall the disembodied spirit find its way to the bowers of bliss without a friendly guide? . . . But the circumstance is by our Saviour made the subject of distinct revelation. The departed saint (He assures us) is at once 'carried by the angels'—by a company of them, as it would seem [8]—'into Abraham's bosom' (St. Luke xvi. 23).

"3. From the same discourse we obtain a clear intimation that there will be *Recognition* in the place whither the departed one will be conducted by his heavenly guides. For Abraham is at once seen, recognised, parleyed with; and Lazarus is also seen, seen 'in his bosom' (St. Luke xvi. 23), and known to be Lazarus. I am inclined to infer from this that we shall carry out of this world a recognisable form; not parting with the semblance of humanity, though the fleshy garment has been laid up in the wardrobe of the grave, laid up against the Resurrec-

---

[8] In Burgon's '*Plain Commentary*' on this verse [*in loc.*] he says, quoting from Isaac Williams and from Ludolphus; "Yesterday, dogs licked his sores: to-day,—'not one angel carries him, but many; for many are eager to bear': 'each rejoicing to touch such a burthen.'"

tion morning. We gather as much from the recognition of Moses and Elijah by the three disciples on the Mount of Transfiguration (St. Matt. xvii. 3). We infer as much from the appearing of Samuel to Saul and the witch of Endor (1 Sam. xxviii. 14). But, in fact, reason cries aloud that so it must needs be. When Abraham, when Isaac, and when Jacob 'gave up the ghost and were buried,' it is significantly added that 'they were gathered to their people' (Gen. xxv. 8, xxxv. 29, xlix. 33). Of what avail would *that* be, if it were not thereby implied that they were severally restored—*consciously* restored —to the society of their lost kindred? Abraham to his Sarah, Isaac to his Rebecca, Jacob to his beloved Rachel?

" 4. It may be confidently gathered from the same discourse of our Lord, that we shall carry with us out of this world recollections of it; that solicitude concerning home and kindred will go along with us. The fundamental truth, in fact, which is observed to underlie the whole parable (and it may not be forgotten that our Lord is the speaker!) is, that the departed carry with them out of this world human loves, fears, hopes, desires. The rich man in the place of pain is solemnly invited by Abraham to call to remembrance what, during his life time, had been the relative estate of himself and of Lazarus. ('Son, remember.') And thus our Lord's discourse helps wonderfully to set before us the solemn truth that this life is but the beginning of the next; the next life but the continuation of the present. No such change, as some seem inclined to imagine, will come over the complexion of our thoughts and over the dispositions of our hearts. Doubtless the eyes will be opened wide to the great realities of our being, but there is no hint anywhere given that we shall become changed in character, temperament, disposition, by the fact that we have been translated. The passionate love, and the strong desire for husband, wife, child, depend upon it, will go on: sublimed, it may be, into the voice of a passionate prayer: but, even in that altered shape, it will still subsist. Of course the tear will be effectually wiped away, and the sigh will be unknown, in the bowers of bliss: the wounds, too, which cruelty or injustice inflicted, cannot possibly go on smarting *there*. But the memory that such things *have been*, will probably never pass away; and (as already suggested) solicitude concerning others will abide with us, until those persons also shall have been gathered into the unseen world, and be themselves eternally at rest.

"5. There is a blissful region, there, a place of refreshment and consolation, where all God's accepted ones who have departed this life are already congregated together. Our Saviour calls it 'Paradise,' implying thereby the recovery procured for our race, in and through and by Himself, 'the second Man,' of that state of entire felicity and lofty privilege from which our first parents by transgression fell. On reaching that blessed region (the whereabouts of which it is impossible even to conjecture reasonably), the departed saint finds himself surrounded by thousands of congenial natures, and by them is eagerly accosted, lovingly welcomed, led about with joy unspeakable. Oh, but it needs the tongue of angels to image forth to one another the very smallest portion of such mysterious blessedness as *that*! For *there* must of necessity be all the holy ones who have ever lived and died, in all but perfect bliss :—'the glorious company of the Apostles, the goodly fellowship of the Prophets, the noble army of Martyrs,'—the four Evangelists (oh, to embrace their feet and ask them a thousand questions!),—yes, all the Saints and Doctors of the Church, from the beginning until yesterday!

"6. Now, familiar intercourse with blessed spirits such as these implies a scarcely imaginable weight of bliss—we are not to forget the evidences of God's goodness, wisdom, power, love, to be again and again elicited from their converse; the removal of unnumbered grounds of perplexity, and the springing up in their place of fresh motives for love, and admiration, and desire. Surely also, we are to picture to ourselves in Paradise a species of polity, heavenly, not earthly in its character and attributes, yet in the strictest sense, human, social, and active, and happy in all its manifold relations, as being of the very essence of that 'Intermediate State' of which we speak. I assume this as certain, and from such considerations as the following: (1) That, as already pointed out, men's and women's natures cannot become essentially and entirely changed by departing out of this world, but must still have objects of love and desire. (2) That the population of Paradise must already be excessive; and that, where myriads of intelligent human beings are congregated together, there must needs be order and subordination, times and places of worship; worship sublimed to any extent you will, but still *worship*. (3) Occupations too there will surely be in that thickly peopled world, though exertion will bring no weariness; and there will be no further regrets, no such thing as disappointment, or sorrow, or unrest. But the passionate prayer will go up like a fountain for every human tie it left behind. And *who* can tell the power and efficacy of the prayers of accepted spirits within the veil, prayers poured forth in the very presence of the Almighty with untiring earnestness, night and day; while angels are standing by, eager to receive their Creator's mandate to minister for any, the very least, of the heirs of Salvation?

"(7) I have said nothing yet of the rapture which will attend the inevitable restoration of every lost tie, even on the very threshold of 'Paradise'; restoration of all that the heart has ever asked for, without the possibility of further severance, further change. But the subject claimed earlier notice, for this will probably be the characteristic blessedness of the wondrous place whereof we speak! . . . . Add to every other source of rapture and of wonder the sense of God's nearness, the partial coming into view of His attributes of glory,—and verily the cup of human joy must altogether flow over. For there will be the certainty, and at no very distant day, of perfect bliss and glory above that of the holy angels themselves, to result upon the redemption of the body from the power of the grave, at the last day.

"(8) Surely no one will complain that such thoughts are lacking in personal application and practical use. It seems to me quite impossible, even in thought, to place oneself within the veil without deriving some practical benefit from the effort. To say that sin straightway hides its hideous form, that unholy desires go out ashamed, that unlovely dispositions slink away abashed—to say all this and more, is not to say much. Surely sorrow straightway lays down half her burthen, and suffering goodness is made to feel more strong. Surely, every holy aspiration becomes hereby encouraged, and faith becomes sensibly confirmed. Surely, instead of cultivating avaricious, or ambitious, or any other form of grovelling desire, we all feel ourselves stirred up to strive to win for ourselves an imperishable crown! And then there springs up a deep, deep sense of confidence in the unspeakable goodness, mysterious wisdom, boundless power of Him with whom we have to do. We feel as children may be supposed to feel, who have been led for once into an unknown region where all is awe and wonder, yet where all is love and promise; and we cling to the strong hand which is guiding us, with a sense of need, insufficiency, confidence, which finds no words. 'Leave me not, neither forsake me, O God of my salvation.' Lord, when my turn comes to depart hence in peace, Thou wilt be faithful and true (wilt Thou not?) to those I shall leave behind! Lord, Thou wilt suffer me—wilt Thou not?—to meet again, and to dwell for ever with, those whom Thy love once gave me: the loved parents, the authors of my being—the husband, the wife of my youth—the children of many prayers—the friends who made the happiness of my life? Lord, I commit them all with undoubting, unswerving confidence to Thee! 'Lord, into Thy hands I commend *my* spirit.'"

INDEX.

ABB

ABBOTSFORD, i. 79.
Abou Simbel, Burgon copies inscription in temple at, i. 304, 305.
Accommodation, doctrine of, i. 198, 269.
Acres, Mr., i. 131.
Acts of the Apostles, Lectures on, i. 95; ii. 16.
Æschylus compared with Shakspeare, i. 137.
Ainsworth's Annotations, ii. 102 and *n.*
'*Akerman's Numismatic Journal,*' Articles in, i. 10, 16.
Allen (the Quaker), i. 105.
Allies, Mr., i. 186, 193.
American Clergyman interviews Burgon, ii. 121, 122.
Amusements, over-indulgence in, by Clergy, ii. 330.
Andrieu, Bertrand (Art. on), i. 71.
'*Anthologia Oxoniensis,*' i. 129.
Antiquities, Burgon sketches his father's collection of, i. 95, 96.
Anziani, Dr., ii. 84.
'*Apostles, The Church of the,*' projected, i. 94.
Archer, Dr. Thos. (Art. on), i. 72.
Armstrong, Bishop, i. 201.
Art, with reference to University Studies, i. 127.
Ashworth, Mrs., ii. 313.
Assaad à Khayat, i. 333, 337.
Athanasian. *See* Creed.
Atlay, Bishop, ii. 38 *n.*
Aubrey, Dr. William (Art. on), i. 72.
αὐτάρκεια occurs only twice in N. T., ii. 332.
Author, letters and communications

BIR

to, i. 164, 233; ii. 11 *n.*, 34 *n.*, 44, 110–112, 115, 121, 125, 126, 132, 144, 163, 194, 275, 276, 279, 286, 297, 299, 302, 309, 311, 312, 339, 347, 353.
Awdry, Canon, ii. 304; letters to author, ii. 125, 126.

B.

Babbage, Mr., i. 272.
Bacon's 'Advancement of Learning,' i. 263.
Baldwin, Mrs., i. 6, 7.
Balston, Archdeacon, ii. 186 *n.*
Bandinel, Dr., i. 60.
Barrow, Dr., i. 256.
Barton, Bernard, i. 69 and *n.*
Bayley, Captain and Mrs., i. 294, 298, 301, 312.
Beauchamp, Earl (the late), ii. 57.
Beds, Glossary of Words in County, i. 214; ii. 349, 381–386.
Bennett, Prebendary, ii. 304.
Benson, Father, ii. 304.
Berkeley, Dr., i. 334.
Berriman's '*Critical Dissertation upon 1 Tim.* iii. 16,' ii. 233 and *n.*
Bible Classes, Sunday Evening, for Undergraduates at Oxford, i. 260; ii. 100–107; for ladies, ii. 116, 117; at Chichester for ladies, ii. 319–323; at Otter College, ii. 308, 323–327.

Bickersteth, Mrs. Samuel, ii. 290; letter to author, ii. 115. *See* Letters.
Biography, truth as to faults in, ii. 357, 358.

Birch, ii. 207.

BLA

Blachford, Lord, i. 62 ; ii. 21.
Bliss, Dr., i. 60, 61.
Blomfield, Bishop, i. 98.
'*Blunt's Undesigned Coincidences,*' ii. 100.
Blunt, Professor, ii. 9 *n.*
Bodleian Picture Gallery, i. 115.
Booth, Mr., i. 31.
Bower, Mr. Henry, i. 86.
Bramley, H. R., ii. 79 *n.*
Brancker, Mr., i. 60, 120, 123.
Brandram, Rev. T. P., letter to author, ii. 347.
Bright, Rev. Canon, ii. 73.
Bright, John, ii. 217 *n.*
Bröndsted, Chevalier, i. 37 *n.*, 38 and *n.*, 40, 51.
Brook, Rev. Arthur, ii. 119.
Broomer family, i. 2.
Brougham, Lord, i. 176.
Browell, Mr., i. 64.
Bruce, John, i. 47.
Buckland, Rev. Dr., i. 62, 64, 265.
Buckle, Henry, i. 334.
Bull, Bishop, i. 159, 272.
Burgon, Emily Mary, death, ii. 48, 49.
Burgon, John, researches into his pedigree, i. 1, 2 ; signification of name, i. 2 ; birth and parentage, i. 8 and *n.* ; family-tree, i. 8 *n.* ; taste for archæology, i. 10 ; talent for drawing, i. 17, 21 ; school-life at Putney, i. 18 ; at Blackheath, i. 18, 19 ; confirmation, i. 20 ; desire to take Holy Orders, i. 22 ; goes into his father's counting-house, i. 22 ; gets a prize at the London University, i. 23 ; society at his father's, i. 24–31 ; intercourse with Samuel Rogers, i. 25 ; trip to Notts. and Derbyshire, i. 31 ; early friendships, i. 31–40 ; wins the Lord Mayor's Prize for essay on Sir Thomas Gresham, i. 36, 59 ; visits Stratford-on-Avon, i. 43 ; sleeps in Shakspeare's house, i. 43 ; special study of and notes on Shakspeare, i. 44–50 ; ii. 378–381 ; correspondence with Mr. Hunter on spelling of Shakspeare's name, i. 46–50 ; journal of his sister Kitty's illness and death, i. 54–59 ; visits Oxford,

BUR

i. 60–65, and Cambridge, i. 60 *n.* ; first literary earnings, i. 65 ; visits Norfolk, i. 66–69 ; tour in Scotland, i. 73–79 ; distaste for business, i. 80 ; his father's failure, i. 90–93 ; draws his father's collection of Greek antiquities before their sale to the British Museum, i. 95 ; goes to Oxford, i. 114 ; to Worcester College, i. 116–121 ; interview with Dr. Pusey, i. 116, 117 ; matriculates, i. 120 ; visit to Newman, i. 123 ; wins the Newdigate Prize, i. 125 ; takes B.A. degree, i. 125, and M.A. i. 125 *n.* ; takes a Second Class, i. 126 ; Fellow of Oriel, i. 131 ; draws frontispiece for '*Anthologia Oxoniensis,*' i. 129 ; gains Ellerton Theological Essay Prize, i. 131 ; connection with the Oxford Movement, i. 134, 135 ; grief at Newman's secession, i. 135 ; sub-librarian of his College, i. 143 ; feelings before Ordination, i. 155, 156 ; ordained Deacon, i. 162 ; his first sermon, i. 162 ; curacy at West Ilsley, i. 163, 181, 182 ; ordained Priest, i. 163, 209 ; his love for his flock, i. 164, 165 ; first extempore sermon, i. 166, 167 ; curacy at Worton, i. 167 ; at Finmere, i. 168–172 ; first sermon before the University, i. 174, 175, 197 ; votes for Gladstone, i. 177, 204, 211 ; withdraws from E.C.U. i. 179 ; maintains doctrine of baptismal regeneration, attacked by Mr. Gorham, i. 179 ; called a 'primitive Tractarian,' i. 179 ; his first baptism, i. 182 ; his mother's death and burial, i. 228–233 ; his father's death, i. 244–246 ; Select Preacher, i. 258 ; his sermons on Inspiration and Interpretation, i. 261–274 ; effect on his hearers, i. 275–279 ; chaplain at Rome for three months, i. 253, 292 ; tour in Egypt and the Holy Land, i. 292–336 ; illness at Jerusalem, i. 294, 331 ; considers his illness a chastisement for leaving his work at Oxford, i. 338; Vicar of St. Mary's, Oxford. ii. 1; refuses the Principalship of Exeter Theological College, ii. 14; votes for Gladstone, but will not join his Committee, ii. 14, 15; removes his sister Kitty's body to Holywell Cemetery, ii. 22-25; appointed Gresham Professor, ii. 26; anecdotes illustrating his impatience in argument, ii. 28 n.; sends a letter to undergraduates against Sunday entertainments, ii. 33; his acquaintance with each individual parishioner, ii. 34; protests against Disestablishment of Irish Church, ii. 35; protests against Dr. Temple's consecration, ii. 36-39; admiration for Bishop Temple's character, i. 149, 150; ii. 42; takes part in the debate on Keble College, ii. 43; candidate for Professorship of Exegesis, ii. 44; protests against an Unitarian being one of the Revisers, ii. 45 n., 64, 65; his sister Emily's death, ii. 48, 49; takes his B.D. degree, ii. 49, 50; visit to Paris, ii. 58, and to Florence, ii. 58; adopts New Lectionary in obedience to authority, ii. 60; his brother's death, ii. 63, 64; protests against Dean Stanley being Select Preacher, ii. 78, 79; offered the Deanery of Chichester, ii. 91, 92; his reasons for accepting it, ii. 92, 93; account of him as Vicar, ii. 99, 100; in intercourse with undergraduates, ii. 100; Bible readings with undergraduates, as Parish Priest, ii. 110-114; classes for young ladies, ii. 114-119; fondness for animals, ii. 119; courtesy to undergraduate guests, ii. 120; sensibility, ii. 121; claims made on him, ii. 121, 122; installed Dean of Chichester, ii. 123; visits Norwich, ii. 123, 127-130; anecdote of conjurer, ii. 127, 128; refuses testimonial, ii. 134, 135; placed on Universities Commission but opposed in Parliament, ii. 136-139; consults Dean Merivale as to whether clergy may assist in a second celebration without again communicating, ii. 140, 141; protest about Oxford lodging-houses, ii. 141-143; disappointment as to Divinity Professorship, ii. 156, 157; not fitted to work with equals, or to be a leader, ii. 163; withdraws from Convocation, ii. 192, 193; Bible-classes at Chichester, ii. 239, 240; in his study, ii. 273; last illness, ii. 290-302; goes to Folkestone, ii. 295, 296; last hours, ii. 299-302; funeral sermon by Bishop, ii. 303; burial, ii. 304; personal reminiscences of him, in his love for children, ii. 309; his Bible-classes, ii. 308-323; his interest in Ordination candidates, and advice to them, ii. 327-334; memorials to him, ii. 334-340; mention in speech of Public Orator, ii. 339; his character, intellectual, moral, and spiritual, ii. 341-377.

— Works of—
'Akerman's Numismatic Journal,' contributions to, i. 10 n.
'Gentleman's Magazine,' contributions to, i. 11 n.
'Life and Times of Sir Thomas Gresham,' i. 23, 66.
'Mémoire sur les Vases Panathénaïques' (transl.), i. 37, 38.
'Memoir of P. F. Tytler,' i. 42.
Articles on Bertrand Andrieu, Dr. T. Archer, and Dr. William Aubrey, in 'New Biog. Dict.,' i. 71, 72.
'Harmony of the Gospels,' i. 112, 172.
Newdigate Prize Poem, 'Petra,' i. 125, 145; ii. 345.
'Remarks on Art with regard to University Studies,' i. 127.
Ellerton Prize Essay on 'The Importance of Translation of the Holy Scriptures,' i. 131.
'Letter to Parishioners of Finmere,' and 'Manual of Prayers,' i. 171.
'Commentary on the Gospels,' i. 173, 201, 237; ii. 95.

- 'Glossary of Bedfordshire Words,' i. 214 ; ii. 349.
- 'Ninety Short Sermons for Family Reading,' i. 234; ii. 95.
- 'Oxford Reformers,' i. 226.
- History of our Lord in coloured engravings, i. 237.
- 'Historical Notices of the Colleges of Oxford,' i. 237, 239-242, 286, 289.
- 'Letters from Rome,' i. 253, 342.
- 'Last Twelve Verses of S. Mark,' i. 257 ; ii. 50, 53-56, 58, 95, 214. See S. Mark.
- 'Christian Inscriptions in the Catacombs,' &c., i. 257.
- 'Inspiration and Interpretation,' i. 260-272, 304, 309.
- 'Treatise on the Pastoral Office,' ii. 6, 8-13.
- 'Expository Lectures on Genesis' (unfinished), ii. 15, 16.
- 'Lectures on the Acts of the Apostles' (unpublished), i. 95 ; ii. 16.
- 'The University Sermon and College Services,' ii. 20.
- 'Mr. Sandford and the University Sermon,' ii. 20 n.
- 'Mr. Kitchin, Mr. Sandford, and the University Sermon,' ii. 20 n.
- 'The Oxford Sunday,' ii. 20.
- 'Lambeth Conference and the Encyclical,' ii. 25.
- 'Disestablishment: the nation's formal rejection of God,' ii. 26, 35.
- 'Plea for a Fifth Final School,' ii. 29, 90.
- 'Plea for the Study of Divinity in Oxford,' ii. 32, 90.
- 'Protests of the Bishops against the Consecration of Dr. Temple,' ii. 36, 37.
- 'Dr. Temple's Explanation examined,' ii. 37.
- 'Review of a Year,' ii. 45, 46.
- 'Woman's Place,' ii. 46, 47.
- 'An Unitarian Reviser of our A. V. intolerable,' ii. 64.
- 'Earnest Remonstrance and Petition to Bishop Ellicott,' ii. 67.
- 'The Athanasian Creed to be retained in its integrity,' &c , ii. 75.
- 'True Principles of Textual Criticism of N. T.' (not finished), ii. 82, 83, 277, 278.
- 'MS. Evangelia in Foreign Libraries,' ii. 84, 198, 231.
- 'Oxford Diocesan Conference; and Romanizing within the Church of England,' ii. 84.
- Chichester Cathedral; suggestions to Commissioners,' i. 124.
- 'Home Missions and Sensational Religion,' ii. 130.
- 'Humility—ad Clerum,' ii. 131.
- 'Our Present Lodging-house System,' &c., ii. 141.
- 'The New Lectionary examined,' &c. (third paper by Burgon), ii. 151.
- 'The Servants of Scripture,' ii. 158.
- 'Nehemiah, a Pattern to Builders,' ii. 161.
- 'Typical Structure of Holy Writ,' ii. 166.
- 'Our Saviour's knowledge of the day of judgment,' ii. 171.
- 'Prophecy not Forecast,' ii. 174 and n.
- 'Disestablishment of Religion in Oxford,' &c., ii. 184.
- 'Divergent Ritual,' &c., ii. 187.
- 'Letter of Friendly Remonstrance to Canon Gregory,' ii. 189-191, 195.
- 'Sacred Greek Codices,' &c., ii. 198.
- 'Revision Revised,' ii. 209.
- 'To educate Young Women with Young Men, inexpedient,' &c., ii. 235.
- 'Poems,' ii. 241. See also Poems.
- 'Articles on the Mosaic Cosmogony; reply to Professor Pritchard,' ii. 246, 268, 270.
- 'Structure and Method of the Prayer Book,' ii. 250, 251.
- 'The New Reformation,' &c., ii. 272.
- 'Lives of Twelve Good Men.' See under Twelve.

Burgon, Katherine Margaret, death, i. 24, 54-58 ; ii. 22-25, 337.
— Mrs. (mother), i. 8 and *n*.; last illness and death, i. 228, 230-233, 286; ii. 23, 337.
— pedigree, i. 8 *n*.
— Thomas, i. 8 and *n*.-15, 51 *n*.; death, i. 246; ii. 23, 337.
— Thomas Charles, death, ii. 63, 64, 337.
Burrows, Mr. Henry, i. 64.
— Montagu, ii. 79 *n*.
Burton, Dr., i. 62.

C.

Cairns, Lord, ii. 243.
Carter, Rev. W. S., letter to author, ii. 276.
Catherwood, Frederick, i. 24.
Ceriani, Dr., ii. 58 *n*., 84, 232.
Chalmers, Dr., i. 98.
Chantrey, i. 30 and *n*.
Chaplin, Mr., i. 331.
Charles Edward, Prince, i. 75.
Chase, Rev. Dr., i. 310, 343; ii. 2, 106, 178, 182 and *n*., 304.
Chequers, visit to, i. 72.
Chichester, Classes at. *See* Bible Classes.
Chichester, Burgon offered the Deanery of, ii. 91 ; reasons for accepting, ii. 92, 93 ; article in the American '*Churchman*' on his appointment, ii. 94; installation, ii. 123; misunderstanding with canons of, ii. 124-127.
— Bishop of. *See* Durnford.
— Cathedral, dedication of memorial window in, ii. 334. *See* Memorials.
— — New statutes to be drawn up for, ii. 226.
— — 'Suggestions to Cathedral Commissioners,' ii. 124.
Children, Burgon's love for, i. 43, 169; ii. 309, 352, 353.
Chretien, Mr., i. 214 *n*., 215 *n*.
Christopher, Mr., ii. 20.
Church teaching, importance of, i. 210 *n*.
Church, Dean, ii. 186 *n*.; letter to author, ii. 194.
Churton, Archdeacon, i. 251, ii. 9 *n*., 7.

Clark, Archdeacon, ii. 220 *n*.
— F. le Gros, ii. 219, 229.
Claughton, Bishop, ii. 38 *n*.
Clergy, laxity of, i. 149.
Clough, Mr., i. 64.
Cockerell, C. R., i. 14-17, 24.
Codex B., Vatican MS., i. 256, 257.
— ℵ, Sinaitic MS., i. 257.
Codices, Sacred Greek, ii. 198.
Coins, current, of England, Art. on, i. 16.
Colenso, Bishop, i. 260 ; ii. 95, 270.
Collett, Rev. E., letter to author, ii. 311, 312.
Colossians ii. 15, reading of, i. 269 *n*.
Combe, Mr. Taylor, i. 14.
Commentary, Plain, i. 173, 201, 220-224, 237; ii. 95.
Commission, Royal, of inquiry with regard to the Universities, i. 175.
Commissioners for the Universities Act, Burgon placed on Oxford list ; opposition in both Houses, consents to withdraw, ii. 136-139, 144, 149.
'*Common-Room, Common-Places*,' Burgon's answer to, i. 225, 226.
Communion, fasting, ii. 85-87.
— Holy, Clergy assisting in, without communicating. *See* Merivale.
— weekly, petition for, from undergraduates, ii. 18.
Compton, Lord Alwyne, ii. 153, 186 *n*.
Conference, Diocesan, at St. Leonard's, ii. 276.
Confession, enforced auricular, ii. 87; Bp. S. Wilberforce on, ii. 87 ; discussion in Convocation on, ii. 88.
Confirmation Classes at Ilsley, i. 170; Worton, i. 195; Finmere, i. 202; Oxford, ii. 116.
Contentment, of Christian growth, no classical word for, ii. 333.
Convocation, Burgon in, ii. 193, 194; withdraws from, ii. 192 ; why he had no following there, ii. 163, 192-195.
Cook, Canon, ii. 56, 211.
Copeland, William Taylor, i. 51.
Corrie, Rev. Dr., i. 91 ; ii. 160.
Cotton, Bishop, ii. 77.

Cotton, Rev. Dr., i. 118, 119.
Cowie, Dean, ii. 186 n.
Cowper (Poet), i. 39, 40.
Cox, G. V., Recollections of Oxford, i. 176, 212, 259.
Coxe, Bishop Cleveland, i. 238; ii. 298, 304.
— Rev. H. O., i. 258.
Cozza-Luzi, Abbate, ii. 207, 232.
Cramer family, i. 2; Catherine Marguerite de, see Burgon, Mrs.; Chevalier de; i. 3; his defence of S. Polycarp's church at Smyrna, i. 4; ii. 272.
— Isaac, i. 3, 4.
Cranbrook, Viscount, ii. 15, 137, 138, 139, 174, 186 n., 195 n., 206, 207. Lines on Burgon, ii. 305, 306. See Letters.
Creation, six ordinary days of, in Burgon's view, ii. 248; correspondence with Mr. Arrowsmith, ii. 253. See also Genesis.
Creed, Athanasian, Burgon's two Sermons on, ii. 75, 76; Bishop Cotton on, ii. 77; Divinity Professors at Oxford on, ii. 73 and n.; Dr. Pusey on, ii. 73; Bp. Thirlwall's speech in Convocation on, ii. 72-74; Bp. S. Wilberforce on, ii. 73; Bp. Christopher Wordsworth on, ii. 73.
Criticism of the N. T., Introduction to, by Dr. Scrivener, ii. 218.
— Textual, of N. T., Burgon's work on, ii. 126, 218, 274, 277, 300, 301, 302; four periods in, ii. 211.
Crosse, Canon, ii. 126, 197, 207. See Letters.
— Mrs., ii. 208; letters to author, ii. 275, 297, 302, 309.
Cust, Dean, ii. 186 n.

D.

Dale, Mr., i. 97, 98.
Daman, Charles, i. 127.
Darby, Mr., i. 309.
Darwin, Dr. Erasmus, i. 88 and n.
— Sir Francis Sacheverell, i. 88, 89.
Days, meaning of in Gen. i., ii. 253; week of seven, ii. 266-269, 391-400.
Deane, Rev. Henry, i. 259, 260; ii. 130, 163; letters to author, ii. 11 n., 34 n.; to Miss Rose, ii. 352.
Deborah, sermon on, ii. 158, 159.
Delphi, oracle at, i. 148 and n.
Deluge, narrative of. See Genesis.
Denison, Archdeacon, i. 178, 212.
Derby, Earl of (the late), i. 177, 207; ii. 35.
'Disestablishment of Religion in Oxford,' ii. 178 n., 184, 209.
Disestablishment of Irish Church, Sermons on, ii. 26 n.; the late Lord Derby on, ii. 35.
Disraeli, Mr., ii. 91, 95.
Divinity, the study of, in Oxford, ii. 32, 90.
Dix, Dr. Morgan, ii. 238.
Dodsworth, Mr., i. 98, 135, 162, 179, 185, 191, 192.
Donaldson, Thomas L., i. 24.
Durnford, Bishop, of Chichester, ii. 161, 303.
— Mrs. Richard, ii. 310.

E.

Earle, Professor, i. 214.
Ecclesfield Church, i. 84.
Eden, Rev. C. P., i. 272; ii. 2, 243, 252.
Education Act, Elementary, opposed by Burgon, ii. 46.
Egina Marbles at Munich, ii. 164.
Egypt, tour in, i. 300-318.
Ellerton Theological Prize Essay, i. 131.
Ellesmere, Lord, i. 207 n.
Ellicott, Bishop, ii. 65, 210, 223; Burgon's reply, ii. 210.
Elliott, Ebenezer, i. 84 n.
Elohim. See under *Jehovah.*
Endemus and Ecdemus, i. 226.
English Church Union, Burgon withdraws from, i. 179.
Epigrams, ii. 34, 43, 223.
Epitaphs, i. 212, 213.
Essays and Reviews, i. 175, 256, 259, 260, 261; ii. 36, 37, 39, 95.
Evangelisterium, the Golden, in S. Catherine's Convent, Mount Sinai, ii. 200.
Evans, Arthur, i. 130 n.
Evidences of Christianity, sermon on, i. 271.

EVO

Evolution, Burgon's views on Darwinian theory of, ii. 220, 230, 289.
Exchange, Royal, burnt, i. 65, 66.
Exchequer documents, i. 102.
Eyre family, i. 2.

F.

Fairbairn, Typology of Scripture, ii. 169, 170 n.
Faithful departed, Burgon's sermon on, ii. 406–411.
Farrar, Archdeacon, '*Life of Christ*,' ii. 366–368.
Fathers, Indices of quotations from N. T. in the, ii. 82 n, 83 n.
Fellowes, Sir Charles, i. 13, 24, 31–37, 97, 104, 106. *See* Letters.
Ffoulkes, Archdeacon, ii. 186 n.
Fialetto, i. 106.
Final School, Fifth. *See* Theology.
Finmere, Curacy at, i. 168, 200-203, 209 ; Archdeacon Palmer's account of Burgon's ministry there, i. 168-172.
Finn, Mr. and Mrs., i. 305, 331, 332, 337.
Finn, Miss, letter to author, ii. 132.
Flood, calendar of the, ii. 268, 391–400.
Forbes, Professor, i. 294, 340, 341 ; ii. 268.
Fox, Bishop, i. 242.
Frankland, Sir Robert, i. 72 n.
Fraser, James Baillie, i. 74.
Fraser, Mrs., i. 75.
Freeman, Archdeacon, ii. 77.
Fremantle, Canon, Burgon's answer to his paper in the *Fortnightly*, ii. 271.
Fridays, observance of, ii. 332.

G.

Gainsborough's '*Boy in Blue*,' i. 27.
Garbett, Mr., i. 144.
Garnier, Rev. T. P., letter to author, ii. 121.
'Gathering host,' office of the, i. 245.
Genesis, Burgon's Lectures on, i. 243, ii. 16 ; account of the Creation in, Professor Pritchard on, ii. 246, 266; Burgon's reply, ii.

HAR

246-249 ; Bishop Harvey Goodwin on, ii. 266 ; Lord Selborne on, ii. 262 ; Professor Forbes on, ii. 268. *See* Sabbath.
Gibson, Bishop, ii. 41 n.
Gladstone, Rt. Hon. W. E., i. 176, 177, 204, 211 ; ii. 14, 15, 36, 201, 203 ; Burgon's letter to, on Oxford Reform, i. 227, 281.
Golightly, Rev. C. P., ii. 79 n.
Goodwin, Bishop Harvey, ii. 267, 269.
Gore, Rev. C., ii. 304, 365, 366, 369, 370, 371.
Gorham case, the, i. 178, 179.
Gospels, Commentary on the, i. 173, 201, 205, 220, 225, 249.
— Harmony of the, i. 112, 172, 201, 208, 213.
Granger, Rev. James, i. 107 n.
— Society, i. 107.
Gray, Bishop, ii. 25.
— (Poet), i. 28–30.
Greenlaw, Mr., i. 18, 294, 340.
Gregory, Canon, ii. 186 n., 189 ; Burgon's '*Friendly Remonstrance*' to, ii. 189 and n., 195.
Gresham Lectures, ii. 307, 311-319.
— Professor of Divinity, Burgon appointed, ii. 27, 52.
— Sir Thomas, Life of, i. 41, 51, 63, 66, 67, 72, 73 ; ii. 27, 343. Portrait of, i. 108-110. Prize for, i. 59.
Greswell, Rev. Richard, i. 125, 127, 128, 130, 144.
Grey, Lady Mary, i. 72 n.
'*Guardian*,' Burgon's letters in, i. 253 ; ii. 198, 231 n., 260, 270, 279.
Guise, Miss Frances, i. 294, 297.
— Sir John, i. 296.
Gwilliam, Rev. G. H., letters to author, ii. 111, 112, 144, 304.

H.

Haddan, Arthur West, i. 127.
Hall, Mr. Ryman, ii. 121.
Hamilton, Bishop, i. 115.
Hampton Court pictures, i. 106.
Hannah, Archdeacon, ii. 297.
— Prebendary, ii. 304.
Hardy, Mr. Gathorne. *See* Cranbrook.

Hargreaves, Miss, ii. 337.
Harrison, Archdeacon, i. 62.
Harrowby, Earl of, i. 207 *n.*
Harwood, Dr., i. 83.
Hatch, Rev. E., ii. 181 *n.*
Hawkins, Dr., Provost of Oriel, i. 234; ii. 208, 327.
— Rebecca, Sextoness of S. Mary's, ii. 88, 89.
Hawtrey, Mr. William, i. 72 *n.*
Heathcote, Sir W., ii. 15.
Heliopolis, obelisk at, i. 310.
Hensley, Rev. Alfred, i. 120, 121, 125–127, 131, 180, 209, 228, 237, 239, 242, 244. *See* Letters.
Herodotus, i. 103, 104, 147, 302.
Heurtley, Dr., i. 260; ii. 20, 73.
Higgins, Charles L., i. 8 *n.*, 219, 231, 337; ii. 51 *n.*, 158 *n.*, 241, 245, 283.
— Mrs., i. 219, 337; ii. 298, 300; letter to author, 286.
Hill, Rowland, ii. 96.
History, Modern, School at Oxford, i. 212 *n.*; ii. 30, 31.
Hobson, Rev. J. P., ii. 207; letter to author, ii. 224.
Hobhouse, Bishop, i. 231; letters to author, i. 164, 233; ii. 353.
Hogarth, i. 105.
Hog, Mr., i. 79.
Holywell Cemetery, Oxford, i. 230, 233, 246; ii. 24, 49, 64, 302, 304, 337.
Honyman, Sir W., ii. 119 *n.*
Hook, Dean, i. 290; ii. 91, 94, 125.
Hooker, i. 148, 160 *n.*, 242; ii. 62 *n.*
Hor, Mount, i. 320.
Horsley, Bishop, i. 272.
Hort, Dr., ii. 229.
Horton, Rev. R. F., ii. 222.
Hoskier, Mr. Herman C., on Dean Burgon, ii. 249.
Houghton Conquest Parsonage, i. 114.
Humboldt, Baron, i. 104.
'*Humility ad clerum*,' Sermon, ii. 131.
Hunt, Rev. C. Jerram, letter to author, ii. 44.
Hunter, Rev. Joseph, i. 34, 46.
Huntingford, Rev. E., ii. 175 *n.*
Hussey, Professor, i. 131.

I.

Ickhard (Icard) Margoton, i. 9 *n.*
Iddesleigh, Earl of, ii. 219, 228.
I.H.S., meaning of, i. 113.
Ilsley, West, Burgon's curacy at, i. 163–167, 181–188, 195–197; ii. 7.
Ince, Rev. Dr., ii. 157.
Inglis, Sir Robert, i. 177.
Ingram, Rev. H. M., ii. 270; letter to author, ii. 279.
'*Inspiration and Interpretation*,' answer to Essays and Reviews, i. 175, 198, 219, 256, 260–279, 294; ii. 209; reviews of, i. 309.
Irish Church, Disestablishment, &c., of, ii. 35.
Irving, Edward, i. 98.
Ivor church, epitaph in, i. 213.

J.

Jackson, Bishop, ii. 37.
— Dean, i. 160 *n.*
Jacobson, Bishop, i. 120, 122, 124, 131.
Jairus' daughter, sermon on, ii. 386.
Jebb, Bishop, i. 309, 341.
Jehovah and *Elohim*, different uses of in Genesis, ii. 270.
Jerusalem, Burgon's stay and illness at, i. 320–329.
Johnson family, i. 2.
— Dr., i. 6, 7.
Jones of Nayland, i. 181, 217.
— Bishop Basil, i. 214, 215 *n.*
— Inigo, i. 143.
Jowett, Dr., ii. 42, 222.
Jubilee service in Westminster Abbey, ii. 273.
Justification and Sanctification, Bp. Bull's theory on, i. 159 and *n.*; Justification prior to Sanctification, Bp. S. Wilberforce on, i. 159, 160 and *n.*

K.

Kafir women, appreciation of sacred pictures, i. 238.
Keble College, Burgon's share in debate on, ii. 43.
Keil on Joshua, i. 324 *n.*

Kempe, C. E., ii. 338.
King, Bishop, ii. 93, 300 n.
Kitchin, Dean, ii. 19.
Kitto, Rev. J. F., letter to author, ii. 311.
Knight, Payne, i. 12.
Knollys, Mr., ii. 134.

L.

Lake, Dean, ii. 186 n.
Lamb, Charles, i. 69 n.
Lambeth Conference, first, ii. 25; Burgon's sermon on, ii. 25.
Lappenberg, Dr., i. 53 and n.
Laud, Archbishop, i. 148.
Laurence, Archbishop, ii. 75, 78.
Law and Modern History, Fourth School at Oxford, i. 175, 211, 212; ii. 30, 31.
Lawson, Rev. R., i. 136, 145, 150.
Lectionary, New, examined, &c., Burgon's Sermon, ii. 151.
Lectionary, the New, Burgon's dislike to, ii. 60; adopts it in obedience to authority, ii. 59, 60, 132; remonstrates with author for not using it till it was compulsory, ii. 61, 133 n.; essay against by Bp. Christopher Wordsworth, Burgon, and author, ii. 62, 63, 151.
Leighton, Dr., Warden of All Souls, i. 166.
Lepsius, Dr., i. 24, 25, 103, 104; ii. 232.
Leslie, i. 26.
Letters to Burgon from—

Arrowsmith, Rev. R., ii. 253.
Beauchamp, Earl, ii. 57.
Churton, the late Archdeacon, i. 251.
Cockerell, C. R., i. 15, 16.
Cook, Canon, ii. 56.
Gladstone, Rt. Hon. W. E., i. 229.
Hunter, Rev. Joseph, i. 49.
King, Bishop, ii. 300.
Liddon, Canon, ii. 67 n., 68, 239.
Northcote, the late Sir Stafford, ii. 219, 228.
Palmer, Rev. W. J., i. 216, 217, 223.
Phillpotts, Bishop, ii. 12, 13.
Pusey, Dr., i. 225 n.

Letters (*continued*)—
Seabury, Professor, ii. 15.
Wordsworth, Bishop Christopher, ii. 55.
Letters from Burgon to—

a Bible-class member, ii. 154, 169.
Circular answering inquiries during illness, ii. 296.
a Friend, ii. 287.
Mrs. ——, ii. 242–246, 257, 260, 263, 265, 282, 284, 285.
his parents, i. 19, 20.
his sisters, i. 81, 115. (*See* Higgins, Rose.)
Arrowsmith, Rev. R., ii. 254.
Bickersteth, Mrs. Samuel, ii. 196, 205. (*See* Williams.)
Bloxam, Rev. Dr., ii. 292.
Chichester, Bishop of, ii. 221.
Clark, F. Le Gros, Esq., ii. 229.
Corrie, Rev. Dr., ii. 160.
Cranbrook, Viscount, ii. 145, 149, 156, 186, 201, 223, 242, 277.
Crosse, Canon, ii. 204, 226, 287.
— Mrs., ii. 282.
Eden, Mrs. C. P., ii. 251.
Fellowes, Sir C., i. 32, 36, 99.
Gladstone, Rt. Hon. W. E., i. 281.
Goulburn, Dean, ii. 61, 172, 256.
Gwilliam, Rev. G. H., ii. 144.
Hensley, Rev. A., i. 126, 209–211, 283–291, 339.
Higgins, C. L., Esq., i. 314.
— Mrs., i. 309, 321, 331, 333; ii. 258.
Hobson, Rev. J. P., ii. 225.
Hunter, Rev. Joseph, i. 46.
Ingram, Rev, H., ii. 279–281.
Knollys, Mr., ii. 134, 135, 154–156.
Lawson, Robert, Esq., i. 145, 150.
Livingstone, Rev. R. G., ii. 289, 291.
Norris, Rev. W. F., ii. 227.
Renouard, Rev. G. C., i. 52, 53, 108, 110–112, 211, 212.
Rose, Rev. Henry John, i. 299, 300, 311, 318; ii. 4.
— Mrs. Henry John, i. 295, 297, 310, 315, 326, 348; ii. 4, 33.

Letters (*continued*)—
  Rose, Mrs. Hugh James, i. 155, 157, 181-209, 280; ii. 3.
  Skeet, Mrs., ii. 295.
  Southey (Poet), i. 39.
  Turner, Mr. Dawson, i. 1, 82, 92, 101, 104, 105, 107, 137, 141-144, 152, 154; ii. 357.
  Valentine, Rev. W., 293.
  Washbourne, Miss, ii. 82, 89, 152, 282.
  Williams, Miss Monier-, ii. 52, 58, 89, 92, 96, 97, 110, 145-148, 151, 153, 157, 164, 165. (*See* Bickersteth.)
Liddell, Dean, i. 62, 127; ii. 79 and *n*.
Liddon, Canon, ii. 20, 44, 51 *n*., 73, 237. *See* Letters.
Linton, Mr., i. 260; ii. 20.
Linwood, '*Anthologia Oxoniensis*,' frontispiece by Burgon, i. 129, 130 *n*.
Litton, Mr., i. 260.
Livingstone, Rev. R. G., i. 275; ii. 6, 43, 100, 160, 304; letter to author, ii. 339.
Lodging-houses at Oxford, Burgon's pamphlet on, ii. 141-143.
Lowe, Mr., ii. 138.
S. Luke xxiv. 13-50, ii. 313-319.
Luther on the Galatians, i. 160.
'*Lux Mundi*,' Rev. C. Gore's Essay in, ii. 365, 366, 369-371.

M.

Macbean, Mrs., i. 292.
M'Caul, Dr., i. 111 and *n*.
Macdonald, Major, i. 323.
Macdonnell, Dean, ii. 217 *n*.
McEwen, W., ii. 169 *n*.
Mackarness, Bishop, ii. 143.
Mackenzie, i. 102.
Mac Neill, Sir John, i. 75.
Magdalen College Chapel, music in, ii. 347.
Magee, the late Archbishop, ii. 38 *n*., 217 *n*.
Mai, Cardinal, i. 342 *n*.
Mair, Josephine, i. 161 *n*., 204, 220, 280 *n*.
Maitland, Rev. Brownlow, ii. 174 *n*.
Maltass, Sarah, i. 9.

Manning, Cardinal, i. 98.
Mansel, Dean, ii. 33, 39, 178, 243, 350; lines on S. Mary's new organ, ii. 34.
Mansell, Captain, i. 333, 337.
— Dr. Francis, i. 241.
'*Manuscripta Evangelia in Foreign Libraries*,' ii. 84. *See* Codices, Sacred.
Manuscripts, cursive, added by Burgon to Dr. Scrivener's list, ii. 59, 198.
S. Mark xiii. 32, Burgon's sermon on, ii. 171.
— last twelve verses of, Burgon on, i. 257; ii. 49-58, 95, 209, 214, 215, 373; Canon Cook on, ii. 56; Revisers on, ii. 49, 50 *n*.; Bp. Christopher Wordsworth on, ii. 55, 56.
Marriage with a deceased wife's sister, Burgon's argument against, ii. 205.
Marriott, Rev. Charles, i. 231; ii. 2, 120, 288, 293.
Marsham, Dr., i. 177, 178 *n*.
S. Mary's Church, Oxford, memorial window to Burgon in, ii. 338.
Mary Queen of Scots, i. 252, 253.
Masaráki, i. 331.
Mass, etymology of, i. 113.
Maydenhithe, John de, his ring found at Chichester, ii. 220.
Melvill, Mr., i. 97, 98.
Memorials to Dean Burgon in Chichester Cathedral, ii. 334-336; Holywell Cemetery, Oxford, ii. 337; proposed west window at S. Mary's Church, Oxford, ii. 338.
Meredith, Mr., i. 333, 334, 337.
Merivale, Dean, Burgon consults him as to whether clergy can assist at a second celebration without again communicating, ii. 139, 140.
Merry, Rev. Dr., his mention of Burgon in his speech, ii. 339.
Methuen, Rev. T., ii. 345 *n*.
Miller, Rev. Edward, ii. 83 *n*., 211, 219, 372, 373.
  Miss, description of Burgon's teaching and preaching, ii. 116-118.

Millingen, James, i. 24, 27 ; ii. 21.
Milton, John, i. 61, 115.
Milton's house, Burgon's visit to, i. 44, 61, 62.
Miracles, Burgon's view on, i. 272.
Missions, Parochial, first inaugurated, i. 243 ; at Henley, Burgon's sermon, i. 243, 244 ; services in North Bucks, i. 246 ; first held at Oxford, ii. 130.
— Foreign, Intercession-Day first appointed, ii. 80.
Missions, Home, &c., Burgon's sermon on, ii. 130, 131 ; Burgon's views on, i. 243 ; ii. 131.
Moberly, Bishop, i. 290.
Molyneux, Sir Capel, i. 320.
Moore, Mr. Niven, i. 334.
— Dr., i. 97.
— Hon. and Rev. E., i. 181, 182, 185, 196.
More, Sir Antonio, i. 108 and *n*.
— Sir Thomas, i. 30, 107.
Morgan, Osborne, ii. 137.
Morley, Earl of, ii. 136, 137.
Mozley, Professor, i. 62.
Muckleston, Mr., i. 119 and *n*.
Müller, Professor Max, ii. 304.
Murdoch family, i. 2.
Murray, Bishop, i. 20, 21, 72.
— John, i. 104, 106 ; ii. 201.

N.

Nash, Mr. F. P., i. 223 *n*.
— Professor, i. 223 *n*.
Neander, i. 118 and *n*., 119 *n*.
Neate, Mr., i. 290 and *n*.
'*Nehemiah*,' Burgon's sermon on, ii. 161.
Nelson, Robert, ii. 9, 13.
Newdigate Prize Poem, '*Petra*,' by Burgon, i. 144.
Newman, John Henry, i. 63, 64, 94, 99, 101, 117, 118, 122, 123, 135, 136, 138 and *n*., 140, 142, 151, 191 ; ii. 1, 132, 188.
'*New Reformation*,' &c., the, Burgon's reply to Canon Fremantle, ii. 272.
Newton, Sir Isaac, i. 28, 29.
Nice, Council of, Fourth Canon requires the consent of the comprovincial Bishop to the consecration of a Bishop, ii. 38.
Nobody's Club, Burgon's maiden speech at, ii. 2.
Norris, Rev. W. F., ii. 208, 209.

O.

Ogilvie, Rev. Dr., ii. 73, 93.
Ollivant, Bishop, ii. 38 *n*.
Oranges, when introduced into England, i. 108.
Oriel College, i. 240 ; Burgon fellow of, i. 131.
Ornaments Rubric, ii. 191.
Orton, Dr., i. 87.
Otter, Bishop, Memorial College at Chichester, ii. 308.
Ottley, Miss, i. 26.
Oxford Colleges, Burgon's Historical Notices of, i. 237, 239 ; ii. 348.
— Diocesan Conference, Burgon's sermon on, ii. 84.
— Movement, Burgon's connection with the, i. 134-136.
— Reformers, Burgon's paper on, i. 226.
— University, not existing distinct from the colleges, i. 281.
— Royal Commission of Inquiry, i. 175, 176, 207 *n*.
— Bill, i. 176 ; — Election, i. 176, 177.

P.

Paget, Rev. F. E., i. 174.
Palgrave, Sir Francis, i. 108.
Palmer, Archdeacon, i. 168 ; ii. 179 *n*., 180 *n*.; letter to author, i. 168.
— Rev. W. J., i. 168, 180, 200, 209, 216.
— Mr., i. 64.
Panathenaïc, Amphora, i. 12, 37, 3
Parallelism the great principle of Hebrew poetry, i. 341.
Parentalia, Burgon's, i. 1, 2, 4, 5 *n*.
Parents, on the death of, i. 245, 246.
Parthenon, Burgon as an infant carried up to the, i. 15.
Pastoral office, Burgon's treatise on, ii. 6, 8-13 ; chronological inaccuracies, ii. 9 *n*.
Pearson, Bishop, ii. 9 *n*., 31, 103, 171.

Pearson, Rev. H. D., letter to author, ii. 119.
Pellew, Dean, i. 68.
Perceval, Mr., i. 177, 178 n.
S. Peter's, Oxford, i. 115.
'*Petra and other Poems*,' ii. 241; Newdigate Prize Poem, i. 125, 145; ii. 345 n.
Petra, rocks at, i. 320, 326, 327 and n.
Phillpotts, the late Bishop, i. 178, 189, 204, 207; ii. 36. See Letters.
'*Philological Club*,' lines on, i. 214, 215.
Pickford, Rev. John, i. 44.
Poems by Burgon, i. 32, 34, 37, 65, 119 n., 234, 241, 251, 254, 327 n., 335; ii. 51, 345.
Pomander, i. 108, 109.
Pott, Archdeacon, ii. 186 n.
Powles, Prebendary, i. 136; letter to author, ii. 215, 335.
Prayer Book, Sermons on structure and method of, ii. 250, 251.
Prayers for the Dead, ii. 246.
Pride Sermon, ii. 131 n., 184.
Princess Imperial visits Chichester, ii. 201, 202.
Prints, Sacred, value of, in missionary work, i. 237.
'*Prints, Sacred, for School and Cottage*,' i. 156, 157, 173, 238.
Pritchard, Professor, ii. 247, 253, 254, 260 n., 262, 266. See Genesis.
'*Prophecy, Argument from*,' by Rev. B. Maitland; its unsoundness though published by S. P. C. K., ii. 176, 177.
'*Prophecy not Forecast*,' Burgon's answer to Rev. B. Maitland, ii. 174.
Psalm cx, Davidic authorship essential to our Lord's argument, ii. 365.
Pusey, Rev. Dr., i. 64, 115-118, 123, 135, 148, 192, 290; ii. 51 n., 73, 77.
— Philip, ii. 51 n., 200.

Q.

Quintard, Bishop, of Tennessee, ii. 298.

R.

Recognition in Paradise, ii. 408.

'*Record*' Newspaper, recollections of Burgon, i. 275.
Reformatory boys, taught by Burgon to recite, ii. 264, 284-286.
Regeneration, Baptismal, doctrine impugned by Mr. Gorham, i. 178, 179; defended by Burgon, i. 179, 189, 190; Bishop of Exeter's letter to Archbishop of Canterbury, i. 178.
Reid, Dr., i. 13.
Reminiscences, personal, of Burgon, i. 133, 168, 233, 275; ii. 28, 34, 42-44, 99, 100-122, 125-127, 132, 144, 193, 194, 249, 275, 276, 294, 297, 299, 301, 302, 309-312, 319, 323-333, 335, 345, 346, 350, 352, 353.
Renouard, Rev. G. C., i. 51-55, 59, 90, 101, 162, 173 and n., 180, 214; ii. 21, 30. See Letters.
'*Review of a Year*,' Burgon's Sermon, ii. 45, 46.
Revised Version of New Testament, ii. 210-219, 277, 291; many alterations in, premature, ii. 216; traces of sceptical *animus* in, ii. 363, 364.
Revision of Authorised Version, Burgon's protest against an Unitarian having part in, ii. 45, 64, 65; letter to Bishop Ellicott, ii. 65, 67; Canon Liddon's letter to Burgon on, ii. 67-72.
'*Revision Revised*,' i. 257; ii. 195, 201, 206, 207, 209-218, 223, 278, 335, 373.
Riff-raff, etymology of, i. 111 and n.
Rigaud, Rev. John, ii. 292.
'*Ritual, Divergent*,' Burgon's Sermon on, ii. 187.
'*Ritualism*,' first appearance in Oxford, ii. 11 n.; Burgon's protest against, ii. 85, 86, 179. See Toleration.
Robsart, Amy, ii. 119 n.
'*Rock*' in S. Matt. xvi. 18, Burgon on, i. 225 n.; Dr. Pusey on, i. 225 n.
Rogers, Sir F. See Blachford.
— Miss, i. 26.
— Samuel, i. 25-31, 141, 144.
— Professor Thorold, ii. 43.

'Romanizing within the Church of England,' ii. 84-86.
Rome, Chaplaincy at, i. 253, 254.
'Rome, Letters from,' i. 253, 261, 342.
Rose family, i. 2, 8 n.
— Misses, ii. 299-301, 352.
— Rev. Henry John, i. 8 n., 71, 90, 91, 114, 115, 117, 118, 156, 157, 168, 231, 237; ii. 80, 82. See Letters.
— Mrs. Henry John, i. 8 n., 184; ii. 1, 82. See Letters.
— Rev. Hugh James, i. 72; ii. 117, 259.
— Hugh James, junior, i. 296 n.; ii. 160.
— Mrs. Hugh James, i. 136, 173, 219, 233, 234; ii. 3. See Letters.
— Rev. W. F., ii. 24-26, 58 and n., 300, 334.
Rossi, Cavaliere, G. B. de, i. 257.
Round, Mr., i. 178 n.
Routh, Dr., i. 233, 234.
Rundle, Dr., ii. 40 n.
Russell, Lord John, i. 176.

S.

Sabbath, antediluvian, ii. 255, 391, 400; law of, expanded and enforced in Exodus and Leviticus, ii. 281; supplanted by the Sunday, ii. 279-281.
St. Helens, Lord, i. 29.
Salisbury, Marquis of, ii. 137, 139, 183.
Saltonstall, Lady Mary, i. 213.
Sandford, Rev. C. W. (Bishop), proposes changes in the hours of Sunday services at Oxford; Burgon opposes them, ii. 18-20.
Scholz, ii. 207.
School Board, established in Oxford, ii. 46.
Schools, changes in Oxford, fourth and fifth Schools added, i. 175, 211, 212; ii. 31, 32.
Scripture, Holy, three aspects of, ii. 321; spiritual aspect, ii. 322.
Scrivener, Dr., ii. 211 n., 257, 277, 286, 372; on Burgon, ii. 53 n.; Burgon's letters to him in the 'Guardian,' ii. 59, 83 and n., 164 n., 231; letter to author, ii. 229.
Seabury, Professor, i. 243; ii. 15 and n.
— Rev. W. J., letter to author, ii. 15 n.
Second sight, stories of, i. 75, 76.
Selborne, Lord, ii. 183, 262.
Selwyn, Bishop G. A., ii. 38 n.
'Sermons for Family Reading,' Burgon's, i. 234, 235, 250; ii. 95.
Sermons, Lenten, at Oxford, i. 239, 290.
'Servants of Scripture,' Burgon's, ii. 88, 158-160.
Sesostris, figure of, cut in the rock between Sardis and Smyrna, i. 103.
Seven Churches, Gresham Lectures on the, ii. 312.
Shairp, Principal, i. 138 n.
Shakspeare, ii. 357 n.; spelling of his name, i. 44, 45; notes and memoranda on, i. 45; n. 378-381.
Shaw, Henry, i. 239.
Sheridan, i. 28.
Silkstone, i. 3, 85.
Sinai, Mount, probable origin of the name, i. 323 n.; Burgon's visit to the Convent of S. Catherine, ii. 199, 200.
Sinaitic MS., ii. 54, 234.
Skeat, Etymological Dictionary, i. 111 n.
Skeet, Mrs., letter to author, ii. 295.
Skeffington, Hon. Henry, ii. 119 n.
Smith, Arthur H., i. 96.
— Miss, ii. 46.
— Professor Henry, ii. 46.
— Dr. Vance, ii. 45 n., 67, 70, 71.
Smyrna. S. Polycarp's Church defended against the Turks, i. 4, 5.
Smyth, ii. 21
Stainer, Sir John, ii. 304.
Stanley, Dean, appointed Select Preacher; Burgon's protest against it, ii. 78, 79.
Stewart, James and Charles, 'The Princes,' i. 74, 75.
Stuart, Cardinal Henry, i. 75.
Students, Unattached, Burgon's proposal with regard to, ii. 185.

umner, Archbishop, i. 224.
Sunday School lesson, Burgon's suggestion for a, ii. 97, 98.
Sussex, Duke of, i. 105.
Sutton, Archdeacon, ii. 296 n., 297.
Sydnope, i. 89.
Symbolism in the Gospel histories, ii. 386.

T.

Taylor, Jeremy, i. 148; ii. 74.
Temple, Bishop, i. 149, 259, 384; Burgon's protest against his consecration as Bishop of Exeter, ii. 36; his explanation; Burgon's reply, ii. 37; Archbishop Tait's manifesto, ii. 36; eight Bishops dissentient, ii. 37, 38 and n.
Testament, New, Burgon's work on text of. *See* Criticism.
— Old, interpreted by the New, ii. 368, 369; suggestions how to read the, i. 150–152.
Teulon, Canon, ii. 304.
Theologian, Burgon as, ii. 362, 372–377.
Theology, Fifth Final School of, Burgon's plea for, ii. 29–32, 90.
Thirlwall, Bishop, on the Athanasian Creed, ii. 72 n., 74–76, 78.
Thomas, Archdeacon, i. 253.
Thompson, i. 78.
Thorpe, Mr., i. 111.
Thursfield, J. R., ii. 181 n.
1 Timothy iii. 16, true reading of, ii. 233.
Toleration of Ritual, address to the Archbishop by ten dignitaries for, ii. 186 and n.
Tract XC, i. 134; Remonstrance of Four Tutors, i. 134.
Tractarian movement in Burgon's view has nothing in common with excess of Ritual, ii. 188.
Trench, Archbishop, i. 157, 290.
Tritton, i. 193, 214.
Turner, Dawson, Mr., i. 7, 34, 66, 67, 68, 69, 71, 72, 97. *See* Letters.
'Twelve Good Men, Lives of,' i. 235, 272; ii. 51 n., 81, 88, 120, 208, 252, 272, 285, 290–293, 341, 344, 350.

Types, Burgon's Sermon on, ii. 166–169, 386.
Tytler, Patrick Fraser, i. 34, 41, 42, 67, 73.
— Burgon's Memoir of, i. 74, 249–252; ii. 344.
William Fraser, i. 77.

U.

Unbelief amongst Oxford tutors, anecdote of, ii. 182 n.
'Unitarian Reviser of Authorised Version intolerable,' Burgon's letter, ii. 64.
Universities, the different measures of the Crown and of Parliament affecting the, i. 284 n.; ii. 136, 178, 179 n., 209.
'University Sermon and College Services,' Burgon's Sermon, his letter and pamphlets on, ii. 20.

V.

Vatican MS., Codex B, i. 256; ii. 54, 55 n., 120, 229.
Venn, Henry, ii. 40 n.
— Rev. John, 41 n.
— Rev. Richard, anecdote of, ii. 40, 41.
Victor of Antioch, ii. 58 n.
Victoria, Princess, i. 26.

W.

Wagner, Mr. Henry, letter to author, ii. 120.
Wailing-place of the Jews at Jerusalem, i. 329.
Washbourne, Miss, ii. 58, 59, 81, 273. *See* Letters.
Watts, Rev. R. E. R., i. 253.
Webb, Miss, i. 292, 294, 295, 298, 299, 301, 312, 316, 320, 330, 332, 334.
Wedderburn, Mrs., i. 75.
Wellesley, Dr., i. 130.
— Lord Charles, i. 207, n. 4.
Wellington, Duke of, i. 175, 177, 207.
Wesley, John, ii. 1.
Westall, i. 26.
West Ilsley. *See* Ilsley.
Westmacott, Sir R., i. 24.
Whewell, Professor, ii. 14.

Wilberforce, Bishop Samuel, i. 158, 159, 204, 239, 244, 246; ii. 38, 73, 87, 88, 208, 342.
Wilkins, Bishop, ii. 9 *n*.
Williams, Miss Monier-, ii. 52, 89, 117 *n*. *See* Letters.
— Professor, ii. 117 *n*.
— Rev. Isaac, i. 222.
Wilson, John Matthias, i. 127.
— Rev. W., i. 194.
Windle, Mr., ii. 23.
Wintle, Miss Mary, ii. 337.
Winton, Archdeacon de, ii. 186 *n*.
Wolff, Dr., i. 85.
'*Woman's Place*,' ii. 46, 47.
Women admitted to University Examinations, Burgon's Sermon against, ii. 234-238.

Woolcombe, Rev. E. C., ii. 79 *n*.
Worcester College, Oxford, i. 117, 241.
Wordsworth, Bishop Charles, ii. 82 *n*.
— Bishop Christopher, i. 224, 290, 342; ii. 55, 62, 63, 72, 74, 120, 135, 160, 202.
— Bishop John, i. 133.
Worship, Public, Facilities Bill, ii. 85.

Worton, curacy at, i. 167, 194, 195; ii. 7.
Wotton, Sir Henry, i. 106.

Y.

York Minster, i. 86, 87.
Yule, Dr., letter to author, ii. 42, 43, 99.

THE END.

Mr. Murray's Forthcoming Works.

Egypt under the Pharaohs. A History derived entirely from the Monuments. By HEINRICH BRUGSCH-BEY. *A New Edition, Condensed and Thoroughly Revised*, by M. BRODRICK. With Maps. 8vo. 18s.

Life of Alexander N. Somerville, D.D. In Scotland, India, America, Australasia, Europe, &c. 1813-1889. By GEORGE SMITH, LL.D. *Popular Edition.* Portrait. Post 8vo. 6s.

Handbook of Greek Archæology. Sculpture. Vases, Bronzes, Gems, Terracottas, Architecture, Mural Paintings, &c. By A. S. MURRAY, Keeper of Greek and Roman Antiquities, British Museum. Illustrations. Crown 8vo.

The Psalter of 1539: A Landmark of English Literature. Comprising the Text, in Black Letter Type. Edited, with Notes, by JOHN EARLE, M.A., Professor of Anglo-Saxon at Oxford. Square 8vo.

UNIVERSITY EXTENSION MANUALS.

TEXT-BOOKS for Study and Reference, in connection with the authorised Courses of University Extension Lectures. Edited by Professor KNIGHT, of St. Andrews.

THE FIRST INSTALMENT JUST PUBLISHED:—

The Philosophy of the Beautiful. By Professor KNIGHT, University of St. Andrews. Post 8vo. 3s. 6d.

English Colonisation and Empire. By A. CALDECOTT, Fellow of St. John's College, Cambridge. Maps and Plans. Post 8vo. 3s. 6d.

The Fine Arts. By Professor G. BALDWIN BROWN, University of Edinburgh. With Illustrations. Post 8vo. 3s. 6d.

The Use and Abuse of Money. By Dr. W.CUNNINGHAM, Fellow of Trinity College, Cambridge; Professor of Economic Science, King's College, London. Post 8vo. 3s.

IN THE PRESS AND NEARLY READY:—

The Realm of Nature. A Manual of Physiography, by HUGH ROBERT MILL, University of Edinburgh. With 19 coloured Maps and many Illustrations.

French Literature. By H. G. KEENE, Wadham College, Oxford; Fellow of the University of Calcutta.

The Elements of Ethics. By JOHN H. MUIRHEAD, Balliol College, Oxford; Lecturer on Moral Science, Royal Holloway College.

The Study of Animal Life. By J. ARTHUR THOMSON, University of Edinburgh. With many Illustrations.

FOR PROSPECTUS APPLY TO THE PUBLISHER.

Other Volumes will be published at short intervals.

JOHN MURRAY, ALBEMARLE STREET.